Detour and Access

Detour and Access

Strategies of Meaning in China and Greece

François Jullien

Translated by Sophie Hawkes

ZONE BOOKS · NEW YORK

2000

The publisher would like to thank the French Ministry of
Culture for its assistance with this translation.

ZONE BOOKS
611 Broadway, Suite 608
New York, NY 10012

Originally published in France as *Le Détour et l'accès: Straté-
gies du sens en Chine, en Grèce* © 1995 Editions Grasset.

Printed in the United States of America.

Distributed by The MIT Press,
Cambridge, Massachusetts, and London, England

Library of Congress Cataloging-in-Publication Data

Jullien, François, 1951–
    [Le détour et l'accès. English]
Detour and access : strategies of meaning in China and
Greece / by François Jullien: translated by Sophie Hawkes.
        p.   cm.
    ISBN 1-890951-10-2.
    1. Philosophy, Chinese. 2. Philosophy, Ancient. 3. China
— Civilization. I. Hawkes, Sophie. II. Title. III. Title. Strate-
gies of meaning in China and Greece
B126.J83513 2000
181'.11—dc21   99–10724
                                                      CIP

Contents

Preface

The questions that interest me can be summarized thus: In what way do we benefit from speaking of things indirectly? How does such a distancing allow us better to discover — and describe — people and objects? How does *distancing* produce an effect? Westerners find it natural and normal to meet the world head-on. But what can we gain from approaching it *obliquely*? In other words, how does detour grant access?

My starting point, in short, has to do with the subtlety of meaning. Ordinary language hints at this quality — so much so, in fact, that it can shroud it in prejudice. When we say "It's in Hebrew," we mean only that there is a language barrier that makes the meaning incomprehensible. But when we say "It's all Chinese to me," we add a layer of complication that overly rarefies the meaning. Figuratively speaking, to be "Chinese" means to be "subtle to the point of excess." But who can measure, we might ask, the extent of this excess? Is it merely a matter of ornamentation? Does not detour — which is anything but gratuitous — exert a certain power, which is all the more forceful for its discretion? I ask these questions about the use of language in China in an attempt to explore how far the subtlety of meaning can go, what its preferred uses are, and what gives it value. In China, even as far back as Antiquity, in poetic texts, public records, and words of wisdom, the subtlety of writing (*wei yan*) was praised by the well-read man. I am not saying that the Chinese have a monopoly on indirection (nor that they cannot express themselves directly); rather, I am taking advantage of this marked taste for indirection to investigate the relation of cultural originality and the production of meaning. For me, this also entails a certain risk: Will I successfully demonstrate how to decipher a discourse to someone who knows neither the language nor the context (for I consider the non-sinologist my primary audience)? How does one interpret "exotic" meaning?

My first point of interest is also a useful one: to be able to "decode" China. But I will not limit myself to this practical purpose: another objective will slowly appear. The vantage point of indirection leads us to examine an entire theoretical plane. It shows us that when we are dealing with the problem of strategies of meaning, the way the mind relates to reality globally is at stake. I was unable to avoid the following questions along the way: What if the world were not an object of representation, and figurative meaning did not tend to represent something — symbolically? What if generalizations were not the goal of thought, or speech tended not to define (to build a universality of essences) but to modify itself — to reflect the circumstances? In short, what if consciousness did not strive to reproduce the real in order to ground it in transcendence (of being or of God)? And what if the purpose of speaking about the world, to make it intelligible, were not to arrive at Truth? A question gradually arose, one that summarized the previous ones and served as a guiding force: Why did the Chinese not constitute the level of essences and spirituality which helped the Greek tradition to structure the Western horizon of meaning? Or, to ask the question the other way around: What are the theoretical biases

8

— which remain beneath the surface — that have conditioned Western modes of interpretation, which, because they seem so obvious, have become confused with Reason?

China is a most fascinating terrain, a site for exploring a rich and complicated civilization. But I was drawn to the study of the Chinese language for another, more speculative reason. Because Chinese lies outside the great Indo-European language groups and uses another form of writing (ideographic, not phonetic), and because Chinese civilization, which is one of the oldest (and was recorded in texts very early on), developed without any borrowings or influences from the European West for a long time, China presents a case study through which to contemplate Western thought from the outside — and, in this way, to bring us out of our atavism. I am not claiming that China is totally foreign, but at least it is other. At first, nothing seems to tally: out of its element, thought has a hard time finding its bearings. But such discomfort presents an opportunity; this disorientation can be beneficial. When I began to study Greek philosophy, I had a strange feeling that because this way of thinking was so familiar to me I could never hope to know it (if indeed I succeeded in identifying it). As different as Greek thought is, all that links Westerners implicitly to it risks preventing us from seeing its originality — from measuring its inventiveness. To break the bonds of kinship, we will have to break away from the family. Thus it is necessary to take a step back. A theoretical distancing is desirable — and this is exactly what China offers.

However, the other point of view that China offers is not immediately accessible and has to be constructed. I have attempted to construct a way to put China and Greece into perspective, on the level of discourse, rather than to trace a parallel between them, for I do not believe in the possibility of dividing the page in half with China on one side and Greece on the other. Or rather, I think that a broad comparison of this type, which immediately claims to situate differences, is unproductive.

Strategies of meaning can only be understood from the inside, by following their internal logic. This explains the itinerant pace that reflection will assume here. Indirect and meandering, full of turns and returns, this work will be a circuitous journey. But from one station to the next, the landscape will change and a panorama will begin to take shape. This is the reason for my occasional appeals to the reader's patience, for the effects of meaning cannot be summarized, and I can only glean the meaning of Chinese texts by plundering their commentaries. With China in full view, and Greece on the periphery, perhaps I am really trying to approach Greece. The more we move forward, in fact, the more we are led to turn back. This voyage to the far-off land of subtlety is also an invitation to retrace Western thought.

Reader's Guide

I have already hinted at why I find it unproductive to list the effects of meaning in predetermined categories, such as by fields — political, poetical, philosophical — or by method: allusion, citation, image. Furthermore, I find the convenience of an index at the end of a book illusory. But since I have chosen to follow the meandering path, it seems useful to plot my itinerary in advance. Why not, then, draw up a map of meaning in China, like the famous seventeenth-century *Carte de Tendre* (Map of the Heart)? Guided by these landmarks, each person will then be able to make his or her own way through the subtlety of meaning.

The second chapter broaches the subject of obliqueness based on strategic differences: phalanxes' facing off in battle is compared with the oblique attack recommended by ancient Chinese military treatises. Such an attack is then explored in the great canonical texts, through, for example, the critiques included in the first collection of Chinese poetry, *The Book of Songs*, and the power of diplomatic quotations from the commentary in public records, *Spring and Autumn Annals*. In chapter 5, I analyze how people identified moral judgments in the slightest mention of facts, a technique that codifies implied meaning. All of this leads, in chapter 6, to a more ideological reflection on the (political) cost of indirection. Herein lies the problem of China (at least as it appeared in comparison with the directness of the Greek *agon* and *agora*): the indirect resulted from a compromise; the indirection that originated in censure was transformed into an artistic effect.

Chapters 7 and 8 again comment on poetic texts, but to orient the discussion in a more theoretical direction, I try to understand why the Chinese, unlike the Greeks, never conceived of the world as an object of representation and, consequently, why their horizon of meaning (revealed among the Greeks by allegorization in myth) is not based on representativeness or the symbolic. I then formulate what the modalities of detour give access to (hence these two chapters in the middle of the book are pivotal). Chapter 7 is a kind of tunnel, since in it I disentangle Chinese conceptions of the poetic indirect; but it leads into what I consider an essential point of difference from the Greeks: the absence of another, spiritual level or world to which the image is supposed to refer.

It is again the absence of this other level, conceived of more precisely as that of abstraction and essences, that I begin to examine in chapter 9. Confucius's *Analects*, forever held up as the model of subtle remarks, here occupies a central position. A double opposition arises from these writings: (Socratic) definition versus (Confucian) modulation and generality versus globality. An idea then begins to emerge: since the detour of Confucian speech does not lead to something else (on the order of the idea), it becomes an end in itself; it never ceases indicatively to illuminate reality. Through the variations of the Sage's remarks, one is constantly aware of the renewal of things; by approaching the real through detour or otherness, one is constantly in touch with its regulation. And this is why *detour* is *also* access.

Whereas *Analects* presents the indicative remarks of the Master, Confucius, *Mencius* presents the indirect journey of the disciple

Mencius's awakening consciousness (as I explain in chapter 12). *Mencius* also provides an opportunity to understand the value of speech that aims to enrich rather than to persuade, or why the Sage avoids philosophical discussions.

Chapter 12 finally raises the possibility of a face-to-face confrontation. On the problem of the ineffable (the absolute and unconditional One), it seems that there are no longer two answers. The neo-Taoist thinker Wang Bi (commenting on *Laozi*) joins the Neoplatonist Plotinus, his contemporary, and the Chinese and the Greeks can enter into a dialogue. Nevertheless, I show how the absence of an ontological perspective among the Chinese modifies the problem of *apophasis* (and hence puts the universality of mysticism into question), for the "great image" characterizing the absolute of the Tao does not correspond to analogy; it does not refer to any reality other than its own and instead detaches us from the exclusive and limiting character of the individual and the concrete. The great image leads not to hypostasis somewhere beyond itself, but to the undifferentiated source of things.

The critique of language with which the other great Taoist text of Antiquity, *Zhuangzi*, culminates allows me to articulate this goal of lack of differentiation more precisely (the subject of chapter 13): the Sage's "clear vision" does not perceive something else, but in it, all perspectives become equivalent, and none is excluded. Here we find once more the ideal of globality (as opposed to partiality), as well as the virtue of the indirect approach — which can vary indefinitely. By oscillating according to the situation, "fluctuating" speech embraces reality from all angles, constantly espousing the spontaneous movement of things, and leads us to a Heaven, which is none other than the natural.

Chapters 14 and 15 show how a literary art favoring a loose or relaxed relationship between the text and its subject matter was built on these foundations. An example from the theater, *The West-*

ern Room, again increases the rift with the Greek tradition, since instead of being interested in how the play represents reality, the Chinese commentator Jin Shengtan reads it in terms of literary detour and sinuosity. I propose the concept of *allusive distance* to articulate this Chinese ideal of writing, and I give an example in the last chapter, in a discussion of the work of Du Fu, of various effects of displacement between the poem and its title: in the distance between them, a diffuse atmosphere is created, and meaning is made pregnant.

The reader could, in fact, begin with these last two chapters, to allow himself or herself to be seduced by the merits of the allusive. The reader more interested in Chinese philosophy could take the philosophical circuit that goes from chapters 9 to 13, while the reader who wants to decode China could follow the initial course that runs from chapters 1 to 6. In any case, the purpose of this journey is the same: to travel as far as possible away from *logos*, to explore how far *difference* can take us.

Chapter One

"He's Chinese,"

"It's All Chinese to Me"

Just over a century ago, the American missionary Arthur Smith devoted an entire chapter of his book, *Chinese Characteristics*, to the talent for indirection. It begins as follows:

> One of the intellectual habits upon which we Anglo-Saxons pride ourselves most is that of going directly to the marrow of a subject, and when we have reached it saying exactly what we mean. Considerable abatements must no doubt be made in any claim set up for such a habit, when we consider the usages of polite society and those of diplomacy, yet it still remains substantially true that the instinct of rectilinearity is the governing one, albeit considerably modified by special circumstances. No very long acquaintance is required with any Asiatic race, however, to satisfy us that their instincts and ours are by no means the same — in fact, that they are at opposite poles. We shall lay no stress upon the redundancy of honorific terms in all Asiatic languages, some of which in this respect are indefinitely more elaborate than the Chinese. Neither do we emphasise the use of circumlocutions, periphrases, and what may be termed aliases, to express ideas which are perfectly simple, but which no one wishes to express with simplicity. Thus a great variety of terms may be used in Chinese to indicate that a person had died,

and not one of the expressions is guilty of the brutality of saying so; nor does the periphrasis depend for its use upon the question whether the person to whom reference is made is an emperor or a coolie, however widely the terms employed may differ in the two cases. Nor are we at present concerned, except in a very general way, with the quality of veracity of language. When every one agrees to use words in "a Pickwickian sense," and every one understands that every one else is doing so, the questions resulting are not those of veracity but of method.

No extended experience of the Chinese is required to enable a foreigner to arrive at the conclusion that it is impossible, from merely hearing what a Chinese says, to tell what he means. This continues to be true, no matter how proficient one may have become in the colloquial — so that he perhaps understands every phrase, and might possibly, if worst came to worst, write down every character which he has heard in a given sentence; and yet he might be unable to decide exactly what the speaker has in mind. The reason of this must of course be that the speaker did not express what he had in mind, but something else more or less cognate to it, from which he wished his meaning or a part of it to be inferred.

Next to a competent knowledge of the Chinese language, large powers of inference are essential to any one who is to deal successfully with the Chinese, and whatever his powers in this direction may be, in many instances he will still go astray, because these powers were not equal to what was required of them. In illustration of this all-pervading phenomenon of Chinese life, let us take as an illustration a case often occurring among those who are the earliest, and often by no means the least important, representatives to us of the whole nation — our servants. One morning the "Boy" puts in an appearance with his usual expressionless visage, merely to mention that one of his "aunts" is ailing, and that he shall be obliged to forego the privilege of doing our work for a few days while he is absent prosecuting his inquiries as to her condition. Now it does not with certainty follow from such a request as this that the "Boy" has no aunt, that she is not sick, and that he has not some more or less remote idea of going to see about her, but it is, to put it mildly, much more probable that the "Boy" and the cook have had some misunderstanding, and that as the prestige of the latter happened in this case to be the greater of the two, his rival takes this oblique method of intimating that he recognises the facts of the case, and retires to give place to another.[1]

One cannot help but feel slightly uneasy when reading these pages today. The author's conviction of the superiority of Western culture is all too clear in too many places (such as when speaking of Western "intellectual habits" or the "Asiatic race"); this ethnocentric prejudice appears all the stronger since it is based, without a trace of contrition, on a colonial relationship ("by no means the least important" representatives of the "whole nation" are said to be coolies). The Chinese are thus placed in the role of the other par excellence, to serve conveniently as the diametric opposite of Westerners. While we look at them with curiosity, we feel confirmed in our own values.

And yet Smith's words are not as transparent as they first appear. Something gradually eludes the initial framework, making the train of thought seem more disturbing and tortuous. Initially, certainly, everything is clear. As Westerners, we express ourselves directly, because we go straight to the marrow of things, guided by an "instinct of rectilinearity," which is also the shortest path to the truth. The Chinese, on the other hand, encumber themselves with circumlocutions, making every effort to express in a roundabout way what might be very "simple" but what no one among them "wishes" to express simply. But can it be left at that? So immersed is Smith in the values of Western culture that, as an eyewitness, he not merely accuses the other of peculiarity but actually suspects him of a certain perversity. Smith, however, is forced to recognize that the so-called unjustified taste for detour is nothing less than a sort of talent and that this continual sleight of hand in communication is presented with an elegance that raises it to an art. It is not enough to study the Chinese language; one must learn to decode the conversations: "large powers of in-ference" are required in China, even with the simplest people and in the most banal day-to-day exchanges. More disturbing still, their immoderate taste for detour makes us confusedly aware, "in a very general way," of a *possible* change of perspective. We dis-cover that another meaning comes to light through detour itself ("a Pickwickian sense," as the author puts it) and that a certain efficacy is therefore at play here, beyond the machinations of mis-chief makers (whom one could easily dispense with by treating them as impostors or sophists): this indirection is based on a con-sensus and might even appear perfectly normal within this other community. Hence the "marrow" of things, as well as the stability of the "subject," escapes us in their presence; our initial criterion becomes confused, and we teeter outside sacrosanct "veracity."

The Chinese counterpart to our attachment to veracity would be something along the lines of "method." This idea remains vague (does Smith really have a specific strategy of meaning in mind?), but we do get a glimpse of something that should be pursued. We think we can safely place the "Chinese" in the role of the other and look at him with curiosity when suddenly, instead of playing the part of the noble savage, he becomes threatening. It would appear, then, that this *indirect* quality, presented as characteristic of Chinese culture, is not so easily mastered. Not only are we con-tinuously led to seek another meaning in conversations, but we are never sure that the inferred meaning is true. Our eyewitness becomes alarmed: if a Chinese person politely refuses the gratuity you offer him, Smith reports later, it may not be for the reasons you initially "deduced," namely, that he wishes to indicate his hope to receive more from you; rather, it may mean, in an even more twisted fashion, that he "prefers to leave it an open question til such time as his own best move is obvious." This disturbs Smith most and appears most dangerous to him: the detour is an attempt not so much to suggest something else (something one dares not mention) as to keep the other in the discomfort of an "open question," thereby arrogating the initiative of action to oneself. Such detour serves not so much to convey alternative information differently as to leave us at a disadvantage. It would tend, dare we say it, to manipulate us.

It is no surprise, therefore, that what in the beginning of Smith's book appears contempt for the other in the name of Anglo-Saxon "intellectual habits" suddenly leads us to acknowledge a possible superiority: not because this art of detour gives someone the ability to manipulate others — Smith, an American missionary, would not dare go down that path — but because it requires a "ready intuition" in different circumstances and makes us more "guarded" in our relations. Smith then presents the following scene:

> Nothing is more amusing than to watch the demeanor of a Chinese who has made up his mind that it is best for him to give an intimation of something unfavorable to someone else. Things must have gone very far indeed when, even under these circumstances, the communication is made in plain and unmistakable terms. What is far more likely to occur is the indirect suggestion, by oblique and devious routes, of something that cannot, which *must* not be told. (p. 68)

Through this "amusing" scene, Smith implies that we may be witnessing a very effective tactic of confusion:

19

> He makes vague introductory remarks, leading up to the revelation
> of apparent importance, and just as he gets to the climax of the case
> he suddenly stops short, suppresses the predicate upon which every-
> thing depends... (p. 68)

But the significance of this behavior ultimately escapes Smith, and
his account lapses into nonsense:

> ... all the while the poor unenlightened foreigner has seen nothing,
> except that there is nothing whatever to see. (p. 68)

I shall not dwell on the many instances Smith finds to denounce invidiously this deeply rooted taste for detour, "which
certainly seems to us both surprising and futile" — for example,
the announcement of bad news in cryptic terms, the allusive yet
coded designations of family members, and the insinuated expressions of insult — for "without the utterance of a word to which
exception could be taken," a Chinese person has only to omit the
slightest gesture within a complex ceremonial code to express,
indirectly but unequivocally, his disapproval or criticism. This
"talent" is also found in discourse:

> All Chinese revile one another when angry, but those whose literary
> talents are adequate to the task delight to convey an abusive meaning
> by such delicate innuendo that the real meaning may for the time
> quite escape observation, requiring to be digested like a sugar-coated
> pill. (p. 71)

According to Smith, the best example of the "Chinese talent for
indirection" is found in the official press, for even a foreigner can
see that some detail about the troubles suffered by an old man-
darin, who "sighs after the day he could have retired from His

Majesty's Service," or some information about a civil servant, who is "invited to return to his post immediately," has other meanings. But how does he find them out? And once he thinks he has one deciphered, is he ever sure?

> Firmly are we persuaded that the individual who can peruse a copy of the Peking *Gazette* and, while reading each document, can form an approximately correct notion as to what is really behind it, knows more of China than can be learned from all the works on this Empire that ever were written. But is there not reason to fear that by the time any outside barbarian shall have reached such a pitch of comprehension of China as this implies, we shall be as much at a loss to know what *he* meant by what *he* said, as if he were really Chinese? (p. 72)

Here the subtlety of detour, by remaining hermetic, makes us into outside barbarians. Even if this last remark is not without irony, it betrays embarrassment, for it reverses one's original position. In a word, which side experiences the "education"? Worse still, once we have entered into this other functioning of meaning, we are cut off from Western logic: we *become* "Chinese."

"China watching," as we see, did not begin yesterday. The *Peking Gazette*, published at the end of the empire, had its counterpart in the *People's Daily* of Communist China. In brief, the official press does not simply offer "perfect illustrations" of detour "every day," as Smith asserts; it also provides us with a firm basis for analysis, for the discourse of those in power illuminates, retrospectively, what its formulations had initially left in the shadows or indirectly implied. Inasmuch as this discourse is continuous and serial, it gives us both a general perspective and reference points by which to interpret it — which the events themselves confirm. Similarly,

21

indirect signification no longer arises in isolation (as in Western relationships with the Chinese) but is visibly integrated into a corpus, which we can learn to decode.

Like any apprentice sinologist, I had the experience of learning to decode Chinese while living in Peking and then in Shanghai from 1975 to 1977. At this time, conflicts of power were at their most violent in China; and the political party line also underwent the greatest upheaval (before and after the death of Mao Zedong, on September 9, 1976, when Chinese policy transformed the revolutionary radicalism imposed by the Gang of Four into the reformist realism of Deng Xiaoping). At the same time, the hegemony of the Chinese Communist Party and the principle of its legitimacy required that the leaders' discourse always appear perfectly unified and consensual, in spite of their dissensions, and that all changes of direction in the historical evolution be dissimulated as much as possible beneath the continuity of its formulaic style. The discourse was thus nearly opaque but deeply fraught with the most divergent concerns; it was nearly unmoored as well, although it had to cover the most convulsive movements. Moreover, beneath the consensual formulation, recognized as canonical, many ulterior motives filtered through. Likewise, in the rehashing of propaganda from one day to the next, countless hidden orientations emerged. This completely stereotyped official discourse does not tell us anything; it is, however, rich in indirect significations and secret warnings, which, for those who know how to read between the lines (since there is nothing to read *on* the lines), are never ambiguous.

I will briefly take as an example the sequence (in discourse) from the elimination to the subsequent return of Deng Xiaoping. One can easily understand that at the beginning of a political movement, when a new orientation is just taking shape, expression is the most shrouded and detour the most extensive. Deng,

first targeted through a critique directed against a fictional character (Song Jiang, from the fourteenth-century novel *The Water
Margin*), was accused by President Mao of "capitulationism." The
denunciation became much less indirect when this campaign
spread through the Revolution in Teaching movement during the
winter of 1975–1976, when people became aware of the "revisionist" positions Deng held on this subject. It became even more
specific when explicit reference was made to "Party heads who
never regretted their errors" — an obvious allusion to the first
elimination of Deng during the Cultural Revolution. Then it cul-
minated in the most laconic expression, which became canonical:
the "critique of Deng" (*pi Deng*). This expression designated him
by name and served as the basic formula for political discourse
until Mao's death: during Mao's last months, every other declaration in China tended toward this formula, confirming it, summing
itself up through it.[2]

Deng's rehabilitation came in a diametrically inverse movement immediately after Mao's death. At first, and after Deng had
already begun his return to politics, one "continued" to criticize
him officially. But by moving away from the above-mentioned formula, the discourse as a whole began to make one suspect that this
formula was outmoded (not only did it let us see this, but it forewarned us, for this formula was logically expected). Instead of
culminating every discourse, the "critique of Deng" formula gradually became isolated: no one touched on it directly, but the adja-
cent formulations that gave consistency to this expression fell
away. Then, having been isolated, the formula became more and
more rare. Finally, it was modified: when one spoke no longer of
the critique of Deng but of his faults, everyone understood perfectly well, though still indirectly, that Deng has been rehabilitated.
(Again, everything first appeared indirectly: the new expression
of Deng's faults began to appear on billboards — the famous *dazi-*

bao — and thus in a more anecdotal and "popular" manner before journalistic discourse made it official.) Similarly, before Deng's rehabilitation had been announced, when the epithet "comrade" Deng Xiaoping was resurging, everyone unambiguously knew that he had again taken control.

I already have stressed that the Party leadership could not permit a rupture in its discourse because, despite all the changes of line, its very legitimacy was at stake. However, this formulaic continuity also brought other advantages. First, since the newspaper reader always understands more than what is explicitly stated, he is placed — in spite of himself — in a relationship of complicity. Indeed, he finds himself already complicitous with the change that is merely insinuated. In attenuating the rupture as much as possible, the Party line always deprives the reader of alternative or choice: such a gradual modification of the formulation keeps him — and again, even if this is in spite of himself — in continuous assent. Something that is always only implied and always only manifests itself by nuance can never allow one to assume an antagonistic position toward it.

In light of this twofold sequence, I think one can schematize such indirect functioning according to two types of signs. In the first case, the official discourse uses detour to *prepare the ground* for establishing a new political line. This is what happened during the critique of Deng, when those whom history will remember as the Gang of Four did everything in their power to eliminate Deng, their principal rival, who was scapegoated to vouchsafe their radicalism before the figure of the Great Helmsman disappeared. In the second case, expression is diverted *to announce gently* a political line that has already been more or less definitively adopted but that too openly contradicts the preceding orientation to be directly acceptable. This is what happened during the rehabilitation of Deng, which was almost an accomplished fact after the fall

24

of the Gang of Four but which took several months to become part of the official discourse.

The first type of sign, which attempts to impose a new line, fulfills a *conative* function (a linguistic term, which means *expressing the idea of effort*); the second, which attenuates a rupture, plays the role of *shock absorber*. In general, the conative sign is issued — under the cover of the most consensual formulations, of course — by the ruling class's attempt to force the course of events and orient them to its own advantage. The shock-absorbing sign, on the other hand, is the tool of a political line that has already triumphed but wants to maintain a facade of coherence in a discourse on which all its legitimacy rests. In this sense, the conative sign is prospective and substantial in content (since it wants to transform the situation to come); while the shock-absorbing sign is retrospective and purely formal (its only goal is to facilitate the absorption of a prior shift).

One can delineate the conative and the shock-absorbing sign only after the fact and, of course, through a reading that is itself retrospective. The reader outside the realm of power often cannot decide if what he perceives as skewing the official discourse is preparing for a future event or part of a past resolution. Indeed, of the two, the indirection of the conative sign is more difficult to detect: if what it wants to suggest gradually imposes itself, the discourse that utters it becomes less and less allusive, thereby making one progressively aware of the previous detour. In the opposite case, however, the discourse is not created serially; the indirect signification lacks a clarifying follow-up and folds in on its own mystery — except when a later critical movement allows it to be cross-checked. How should one understand, for example, an article that appeared on the third page of the *People's Daily* on June 19, 1976 (penned by a "young militiawoman" from Shanghai), praising the benefits of the militia's "unified command"? There

25

was no immediate follow-up in the daily paper. But after the fall of the Gang of Four, an accusation published in the same newspaper reported that one of the Four (Wang Hongwen) had wanted to set up a unified command of the militia, of which he had seized control. The detour fabricated by the article attributed to the "young militiawoman" from Shanghai can thus be interpreted, retrospectively, as an initial conative sign, on the leader's part, whose aim was to create this unified command.[3]

Another distinction is in order if one is to understand how this mode of discourse is established: indirect expression functions either through a *borrowing* of external elements or through internal *difference*. In the first case, one speaks of real *detour*, while in the second case, the effect is more of *meandering*. External supports of detour include: first, everything that aids the functioning of the image or whose motif is borrowed from the past, such as when Deng is referred to through a fictional character (or Zhou Enlai through Confucius). Second, there is the anecdote, such as when someone recounts (or invents) a story in which certain details reveal a decisive signification. By its mere mention, this anecdote can, beneath a harmless surface, assume the qualities of a paradigm and serve as a warning (such as the edifying stories told by many newspapers in the spring of 1979, which are full of premonitions of the halt of the democratic process). Third, there is the quotation: someone reports (or pretends to report) the opinion of a third party (or someone quotes a letter or a conversation) in such a way as to divert the desired direction (thus, still at the beginning of the movement of antidemocratic repression, two letters cited in the Readers' Letters of the *People's Daily* for the first time denounced, in the guise of "freedom of opinion," the "unhealthy" imitation of foreign ways — thereby signaling the need for a return to socialist morality). One often finds this detour between one level of discourse and another, discreetly sketching or indicating on the periphery what will soon resonate in the center. University and provincial newspapers were used to disseminate a message that would only later be made official on a national level.[4]

I have already cited one of the most common ways that expression is diverted by internal difference: rarefaction. The *People's Daily* provided one of the finest examples of this at the beginning of de-Maoization in early 1978. One day, January 10, 1978, to be exact, the Marx quotation disappeared from its place at the top of the newspaper (but it reappeared in the following days). Another day, the Mao quotations ceased to be printed in bold type; and on yet another, the Mao quotations were no longer on the first page of the daily — even though they were still printed on the inside pages. At this moment, no one could openly question the infallibility of the Great Helmsman (a process that did not begin until June of the same year, with the debate over the "criterion of truth"); but everyone could understand — was forced to understand — that de-Maoization was in progress. Inasmuch as it reveals a very concrete intention, this rarefaction of the quotation is not merely a symptom but works also as a sign. (Is it conative first, and a shock absorber later — once the political line has definitively shifted?)

Generally speaking, direct expression, meaning the type of expression to which Westerners are accustomed, usually suggests modification by highlighting what has changed. Indirect expression, as practiced by the official press in China, illuminates a modification *by default* by continuing to speak of *things that have not changed* (thus allowing a glimpse — by deduction — of what might have changed). Such is the deliberate effect of the gap, the lacuna, the silence. The most radical case of this is suppression, pure and simple. I think here of the first signs of the thaw between China and the Soviet Union. On May 10, 1979, the Chinese news agency (as quoted by the *People's Daily*) announced Tito's visit to the

27

USSR by directly citing the communiqué of the Yugoslavian news agency, which, of course, did not mention the term *revisionist* (with which the Chinese had always qualified the Soviet Union until that point). On May 16, the *People's Daily*, announcing Tito's arrival in Moscow, designated Brezhnev simply as the "head of the Party and the State." The sign was made all the clearer, since this time it was the Chinese news agency itself that, no longer passing through the detour of a quotation, suppressed the epithet *disgraceful*. The next day, the *People's Daily* announced the arrival of a Soviet Communist Party delegation in Israel, calling it merely by its official and neutral title: the sign is too systematically developed not to be clear — even if the commentary that followed continued to affirm the eminently "revisionist" nature of the Soviet Party. A certain shock absorption was necessary in regard to public opinion (after so many years of anti-Soviet slogans). The Chinese government took advantage of the ambiguity that it had thus maintained, through these very signs of opening, so as to bear — in a *conative* fashion — on the negotiations under way.[5] (I am, of course, merely providing a sketch of the situation and leave historians the task of supplying the details.)

This last example leads to the specific case where the internal difference causing indirect signification is pushed to the point of contradiction. This is one of the most interesting forms of detour to analyze, for its effect is most circuitous. A good example of this was when Mao was used against Mao. According to Mao, the only criterion of truth was "practice": hence, resorting to this criterion made it possible to separate oneself from "Mao's thought" while pretending to "preserve" it and "unfurl the great flag of President Mao over China." During the summer of 1978, quite a few magnificently (and intentionally) convoluted articles in this vein appeared.[6] A little later, when de-Maoization was under way, a political poster on a wall in Wuhan reevaluated the

28

work of Mao: it began by citing Deng's now canonical formula ("seven-tenths good, three-tenths bad"), but then quickly passed over the positive role Mao played before the Revolution to insist at great length, point by point, on the serious faults he committed afterward. It was clear by then that the commentary attached to Deng's formula was not at all in proportion to what it implied and that, consequently, the criticisms set forth far surpassed the "three-tenths" to which they were supposed to be confined. Under the cover of the official formula, and even gaining authority from it, the commentary went beyond its stated position and intentionally subverted it. Without openly asserting that Mao's role was essentially negative, which would have cost a publicist his head, the author of the poster claimed this, although indirectly, through the device of imbalance. I shall conclude with a similar example taken from photography. When the position of the Party leader Wang Dong-xing was beginning to weaken, the *People's Daily* still listed him among the top five leaders (see, for example, August 1, 1978), but Wang no longer appeared in the accompanying photograph. Thus we were left to understand that his luck had changed.[7]

As a Westerner, to view China from the inside was somewhat baffling, since at that time I had almost no direct contact with the Chinese; and when I did speak with them, they unfailingly tended to reproduce the official formulas (so great was their fear of compromising themselves with me). Today, the official discourse in China is much less stereotyped. But has it shed its indirect character?[8] I return briefly to this experience because, although limited, it gives us something to think about, for, while it was in many ways unpleasant, it remains somehow fascinating. Indeed, one might sum up the discourse of that period in the following way: the more it seemed transparent or redundant, the more it

29

might indirectly signify, the more filled it was with allusions and hidden meanings. In other words, the less it seemed to say, the more it told. Of course, such a discourse presents itself as explicit — but in fact, it only exists in an implicit mode. To grasp the allusions, however, the newspaper reader had always to know more than what was written. He became a scholar of sorts, remembering past quotations, considering the text in its context each time, and being ever vigilant to notice the slightest deviation. To penetrate this party line, an art of reading was necessary.

One might be surprised, therefore, that there has been so little systematic literary analysis of Chinese political expression. Those who have broached the question (Alan Liu, Merle Goldman, Lucian Pye) certainly understand — especially in the time of Maoism — that this indirect mode was due to censorship and, consequently, was comparable to the official press of all countries ruled by dictators. Nonetheless, they could not help but notice certain features specific to China, such as that it was not only public opinion that was in an inferior position — and therefore condemned to dissimulate through indirect expression. Indeed, the ruling power itself delivered its orders cryptically. (Did Mao ever specify *whom* among his contemporaries he had in mind when he denounced the character in the novel *The Water Margin*?) On the other hand, in China, much more than elsewhere, a partisan or particularized interest cannot be expressed except in the guise of a consensual formulation and therefore insidiously and subtly. (All the while, as far as I could tell, Chinese officials expressed themselves in as formulaic and coded a way in private as they did in public.) Furthermore, when taking stock of the surprisingly esoteric character of communication, specialists in Chinese political discourse have the habit of speaking of the "traditional Chinese cultural pattern" and invoking "conservative forces" and a "powerful continuity." According to one of them, "Mao's style of using aphorisms and slogans as means for communicating policy directives conformed to the imperial tradition."[9] Having reached this point, the scholar of contemporary Chinese politics seems to have perfected his analysis: he has tied the present to the past, found a guiding thread in spite of revolutions and an explanation through integration. Nevertheless, the question remains: Can one leave it at that and so simply — I would even say naively — invoke what is called tradition? What does tradition, in a word, have to do with it?

In short, I wonder whether it is too convenient to claim to group, under the common heading of Chinese tradition, all that cannot be accounted for otherwise. Will one not then be forced to grope confusedly in this great sack, to be rid (all the better) of everything for which there is no specific explanation, simply because one does not know how to analyze it closely? Tradition encompasses everything that eludes us, covering it with a facile wave of the hand, as if it enables us to get to the "basis" of things, as if it had stability in and of itself, for in the Western imagination, the basis of things retains a certain substantial prestige. Since the idea of continual transmission (from the Latin *tradere*), occurring anonymously from era to era, from hand to hand, is more intellectually reassuring, tradition gives us the impression of grounding ourselves in reality. But how can we believe that tradition alone is enough to uncover the links between things, which have remained hidden, to form a unity that is not artificial, and to produce coherence?

On the other hand, is it easy to eliminate this notion of tradition, which has become untenable? Even though, in great part due to Foucault's analyses, there is now more recognition of historical discontinuities, there is also more awareness that any spectacle is not perceived in the same way from the outside as it is from within (the lesson of Lévi-Strauss). We can apprehend ruptures from within, but coherence appears from the outside. Thus, any

Western sinologist understands that a sort of experience or craft is acquired in silence, through the continuous reading of Chinese materials, a sense of which cannot be reduced to an organized system yet which conditions nonetheless one's capacity for analysis in every circumstance. It is because I have never found a Chinese book that treats Chinese indirection globally that I have, from the outside, undertaken this study. Unfortunately, I always confronted reticence in my Chinese interlocutors when I mentioned this project (they could have offered some suggestions, but they never broached the subject). My objective, nevertheless, has been to try to bring to light certain methods of linguistic functioning so widespread in China that they almost go unnoticed. Since they are intended to remain implicit, I think that the meaning of such utterances can only be made visible by comparing them with other logical configurations — and thus by a continuous exchange between an *outside* and an *inside*. This amounts to reclaiming the right of an actively (or *positively*) Western sinology (that is, one that profits from its external perspective) that knows how to take advantage of the possibility for a comparative reading. The analysis that follows will be a test of this possibility.

I began this chapter by citing Arthur Smith and his *Chinese Characteristics*. I did so not so much to find an antecedent to the surprisingly cryptic and circuitous writing of the official press in contemporary China or to presume some sort of continuity on that basis. Instead, I lingered on those passages because of the malaise they cannot fail to provoke — so great is the mingling of Smith's incomprehension and certain insight, so much does his "curious" perspective remain, beyond his basic ethnocentrism, profoundly ambiguous. Smith's words leave us with an undeniable ideological deficit, which may be all the more serious because sinology has not helped us move much beyond it since then. In seeking to establish itself as a body of knowledge for a century now, sinology has focused mainly on the signified (and primarily on the signified par excellence, the historical signified), while neglecting all that relates to the signifier in travel literature as well as in private reflections. More recently, in distributing itself over the gamut of human sciences, and thus modeling itself on each of these disciplines (as well as once again separating classical China and modern China), sinology has tended to take nothing into account except definite objects of knowledge, thereby losing sight of the acculturation, or the "craft," that gives access to them (although all sinologists *have been obliged* to deal with the indirect expression of the Chinese in some way).[10] Moreover, sinology has left gaping wide the lacuna so poorly filled by Smith's pages.

I speak of an ideological deficit in sinology, and perhaps in orientalism in general, because there is now an awareness that the difference in question cannot be effectively treated in terms of race (Asiatic) or instinct (nor in terms of their surrogates, such as mentality). Hence the goal of this book is to situate the phenomena here under study on their proper level. Indirect expression in China is of the order of rhetoric, even if it first seems antirhetoric (because it favors the symbolic or the subtle, as opposed to discourse). It is, therefore, from this vantage point that I shall consider the phenomena. And indeed, nothing leads us to believe that this antirhetoric does not exist, to some extent, in Western culture as well, even though the rhetorical tradition predominates or, at least, is more visible. Most importantly, there is no reason to think that this other functioning cannot be grasped logically, with no residual effects. To deem something impossible, or "Chinese to me" (when speaking not of language but of discourse), is senseless. To concede as a last resort that "he is Chinese" (as Khrushchev did to Mao), hence isolating the other in his absurdity, is equally idiotic. The danger, as was evident in my reading of Smith, is to allow difference to be established in kind. Difference is not

33

something to be imposed (by forcing the Chinese to play the role of the other par excellence) nor something to be leveled at all costs (in the name of a humanist universalism, too immediate and too lazy) — but something to *be made intelligible.* In the following pages, I will attempt to describe the forms of utterance, and will ultimately present them in an alternative way that will reveal their coherence, by taking advantage of the effect of contrast. For this reason, I begin with a consideration of the question of detour by situating myself at a vantage point in which operational models are set into play — that is, by beginning with opposing strategies.

CHAPTER TWO

Frontal Versus Oblique Attack

Military strategy was much more than a specific technique in ancient China. It reflected some of the most radical elements of Chinese thought and informed many other disciplines when elaborated into theory. If there is one basic principle on which all ancient Chinese military treatises insist, it is that of avoiding direct confrontation with an armed enemy. A frontal clash, in which two armies are engaged face-to-face, was always considered eminently risky and destructive. The whole art of war was crafted with the intention of depriving the other of his ability to defend himself and undermining him from within, even before the confrontation took place, so that at the moment of confrontation the enemy collapsed of his own accord. "To carry one hundred victories for every hundred battles," wrote one of the oldest masters of the art of war, "is not an end in itself, whereas to subjugate the enemy without having engaged in combat is the height of excellence."[1] "The best general is he whose merits one does not even dream of praising, since he vanquishes an already defeated enemy."[2] Rather than glorifying the battle, the art of war taught how to triumph by avoiding battle altogether.

Strategy also consisted in attacking the enemy's plans, or ideas, rather than his troops by physical force. The best strategist was the one always able to anticipate the course of events, the one who could situate himself before their conception and thereby thwart maneuvers as the enemy planned them. Conversely, the worst way to engage in battle was to end up in a face-to-face immobilization of armies, such as a siege. Such cases lessened initiative and lost flexibility. It is hardly surprising, then, that Chinese theorists of military strategy advise not the destruction of the enemy (for this would deprive him of his resources, which are better to use to one's own advantage) but his *destructuration*. By striking at the level of the "brain"[a] rather than at deployed forces, the good strategist inhibited his enemy; it was enough for him to deprive the enemy of his ability to react, to paralyze his movements. This is why he who "dexterously handles his troops ... subjugates the enemy without combat and takes his positions without attack."[3] The internal disintegration to which the adversary was initially subjected precluded the necessity of confronting him later: such an enemy was always immediately vanquished, since he was continuously disabled.

Two pairs of concepts underlie this theory of thwarting at the core of ancient Chinese military writings: the "direct" versus the "oblique" and the "straight" versus the "circuitous."[b] The first pair has an essentially strategic function, while the second is more limited to the description of tactical operations. But whatever the application, the resource exploited by Chinese military art always rests on the relationship of direct and indirect. When maneuvering troops, it might be just as advisable to make the enemy's advances excessively long and tortuous, so as to exhaust him, by luring him with false bait as to make one's own progress circuitous and keep one's plans secret in order to surprise the enemy.[4] Similarly, the most general strategy can be summed up as follows: "an encounter takes place frontally, while victory is gained obliquely."[5] According to a series of commentators, "frontally" signifies

36

not only facing the enemy but doing so in a normal, ordinary, pre-dictable way. Similarly, "obliquely" means not only approaching from the side but doing so in an extraordinary way: unexpected by the enemy, reaching him when he is least prepared. The attack is indirect, operating in secret.

But even in such explicit terms, the distinction remains too crude, for it imagines the opposition from the outside without taking into account the internal differences between the two processes. Another treatise from Antiquity allows us to pene-trate more deeply into the logic of this correlation by placing it within a more general perspective of the way things come about: "When [something] that has occurred and assumed a shape cor-responds to [something] that has likewise assumed a shape, we have a frontal relationship; but when, without having assumed a shape, [this] reacts to [that which] has assumed a shape, then we have an oblique relationship."[c6] If I make this statement more specific by relating it to the military arts and to operations on the ground, then positioning one's troops in response to the enemy's position would represent a frontal relationship, whereas domi-nating the adversary's troops' position without taking a position would represent an oblique relationship. In other words, through the absence of positioning, I control the positioning of the ene-my. In the frontal relationship, the two realities that "correspond to each other" are limited by their concrete and specific charac-teristics; at the same time, each offers the other a hold on it by allowing itself to be seen as identifiable, as a target. It is easy to define, by way of contrast, the oblique relationship and what characterizes its superiority: that is, what has not yet occurred and taken concrete form benefits from possible expedients and escapes the outside assessment that might allow for opposition. In operating on the virtual level, the oblique relationship makes it possible to keep one's initiative intact while remaining unattackable. This is why the oblique relationship upsets the enemy's maneuvers.

The same treatise asserts that, insofar as one adversary is the same as the other, the one cannot triumph over the other; therefore, the relationship in which one differs most from the other constitutes, in a figurative and purely trajectorial way, an "oblique" relationship,[d] which allows one to overpower the other. This treatise also represents the differences at play as an opposition of stages: "the stage of deployment represents a frontal relationship, the stage that precedes deployment is the oblique relationship."[e7] If we follow the logic of this remark as far as it will go, we end up with something that seems a paradox but represents the most profound intuition: "When the oblique relationship is in effect, not to respond [in kind] makes a victory possible."[f] Indeed, if the enemy attacks me obliquely, it is by responding frontally that I neutralize him. To maintain my oblique capacity, I must renew the oblique through the frontal relationship and not immobilize myself in it. As a Tang emperor explained, the art of war "consists in creating a frontal relationship from an oblique relationship in such a way that the enemy, seeing it as a frontal relationship, allows me to surprise him obliquely and likewise creating an oblique relationship from a frontal relationship in such a way that the enemy, seeing it as an oblique relationship, allows me to attack him frontally."[8] Thus by countering frontally he who thinks to surprise me obliquely, I take him obliquely. As the above passage concludes, the victor will always be the one with a "surplus of oblique moves" (that is, the one with "one more" oblique move "left over").[g9] In other words, as the first treatise cited maintains, he who is apt to "produce an oblique move" is as "inexhaustible" as "the heavens and the earth" (in their continual renewal) and as "unfailing" as the "streams and rivers."[10] This "surplus of oblique moves" thus captures most precisely the content of the strategic

38

principles mentioned above: to preserve the initiative while the enemy is crippled and to remain impenetrable.

Under the influence of Western thought, twentieth-century Chinese philosophers have described the conceptual relationship at work here (as well as in the other great dyads in Chinese thought, such as rest and movement, modification and continuity) as dialectical — in the Hegelian-Marxist sense. But clearly, the two types of relationships opposed, frontal and oblique, never lead to anything other than themselves (and thus never transcend their opposition) — they also never cease to converge and, in so doing, renew themselves. One intuition at the core of Chinese thought is the concept that everything that actualizes itself through opposition always latently contains its opposite, so that opposites, by remaining linked, alternate between themselves; hence, an uninterrupted dynamism flows from their reversion. The theorist of military strategies contemplates the constant renewal of this dynamism in the great disposition of the world, through the incessant comings and goings of the sun and the moon and the changing of seasons. It is this dynamism that the strategist will reproduce, to his advantage, on the battlefield, for the ability to function through immanence is the same in both cases. It is therefore enough for him to allow the strategic arrangement to operate only through the frontal or the oblique attack. Just as sounds, colors, and smells "are all five in number," according to the traditional Chinese nomenclature, but "are never ending in their variations," the "strategic potential" always rests on these two possibilities alone, though the variations obtained through them are inexhaustible. Such serial continuity is illustrated by the figure of the ring: "oblique and frontal relationships engender each other, like a ring forever following itself, with no head and no tail; who could ever reach the end?"[11]

Through continuous conversion, the frontal and oblique approaches are equally necessary to permitting the *endless* renewal of strategic potential. But we also have seen that of the two, the oblique is preponderant, since it functions through both relationships, with the frontal gaining its validity through the oblique. As a classical war veteran noted, it is always through an oblique relationship that victory is achieved: when I attack frontally, it is to surprise my enemy's oblique approach with an oblique approach of my own. Hence, since it always situates me on a level prior to actualization, the oblique relationship allows me to manipulate the other as I please, while remaining unfathomable myself. Moreover, inasmuch as I always retain an oblique move as a "leftover" — because of the unending alternation between one approach and the other — my ability to attack remains intact and my potential inexhaustible.[12] This strategic concept, formulated quasi-definitively in the fifth and sixth centuries of Chinese Antiquity, has ceaselessly been reformulated and commented on, to the point that it has become proverbial and seems no longer to require justification. In the twentieth century, Mao referred to it once again in his military treatises (which remain, in my opinion, the best part of his oeuvre and greatly illuminate his political conduct): to conquer the enemy, one must first disorient him, "make noise in the east to attack in the west."[13] The whole of Chinese military strategy can be summed up in this oblique phrase.

I would like to make these concepts come alive and shake up the context in which they have usually been contained by briefly comparing them with what the ancient-military scholars John Keegan and Victor Davis Hanson have described as the Western model of war. This model is thought to have been almost definitively formulated by the ancient Greeks. But the concept it puts forth is diametrically opposed to the Chinese model, because it rests on directly facing the enemy in pitched battle. Around the seventh century B.C., the conduct of war in Greece underwent profound changes: gone were the days of skirmishes and ambushes, the one-on-one confrontations between enraged heroes of the sort Homer sang about. A new structure was put into place — the phalanx — according to which two bodies of heavily armed and cuirassed hoplites, arranged in lines one behind the other and marching in step to the rhythm of the fife, advanced in tight formation, with no possibility of fleeing. This face-to-face could lead only to a massive and destructive clash, for the sole effort of these men on each side was in the "thrust" *(ōthismos);* the first ranks, which directly sustained the enemy's charge, were supported by the accumulated pressure of the ranks behind them. Indeed, the deeper the column and the tighter its ranks, the better it weighed on the enemy and the more striking its power and momentum.

Hanson has demonstrated that what might appear pure carnage in this frontal clash corresponds to a principle of economy:[14] reducing the ravages of a protracted war, which spares neither goods nor families in the "all or nothing of the pitched battle," to obtain, through a brief and direct confrontation between the political bodies that represent cities, the quickest and least equivocal decision possible. This is why adversaries engaged in combat, according to the rules, by setting the rigid order of the phalanx into motion on an exposed site cleared of obstacles and agreed on by both parties. Disdained were the dilatory operations in which dodging and harassing were alternately used to tire the enemy out, since their circuitousness diluted the rapidity and definitiveness of the single assault. Moreover, all arms that were used from afar or by surprise, such as arrows and javelins, were rejected in favor of lances, which were the arm par excellence of face-to-face combat. "The Greeks thought," Polybius explains, "that it was only a hand-to-hand battle at close quarters which was truly deci-

41

sive."[15] Skill in maneuvers became less important; all that really mattered was the courage exhibited at the crucial moment. As such, weakening the enemy in advance was not even attempted: Agesilas decided, Xenophon states, that it was better to let one's enemies regroup, no matter their number, and "allow the two hostile forces to come together, in case they wished to fight, to conduct the battle in regular fashion and in the open."[16] Taken to such an extreme, Greek military strategy offers a sharp contrast with Chinese military strategy: the Greeks would have resolutely ignored the infinite expedients of oblique confrontation, relying instead on the violent clash of a victorious or fatal encounter. On the one side, we have mass weight, on the other, the strategy of detour: physical pressure is opposed to the art of thwarting. The Greek model of war, Hanson explains, did not die with the Greeks. The Americans, who, in Vietnam, were put in the impossible position of engaging in a confrontation of this type, "were the most recent prisoners of this ancient heritage."

This picture needs to be clarified: we should not imagine that the Greeks were unaware of the expedients of detour or were not cunning. Their taste for strategems is well documented. Marcel Detienne and Jean-Pierre Vernant have brilliantly demonstrated the importance to them of *mētis*, or cunning intelligence, with which the gods themselves were richly endowed and which combines "intuition," "foresight," "feint," "various skills," and "a sense of opportunity." It is nonetheless important to note that it was not by deliberately resorting to *mētis* that the Greeks regulated their armed conflicts. More importantly still, the kind of intelligence manifested in this taste for detour, this *agnkulomētēs*, "always appeared more or less 'submerged,'" Detienne and Vernant explain, "immersed in a practice that never seeks, even as it uses it, to explain its nature or to justify its actions."[17] Unlike Chinese obliqueness, *mētis* remains in the shadows of reason, appearing clearly only in myth. Repressed by speculative thought, it is not the object of any Greek theory.[18]

This comment on *mētis* deserves to be generalized, since it allows us to understand that the comparison just outlined remains tentative because it draws a parallel between military strategies (among the Chinese) and a way of enacting war, not of thinking about it, as the Greek historians have reported it. I have not made this comparison more rigorously, simply because there are no Greek military strategy texts on this subject that are comparable to the Chinese treatises. Certainly, there is an abundant literature on Greek military *technē*, but this is never philosophical (nor has it influenced, to my knowledge, other areas of Greek thought). Moreover, the Hellenists do not seem concerned to exploit it (as proof, there are the largely undeveloped treatises of Aelianus and Arrian). One might go so far as to ask: What would be the specifically strategic interest of a theory of war that favored frontal confrontation and shunned the infinite expedients of the oblique? (Or to take it one step further: Does the thought of even a Carl von Clausewitz, recognized as the greatest theorist of war in Europe, constitute a work on strategy?)

Furthermore, the Greek texts that focus only on tactics lead one to refine the model of confrontation elaborated by Hanson rather than to question it. In Asclepiodotus's succinct and almost mathematical description of the phalanx, he envisions an "oblique" arrangement (*lochos*) as opposed to a "frontal" formation (*plagia, orthia*), but he does not draw any conclusions on this subject. Aeneas the tactician occasionally advises not to confront the adversary immediately but to wait until, emboldened by the deviation, he begins to let down his guard (Xenophon, in *Horsemanship*, and Frontinus, in *Stratagems*, give the same advice). He also recommends that one know how to create a diversion the better to attack the adversary by surprise and that one not neglect secret

43

sallies or other cunning means (spying and disinformation existed in Greece, and people have been wrong to consider them Chinese attributes).[19] But although this practice of detour was always present in Greek strategy, unlike in China it was considered a last resort. One can very well give such advice, but the Greek concept of war was not *based on these concepts*. Detienne's work on the phalanx confirms the importance of the Greek style of confrontation all the more because it allows us to see the direct link between the phalanx and the organization of the city. There is even a homology between the structure of the two: through the uniformity of equipment, the equivalence of positions, and even the types of required behavior, the foot soldiers of the phalanx were reduced to "interchangeable elements" that corresponded exactly to their position as citizens in the egalitarian framework of political life.[20] It therefore appears that the phalanx, and with it the logic of a frontal approach, could indicate a choice of Greek culture. Let us, then, see if the comparison can be drawn out further and if what we have demonstrated with the phalanx can orient us toward a more general opposition.

I hazard a question: Does this face-to-face confrontation of phalanxes on the battlefield have an equivalent in the face-to-face discussion around which the city was organized? I use the word "equivalent" and not merely "analogy"; the *agonistic* structure of armed confrontation also existed in the organization of the theater (tragedy or comedy), the tribunal, and the assembly. Indeed, whether in the dramatic, the judicial, or the political realm, the debate manifested itself like a force pressing for or against something, in which the upper hand was gained only by the sheer strength and number of arguments either side amassed. Hence if there is homology between the phalanx and the city, it is not only because they shared participants (as citizen-soldiers) but also

44

because their structures caused them both to make decisions in the same way. We just saw how the confrontation of phalanxes strove to obtain a decision as quickly and unequivocally as possible; the face-to-face arguments at the heart of antithetical discussions, as the Greeks conceived of them, whether in the theater, the tribunal, or the assembly, had the same end in mind. Orators made their cases in front of each other, in full view and knowledge of everyone and in a limited time frame, and every witness could draw his own conclusions. This antagonistic thrust in either direction would then be translated into a majority vote. In this respect, the face-to-face confrontation of speeches is tightly bound to the Western democratic organization. (To convince ourselves of this point, we need merely consider the importance of televised debates in modern political life.) Hence we might ask: To what extent does the privilege that the Chinese tradition accords the oblique approach thwart the democratic process in China today? (And, more ironically, when will the candidates for power in China confront each other in organized debates?) Although contrary to Western ideology, in which voting and freedom are so closely associated, it seems to me that decision making arrived at by a simple vote would *logically* have difficulty taking root in a political system dominated by obliqueness.

The face-to-face confrontation of arguments, which Westerners take for granted, is therefore not as obvious as one might think. It underlines, like the vote that is its culmination, a cultural circumstance that, in comparison with China, appears rather particular. One might therefore assert the principle: while an isolated argument frees up ideas, two antithetical arguments, by opposing ideas, bind them all the closer. And we know, at least in general, the origin of oratorical debate (*agōn logōn*), as it was established in Greece in the fifth century B.C. Clearly, one tradition began with Protagoras, who not only attempted, according to Aristotle, "to make the weakest of two arguments the strongest" but also conceived of the idea that "for any question there exist two discourses or two contrary arguments." ("He was the first to say that everything had two opposing arguments," Diogenes Laertius states.[21] Clement of Alexandria confirms this: "The Greeks claim, after Protagoras, that in regard to any discourse there exists another that is opposed to it."[22] From this principle follows, to a great extent, the Western conception of *logos*. If an opposite position can always be argued, the art of debate, which developed simultaneously with the formation of reason, would essentially consist in advancing arguments opposed to those presented and making them more persuasive.

It is quite evident, since Greek orators made such frequent use of it, what this discursive procedure of confrontation consists in. Among the means most frequently used to reverse an argument, the simplest is refutation, which consists in showing that the adversary's argument is erroneous; there is also compensation, which attempts to annul the adversary's argument, and reversal, where one demonstrates that what an adversary thought to be in his favor is, in fact, not in his favor or is favorable to us (which is accomplished by twisting his argument). Whatever the route taken, the whole art consists in sticking as close as possible to the opposing arguments (and reusing the adversary's facts, words, and ideas as much as possible) while arriving at opposite conclusions. As Jacqueline de Romilly has clearly shown about Thucydides' antilogies, the responding argument in this verbal confrontation must align itself strictly to that to which it is responding (*logos para logon*; and in an opening argument, the orator must anticipate the arguments that will be thrown back at him) in such a way that each speech provides the closest possible argumentation (*logoi antikatateinantes*, as Thucydides calls it: these "discourses" are "hurled forcefully against each other").[23] I think that one can even formulate an essential principle of *logos*, as it originated in Greece, based on the functioning of antilogy, thereafter so common: the aim of *logos* is to grasp its object *as closely as possible*. Inversely, the aim of Chinese expression (characterized by *wen*) is, by oblique means, to achieve suppleness and elusiveness, to keep the grip "slack"[i] to maintain an *allusive distance* to the object in view.

This figure of confrontation highlights the nature of the antagonistic *thrust*. Inevitably, certain tactical aspects discussed earlier reemerge. Once two lists enumerating the advantages on two sides of an argument have been established like two opposing phalanxes, one settles the question merely "by saying which list is longer or presents greater advantages." The comparison (and the ensuing decision) will be all the more probing and swift when its elements are similar. The isonomic principle in the structure of the phalanx thus appears just as necessary. The rigor of antilogy tends "to transform all the elements of argumentation into comparable givens, subject to addition or subtraction, and thus interchangeable"; one arranges the arguments in facing units, "as one does with numbers."[24] Confrontation and calculation are thus the basis of this conflict of words, and it is always by *surplus* — of arguments presented, not of secret obliqueness — that a victory is won. "So," Thucydides has one of his Peloponnesian leaders, facing an enemy, say, "when you think of their greater experience you must also think of your own greater courage, and when you feel frightened because of the defeat you have suffered, you must remember that at that time you were caught off your guard and unprepared. There are solid advantages on your side — you have the bigger fleet: you are fighting off your own native shores..."[25] "Here," notes de Romilly, "the same words describe the two parallel columns *(antitaxasthē)*, making it possible to see the arithmetical conclusions clearly: the neutral comparatives correspond well to the advantages of either side."[26] The arguments are thus evaluated like weighed quantities. It is also revealing on this point that the same Greek term, *logiksesthai*, means both *to think* and *to count*.

Thus the organized face-to-face confrontation of arguments was more than rhetorical play for the Greeks. It was a veritable intellectual instrument. Sustaining or turning an argument around, proceeding via thesis and antithesis appeared the best method to bring out, before a listener, the sought-after truth. Later, the very strict, and thus very rigid, treatment of antilogy, which one finds in all the fifth-century genres — not only in oratory but also in drama and the writing of history — became much more supple. In transforming itself, this *antilogy* would lead, notably, to the philosophical *dialogue*, for pure antilogy as an exercise risked giving the impression that all things could be defended equally and, in this way, could become morally dangerous or lead to skepticism. Furthermore, the procedure, as Plato criticizes it in *The Republic* (1.348A), implies continual and successive arguments and requires the presence of a third party to act as judge. This antithetical construction of discourse will not, consequently, be constantly reworked and is destined from the start to the endless adventures of dialectic. But in this face-to-face antagonism, can we not detect not simply a point of departure but a chosen *position* continuously at work in Western logic?

The characteristics of military art described above should serve as illustrations. I have begun by accentuating the distance between Chinese and Greek cultures to try to establish a more general alternative (one that might be of use within both a Western and a Chinese framework) — the goal being to gain a better perception of what the economics of meaning rests on, as well as to explore the broadest range of its possibilities. (I am conscious of saying *meaning* in the singular: the effect of meaning, even the most exotic, is something that *becomes* intelligible to us.) Thus I was led to presume that the invention and the perfecting of antithetical discourse in classical Greece found its counterpoint in the confrontation of phalanxes on the battlefield. At the same time, an occasion arose to test a metaphor: that of the strategy of meaning.

Indeed, even in its vocabulary, Greek rhetoric encourages us to imagine the confrontation of arguments in terms of battle.[27] This is all the more obvious among the Chinese. A military expression turned proverb — "to kill the horse to reach the horseman" — is still widely used in Chinese political life to recommend indirectly criticizing a leader through his subordinates (the defensive formulation being the opposite: "to abandon the horse and carriage to protect the general"). Another common expression, still used as we saw by Mao in his thoughts on guerrilla warfare — "make noise in the east to attack in the west" — also applies to discourse. On one side are explicit statements that serve only as diversions (for example, in the official press, the redundant use of set formulas); on the other side is the nuance that dissimulates the polemical charge beneath this cover. This tactical expression finds its perfect homology in another formula that applies only to the art of verbal attack: "to point at the chicken to insult the dog" (or "to point at the mulberry to insult the sophora"[j]). One thing is said to indicate another: the *one* is merely an occasion for detour — and, as such, openly manifested — with the aim of reaching the *other* secretly.

Thus the obliquity recommended in the art of war corresponds to an obliquity in speech. We can complete the picture while continuing to rely on this single contrast: to the thrust of the hand-to-hand or face-to-face confrontation of soldiers or arguments the Chinese prefer detour, which frees up the field for maneuvers, the crafty tactics that will rout the enemy without exposing oneself. Dodging and harrying are once again the goal: instead of presenting arguments so clearly that the other can retort, I use a circuitous expression, which allows me to dodge

49

any frontal attack that might require self-justification while working as my defense. At the same time, I can harry an opponent
ceaselessly by threatening him through allusion — thus pressuring
him by insinuation. As in military strategy, in verbal confrontation the subtlety of the oblique approach opens the way to infinite
games of manipulation. A good military strategist, as we saw,
anticipated the unfolding of events and was better able to domi-
nate his adversary's position for not having taken a position himself. Likewise, criticism gains by evoking the purely suggestive,
inchoate stage of the statement, since a lightly sketched affirmation does not force me to defend a position but rather allows me
to evolve as I will, while remaining master of the game; the adversary is forced to depend on my taking the verbal initiative and is
therefore reduced to passivity. This sort of ever-emerging meaning is all the more menacing since it is never clear where we are
heading. And this barely sketched criticism is all the more dangerous because it never exposes itself, thereby avoiding any grounds
for refutation. Thus there is more than a simple parallel between
the obliquity of discourse and that of military strategy: both relate
to the same economy and contain the same logical justifications.[28]

Let us examine how Liang Shiqiu, a Chinese scholar from the
beginning of the twentieth century who was a great translator of
Shakespeare, depicted the "art of the invective" (an expression
that has become popular in China). On returning from the United
States (the land of "direct talk"), he wrote a few pages perhaps
responding to a need to justify the indirect. After a few general
considerations, Liang begins the fourth paragraph, titled "Strike
from the Side and Attack Obliquely,"[k] as follows:

> If someone steals from you and you say, in accusing him, that he is
> a thief, or if someone robs you and you say, in accusation, that he is
> a bandit, this is stupid. When one wants to accuse someone, one

must first put into practice the art of the empty and the full, the veil and the reflection; one should therefore suggest indirectly and approach laterally, strike from the side and attack obliquely: when you have arrived at the crucial point, you will need but a single word to finish him off, and your opponent, as they say, will have a knife to his throat.[29]

As in Chinese military art, victory can be won before the first battle takes place, before the first words of the argument are spoken (when one begins to fight, the enemy is already defeated; when one releases a word, it is the coup de grâce for the adversary). The efficacy of the invective thus originates in the condition in which the adversary is placed beforehand and is expressed, naturally, in terms of military strategy. Among the titles in Liang's commentary, we find, in addition to the one mentioned above, "Conquering by Withdrawing" and "Preparing Ambushes." At the same time, this terminology of military operations is mixed with aesthetic terms: "full" and "empty" not only are opposed in the theory of military strategy, with points of resistance being full and those of penetration, or gaps, being empty; they also evoke, in the language of painting, the fecund relationship between the fullness of the line and the whiteness of the paper that surrounds and animates it. Similarly, "reflection" and "veil" designate the discreet art of suggestion, which leaves things transparent or masks them and never gives us more than a glimpse. Military strategy and aesthetics are thus considered closely related. Just as strategic potential never ceases to be transformed by alternation, the aesthetic potential continuously renews itself by a variation between presence and evanescence, manifestation and retreat. The critique constantly oscillates between the explicit and the implicit, just as the art of war oscillates between frontal and oblique attacks.

The efficacy of each stems from the same principle. If one

begins with a reproach, everything has already been said; there is nothing more to add, unless one exploits the Greek method mentioned above and engages in a formal demonstration. Speech becomes closed to further development; it has no future and, by betraying its limitations, becomes sterile. Meanwhile, the adversary already knows what he is up against and so has nothing to worry about: in exposing oneself, one is deprived of all resources, while the other gains the means to defend himself. This is precisely what the strategy of detour mitigates: by keeping critical signification purely suggestive and inchoate, it prolongs its virtuality, thereby preserving its offensive capacity as long as possible. Furthermore, the adversary is pressured with something that is not localized in time or space, as in the frontal attack, but prolonged and diffused — all-encompassing and invasive. One suspects that this evasive strategy in speech is much more than an art of litotes; by refusing the fireworks of direct statement, spectacular but immediately depleted, one acquires the possibility of transforming the antagonistic relationship (in which the adversaries are face-to-face and on an equal footing) into a process whose unfolding, by giving more room to maneuver, opens up obliquity's infinite resources. By insinuating suspicion, provoking anxiety, one disables the other.

In the art of invective, therefore, are two characteristics central to Chinese military strategy. The oblique approach gives the one who is criticizing, like the one who is fighting, a means not to expose himself, a means to remain unfathomable, while rendering his power of attack inexhaustible. By always having something else to say in reserve, criticism, alternating moments when the innuendo is more direct with moments when it is more veiled, works on the principle of endless oscillation: it can continue to snake back and forth, never reaching the end of its meanderings.

At the same time, we have grasped the tenor of this detour: the *oblique approach* in military strategy becomes the *implicit* in discourse; the *obliquity* of the trajectory leads to a *depth* of meaning. Hence we should not be surprised that the discussion of the art of invective is followed by praise of the implicit. I quote first the way Arthur Smith conceives of this situation: "All Chinese revile one another when angry, but those whose literary talents are adequate to the task delight to convey an abusive meaning by such delicate innuendo that the real meaning may for the time quite escape observation, requiring to be digested like a sugar-coated pill."[30] As a counterpart to this, the Chinese scholar Liang illuminates this strategy from the inside:

> When one inveighs against someone, it must be done in an infinitely subtle manner, and its meaning must remain implicit. The other should not at first notice that he is being insulted; only after a certain amount of reflection should he progressively realize that these words were not well intentioned, in such a way that his face, which was at first smiling, goes from white to red, and from red to purple, and then from purple to gray. This is the highest level of the art of invective.

He concludes: "Avoid day-to-day language because it is exhausted quickly.[l] It is no match for literary language, whose indirect nature is rich in implicit meaning."[m31]

The basic principle of aesthetics in China, in both painting and poetry, is for the meaning, the pleasure, "not to exhaust itself at first glance" but to develop endlessly. This is why the invective is also an art. Because of its obliquity, the verbal attack has this extra, this surplus, that ensures its depth and opens onto another realm, offering us something into which to delve more deeply. One need only consider the way Chinese scholars for two thousand years read their first literary work, *The Book of Songs*, to take stock of this effect.

53

CHAPTER THREE

Under the Cover of the Image:

Insinuated Criticism

When comparing two civilizations, it is difficult to discern that which is absent in either one. Such absences are often the most telling, since a lack of symmetry serves to illuminate implicit choices. China, for example, is one of the only ancient civilizations not to have an epic at the beginning of its literature: no grand tale of heroic exploits, few evocations of the marvelous. In short, China had no Homer. Its first literary work is an anthology of poems. *The Book of Songs (Shijing)* dates from the ninth to the sixth century B.C., and its last selection is attributed to Confucius. These short poems, recounting few exploits or myths, express sentiments of the people and were used for ritual celebrations during court ceremonies and sacrifices.

With the advent of philosophy, the Greeks had to attempt to justify the Homeric episodes whose treatment of the gods appeared absurd, if not dangerously immoral. They were led to perfect a new type of reading, the allegorical, which in turn led them to conceive of a theoretical lesson behind the imagery invented by the poet (*hyponoia*). This lesson established coherence on another level and rendered the meaning acceptable. According to the classical definition, allegory "signifies" something other than that which it expresses "verbally"; it "seeks" to make us "understand" otherwise: "aliud verbis, aliud sensu ostendit; aliud dicere, aliud intellegi velle" (Quintilian). Moreover, the meaning interpreted allegorically can relate to the physical world (after Theagenes of Rhegium and in the Stoic tradition), or it can be moral and psychological (after Anaxagoras, in particular, and in Antisthenes). The battles fought by the Homeric gods are no longer scandalous when one understands that they represent the natural elements or the conditions of the soul. This allegorical sense has a metaphysical thrust in Neoplatonic thinking, in particular Plotinus. Chronos's enchainment by Zeus, Hesiod explains, demonstrates that intelligence is immutably attached to the realm of intelligibility, with neither the possibility nor the desire to fall into the domain of the sensible. Or Saturn can represent time. He devours his children because infinity tirelessly swallows the years (according to the stoic Balbus, in Cicero's *De natura deorum*). He is enchained by Jupiter because the stars bind him to a regular flow. In their various productions, including those that appear most indecent, the ancient poets Homer and Hesiod presumably send a message about the principles of life and the world, exposing a truth of another order, constructing a "theology."[1]

Allegory, that *other* meaning which the text communicates indirectly through imagery or fiction, or rather, that meaning with which commentators endow the text to accommodate their views, saves the ancient Greek poets from their "irrationality" and cleanses them of all impiety. When read allegorically, Homer and Hesiod remain, with good reason, the "educators" of Hellas — in spite of Plato. Chinese scholars also had to legitimize the canonical status of their ancient *Book of Songs* by seeing in its poems more than anecdotal or circumstantial meanings (especially in the first two parts of the collection, "Feng" and "Xiaoya"). They were to uncover lessons there. To justify the authority stemming from its antiquity (especially since in China tradition is considered sacred) and to confirm the patronage of Confucius — the sage par excellence — assigned to this anthology, they had no choice but to reveal the essential between its covers.

But the essential is not the same in China as in Greece. In keeping with their intellectual and ideological framework, Chinese commentators sought another meaning at the heart of the poetic text that does not touch on the status of the soul or of the divine; it does not attempt to reveal any "truth." The meaning they uncover is social, both moral and political. This means that its morality is conceived of not from an individual and psychological point of view, based on questions of the soul, but from a collective point of view, that of the harmonious regulation of human relationships. The lesson they find in the circumstantial meaning of a poem concerns the order, or disorder, of the family and society. Hence this other meaning does not refer to *another level*, as in Greek allegory; it is entirely extracted from the contextual, historical reference assigned to each poem.[2] In a poem's evocation of emotions and beneath its imaged language, the commentators discern the expression of praise or blame, serving as an example and bearing on the contemporary situation and mores. Thus poetic language becomes the indirect expression of a political meaning. And since they belonged to a political world that was strongly censored (the official commentary on *The Book of Songs* began with the Chinese empire, two thousand years ago), they were inclined to conceive of this political meaning as the indirect expression of a criticism of those in power that could not be expressed openly. The poetic language allowed for the veiling of what might be too offensive in the remonstrance. Under the cover of imagery, the criticism is all the better insinuated.

Thus by following the generations of commentary, we can learn to read in China's first literary work, its most ancient and most influential book, what I have begun to suggest as an art of oblique attack, for poetry is oblique speech par excellence. And obliquity is, in fact, an art: the detour involved in the poetic expression of political criticism has its own efficacy. It is not only justified by the poet's not being able to express his remonstrances more openly for fear of offending the authorities; it also benefits from the dimension of infinity proper to poetic speech. As commentators on *The Book of Songs* note: "When criticisms are expressed openly, one can easily discern their end; but when they follow a circuitous path, they become inexhaustible."[a3] Clearly, the principal advantage of poetic language, as of military strategy, is obliquity: since it is expressed indirectly, the criticism becomes inexhaustible. This detour does not represent only a constraint (since one *may not* express oneself directly); it valorizes the criticism as well, heightening its effect.

In the commentaries on this ancient *Book of Songs*, we see once again the two paths of indirect expression previously noted: the criticism is expressed either through a borrowing (as detour) or as an effect of internal difference (leading to its sinuousness). The poetic borrowing par excellence, of course, is the image. When a poem begins with the following lines:

> Big rat, big rat
> Do not gobble our millet!
> Three years we have slaved for you[4] (113)

the image of the rat represents the rapacity of the extortioners, which is being denounced. Another form of borrowing involves not a transfer from one level of reality to another, as in metaphor, but a transfer that operates in time. Of *The Book of Songs*, the commentators note that the poems "expose the past" "in order to criticize the present."[b]

As a stereotyped effect, borrowing would appear peculiar to the Chinese. We also saw that it remains a constant in contemporary political movements. But a more original aspect stems from the way the commentators seize on an insidious meaning through poetic subtleties. The three stanzas of poem 47 celebrate the beauty of a queen using superlatives, describing not only her finery but also her dignity and majestic air. One would be inclined to believe this a song of praise were it not for the last two lines of the first stanza, which undermine such an obvious reading:

> That our lady is not a fine lady
> How can any man say?

This doubt, expressed as a detour of the praise, carries all the meaning of the poem. While "the poem," one commentator explains, "only describes the magnificence of her finery and dress," these last two lines of the first stanza "make visible through detour" the critical design.[5] And "the more the expression detours," another commentator states about the same poem, "the more the meaning gains in depth."[6]

Thus the remark, the detail slipped into the eulogy, becomes the essential. This indication of a polemical intention can sometimes be even subtler. Poem 106 ostensibly praises an accomplished prince. It praises his height, gaze, and bearing; it celebrates his adeptness at archery, speaking, and dancing. There is no word in this description that is not positive, no note in this eulogy that strikes a tone of dissonance. Only a "Hey-ho," which begins each verse, allows us to hear a sigh:

> Hey-ho, he is splendid!
> Magnificent in stature,
> Noble his brow.

This sigh is so discreet that modern Chinese commentators refuse to hear it; they consider this poem a genuine eulogy and take this semantically ambiguous "hey-ho" to be an admiring exclamation. On the other hand, classical commentators, including Zheng Xuan, Zhu Xi, Yan Can, and Shen Deqian, are unanimous, according to the short preface, in deeming this single exclamation sufficient to undermine the homage, questioning the entire display of qualities (in her French translation, Séraphin Couvreur uses the term *hélas* (alas).[7] "The situation," notes Yan Can, "is difficult to assess" (here the prince is criticized, since his mother, Wen Jiang, has conducted herself licentiously and he has not restrained her excesses); also "the meaning was subtly implied at the beginning of each stanza, in the 'Hey-ho!'" "After this 'Hey-ho!' all the verses praise the prince, but there are so many signs of dissatisfaction": the expression is not "pressing," that is, it does not press the meaning closely, but "the signification is profound and appropriate."[8]

Although it is the poem's intention, according to the classical commentators, the criticism is introduced only incidentally — but all the more insidiously — by the obliquity of a detail that contrasts with the text's coherence. The incoherent effect, barely sketched yet enough to lead one to suspect the opposite of what is being said, can be carried to the point of contradiction. Poem 34 criticizes marriages too hastily abandoned. The first, third, and fourth stanzas bring up different points of view, all the norm: "The ford is deep to wade," the first stanza concludes, "If a ford is deep there are stepping stones; if it is shallow, you can tuck up your skirts." But the second stanza continues:

> The ford is in full flood,
> And baleful is the pheasant's cry.
> The ford is not deep enough to wet your axles;
> The pheasant cried to find her mate.

"These last lines," Shen Deqian explains, "make words leap from the shadows to express criticism (indirectly). The rest of the poem evokes the reason for things in such a way that people, in hearing what is correct, understand for themselves what is wrong."[9] Even if it is raised only in passing, a contradiction shatters the stability of a poem and raises doubt: it is enough to point toward the disorder that the apparent order of things cannot hide.

In short, one can imagine a criticism without critical terms, with no suspicious connotation, in which everything serves the most insistent celebration. For example, poem 57 praises the queen by describing the nobility of her family, the beauty of her face, the perfection of her bearing, the wealth of her country of origin. Nonetheless, the ancient commentators note, "not a word is said about her husband," "which makes one imagine beyond the words."[10] In this extreme case, what is significant is the omission; all the meaning lies to one side. This poem is aimed at denouncing the behavior of the prince Zhuang of Wei, who, smitten with a concubine, left his wife, with whom he had still not had a child. Nothing in this poem broaches this delicate subject (modern commentators, breaking with the tradition of an insidious poetic meaning, refuse to see anything in the poem other than what is said and read it — no doubt, rightly so — as an epithalamium). But according to the classical reading, by mentioning everything but the subject, yet broaching it from every direction, this poem is better able to make its true subject clear. The meaning is submerged, it operates by default, and the effect depends on silence.

Nuance, tension, silence — all these deviations are oblique ways of carving out an insidious signification beneath the words, and ultimately they undermine what apparently is being said. Such sinuosity, which the traditional commentators enjoyed deciphering — or projecting — is not unrelated to what we have

61

already noted about the official press: a remark slipped in surreptitiously can be more important than the conventional development around it; or what is not said can affect the things that are said and draw attention to itself. Contradiction, in short, is not a symptom of logical inconsistency (as if the Chinese had another mentality or lacked rationality); rather, it is the sign of an opinion asserting — or twisting — itself the better to impose itself by dissimulation. The strategy of the indirect therefore corresponds to a rhetoric, and this is what the first theorists began to define in relation to *The Book of Songs*.

It is remarkable that people began to analyze the nature of poetic language in China through the opposition between the direct and the indirect. The preface to *The Book of Songs* from the Han era (two thousand years ago), which was the first general reflection on the nature of poetry, distinguishes three modes of expression (which I introduce here as they were understood by Zheng Xuan): the first (*fu*) is "direct exposition" of the "contemporary political and moral situation in its good and bad aspects";[c] the second (*bi*) is characterized, conversely, by the fact that "faced with the defects of the present time, which one does not dare criticize openly, one expresses them through comparison";[d] and the third (*xing*) is characterized symmetrically by the fact that "in front of all that is good in the present time, since one does not want to fall into flattery, one expresses oneself analogically by resorting to other positive realities, by way of exhortation."[e] Compared with the first mode of expression, direct exposition of meaning, the other two designate an indirect expression that aims at sparing, or treating with caution, the susceptibility of the listener. But the real reason a speaker might express himself by detour has more to do with a fear of taking chances than with a desire to avoid being too obvious or flattering. The distinction between the second and

62

third modes of expression, however, cannot hold, at least as it is understood here (where it essentially rests on a formal effect of symmetry that presents praise and blame in equal parts), and the later commentators did not retain it. Indeed, the first mode of expression, as it was later defined, consists in "directly expressing things without censor." The second, on the other hand, consists in "expressing oneself with imagery, without daring to speak directly, as if one were afraid." From this perspective, the indirection of poetic language is reduced to mere prudence: it seeks to veil with imagery, and by this means attenuate, the offensiveness of a criticism that might endanger its author.

I do not know if one could take the subjection of poetic meaning to political constraints any further than this. Poetic expression is indirect, the commentators say, because it cannot express itself openly and does not dare to confront the authorities head-on. But we have also seen that one Chinese poetic theorist recommends the indirect expression of criticism for its own sake. Theoretical reflection expressed the value of indirect communication, whose richness was considered inexhaustible, through one of the most ancient Chinese representations — not really a notion but an image, which never ceases to speak to our imaginations — the wind, for the wind fills all the earth's cavities; it is the source of a musical infinity (see chapter 2 of *Zhuangzi*). Moreover, the wind is imperceptible, cannot be apprehended directly, but exercises a perceptible influence everywhere it goes; where there is wind, "the grass must bend" (Confucius, *Analects* 12.19); only its vibration outside tells us of its passing.[11] Finally, the wind penetrates everywhere, since it is impalpable; it diffusely surrounds us, insinuating itself into the heart of things (see the trigram *xun* in *The Book of Changes*). By exploiting this image, Chinese thinking in Antiquity never ceases to make us dream of the wind's power: its invisible aspiration, blowing across the countryside, shakes the slightest shoot and sets it in motion; its immaterial presence never ceases to invade and animate.

The Chinese conceived of the poetic word as discreet influence — endless penetration — like the wind's ceaseless haunting of the world. Already in *The Book of Songs*, one poem's author concludes:

> So Ji-fu [Jifu] made this ballad,
> Its words very grand,
> [May it be excellent as the wind]
> As a present to the Lord of Shen! (259)

Ancient commentators, notably Yan Can, interpret this wind image, in parallel, as *poem* and as *wind*, as a beneficial influence that fills the sensibility of the recipient and orients it positively. The following poem ends with a similar desire:

> Ji-fu [Jifu] made this ballad
> Gentle as a clean breeze.
> Zhong Shan Fu [Shanfu] has long been burdened with care;
> May this calm his breast. (260)

The first part of *The Book of Songs* bears the emblematic title "Guofeng," winds of the land. The image of the wind is used to suggest a moral influence that, emanating from the sovereign, spreads through each region and characterizes it. Finally, at the beginning of the empire, when the Great Historian, Sima Qian, sought to define each of the classics, again it was by reference to the wind that he summarized the excellence of *The Book of Songs*, which he thought represented the originality of the poetic.[12]

From then on, reference to the wind served to distinguish between two types of speech: "instructive,"[f] political speech, which exerts pressure directly on the listener by giving orders; and poetic speech, which influences its recipient discreetly, moves him, and penetrates him all the more deeply by working indirectly. The wind bends the course of thoughts; instead of imposing itself on them, it insinuates itself gently. Offering no definite, explicit meaning, it reveals itself diffusely to a sensitivity that it moves, rather than showing itself explicitly through injunction. And since it has no fixed (or finite, limited, or sharp-edged) contents, it cannot encounter any resistance. With its infinitely supple and unfettered trajectory, it invades consciousness: hence it surreptitiously directs it — but generally and continuously, and thus all the more effectively.

In the preface to *The Book of Songs*, the value of indirect expression is understood in terms of this *insinuation* of poetic speech. The wind rises and falls; thus it can accompany a hierarchical relationship in either direction. From the prince to his subjects: the exemplary behavior of the prince exerts a far-reaching and discreet influence — hence the image of the wind (*fenghua*) — on all his people and civilizes them; it progressively opens them to the consciousness of morality even before the prince has commanded it.[g] This influence, which can also be negative,[h] is manifest in the poems of *The Book of Songs*, since they are reputed to have been collected from the heart of each principality to serve as a mirror of its mores and were registered under the various rubrics of the "winds of the land." From the subjects to their prince: the subject composes his work by exploiting the "musical harmony" that serves as the "principal" support to the poetic text, even as he expresses his criticism indirectly "through circumlocution"[i] (still through the image of the wind, *fengci*[j]). Like the wind, this criticism is only visible in the way that it rouses and provokes a reaction by insinuating itself. It is not directly perceptible but is all the more invasive. And because it cannot be pinned down, it can be neither fixed nor circumscribed; its influence is without bounds: it can haunt inexhaustibly and powerfully bend within.

In this case, continues the preface:

> He who expresses himself does not commit an offense, while at the same time his listener hears enough to be warned. Such is the meaning of the term "wind."

Thus the indirection of poetic expression offers a compromise between the speaker and the authority addressed. It falls to poetry to organize this oblique relationship through which one partner stealthily exerts his initiative over the other and influences him, without confronting him. Under the cover of imagery, through the circuitousness of meaning, criticism operates strategically: it implicitly exerts itself from a distance and offers no grip through which the authority can defend itself or posit condemnation. One might even say that it is all the more cunning as it leads its revered recipient, in spite of himself, into a process of interpretation, obliging him to be guided through detour to pierce its relative obscurity — thus reversing the subjugation: before grasping where the other is leading, the prince finds himself uneasy. Poetry thus profits from its vague and indeterminate qualities and can risk a seditious meaning. But here the oblique relationship is presented officially and therefore ideally. It is above all suspicion and unaware (or so it pretends) of any ulterior motive. The prince and the scholar get along splendidly: the latter has said enough to make himself understood, yet not enough to risk his head. Poetic detour lessens the shock on each side: it softens the blame for the latter, the shame for the former. For its subject matter, it chooses between righteous courage and foolish recklessness, allowing the scholar to fulfill his duty to admonish while respecting authority.

Furthermore, its half measure is a just balance between the implicit and the explicit: it draws a sketch without insisting on it, orients without stopping. This poetic detour lets criticism resonate in the way the wind echoes. In this way, detour *gets its point across*: it communicates criticism effectively, just as the wind never ceases passing between things, and it softens the criticism, making it palatable.

The obliquity of poetic language might be no more than the political convenience of the implicit. This compromise between the scholar and authority figures would become the object in China of a surprising consensus, for the formula was repeated without end for two millennia; through the detour authorized by poetry, he who expressed himself avoided running risks, and his reader heard enough to know what was going on. This characteristic is all the more striking when compared with the situation in Greece. We find almost no trace of it among the theorists of oratory, who consider the detour of the image only as it relates to its proper functioning in *lexis*. Only at Delphi, on the Pythian tripod, does the obliquity of the poetic formulation meet political interests. Plutarch, in approving the recent evolution of the oracles toward clarity, nonetheless recognized that indirect expression was justified by prudence, for the Delphic oracles addressed cities, not kings: to contradict them head-on would not have been favorable to the prosperity of the ministers of Apollo. Plutarch was among them and conscious of the danger:

> For this reason, the god, without consenting to hide the truth, manifests it indirectly: by putting it in poetic form — as one would do to a luminous ray by reflecting it and by dividing it several times — he removes the things that are hurtful and hard.... Hence he surrounds the revelations with implications and circumlocutions, which conceal the oracle's meaning from others without escaping

the interested parties and without abusing them, when they try to understand it.[13]

Apollo the Oblique (*loxias*) envisioned a balance between the implicit and the explicit, prudence and truth; through the detour of poetic formulation, he sought to come to terms with the power of men and cities. But this case, which confirms the Chinese position so well (only the comparison to reflection is characteristic of Greek wisdom), appears rather isolated within Hellenism. It concerns an extreme case among the Greeks (the exceptional circumstance of divination) but a most banal one among the Chinese, who lack the category of poet as separate among men and inspired by the gods, as imaged in the West by the myth of Orpheus and the figure of Homer. Any civil servant in China is necessarily a "poet": poetic formulation is used in political life, and only the ambiguity of the image allows the scholar to protect himself.

The indirect criticism that classical commentators explain how to read in *The Book of Songs* is found throughout the history of Chinese poetry. When a poet of the Tang epoch (seventh to ninth centuries) mentions events from the first great Chinese dynasty, the Han (at the beginning of this era), most often it is not because he is interested in this historical moment but because he seeks to criticize through detour some vice in the politics of his own time too dangerous to state: this *translatio temporum* is too common, too generally acknowledged, for anyone to hesitate in its interpretation. Consequently, Chinese poetry is read with a watchful eye; one learns to *suspect* the meaning. The "realistic," descriptive account is always suspected of hiding beneath its innocent airs a less acknowledged intention; any eulogy risks being considered a roundabout criticism — one that remains submerged. In short, words are heavy with silence. The things revealed drag their shadows behind them. Even when one of the epoch's greatest poets, Du Fu, emotionally celebrates the poetry of his friend Li Bo — himself a poetic genius — it is still necessary to uncover, as the commentator Jin Shengtan painstakingly invites us to, the meaning expressed within the cracks and by default.[14] Such a laudatory expression allows a less favorable evaluation to resonate *on the side*. It is also enough for Du Fu, a great master of the art of detour, to describe at the beginning of a ballad crows that

At night fly over the Gate-to-welcome-autumn cawing,[15]

for the scene to remind us of the flight through this gate of a past emperor escaping from rebels (July 756): the cawing of the crows primly covers the more disparaging aspects of the reference but also raises a note of shame and remorse and charges the scene with an ignominious meaning. "One can see," Jin Shengtan states, "with what art he wielded his brush indirectly to avoid telling."[k]

It must be asked: Has China ever referred to contemporary injustices through poetry without detour? Bo Juyi, poet of the eighth and ninth centuries, a little later than Du Fu, remained famous for his violent denunciation, more direct since it is more prosaic (in imitation of ancient popular songs), of the authorities' exactions and the woes of the people. But in this case, too, detour is not lacking, and the obliquity missing from expression resurfaces in the communication. As Bo Juyi himself explains:

> Aside from the official relations that corresponded to my duty as
> adviser to the emperor, when cases arose in which I thought that one
> could ease the suffering of the people or correct some defect in the
> contemporary situation but which were delicate to broach, I com-
> posed a poem, in the hopes that it would be transmitted progres-
> sively and ultimately reach the authorities.[16]

69

The indirect vocation of poetry is here manifest in how the word is transmitted: its polemical meaning is attenuated by its diffuse propagation. Given the impossibility of addressing the emperor directly, the poet relies on vox populi to spread his poems, thus reproducing the ideal mode of communication inaugurated by *The Book of Songs*. Indeed, *The Book of Songs* was supposed to have emanated spontaneously from popular consciousness, thus propagating common complaint as far as the governor's ears. Forced to hear reliable witness to the people's situation and frame of mind, the prince could not fail to find indications in these poems as to the necessary reform of his conduct.[17] Supplementing official proclamations — the reports addressed to the court — poetry remained the legitimate vehicle through which to make audible, in this case most anonymously, under the cover of rumor, the things that could not be said openly. This is why Bo Juyi was able, in the letter quoted above, to accept the following credo of scholars: he who expresses himself in this fashion does not offend anyone, and his reader hears just enough to be forewarned; hence "each of them," he concludes, "completely fulfills his duty." The only difference, in short, is that here the detour of poetic meaning becomes the *circuit* through which the poem reaches its destination; and the softening effect of the insinuation takes the form of a *murmur*.

Let us imagine, finally, a poet who kept a distance from the political problems of his time and took pleasure in his own imaginings. Such a case does exist in China, almost contemporaneously, and it involves one of the finest geniuses of Chinese poetry, Li He, who died at the age of twenty-seven. Drawing inspiration from other sources (not *The Book of Songs* but the shamanic poetry of *Lisao*, and not Confucius's works but Buddhist sutras) and breaking away from conventional associations through abrupt contrasts in his language by highlighting the troubling and paradoxical encounters that upset and threaten the traditional harmonies (for it is harmony that surrounds and contains all Chinese ideology), Li He invents a fantastic world in which the insufficiencies of the great natural Regulation are repaired and the real is transfigured. This poetic world is not limited to the relation between the natural and the social, as is the custom in China, but opens to that outside, the life of the gods, a world that is carried along not by the rhythm of the seasons but by dreams of eternity.

Subsequent Chinese tradition was not content to correct Li He's work by expurgating the jarring elements produced by his art of dissonance; it also never ceased to fit this imaginary world into the mold of a voluntarily indirect political criticism. To those tempted to reject Li He's poetry as too extraordinary and confusing, the conscientious exegete periodically responds that even this sort of poetry is no exception. What appears pure imaginative delirium, or even veritable debauchery of the spirit, with its exacerbated and unwholesome taste for the unusual, can be perfectly understood and recuperated, provided one carefully identify the political reference that is insinuated (as did Song Wan under the Song dynasty and Yao Wenxie under the Qing). Li He, too, can thus be brought back into line, for he merely denounced the dark sides of contemporary politics, the long list of which is repeated century after century: "the damage wrought by pacifism, the foolish quest for immortality to which the emperor devotes himself, the autocratic power of the provincial governors, the military power of the eunuchs, the governmental cliques and the misfortunes of invasion."[18] But the insignificance of his responsibilities at court prevented him from expressing his remonstrances more openly, his zealous defender explains, so he was forced to deliver them in a language that is "obscure and delirious, dangerous and resistant to our comprehension." We should be nonetheless reassured: in spite of his fantastic manners, his "phantom," bad genie–like presence, this poet has not lost his mind. He has simply

buried more deeply than the others — beneath the apparent vagueness of his speech — a historical meaning. He, too, like any loyal
subject, sought to denounce political misdeeds via the detour of
poetry. Poetic detour is more complicated in his case; to reach the
mark, the meanderings of interpretation are more circuitous.

Hence Li He describes the immortals' happy life in "Ballad of
the Heavens," Song Wan explains, to blame the reigning emperor,
Xianzong, for inviting all the empire's Taoists to his court in
hopes of obtaining a draught of immortality from them. These are
the true immortals, the poet would say, how can we hope to imitate them? Similarly, his marvelous "Lamentation of the Bronze
Camels," which depicts the eternal repetition of time, is reduced
to a denunciation of the powers of the eunuchs , whom the poet
predicts will lead the empire to its ruin once again. When Li He
paints a surreal picture of the "cold of the North" — fish and dragons dead in the ice, gigantic rimy crystals, and the impenetrable
opacity of the sky — it is purportedly to criticize the lack of rigor
in the Imperial Army, which, under the eunuchs' command, would
be fatally incapable of confronting an invasion. No symbolic value
can resist this type of reading; the commentator, instead of explaining what the image means in the context of the poem, contrives to
provide the keys to its understanding: the poem refers to some
concubine who disappeared prematurely, some unlucky nomina-
tion at the head of the armies, some unjust exile of a loyal subject.
Beneath the enchantment of the images, the poet is seen as always
expressing his resentments. Hence Yao Wenxie can conclude:

> His poetry, as much in the words and meaning as in the theme,
> deeply criticizes the mores of the time and reaches to the heart of its
> most veiled aspects; but had he not deeply buried his intentions, he
> would certainly have suffered the worst punishments. Hence the
> ever more far-off and indirect, subtle and elliptical character of his

expression: he hides all the violence of his inner imagination in the smallest formula in such a way that he who is expressing himself does not offend anyone and the recipient cannot tell whence it comes.[19]

We keep returning to the same formula of compromise between the scholar and the authorities, except that the scholar's camouflage is apparently greater here. Instead of hearing enough to be forewarned, the recipient has no idea whence the meaning comes; he does not notice the allusions. Thus detour has become too costly; indirect communication no longer functions well. This is why Li He was progressively neglected by the history of Chinese poetry and even omitted from anthologies. At the end of the nineteenth century, it took the opening to the West and the discovery of Western notions of romanticism for the Chinese to reexamine this poet, allowing the symbolism of his poems to speak at last, freeing his imaginary world from the never-ending quest for insinuations.

The fate of Li He's poetry is one measure of how the practice of detour is anchored at the very core of the Chinese tradition, to the point of imposing a way of reading, burying originality, and erasing difference. Literature clearly overflows with this practice and draws poetry away from its own game: it exerts a power. I will consider this aspect more closely, within the framework of life at court and of diplomacy, by returning to the ancient *Book of Songs*.

73

CHAPTER FOUR

Quotations as Proxy:

The Power to Unsettle

The questions we have examined within the tradition of poetic commentary may be applied more generally: In what ways is detour effective, and what kind of power is derived from it? By bringing distance into play, what conditions does the detour impose that enable it more intimately to penetrate or take possession of the recipient's spirit? What does it reach or unsettle in the other (in his capacity for volition and decision making) that direct discourse through argument cannot access? The way the practice of quotation developed in ancient China can elucidate this point. Here detour is set into play before our very eyes, and the stakes are clear. Previously, we were dealing more with a reconstruction, that of the commentators who demonstrated through their readings of *The Book of Songs* how to let meaning discreetly find its path. We have yet to see this detour at work in a context where a poem known by all is used by political protagonists to make their desires known and to influence a decision.

After the seventh century B.C., China evolved in a way that has an analogy in ancient Greece. The ancient royalty had lost its influence, while the former fiefs gained independence. Like the situation in Greece among city-states, each new principality struggled to exert its hegemony. Leagues and confederations were formed, and an intense diplomatic activity came into being that, in alternation with military operations, set another type of strategy into play. These diplomatic encounters were not, however, an occasion for opposing arguments delivered face-to-face, as one reads of in Thucydides (and as he rewrote them). Instead, as the ancient chronicles report, a number of such interviews took place as exchanges of canonical quotations. Often without reporting any other direct discourse, these documents record only the results of the decision. These quotations were borrowed from the sole literary corpus of the time, which later became *The Book of Songs*, whose motifs a good ambassador had to know in depth. By drawing from this well-known repertory, the person "quoting," that is, the one singing or executing a poem[a] (there is no equivalent term in English to designate this practice), in part or in its entirety, not only appealed to a hallowed authority but also used these phrases as more than simple illustration. Since his intervention in the encounter was most often limited to this quotation, he could only express his desires through the circuitous route of these conventional motifs.

Covering more than a century, from 626 B.C. (Xi *gong*, twenty-third year) to 516 B.C. (Zhao *gong*, twenty-fifth year), *Zuozhuan*, the main commentary on the most ancient Chinese public records, the Lu principality's *Spring and Autumn Annals*, reports thirty or so interviews of this type, some of which merely follow protocol and aim only at reasserting alliances, while the majority are actual negotiations. During any given conference, through the poems he cited, one protagonist bent the will of the other and won him over to his point of view. For example, in 613 B.C. (Wen *gong*, thirteenth year), the prince of Lu went into the powerful Jin principality to renew his alliance with it (in opposition to the rival Qi principality). As he was returning home, the prince of Wei and then the prince of Zheng met up with him and begged him to intercede on their behalf and procure peace for them with Jin. On this occasion, the annals recount, the prince of Zheng offered a meal to the prince of Lu at Fei. A ranking officer of Zheng sang "The Wild Geese Are Flying" (*Book of Songs* 181). A ranking officer of Lu answered him simply, "Our prince is not yet carefree enough for that," and sang in response "The Fourth Month" (204). The ranking officer of Zheng then sang the fourth stanza of "Gallop" (54), and the ranking officer of Lu answered him with "Plucking Bracken" (167). The outcome of the interview is reported laconically: the prince of Zheng gave a salutation; the prince of Lu saluted him in turn.

A closer look at the poems used in this exchange reveals how the negotiation evolved and the success to which it led. The first poem quoted speaks of flying wild geese that cry plaintively about past sufferings. Through this poem, the ranking officer called on the kindness of the prince of Lu, asking him to intercede in favor of his principality. The poem sung in response gives a lengthy account of the sufferings encountered by an officer in the exercise of duty. In this way, the ranking officer of Lu made it understood that his prince could not displace himself yet again for a new negotiation. The third poem cited is an appeal to a more compelling pity than in the first poem: the tradition attributes it to a married princess in a foreign court whose parents are dead and who learns that her family's principality has been ravaged. She wants to console her brother, but custom does not allow a married woman to return to her parental home after the death of her parents; thus, stopped on the road by a high commissioner, she expresses her unhappiness and looks for succor. The request is insistent, the tone pathetic. Finally, the fourth stanza of the poem quoted in response describes the beginning of an expedition and ends with the following lines: "His war-chariot ready yoked /

With its four steeds so eager. / How should we dare stop or tarry? / In one month we have had three alarms" (167). This stanza, in the mouth of a ranking officer from Lu, signifies an acceptance: the prince of Lu is ready to set out again to negotiate. The prince of Zheng has understood, with no further explanation, and he thanks him.

Through this exchange of canonical quotations, the prince of Zheng reversed the resolution of the prince of Lu, without needing to explain the situation any more fully or to specify his request. "At each moment," a Chinese commentator explains, "nothing is said but everything is understood,"[b] and the message is passed on.[1] The poetic images allow each party to make its interests known but dispense with their justification. They hint at the position held by each side, without leading to a confrontation. Each person is freer to maneuver since he does so at a distance, under the cover of borrowed formulas. At the same time, these hallowed formulas lend each side of the exchange much more weight than anything personal that could be said. The motif set into play by the canonical formulation not only makes it possible to conceal desire or diffuse conflict; it also facilitates the compliance of others through its conventionality, its anonymous allure. It even exerts surreptitious pressure on the other by allowing the full potential of the image to come into play on its user's behalf. Instead of listing arguments, it mobilizes energies; the art is less to persuade the other through reasoning than to shake his resolve.

One can measure the effectiveness of this rhetoric of quotation through one of the more delicate negotiations related in the annals. No issue could be more sensitive in the relationships among princes than that of imprisonment. In this case, in 546 B.C. (Xiang *gong*, twenty-sixth year), the prince of Jin arrested the prince of Wei in reprisal. The princes from Qi and Zheng then went to Jin on behalf of the imprisoned prince, but at the banquet

78

held on their arrival the true subject of the interview was not broached. To welcome his guests, the prince of Jin sang a poem (249) that praises the good sovereign and shows how the heavens heap favors on him. A ranking officer from Qi answered with another solemn poem (173), which, beneath its image of the southernwood drenched with dew, implies that the kind protection of Jin covers all the other princes and favors their prosperity; a ranking officer from Zheng, in the name of his prince, also sang a poem (75), in which the last two lines in particular — "Let us go to where you lodge / And there I will hand food to you" — serve as a declaration: the small Zheng principality will remain allied with Jin. The minister of Jin then told his prince to salute his guests as a sign of thanks: to the first, for "having procured peace by means of his ancestors' tablets"; to the other, for remaining loyal to him.

There ensued a second act in the wings, in which the ranking officers of these principalities informed each other through intermediaries of their respective grievances. Other poems were quoted during a second interview. The first among them has been lost, but its meaning, as reconstructed by a commentator, is that through magnanimous policies peace is established among princes, just as a fiery horse is best led with slack reins.[2] The second poem (76), sung by the officer from Zheng, describes a young girl's resistance to her suitor's desires and ends with the following stanza:

I beg of you, Zhong Zi,
Do not climb into our garden,
Do not break the hard-wood we have planted.
Not that I mind about the hard-wood,
But I am afraid of what people will say.
Zhong Zi I dearly love;

> But of all that people will say
> Indeed I am afraid.

This is a clever quotation: it indicates esteem and attachment (which the prince of Zheng should feel toward the prince of Jin), while insinuating that the other should not go too far (as Jin did by keeping the prince of Wei prisoner). Above all, it predicts the evil rumors that will arise if the other persists in his behavior (and that the speaker, in spite of his sincere attachment, was obliged to note). The attitude adopted here is irreproachable, but it hints at threat; and the prince of Jin was sensitive to this, since he immediately consented to freeing his prisoner.

"The detaining of a prince," one commentator states,

> inevitably elicits deep resentment and strong hatred. How, in such a circumstance, can one do battle with words (in discussion)? Here princes are adept at resolving differences. It is enough for them, between draughts of wine, to quote poems to soften the critical implication[c] indirectly, for the wrath of the prince of Jin to be appeased. That the delicate Wei affair was resolved so promptly shows the ability of poetic citation to touch people's sentiments.[3]

In Chinese, this last phrase is doubly expressive: it means that the citing of poems both alters the sentiments of others and modifies their states of mind. The articulation of these two meanings through the same verb[d] leads me to believe that the circuitousness of the citation, by shifting the interlocutor's attention, changes his mind by making him turn aside from his own opinions. There is a term of particular usefulness on this point: *motif*.[4] Without knowing to what extent the relationship between the psychological and the aesthetic meaning of the word is justified by ordinary usage (between motif as motive and motif as theme), however, I have seized the opportunity here for breaking down these distinctions, an opportunity provided by the language itself. I thus hope to communicate by suggestion something that is awkward to say and that resists discursive analysis. In the small particle represented by this word, a decisive junction takes place — between levels of meaning — which, though not concrete, is precisely the thing at which this Chinese practice of citation is constantly hinting. A communication is thus discovered from one sphere to another — a communication I shall henceforth explore and exploit. The poems in *The Book of Songs* serve as literary motifs for those who cite them, by providing them with patterns that often repeat themselves or are subjected to variations from stanza to stanza and are relatively standardized. Through them, the speaker allows his wishes to be inferred, while aiming to communicate. At the same time, these motifs are *mobile;* their motivations set the will in motion. Through a poem's motif, one seeks to change an inner disposition in the listener in such a way as to make him act, or rather react — the relation is less mediated — in the desired fashion.

Spring and Autumn Annals is sufficiently precise, especially toward the middle of the sixth century (under the reign of Xiang *gong* and the beginning of Zhao *gong*) to allow us to glimpse the personalities of some of these skilled diplomats, these formidable opponents. The practice of citation is an art, and princes and great vassals are not equally skillful at it. One who demonstrates the most talent, and who is most often cited in the annals, is a high officer of Lu named Mu Shu (alias Shu Sunbao). Mu Shu spent his life endeavoring to reinforce the alliance between the small Lu principality and the powerful Jin principality, to keep the imperialistic maneuvers of the Qi principality to the north in check. In 556 B.C. (Xiang *gong*, sixteenth year), he went to Jin to complain once again of the extortions of Qi, but the officers of Jin invoked various pretexts to avoid becoming involved, and his call for help, though moving in its eloquence, remained unanswered. Thus he changed tactics and called on the ministers separately. Instead of pleading the cause of Lu, he sang, in the presence of one of them, a poem (185) in which soldiers complain that the ministers of war "roll us on from misery to misery," "giving us no place to stop in or take rest." The minister, unsettled by this picture, "recognized his culpability" and pledged his support. Then, going to the next minister, Mu Shu sang the last stanza of the poem "The Wild Geese Are Flying," which, as we have seen, describes the plaintive cry of geese and the suffering of a people who have been dispersed. The minister acknowledged himself as justly targeted by the poem and concluded that he would not let the Lu people fall into such dire circumstances. Through the mobilizing effect of familiar poetic motifs, Mu Shu accomplished something that a direct discussion, no matter how passionate, could not have achieved.

Three years later (Xiang *gong*, nineteenth year), after Jin had attacked Qi to defend Lu, Qi made peace with Jin, and Lu was again fearful. The high officer of Lu had to renegotiate with Jin. Once again he met with a minister of the principality, once again he cited a poem (54), once again he received support. In the infinitely subtle game of diplomatic citations, this officer was, without a doubt, one of the best. He demonstrated these abilities again when, wishing to honor the prime minister of Jin during a banquet (Zhao *gong*, first year), he sang "Magpie's Nest" (12). At first glance, this poem might seem to have no bearing on the situation, since it is entirely devoted to the celebration of a young girl's marriage, of which it describes the large procession; but the image with which the poem begins,

Now a magpie had a nest
But the cuckoo lived in it

provides a useful angle. Just as the cuckoo lives in the nest, even
though it does not belong there, the prime minister of Jin, the
diplomat implied, retains the essence of power in Lu. Simply by
citing the poem's opening lines, the officer from Lu was able to
insinuate the highest eulogy (showing this minister to surpass his
prince, which would not be lost on the interlocutor) without,
however, falling into mere flattery or making his eulogy too risky.

This skill in using poetic motifs requires an equal talent to
decode them. In the above-mentioned example, the prime minister of Jin was invited to a banquet and sang "Gourd Leaves" (231),
in thanks for the invitation. Only the official from Lu interpreted
the poem correctly and detected the threat: at the banquet
offered in his honor, the prime minister desired to be treated
simply, not wishing to give umbrage to the prestige of his prince
(such a display of modesty makes all the more necessary the discretion of the eulogy that we just read by the official from Lu).
The prime minister of Jin, Zhao Meng, also exhibited his ability
to decipher the hidden intentions that were presented to him
through the poetic motifs. He went so far as to make it a diplomatic game, to which he courteously invited his hosts, although
he did not approach this game with disinterest; it was politically
revealing to him. Through the chosen citation of each person,
Zhao Meng was able to evaluate his ambitions, understand his
inner thoughts, and even measure certain secret ploys. This happened in a particularly solemn way in 545 B.C. (Xiang *gong*, twenty-
seventh year), when Zhao Meng was received at the court of Zheng
(one finds this type of episode, in abbreviated form, in Zhao *gong*,
sixteenth year). The prime minister commented on each poetic
citation made by the seven officials participating in the banquet by

83

evaluating his impression of the messages each conveyed. Some he praised for the good example they were supposed to inspire; while he expressed reserve for those that indirectly addressed him with an homage too exaggerated not to embarrass him, going so far as to condemn one of them for a seditious and compromising implication. One of the guests cited the brief poem "How the Quails Bicker" (49) to contrast the natural coupling of animals with the shameless behavior of a prince and a princess. At the end of the meal, the prime minister confided that he considered the official's citation an explicit attempt to insult his prince (but perhaps this same citation insinuates, as Marcel Granet has proposed, the idea of a secret alliance through the image of a necessary coupling?).[5] During the banquet, the minister was content to blame the choice of poem, arguing its inappropriateness: the song touches on issues too intimate (amorous relations) to be raised in public. On the spot, he predicted a dishonorable demise for this ambitious fellow. As for the others, during this round of citations, Zhao Meng not only evaluated their respective situations but also plumbed their inner natures, analyzing their motivations: the citations served as both indication and avowal.

Other episodes in the annals make it clear that the art of citation is a mark of education. A barbarian from the provinces, civilized through contact with the Chinese, might prove adept at it, while a high official from an interior principality might remain insulated from it. In 557 B.C. (Xiang *gong*, fourteenth year), at a conference of principality heads, a minister from Jin, irritated about his principality's recent defeats, openly blamed the leader of a barbarian people, the Rong, who had allied with Jin, and threatened to have him arrested. The Rong leader remonstratively answered his reproaches point by point; before he withdrew, he cited a short poem, "The Bluebottles" (219), which advises not to heed calumny, comparing it to the buzzing of flies. The cited poem could seem a simple illustration of his preceding speech, since it keeps the transposition to a minimum, its application is clear, and it seems almost directly to validate the argument. This time, the speaker relied on vigorously demonstrated reasons and minimized the degree of detour. But the text of the annals explains that there is an epithet in the poem that touched the adversary and turned the situation around. While this brief poem is a categorical denunciation of calumny, the end of the first stanza is addressed to a respected interlocutor, who is referred to as "my blessed lord" and is begged not to allow himself to be influenced by these rumors. While calumny is criticized, a discreet appeal is directed to the listener to restore confidence. A person who cites the poem opens the door for a new understanding. It is worthwhile to follow Lao Xiaoyu's analysis on this point:

> The citation of the poem "The Bluebottles" is a clear denunciation that proceeds openly. But what touches and moves the minister from Jin are the words "my blessed lord," which penetrate to the depths of his heart and melt his resolve. What people call moral education operates through gentleness, for the text of the annals is not written lightly and demonstrates well that the plea of the leader of the Rong draws its strength from these few words.
>
> Furthermore, seeing the ability of a barbarian in this type of citation, one is made aware of the extent, in this epoch, to which education linked to poetry had profoundly affected men. [6]

More than a long plea, these little words slipped into a stanza set a favorable reaction into motion. The antagonistic position taking was deftly and obliquely crossed by a sign of conciliation. This allowed the conflict to be resolved and altered the listener's mind. By contrast, alongside the well-sinicized rhetorical skill of a barbarian, the annals twice show an official from Qi who was too obtuse to perceive the reproach addressed to him in a citation. The first time (Xiang *gong*, twenty-seventh year), when invited to a meal, he lacked respect for his host; the latter sang "Look at the Rat!" (52), but the other did not understand. The episode was repeated the following year between the same protagonists, except the poem was different. With this boor, indirect communication always failed. Only between equals is detour worthwhile.

The diplomats had only contempt for those among them who remained closed to this art of citation, and they abandoned them pitilessly to their sad fate (another example is found with an envoy from Song [Zhao *gong*, twelfth year]). At the same time, it could be extremely tactical to pretend not to understand, for example, when a diplomat wanted to teach a lesson without having to speak his reproaches directly. Thus, in 622 B.C. (Wen *gong*, fourth year), the envoy from Wei, who was received at the court of Lu, feigned indifference the two poems executed in his presence (174 and 175). Questioned in private, he explained that these poems had previously been sung only at the emperor's court; hence he indirectly criticized the presumption of the Lu principality in taking on such solemn rites. This episode was repeated fifty years later (Xiang *gong*, fourth year), but this time it was the official from Lu, whose addresses we have many times admired, who demonstrated his disapproval of the court of Jin: he did not salute when the first poems ended, then saluted the end of others. This gave his hosts a detailed lesson on ritual; it also bears witness, according to the commentator, to a large diffusion of this art of citation from one epoch to another. At the middle of the sixth century, the art was sufficiently developed to constitute a rhetoric.

From these reports of indirect communication in the annals, let us go back to the source of its efficacy. In general, what conditions this art of citation and makes its rhetorical use possible is that

86

these poems were never cited during diplomatic interviews for their literal meaning. He who cited did not pretend to interpret the original meaning of the poem and would not dream of proposing a new interpretation. The point was merely, according to the expression already formulated in *Zuozhuan* (Xiang *gong*, twenty-eighth year), "to deviate from the text to grasp its meaning" (or, more exactly, "to give it meaning"): the poetic text constituted a sort of emotional base — of rhythms and images — that each person exploited as he saw fit.[7] The poems in *The Book of Songs* were convenient for this purpose because most of them are anonymous and few have circumstantial references. They are also presented as a repertory of formulas and stock images that the user can appropriate both to shield his goal and to give it more weight. To offer a mere glimpse of one's goal is the most efficient approach, since the recipient is less informed than *called* or *drawn in* to it, and the intention implied therein thus becomes an invitation to participate. The more a poetic image is known and free of specific references, the more autonomy to maneuver it grants speakers in a situation; the more the communication takes place discreetly, in the shadow of borrowed formulas and in the depths of images, the more complicity it allows. This is why, during diplomatic interviews, the cited poems led not to long deliberations but to action being taken: they attempted less to convince than to rally. The image mobilizes the conscience; the consecrated formula "makes the intention less partial": beneath the anonymous crafting of the expression, everyone's judgment is called into play. Because of the canonical, definitive nature of the formula, it is as if the situation had already been settled. Thus in spite of the distance created in a situation by the poetic motif, the mediation it effects allows it to penetrate more intimately into the spirit of its recipient — which may be possessed all the better through roundabout means.

The protagonists of these diplomatic encounters were seeking, in short, neither to decipher the poem cited nor to project another meaning onto it; they were using the poetic motif to their own advantage. It is true that, according to the examples reported in the annals, a number of poems used in these diplomatic games have a more or less coded significance. "The Wild Geese Are Flying" (181) was cited twice to ask for assistance (Wen *gong*, thirteenth year, and Xiang *gong*, sixteenth year). The same goes for "Gallop" (54), in which the request is more pressing (Wen *gong*, thirteenth year, and Xiang *gong*, nineteenth year). Two times again, "Young Millet" (227) served, based on the first two lines ("Lusty is the young millet; / Copious rains have fattened it"), to eulogize a prince or a great lord (Xiang *gong*, nineteenth and twenty-seventh year). Similarly, "Cherry-Tree" (164) celebrates friendship (Xiang *gong*, twentieth year, and Zhao *gong*, first year). Nevertheless, though used in the same way, these references remain supple. A poem such as "The Sixth Month" (177) has a military expedition as its theme: in one case, it was cited as thanks for an expedition that had just taken place (after Jin came to the rescue of Lu against Qi [Xiang *gong*, nineteenth year]); while in another case, which is also the first occurrence of this type of interview in the annals (Xi *gong*, twenty-third year), it was used by the prince of Qi to imply to his listener, who had been chased from his principality, that he would lend him military assistance.[8] The flexibility in the use of these poetic citations also can be seen in the ability of two poems to indicate the same situation but relate it differently (as in Cheng *gong*, ninth year). In this case, Lao Xiaoyu notes, the first poem "sticks" to the situation, while the second "crystallizes the event and gives it meaning," letting the situation be seen from a less concrete angle by revealing its moral contents.[9] "In Antiquity," the commentator concludes, "people did not proceed in a stereotyped fashion"; and this is certainly what allowed this practice to become an art.

Lastly, the reason for citing a poem can remain resolutely ambiguous (Xiang *gong*, twentieth year). The leader of a principal Lu clan, whose power gave umbrage to the prince, was received with great honors in a foreign court. On the return of this ambassador, the prince of Lu held a banquet in his honor. This great lord thanked him by citing a poem (170), that, while paying homage to the meal offered, implied — just as the poem concludes, that "things they have in plenty" — that his mission had gone extremely well. The prince answered him with a poem that praises great lords:

Happiness to our lord
That is the groundwork of land and home!
Happiness to our lord!
May he live for evermore. (172)

This wish is repeated from one stanza to the next with slight variations: "May his fair fame be for ever," and, "To your descendants, safety and peace!" One can, of course, attribute the citing of the poem in such a circumstance to its obvious intention of eulogy (as certain ancient exegetes have done, notably Du Yu).[10] But one can also, as Lao Xiaoyu invites us to do, suspect a critical sense beneath this eulogy.[11] In this case, the poem would be a warning from the prince to his vassal that if he pushes his independence too far, the prince would be forced to deal severely with him, and the fate of his descendants might be compromised. The end of the episode, moreover, does not make it any less ambiguous. The annals merely mention that the great lord left the banquet saying, "I cannot bear this!" Does he mean that he cannot bear the eulogy, out of modesty, deeming it excessive? Or is this a form of coding, as the preceding commentator imagined, resulting from this lord's having grasped the warning? Again, this poetic citation, which appears so conventional, suddenly opens up an abyss: it oscillates between eulogy and threat, and facile assurance gives way to endless defiance between the two interlocutors.

Depending on the occasion, the poems fulfill different functions. The most simple, at least in appearance, is that of eulogy, but we have seen how ambiguous this can be and how fraught with ulterior motives. A second function, more charged with an imperative, is that of warning, which runs the gamut from discreet announcement to the most pressing advice. When the prime minister of the powerful Chu principality received the prime minister of the no less powerful Jin principality (Zhao *gong*, first year), the stanza he sang (236), which describes the granting of an imperial mandate to the most worthy, restrained his ambition. The prime minister of Jin answered with a poem (196), that, through the images of the dove and the wagtail, reminded his interlocutor of more modest views and placed him on his guard. (Indeed, the poem concludes, "Be careful, be cautious, / As if you were treading on thin ice...."). Faced with this hubris, which it would be dangerous to contradict and which might not listen to reason, the minister of Jin had no choice but to play the opposite register: only images of prudence and wisdom and proverbial formulations could reach such pride and modify it. Furthermore, this function as advice, expressed through a poem, could even operate in the heat of action. "The troops, having arrived on the banks of the river," the annals recount, "did not want to cross it" (Xiang *gong*, fourteenth year). Their general went to see the high official of the Lu principality (still the famous Mu Shu), who then sang "The Gourd Has Bitter Leaves" (34) — which describes the crossing of a ford. This was enough to make up the general's mind, and the annals add only, "He withdrew and procured boats."

Continuing in the injunctive direction of this inventory, we arrive, after the advice function, at the last — and most decisive —

function of the poetic citation: dissuasion. We have seen the Rong leader use dissuasion to conclude a very argumentative plea by citing a poem that, through the vehement denunciation of calumny, slips in a few words that opened the door to reconciliation. Similarly, when the prince of Lu, on a journey abroad, learned that one of his great vassals had rebelled, he was reluctant to return home. His minister at first argued in favor of returning, but the prince remained undecided. Another minister then sang a brief poem (36), whose two stanzas are a variation on the following motif:

> How few of us are left, how few!
> Why do we not go back?
> Were it not for our prince and his concerns,
> What should we be doing here in the dew?

The annals merely add laconically, "So he went back." In both cases, following a direct explanation that failed to convince, the interlocutor called on the citation of a poem as a last resort. One does find arguments developed frontally in the annals, for example, when Zhao Meng pleaded in favor of Mu Shu (Zhao *gong*, first year). But this resource is limited and does not act directly on the other's will; through the detour of poetic citation, on the other hand, one *incites* the interlocutor by wielding the power to *unsettle* him.

This power is judged legitimate. Its use during diplomatic interviews is recognized as an attribute of the ancient poems. Confucius charges his son first to study *The Book of Songs*, because "If you do not learn the Odes, you will not be fit to converse with" (*Analects* 16.13). Furthermore, he says, he who can recite "the three hundred odes" from *The Book of Songs* but who, when "entrusted with a governmental charge," "knows not how to act" possesses an empty knowledge (*Analects* 13.5). *Official History* likewise follows this tradition:

> In the past, during diplomatic encounters with neighboring countries, the princes and their high officials used subtle means to move others.[e] During the ritual salutations, they were required to recite the poems (from *The Book of Songs*) to make their aspirations known.[12]

Note that these subtle means to move one's interlocutors are precisely the same poetic quotations that make known one's aspirations. Marcel Granet used a wealth of striking formulations to trace this use of citation to the originality of the Chinese language. In fact, he goes so far as to say that the Chinese language was marked by this diplomatic practice: "Chinese, it is true, possesses an admirable strength in communicating emotional shock, in inviting others to participate in it. This language is both rough and refined; one senses that it was formed by palavers between artful wills at odds with each other."[13] He insists, moreover, that these "centos" through their "stereotyped formulas" possess, in *The Book of Songs* in particular, an infinite power of "suggestion." From a more general standpoint, the question becomes: How can the most neutral and anonymous formulation convey the most precise and personal meaning? The problem in this art of poetic citation hides another, vaster problem, one that touches on the nature of discourse: In what way(s) does it relate the general and the particular? More precisely, how can a personal aim be expressed through a stock formulation or a value judgment through a purely factual mode? On these points, the Chinese tradition has attempted solutions that have been at times extreme and, as we shall see, have the power to astonish. The voyage has only just begun.

CHAPTER FIVE

Insinuating and Avoiding to Say, or

How to Read Between the Lines

The account of diplomatic negotiations conducted through poetic quotations discussed in chapter 4 is presented as the explanatory commentary (*Zuozhuan*) of a much more concise text, *Spring and Autumn Annals* (*Chunqiu*), in which only events are related, with no connection made between them. In accordance with the political and religious role of recording held by scribes in Antiquity, this initial account, which is brief and purely annalistic, mentions only events, be they natural or social, as they happened: meetings between princes, military expeditions, and treatises, as well as droughts, floods, and fires. The year, season, and day of the event are recorded, but no judgment is passed on it: the murder of a sovereign is treated with the same neutrality as a natural event, such as an eclipse; the scribes document these events without straying from a ritual impassiveness. The only extant annals from this epoch, whose composition is attributed to Confucius, are those of the small Lu principality, which were later considered a personal work of this "author." Confucius, according to Mencius (3.2.9), "feared" the decadence of his time, which was marked by a rise in conspiracies and usurpations.[1] His was an outrageous time that saw the vassal kill his prince and the son his father, and supposedly Confucius "shaped" the annals so that they might

93

serve as a lesson to those in power. Thus through the mere mention of facts, the work is considered a moral code addressed to posterity.

One can well understand the surprise of the first Western translators. How could such passionless and colorless descriptions, which lack any indication of their author's sentiments, serve as a message regarding proper conduct and presume to reshape the world? With our Western ideas of "what History should be," we experience, according to James Legge, "an intense feeling of disappointment" after reading the annals.[2] Indeed, Edouard Chavannes recognizes that "the admiration the Chinese have always felt for this classic is something that the European reader can hardly share; these dry and dead annals cannot be compared with Herodotus's masterpieces, which date from only a half century later."[3] Furthermore, unable to make this dryness tally with all the praise traditionally granted this text, some Western commentators (such as Legge and, more recently, Piet Van der Loon) have gone so far as to doubt that we are dealing with the same text. This, however, is merely the last resort of philologists in distress. Not only is there nothing in Chinese tradition to support the idea that the original work referred to by Mencius may have been lost; but more importantly, whole generations of ancient commentators have taken great pains to show how to read the purely factual account of the annals for them to express a moral judgment. If it is true that an opinion is always being communicated in the mere mention of an event, this is certainly expressed indirectly, though systematically, through a circuitous route.

Thus a special case becomes a typical case, which points to a possibility with which we are already familiar through the various plays on meaning in *The Book of Songs*. Does one always have to state one's opinion to communicate it to others? Why do we feel a need to make it a matter of discourse, to put it on display? Why

94

always say, "In my opinion…"? An ambiguous exclamation or even a silence in a poem is enough to insinuate criticism; furthermore, the mere recounting of an event, even if it is purely factual, implies an assumed point of view. Within the framework of the ancient Chinese annals, this technique was taken particularly far (to the point of appearing hard to believe); but it rests on a general and not at all paradoxical acknowledgment: to mention something, to prefer speaking to remaining silent, is already to take sides, for saying is always choosing to say; there is consequently no such thing as pure denotation, free of judgment. As soon as I speak of the world, I express an opinion on it. If I mention something, even if only in passing, it is because I have already judged it worthy of mention, because I take some interest in it; whatever I say conveys my opinion — no declaration is disinterested. Based on this perception of the word, a technique of expression was developed in China that, as we shall see, was very concentrated. (While some do not believe that it was intended by Confucius, tradition has justified it as such.) From it, we shall learn how the facts themselves, as soon as they were announced (denounced), served obliquely to pronounce a judgment; in other words, neutrality becomes a trap that functions through indirection.

Let us begin with some examples. When *Annals* merely mentions that in "the fiftieth year, in the spring, the duke ordered fishing implements from Tang" (Yin *gong*, fifth year), this, *Zuozhuan* explains, is meant to imply that the duke infringed on etiquette, since the place was "too far away." Similarly, when, four years later (Yin *gong*, ninth year), the annals note laconically, "Fortification of Lang in the summer," this is "mentioned," according to the commentary, because it was "not the season" (the summer being reserved for working the fields). Inversely, when it is noted, "In winter, fortification of Xiang" (Huan *gong*, sixteenth year), it is to approve of the chosen moment and set it up as an example. Yet again, when the annals mention, "Great celebration in autumn to ask for rain" (Huan *gong*, fifth year), this means that this celebration was not at the correct time. Each sacrifice corresponded to a season; thus if a sacrifice is mentioned, it is to suggest blame by implying that a departure from custom took place.

These examples confirm a principle of writing: merely mentioning a fact implies an appraisal, either praise or blame, of the event. But usually, as we saw earlier, *Zuozhuan* prefers to take stock of the events mentioned by developing the account in such a way as to bring them to life. Two other commentaries on Antiquity, on the other hand, are devoted to the systematic justification of the canonical text: *Gongyang* and *Guliang*. (It is to *Gongyang* that I shall henceforth show preference in my citations.) When reading the annals, two questions come up again and again: Why is this event mentioned? And why is it phrased in this way and not another? The annals begin as follows: "The duke Yin, the first year, in the spring, of the king the first month." In response, *Gongyang* unleashes a litany of questions: "Why does it say 'the first year'? Why does it say 'in the spring'? What does it mean by the 'king'? Why does it mention 'king' before 'the first month'?" and so on. Each word and its placement are passed through a sieve, while the things that are not said are scrupulously examined. For example, why is the fact that the duke has ascended the throne not mentioned? Once the machinery of the commentary is set into motion, any purely event-related indication, as well as any notable absence of indication, in the annals is supposed to reveal an intention. According to the commentary, the annals attempt to "praise" or to "blame," to confer "importance" or to "criticize" and make note of their "aversion." Only facts are registered, but each one indicates an option on the part of the one relating them (Confucius): these facts, though simply cited, are value judgments.

We have seen that stating something is already to bring it into relief, to judge its effect. According to the annals, "In winter, the tenth month, the day of *jia wu*, Shusun Dechen defeated the Di at Xian" (Wen *gong*, eleventh year). The commentary adds:

> Why does it say "defeated"? To express the importance of the fact. Why is the day mentioned? To express the importance of the fact. Why is the place mentioned? To express the importance of the fact. Why, lastly, is the fact itself mentioned? To report that it was out of the ordinary.

To say something is to draw it out of silence, to pronounce on its importance, to highlight it. I deem something worth saying because I consider it not exactly ordinary, as standing out, however little, from the usual. The same goes for natural phenomena: the annals state that "in winter, in the tenth month, there was no rain" (Xi *gong*, second and third years) because it was considered abnormal. Similarly, day-to-day events in the social and political order, the commentary explains, were not generally recorded. The annals mention an event that took place at the court because it merits our attention; even if it is a small detail, we must figure out what makes this event remarkable, what judgment is being passed on it to justify its inclusion. "In winter," note the annals, "the prince of Lu went to Qi to bring engagement presents" (Zhuang *gong*, twenty-second year). The commentary explains:

> Usually the giving of engagement presents is not mentioned. Why is it mentioned here? To criticize, but to criticize what? That the duke went in person to give these presents does not conform with custom.

If something that appears normal (and therefore should not be mentioned) is mentioned, we should suspect something abnormal beneath the apparent normalcy. Here, a detail (that the duke went in person) is enough to express, indirectly but rigorously, disapproval.

Yet inclusion in the annals is not based on deviation alone (in relation to the norm or custom); events are also noted to serve as examples. If the annals mention that the duke of Lu went on a hunt in winter with the marquess of Qi (Zhuang *gong*, fourth year), it is because they deem this event, which appears secondary politically, significant morally. Since the marquess of Qi had his predecessor killed, the duke of Lu should hate him. Still, not only had they already attacked another principality together (and would join together in the future to besiege a stronghold), which could be attributed to political necessity, but they also shared the pleasures of the hunt. *Gongyang* explains it as follows: in both instances, the duke of Lu committed the same error, but to criticize him once is enough, provided that this criticism, by putting a finger on what is serious, is well chosen. One can hardly criticize every instance; "all the other instances become understandable on the basis of this one." This selection made among events of the same order therefore does not correspond merely to a principle of economy; it proves another way for the chronicler indirectly to make known his appraisal of the event.

Since an event is mentioned for its characteristic deviation, one might expect a negative interpretation to predominate in this type of reading (and in this decadence-obsessed ideology). The mention of a fact is most often supposed to express a moral deviation, a departure from the rules; from there, the commentary tends to become stereotyped. Whatever the question posed (why mention that he "asked to participate in a funeral"? or that "the marquess of Qi accompanied his daughter to Huan"? or that "the son of the heavens sent Lu to look for carriages"? or that a great administrator "crossed a border to meet his bride"? and so on), the commentary always gives the same answer, "to criticize." Each time, the reason for the criticism, according to the commentary, is that something occurred that was "contrary to custom." In short, Confucius composed *Annals* to expose the most significant faults that had led the world, over time, into its detestable state. This is why a favored formula in the commentary is to make the criticism more precise by indicating that it was "the first time" someone had acted in such a way (the first time someone had not gone in person to meet his spouse, or that someone had usurped the rank of princes, or that mourning was not observed for three years, or that a tax by acreage was adopted). From this perspective, Confucius becomes a historian again, and the judgment expressed through the events carries all the more weight because it constitutes a system.

But the commentary inevitably exposes itself to danger on this path: it repeats itself, with no chance of renewal, and risks wearing itself out.[4] Indeed, if the annals mention that "in spring, the duke went to see the fish in Tang" (Yin *gong*, fifth year), it is, according to the commentary, "to criticize," "because it is far away." Likewise, if the annals mention, about the duke's successor, that "in the spring, he went hunting in Lang" (Huan *gong*, fourth year), it is again "to criticize" and "again because it is far away." Only when the description is less laconic can the commentary give an event a particular justification and get out of its rut. For example, a sacrifice is noted after a fire in the royal granaries (Huan *gong*, fourteenth year). Its mention implies that it was inappropriate in a time of shortage; earlier, another sacrifice was mentioned several times (Huan *gong*, eighth year), but this was to criticize its frequency, since it was thought to lead to "disrespect." The argument is not uninteresting: if common things are unwor-

99

thy of mention, that which is *too* common deserves mention, since it is criticized.

This observation holds true more generally and leads surreptitiously to an overturning of the rules of interpretation. Clearly, the more deviation is repeated, the less remarkable it appears; at that point, proper conduct represents a divergence. When a negative judgment, expressed through events, becomes common and banal, noting normalcy becomes significant. Thus when the annals mention that the troops of various principalities "accompanied the king on his expedition against Zheng" (Huan *gong*, fifth year), they do so because the expedition is "correct," the commentary explains. Similarly, so apparently trivial a detail as "the duke's going to Qi to meet his fiancée" (Zhuang *gong*, twenty-fourth year) deserves mention because, after so many pages of events that do not conform to custom, this conformity becomes unusual and serves as a lesson. In this history of decadence, it is logical that the ordinary and the extraordinary gradually change places: abnormality becomes the norm, and normalcy becomes exceptional and noteworthy.

Given how the extraordinary thus changes sides, being first praised and then criticized, and how what is normal can change meaning, indicating at times what is common, at other times what is correct, one might think that the criteria for reading become unclear and that the interpretation vacillates. Would not the moral judgment on the reported event thus be whimsical? Would not the search for praise or blame, ceaselessly pursued through the annals, prove a vain effort to save the text from its flat aridity? The modern commentator Legge states plainly, "I have demonstrated a hundred times in my notes the extent of the absurdity into which such a method leads us."[5] All too often the indications allowing one to perceive an indirect judgment through mentioning an event contradict each other, depending on the event.[6] It is true that the ancient commentary produced no definitive rules of interpretation that might assure us of grasping these indirect meanings in every case. Nonetheless, the question remains open: In the absence of established codifications, is there not some more discreet relationship in the fastidious listings of the events that might make it possible to group the examples, to map out some patterns? And can one imagine a subtlety of meaning that would be free, a priori, of all ambiguity? It is normal for the reader not to be able to decode mechanically this subtlety of meaning expressed indirectly through facts; it demands a silent familiarization, which I shall try to practice.

One of the most characteristic indications of praise or blame through the mentioning of facts is the way people are named. Is there an implicit typology in this? The use of title is the clearest case. To call someone by his title is to honor him, as we saw with the official from Jin (Min *gong*, first year); inversely, omitting a title is disparaging. When the annals mention the military expeditions of Hui, *Gongyang* explains this twice (Yin *gong*, fourth year):

> Who is this Hui? It is Hui, the duke's son. Why is he not called the duke's son? To abase him. Why abase him? Because he took part [later] in the duke's assassination.

Or again, to call someone anonymously "a man" is, systematically, to express blame. When the annals note, "A man (or some people) from Qi attacked the mountain people" (Zhuang *gong*, thirtieth year); or, "A man (or some people) from Chu" sent an ambassador (Xi *gong*, twenty-first year), these apparently vague formulations designate the princes of Qi and Chu whose conduct is being criticized.[7] But the system of examples is not limited to this possibility: it may be that the title of the duke of Lu is omitted not to express reserve but because the duke is dealing with someone of a lower rank, and the annals prefer discretion on this type of abasement.

Similarly, the absence of a clan name can imply disapproval; this is especially true in reference to princesses. The annals need only say "the wife went back to Qi" to convey that this woman leads a disgraceful life. Inversely, there are cases in which the indication of a clan name takes on a negative meaning. One might think that the rule is being flouted here, but in considering these cases more closely, one finds they have an individual justification. If the annals designate an emperor's high official by his clan, this is to criticize, according to the commentary, that such a position is transmitted through heredity (Yin *gong*, third year); or it could be that the official is carrying out duties without having been invested with the office.

While systematization proves possible, it remains open-ended; it allows for particular interpretations, but its efforts at refinement threaten to undermine its integrity. The last case to consider is personal names. Most often, the absence of a proper name is understood as a mark of esteem, while its mention is a mark of disapproval. But outside this general principle are special cases: the personal name can be a social name, which serves to express praise (see Yin *gong*, first year); or not calling someone by name can be a way to avoid stooping to his level. What creates a subtlety of meaning, as these examples demonstrate, is that, while invoking the more general codifications and even lending itself to their efforts to create order, the meaning is not entirely resolved by them but requires individual consideration in which neither the course nor the outcome is predictable. It is not, therefore, that the particular case contradicts the general framework nor, inversely, that the exception confirms the rule but that there remains an inalienable rift in all the familiar routes that makes way for nuance. In attacking the absurdity he finds in the commentary on the annals, Legge seems unable to see that they possess their own geometry, although this geometry is variable; or rather, there is a continual geometrization that assumes a new configuration in each case.[8] Here, as at the core of Chinese culture, if there is a system, it does not reveal itself right away panoramically, in a theoretical vision or complete overview (in accordance with the general perspective of Greek speculation); rather, it is discovered along the way — by progressive trial and error, successive definitions, and accumulated experience.

I find an example of this subtle meandering of interpretation, as well as the experience accumulated by it, in the commentary on the last pages of the annals: "The duke of Lu had a diplomatic encounter with the prince of Jin as well as the viscount of Wu in Huangchi" (Ai *gong*, thirteenth year). The indication is laconic, but the commentary carefully justifies all its terms to explore its intention:

> Why is [the lord] of Wu called viscount? Because Wu presided over the encounter. But if Wu presided over the encounter, why mention Jin first? In order not to grant a barbarian principality [such as Wu] precedence over the principalities of the center [such as Jin and Lu]. But what does "as well as" mean before "viscount of Wu"? It serves to tell us that the encounter was made under this double patronage. But since one does not grant a barbarian principality precedence over the central principalities, why is the encounter presented under a double patronage? Because of the weight attributed to Wu. But why does Wu carry so much weight? Because, with Wu there, the other princes did not dare not to come.

These lines show that even the most neutral-seeming factual mention can convey a finely elaborated judgment which takes into account not only the order of values but also the relationships of power. Taken together, the three indications — the use of titles, the enumeration, and the mode of coordination used — lead to a complex point of view, according to which the same power (Wu, a barbarian principality, that is, more recently civilized) is simultaneously superior and inferior to the other (inferior in rank to Jin, one of the most prestigious central principalities, but superior in power). In this decadent time, the ancient sovereignties were questioned. It was necessary to make concessions to the new powers, and this compromise remained precarious. One can also detect through this single notation its alleged author's appreciation for the evolution of the time — his nostalgia for traditional hierarchy, which rested on the antiquity of the civilization, as well as his distrust of the new hegemonies, which had overturned the established order.

This system of interpretation, which underlies the commentary on the annals and underscores their moral judgment, emerges in the intricate grid of readings that from time to time the exegete takes the trouble to explain. Two of them in particular merit citation. In reference to the mention "Hu, the prince heir of Zheng, went back to Zheng again" (Huan *gong*, fifteenth year), *Gongyang* distinguishes four possible cases:

> Why do people sometimes say "went back" or "went back again"? "Went back again" means that when he left he was at fault but that when he returned home he was without fault, while "went home again" means that when he left he was without fault but that when he returned he was at fault. "To go home" simply means that in both cases he was at fault, while "to return" simply means that in both cases he was without fault.

As a result of this typology, the most strictly denotative expression, such as "went back again," abandons its neutrality to imply a judgment of character: Zheng's flight was shameful, but his return rehabilitated him. Similarly, apropos the mention "In autumn, the Wei troops entered Sheng" (Yin *gong*, fifth year), the commentary distinguishes a new series of cases: when the general is prestigious and the troops numerous, one says, "So-and-so leads the troops"; when the general is prestigious and the troops few, one says, "the general"; when the general is not prestigious and the troops many, one says "the troops"; when the general is not prestigious and the troops few, one says "some men"; but when the prince himself fulfills the duties of the general, one does not say "led the troops," to indicate the importance of the fact. It becomes easy to read the implicit judgment brought to bear on the present expedition: the troops were many, but their general without great merit. The system of evaluation is carefully defused (is it not inappropriate, if not dangerous, to bring the prince into this framework?); while the first four relate to one another and form a closed unit, the fifth throws open the system and overflows the boundaries of possibility, so that the meaning is destabilized.

In his search for a message addressed to the world, the commentator scrutinizes every notation, for nothing in the mention of an event is seen as either fortuitous or innocuous. A moral assessment is revealed in each word, in the order of the words, and in the void of their absence.[9] Just as in psychoanalysis the smallest slip is supposed to be revealing, the tiniest detail of these annals is deemed rich in instruction. Unlike in psychoanalysis, however, here one is situated on the level of intention and judgment, on the level of signs, not symptoms. Hence in raising these annals, with their dry style, to the level of a canonical text, the later tradition celebrated the scrupulosity of their delivery and justified them in the most minute fashion. There are two famous examples of this.[10]

"In spring," one reads in the annals, "in the first month of the royal calendar, the day of *mao shen*, the first day of the month, fell stones in Song, five in number" (Xi *gong*, sixteenth year). The commentary is particularly precise on this account:

> Why does it say "fell" before "stones"? The falling of stones repeats the way it is heard: one hears the noise of something falling, and in looking at the thing that has fallen, one sees that it is stones; in looking at them closer, one can count that there are five.

There is a parallel example of this in a description of the sky, just as hearing precedes sight. The annals next note that "the same month, six herons, flying backward, passed over the capital of Song" because one first notices six birds, then on looking closer, one notices they are herons, then on even closer inspection, one notices they are flying backward. Could the attention to event-related exactitude, the concern not to invent anything, which is obsessive in this case, be taken any further? One can see from this example why the Confucian tradition kept a distance from myth and censored fiction. Here the order of the sentence is supposed to follow the unfolding of the process, to reproduce it at every step, as if the description could be limited to the pure recording of facts, in an absolutely trustworthy fashion, so as not to deviate from reality.

At the same time, this factual exactitude is charged with another imperative — to pass a value judgment. When the annals mention, "In summer, in the fifth month, the day of *ren chen*, the Pheasant Gate as well as two towers were destroyed by fire" (Ding *gong*, second year), *Gongyang* adds:

> Why does it say "the Pheasant Gate as well as two towers were destroyed by fire"? Because the two towers are less important. Why

106

not say that the fire that destroyed the Pheasant Gate also destroyed the two towers? Because the principal site of the fire was at the towers. But if the towers burned first, why are they mentioned afterward? Because [in the way facts are related] one does not proceed from the least important to the most important.

Although in the second example the care with which the text is justified is carried as far as it is in the first, two requirements enter into consideration and become superimposed: factual rigorousness and value judgment. Event-related priority must accord with axiological priority. What leads to this reversal may seem a paradox: while they are so concerned about the exactitude of facts, the annals, in satisfying another requirement, can leave the facts behind or bring them up only indirectly. From this point on, it is not the judgment but the event on which this judgment is based that is implied indirectly (and does not the judgment thereby become more transparent?). The logic of detour thus becomes more complicated: events are reported only indirectly, but so much obliquity, in the historian's need for veracity, is indirectly and conveniently useful to the expression of morality.

To insinuate is to avoid having to say (since it is to avoid saying that I insinuate something). And on this point, at least, the principles are set forth clearly. "With regard to the outside," the commentary explains, "the annals mention the large flaws but not the small ones; with regard to the inside, they avoid mentioning the large flaws and mention the small ones" (Yin *gong*, tenth year). This inside is represented primarily by the Lu principality, whose cause Confucius, as a loyal subject, was supposed to adopt; and the outside is thus the other principalities. But the concern *for avoiding having to say* (the notion of *hui*[a]) also covers those of high rank, those who are esteemed, and parents: from this split in perspective between outside and inside, there results a double regimen of narration that, as we shall see, illuminates the position of the chronicler through its internal differences.

The most common manifestation of avoiding having to say is euphemism, which, of course, is used all over the world to a greater or lesser extent in military operations. Even Tolstoy's characters know how to read between the lines of the Russian government's report concerning the campaigns against Napoleon at Austerlitz. In the ancient Chinese annals, this principle is in full force. Out of consideration for the vanquished, one says that he "completely abandoned his territory," not that he was completely crushed, or one says that there has been a "battle," not that there has been a defeat. Out of consideration for the assailant, inversely, to "penetrate" means to annihilate, and to "fortify a position" means to occupy it. Each time decency requires it, the expression is veiled and the meaning obscured. Although it is so well coded, this system can once more turn in on itself, adapt to the circumstances, and open up to the exception, which becomes all the more significant. While it is agreed that, in regard to the Lu principality, one must never speak of defeat, openly admitting that the principality was defeated (Zhuang *gong*, ninth year) is enough to accuse it of being boastful and having deserved its defeat.

This discretion can be taken even further and obscure the truth. Not hiding it, properly speaking, but leaving it in shadow (the notion of *yin*[b]). The same is true when one speaks of an annihilation without saying who was annihilated, out of consideration for him. Similarly, when the annals note that "the duke of Lu pursued the Rong to the west of the Ji" (Zhuang *gong*, eighteenth year; see *Zuozhuan*), we must infer a preliminary proposition from this one, which is that these barbarians had come to invade this territory. Sometimes this abbreviation in the reporting can be considerable. Thus, when the annals say that "in the spring the people from Zheng came [to Lu] to make peaceful overtures" (Yin *gong*, sixth year), the negotiation as reported implies a prior battle, which is not mentioned out of consideration for the duke of Lu, who was taken prisoner. In such a case, the account is kept to a minimum so that dissimulation is not complete.

The dishonor that accompanied the murder of the sovereign must at all costs remain hidden, but the act was ceaselessly reproduced from generation to generation in Chinese Antiquity. This was the most serious crime, since it openly contradicted the filial piety the vassal was supposed to feel for his king and undermined the political order, the basic principle of which, according to Confucius, was confidence. On this topic, the chronicler is most likely to proceed by indirection, and the veil over the event tends to be the most opaque. The entry on the first prince mentioned in the annals ends in the following way: "In winter, in the eleventh month, the day of *ren chen*, the duke died." How could one suspect, Legge asks indignantly, that the duke did not die from natural causes but was assassinated? The "foreign student" finds a fair amount to doubt in the "merits of Confucius as a historian."[11] Indeed, the Chinese chroniclers of Antiquity had already responded to this criticism (and Legge is well aware of this, but he sees this merely as a "riddle," "which two men will not guess alike"). While not wishing to bring to light such an enormous offense committed in his own principality and out of concern for saving face (and in conformity with the principle of discrimination between the outside and the inside), Confucius nevertheless implies that the duke had been killed: that he does not speak of the funeral and does not indicate the place of death make his silence eloquent. The void with which this death is willfully surrounded makes it seem all the more suspicious. Is not such a silence more definitively reproachful that any explicit denunciation?

The only way to cut through the debate is to examine whether the clues in the narration (while serving to show that the duke was assassinated) are consistent: we can evaluate this in the account of the second duke mentioned in the annals, who also was killed (as were a number of his successors; during this time of exacerbated political ambitions, there were continual usurpations of power). On the subject of this prince, the account in the annals is a little more detailed: "In the spring, the first month of the royal calendar, the duke [of Lu] had a meeting with the marquess of Qi on the banks of the Luo river. The duke and his wife, the lady Jiang, then went back to Qi." The following line reads: "In summer, in the fourth month, on the day of *bing zi*, the duke died in Qi; and on the day of *ding you*, his coffin returned to Qi." We know from other sources what really happened. The duke of Lu's wife had sinful relations with her brother, the marquess of Qi. The duke reproached his wife, who complained to the marquess. When they met in Qi, the marquess held a banquet for the duke, and then, when he was drunk, took him in his carriage, where the duke was assassinated. Then, to satisfy the public outcry, the murderer was put to death. There is enough material here for a good novel of the heinous, scabrous, and violent sort. How much more discreet is Confucius's account! Nonetheless, the commentators assure us, all the facts are there: the little "and" ("the duke and his wife") instead of "with" (more expected perhaps?) is enough to imply that this woman was already separated from her husband; next, that the new duke's accession to power at the beginning of the next reign is not mentioned suggests that this accession was due to a forfeiture. Furthermore, that it is then noted that the wife of the preceding duke "withdrew" to Qi (another euphemism to say she fled) implies that she was seriously implicated in the events. Not only are these indications sufficient, but a Chinese commentator concludes that here Confucius gives a "direct" account and his judgment "rests on the facts themselves." With

the events laid out before our eyes, he continues, we can understand the nature of the events "without any commentary."

Can we really believe, however, that everything is so clear that
there is nothing to decode? First of all, that the place of death is
passed over in silence when it occurs within the borders is not
always the sign of an assassination, since at least at one other time
in the annals the indication of the place suggests that the prince
was killed (Xiang *gong*, seventh year).[12] On the other hand, the
annals mention the murder of a prince by his son when the son
did not intentionally kill him, only unwittingly giving him a fatal
potion (Zhao *gong*, nineteenth year). Of course, the chronicler
was seeking not to stretch the truth but to underline the responsibility of this unworthy son. Furthermore, as the commentary
subtly remarks, the annals then mention the honors paid to the
deceased, which is the sign (see the criterion established above)
that it was not really a murder. The two apparently contradictory
indications in the annals (of a murder and a funeral) are thus combined to express a more complex perspective: Confucius blames
this son for being morally guilty of his father's death but forgives
him. As a "writer," Confucius took indirect expression to its limit,
and the tangency that he chose in the narration of events enhanced
his ability to make the necessity of a moral interpretation felt.

In the Greek tradition as well, the way a historian reports an event
also conveys a judgment. This is especially the case with Thucydides. People often have noted how he framed an episode, introduced breaks, used digressions, and organized reversals of situation,
which allowed him indirectly to express a personal interpretation.
A reader as early as Plutarch noted this effect in the Gylippus
episode, for example (as a bridge between books 6 and 7 of
The Peloponnesian War): without making the slightest remark and
by using a narrative that never strays from its objectivity or rigor,

Thucydides' judgment on the event "is read as clearly" as if he had expressed it in the first person. The smallest details come to reveal an intention and to imply a valuation. This is only possible, Jacqueline de Romilly notes, "thanks to this remarkable peculiarity of Thucydides' history," whereby "the interpretation and the judgment are entirely expressed by means of a single account, with no visible intervention by the author."[13]

Can there be any doubt, indeed, that Thucydides' expression requires an ever more attentive reading and possesses an extreme subtlety? What, then, is the difference? With the Greek historian, the indirection derives essentially from the construction of his narrative. With him, indirection comes through in each episode; interpretation begins to show through a series of echoes, reminders, and contrasts in each sequence. Through the arrangement of his account, the historian delivers an analysis. The modern novelist, in turn, does not act any differently, as Maurice Merleau-Ponty so aptly demonstrated in an analysis of Stendhal's "indirect language."[14] In the Lu principality *Annals*, on the other hand, there is almost no organized account but rather successive mentions: the indirect quality is not the result of construction but rather flows from the projected intention — such, at least, as its commentators have decoded it or imagined to do so. This obliquity is only perceptible through a biased reading (which was adopted by the entire Chinese tradition after Mencius): Confucius, by reporting these events, wanted to deliver a message and re-create the world. Once this critical position is adopted, nothing in the text escapes the logic of obliquity. Like the classical allegorists who were always ready to read each line of Homer or Hesiod in "another way," with a philosophical or a theological slant, the Chinese moralists exposed a hidden meaning beneath each event — which for them, taking into account their ideological framework, could only be an expression of praise or blame, a value judgment.

The important thing is not so much to know whether the Chinese moralists were right to interpret the annals in this way (the question does not make any more sense if asked of the Greek allegorists) as it is to observe how this type of reading, in becoming the accepted interpretation (along with the canonization of the book), led to the formation of a specific type of writing (which, since then, bears its name).[c] Many of the expressions joined by conjunction in the oldest commentary, *Zuozhuan* (Cheng *gong,* fourteenth year), which have been constantly repeated since then, allow for an appreciation of the annals' originality by highlighting their characteristic tension.[15] In this network of formulas used to describe the annals, it is always a simultaneity of opposites, a transitory state, that one is seeking to indicate; the writing in the annals is called both "subtle and clear"; it "expresses what one wants to say, but in a veiled way"; it "is indirect while at the same time clear"[d] (Zhao *gong,* thirty-first year). Between the poles of *hidden* and *revealed,* the scale is poised, the equilibrium maintained. Shadow and light alternate and counterbalance each other: the semidarkness attenuates, the chiaroscuro barely reveals its meaning. This writing is not cryptic, nor is it transparent: the writer in fact expresses himself, addressing all, but reservedly. In this in-between state of *glimpsing,* the meaning becomes valorized, while an allowance is made for prudence.

This sort of writing is found in particular in the first author of *Official History,* Sima Qian, who wrote under the Han in the first century B.C. The Great Historian, for such was his title, is aware of the originality of *Annals,* which he compares with *Yiking* (*I-Ching*), the famous *Book of Changes;* while the latter "bases" itself on the things that are "hidden" to us (the principles of the course of the world and our lives) to make them manifest, *Annals* "unfolds" what is "visible" to us (events that have happened) to reach its "hidden"[e] meaning.[16] It is always in this give-and-take, not between appearance and reality but between the latent and manifest aspects of things, that the advent of meaning and the exploration of the real are conceived of by the Chinese. Indeed, while composing his work, as soon as he touches on some delicate point of the contemporary situation, the Great Historian resorts to the mode of very "subtle"[f] expression, which he attributes to the annals — such as when he brings up the rash, overly adventurous policies carried out against the barbarian populations, the excessive luxury of the court, or the autocratic power of the sovereign.[17] This surreptitious transformation of a traditionally pejorative expression, "empty words," allows us to glimpse his intention. Far from being ineffectual and empty, this "proposition," this empty "text"[g] that the historian "transmits" to posterity, conveys, without any specific references and through the mere reporting of facts, the appropriate judgment.[18] *Empty* now signifies that the essential remains implicit; hollow means that it is in the depths of the text that the meaning can be gleaned.

Dedicated first and foremost to expressing criticism or resentment, this type of writing was nearly lost in the later *Dynastic History*, which was heavily censured. It is found abundantly, on the other hand, in the type of discourse that is the privileged site of indirection, especially in China: poetic expression. One commentator considered the following Tang poem "related to" the type of writing in *Annals* (the day of "cold eating" in the spring is the feast of the dead, when the fire was rekindled only in the evening):

The town in spring: nowhere are flowers not blowing.
The day of cold eating: under the east wind the imperial
willows bend.
Night is falling: the Han palace is lit up with candles.
Their light smoke disperses and penetrates the houses of the
five marquesses.[19]

One might think these lines are meant to describe a scene, creating a tableau of a landscape, for no emotion is expressed, and the tone is neutral and descriptive. But as we know, according to the theory of Chinese literature, "one word" suffices to allow the meaning, praise or blame, to appear through the event recorded.[h20] Here the expression that reveals the blame, and is the "eye" of the poem, is the final reference to the five marquesses. Under the later Han in the second century A.D., these designate the five heads of the eunuch clans, who, after having ousted the men of letters' party, were rewarded by the emperor, who granted them marquessates. The *translatio temporum* from the Han to the Tang is too obvious for the allusion not to be clear: under the cover of describing a holiday, this poem denounces the eunuchs, who, in the reign of the emperor Dezong at the end of the eighth century, spread their influence to the court. One need only reread the poem to notice how, from line to line, the diffusion of imperial favor is indicated ever more suspiciously. As the coordinates become more precise, the animation that flows through each line is more clearly oriented. The reader's attention, at first free and undirected, is soon steered in the same direction: we move from the light fluttering of flowers to the bending of the willows, from the diffusion of lights and their dispersion in smoke to a precise and definitive culmination — the homes of the five marquesses.[21] This smoke (suggesting the sovereign's favors) is not lost for everyone; it concentrates only on the favorites. The implication with which the poem ends is heavy with reprobation. According to the classical formula, the meaning is both "subtle and clear": the critique reaches its mark while remaining disguised. The effect is successful, the blame deftly insinuated. And yet we cannot help but wonder if the indirectness of the remonstrance aimed at the prince actually protected the man of letters.

CHAPTER SIX

The Impossibility of Dissidence

(The Ideology of Indirection)

We can no longer avoid asking whether the art of indirection practiced by the Chinese man of letters, whereby one may convey an opinion through hints, might not also have another, ideological connotation. In other words: What might be the political price of this subtlety? It is possible that the Chinese man of letters became the victim of his own cleverness. By being indirect with power, by disguising his censure, did he not renounce the power of speech, which liberates by contesting? This implicit understanding between the literati and the authorities creates an objective complicity; it precludes confrontation and makes dissidence impossible. One might counter by saying that the Chinese literati were forced into this position or that prudence made it necessary to "speak covertly," as the saying goes. But one might also ask whether this discreet, artistically veiled whisper of protest did not ultimately disarm the man of letters more than it protected him. In any case, there is enough here to let us see why, for this and other reasons, the Chinese man of letters experienced (and perhaps still does experience?) so much difficulty in modernizing himself, by which I mean recasting himself as an intellectual, and why today the Chinese remain reluctant, to say the least — in spite of abandoning all Communist conviction — to embrace democracy.

Once again the example of Confucius, the "patron of literary men," serves as a starting point. In his conversations with the lords of his time and in the advice given to his disciples, which have been passed down in the famous collection *Analects* (*Lunyu*), we find a desire to "flee" the truth in order to "avoid saying" (the notion of *yin*ᵃ), which, as we have seen, is also the guiding principle of *Annals*. But here the principle is internalized and presented as a moral imperative:

> The duke of Sheh [She] informed Confucius, saying, "Among us here there are those who may be styled upright in their conduct. If their father has stolen a sheep, they will bear witness to the fact." Confucius said, "Among us, in my part of the country, those who are upright are different from this. The father conceals the misconduct of the son, and the son conceals the misconduct of the father. Uprightness is found in this." (13.18)[1]

To justify Confucius's position, the commentators argue that filial piety and paternal benevolence are the cardinal virtues supporting the social structure, producing the moral influence that renews tradition and assures political cohesion. Might not a better defense be that the intimacy of personal bonds, marked by love (such as that between father and son), legitimizes a certain partiality and even complicity? The fact remains that here Confucius downplays truthfulness or at least makes it secondary to another value. This stance is likewise found in politics. The duke Lu married a princess from another principality who had the same family name; to disguise that fact, he called her by another name (*Analects* 7.30). This went against custom, and Confucius knew this better than anyone else. But when a minister of justice from a foreign court taunted Confucius by asking whether or not his sovereign "knew propriety," he responded resolutely in the affirmative.

118

Later, in front of his disciples, he acknowledged his error, without, however, trying to justify himself, as if resigned in advance to the accusation. There is certainly greatness in this sense of allegiance, experienced as an inner force, but can one really believe that it is without danger?

Inevitably, the result is that, out of respect for authority, no one dares openly to express an opinion. An anecdote from *Analects* is typical. The new duke of Wei was struggling with his father, who, driven from his principality long ago, had returned to reclaim the throne. As Confucius was passing through Wei, two disciples wondered whether their Master was for the current duke (the son), his host, but they did not dare ask so delicate a question directly. Zigong went to find Confucius and asked:

> "What sort of men were Po-î [Boyi] and Shû-ch'î [Shuqi]?" "They were ancient worthies," said the Master. "Did they have any repinings *because of their course?*" The Master again replied, "They sought to act virtuously, and they did so; what was there for them to repine about?" On this, Tsze-kung [Zigong] went out and said, "Our Master is not for him." (7.14)

The detour is clear: to probe the Master's political opinion, the disciple resorted to a commonplace, the story of two famous brothers (Boyi and Shuqi), each of whom wanted to cede the throne to the other. By means of this counterexample, the disciple proposed to evaluate what Confucius thought of the struggle for power between father and son at the court of Wei. Confucius, of course, understood the allusion. In praising these sages from the past, as was appropriate, and in insisting that their virtue was its own reward, he insinuated his lack of respect for the prince, his host. "In his position," says the commentator Zhu Xi, "a man of good breeding refrained from criticizing high officials, in this case, the prince. This is why Zigong does not speak openly about the prince of Wei but questions Confucius by speaking of Boyi and Shuqi. Through the Master's response, we see that he does not support the duke."

Such an indirect expression of political opinion is not only deemed entirely satisfactory; it is also judged the only acceptable moral stance. Hence we are led to suspect the same type of indirect exchange in other passages of *Analects*, whose meaning, at first glance, is not very convincing. For example, someone "questioned" Confucius by proposing the following parallel: on the one hand are two figures from the past who became famous, one through his skill at archery, the other through the art of boatmanship, but who died violent deaths; on the other are two figures no less famous who "wrought at the toils of husbandry" and "became possessors of the kingdom" (14.6). According to Zhu Xi, Confucius's interlocutor was not merely contrasting two types of merit, technical skill and moral rectitude. His proposition also contained a hidden application: the first case targets people in power at the time, while the second serves to praise Confucius. This is why Confucius, sensitive to the allusion, did not immediately respond (but is not this silence a response?) and waited until the other had left to praise him, as proof that they had understood each other and that the message had been passed between them. Similarly, when a disciple of Confucius openly disapproved of the reconstruction of a building in Lu, one might see nothing more than a conventional expression of attachment to the past. But considering Confucius's praise ("That man seldom speaks; when he does, he is sure to hit the point" [11.13]), we are led to infer, as certain commentators have done, that the remark conceals a more significant position. The building was the Long Treasury, which, as we know from *Annals*, was used as the defensive base of the sovereign of Lu against the subversive attacks of a usurper. The disciple's stance, which could be deemed insignificant in its conformism, can thus be read as a veiled expression of his support of legitimate authority.

Indirection becomes even more subtle when communication is complicated by the speakers' political motivations and personal interests. In such cases, emblematic figures from the past are replaced by proverbial expressions. The principle remains the same: beneath an apparently neutral and general formulation, along the lines of a commonplace, a "subtle" intention, the commentator explains, is slipped in, which attempts to "upset" the other and thereby produce the desired effect. A minister of Wei repeated a saying to Confucius and asked him what it meant: "'It is better to pay court to the furnace than the southwest corner.' The Master said, 'Not so. He who offends against Heaven has none to whom he can pray'" (3.13). The proverb contrasts two symbolic places. On the one hand, there is the most secluded and quiet place in the house, the southwest corner, which is also the place of honor; on the other, there is the furnace, where people bustle about and eat. Based on this, two interpretations are possible. Some commentators think that in a veiled way the minister was asking advice about his career: Should he seek the good graces of the prince or a favorite woman or lover? According to the more common interpretation, this powerful minister was not soliciting advice but giving a warning: if someone wants to succeed in the court of Wei, he must directly address the minister of Wei, who considers himself the furnace, since he takes care of immediate business, while the southwest corner represents the prince's friends, who are more respected but lack real power. Hence Confucius's abrupt response, in which "Heaven" refers to the prince; only from him, and not from any faction of the court, did he seek recognition.

Indirectly communicating political opinion responded to

a concern for decorum, due to the customary respect for authority. It was also justified in relationships of force as a way to avoid
the shock of confrontation. The following brief dialogue at first
seems flat, but it is charged from beginning to end with implicit
warnings:

> Chî Tsze-zan [Ji Ziran] asked whether Chung Yû [Zilu] and Zan
> Ch'iû [Ran Qiu] could be called great ministers. The Master said, "I
> thought you would ask about some extraordinary individuals, and
> you ask about Yû [Zilu] and Ch'iû [Ran Qiu]. What is called a great
> minister is one who serves his prince according to what is right, and
> when he finds he cannot do so, retires. Now, as to Yû [Zilu] and
> Ch'iû [Ran Qiu], they may be called ordinary ministers." Tsze-zan [Ji
> Ziran] said, "Then they will always follow their chief—will they?"
> The Master said, "In an act of patricide or regicide, they would not
> follow him." (11.23)

Confucius's interlocutor belonged to the most powerful Lu clan,
whose ambition was to overthrow the prince. On this occasion,
he showed himself proud to have employed two of the Master's
disciples (Zilu and Ran Qiu). Showing surprise at the pettiness of
the question and then ostensibly diminishing the merit of his own
disciples, Confucius began by disparaging this great lord's arro-
gance. Next, through his definition of *great ministers*, he implied
that his disciples' fault was not to have withdrawn in time, which
was an indirect condemnation of their employer. Lastly, this disapproval becomes a warning in the final response: if the powerful
lord goes too far along the path of usurpation, his disciples will
oppose his ambitions.

Such examples (and we must rely on examples, since *Analects*
is based on them and resists theorizing) reveal the ambiguous
nature of the relationship between the Master and authority. On

the one hand, Confucius consented to bend to authority; on the other, he remained attached to his convictions: we see both the desire to conform to political reality and intransigence. That Confucius accepted challenging those in power in this way could lead him into comical situations, which leave the reader with an image of a Master somewhat crafty (even though this image has never tarnished tradition's universal praise): one day, for example, an ambitious fellow who sought the support of Confucius sent him a pig. Confucius, who did not want to give in to his solicitations, chose a moment he was not at home to thank him. In a stroke of bad luck, he met him along the way (17.1). In contrast, but with no real contradiction, Confucius made the following retort to one of his closest disciples, Zilu (with whose audacity we are familiar): to serve one's prince, "Do not impose on him, and moreover, withstand him to his face" (14.23). In principle, the distinction usually made between periods of order and disorder, which basically represent the only alternatives in Chinese political thought, attempts to reconcile the demands of honor and prudence. When good government prevails, Confucius says, people are able to speak openly and act uprightly, making no concessions; when it does not, one must continue to act uprightly but speak with reserve (14.4).[2] While the man of letters should remain imperturbable in his actions, he should also know, the exegete explains, "not to dare go all the way" with his thoughts, "to avoid trouble."

Here Confucius is simply reworking an ancient theme from *The Book of Songs* (260): to be "clear-sighted" helps to "assure [one's] own safety." As another great text from the Confucian tradition comments, in an attempt to define the golden mean: "When the world is well governed, words encourage [morality]; when it is ill governed, silence allows such a situation to be tolerated" (*Zhongyong* 27). Thus a compromise is reached between insubordination and cowardice: the demands of honor and prudence are reconciled. However, this delicate equilibrium, counterbalancing inflexibility with suppleness, bringing conviction and precaution together, can only be fragile, for although it can remain an inner demand, idealized by the Sage, this equilibrium proves difficult to institutionalize. The later tradition, after Antiquity, tended to lean in one direction only, docility.

The last centuries of Antiquity represent an exceptional moment in Chinese history. At this time, the fetters of the ancient feudal structures were loosening, and the new political system of the empire was not yet established. This transitional period was one of great collective and personal freedom. Since the principalities were now independent, there were multiple centers of power, comparable to contemporaneous Greek city-states; that the princes vied among themselves to obtain hegemony and restore monarchic unity produced a rivalry that favored the mobility of the population as well as currents of thoughts. These changes also benefited Chinese men of letters: heredity gave way to talent, and the granting of lands gave way to the allocation of salaries; in short, in this period of crisis, the governments were seeking any recipes that might assure them of power and prosperity. A new social type thus appeared: the court counselor who traveled from one principality to another (*youshi*[b]) to offer his lessons to the prince and be employed by him.

The establishment of the empire in 221 B.C. constitutes an essential break, since it resulted in a general unification of the territory as well as the concentration of power in the hands of a single man. Likewise, the status of the man of letters, condemned to be little more than a cog in the state's machine, was strongly devalued, while his independence of thought was subjected to the autocrat's often high-handed censorship. A number of these new men of letters, such as Sima Qian, under the Former, or Western,

Han dynasty in the last two centuries B.C., still dared to draw a parallel between past and present situations and to convey their resentment. But afterward, as Xu Fuguan has analyzed so well, the Chinese men of letters "became accustomed," and their feeling of oppression was progressively "anesthetized."[3] Instead of blaming the new regime, they did not think of complaining, except about things that impeded its good functioning (thus Sima Qian led to Ban Gu, who wrote not to express resentment but out of concern for literary glory). In their confrontation with authority, the literati were reduced to passivity.

The point of clear difference where the rift is greatest between China and Greece is in the Chinese's never having imagined any regime other than the "royal path," or monarchy. The Chinese never thought to oppose monarchy with different political forms such as oligarchy and democracy (and the forms that derive from them). As we have seen, they conceived only of periods of order, when the prince was well advised and spread his benevolent influence over the world, and disorder, when he became victim to his entourage and vices, renounced his moral standards, and plunged the world into chaos. The principle of government by a single man was never questioned in China (and still is not, it seems to me, since, in spite of the disappearance of Communist ideology, the Chinese Communist Party continues to monopolize power, as if there were no alternative). There was, nevertheless, a political practice that the Chinese tried to institutionalize to guarantee the smooth functioning of monarchic power, one that would give the literati their legitimacy back: the "remonstrance"[c] addressed to the prince, which was part of one's duty as adviser to him. Clearly, it is this principle of remonstrance that still motivates the tradition of mural posters, the *dazibao*, and that contemporary Chinese thinkers have presented, in a world where the idea of voting has never seen the light of day, as the Chinese form of democracy.

The principle of remonstrance has been valued since Antiquity. A minister was praised in the ancient annals, for example, because after "his prince had acted poorly, he did not neglect to address remonstrances to him in the name of morality"; he was thought to be protected by the heavens.[4] Inversely, a presumptuous general, who forbade that remonstrances be addressed to him, is presented as lost from the start.[5] But it was at the beginning of the empire, when the court counselor's influence was considerably reduced, that ritualists and moralists made a theory of it. Once more, people were tempted to reconstruct formally, that is, to *reconcile ideologically*, what proved too contradictory and impossible in reality. From this arose the detailed codifications that were called on to weave the web of a utopia, for the principle of remonstrance was supposed to cross social strata, while at the same time scrupulously to respect its hierarchy. The same model is found in an increasingly reduced form as one descends the ladder; the proportions remain equitable and the geometry simple. Nothing henceforth can escape this type of inventory, this great labeling of categories, modulated on each level:

> If the Son of the heavens has seven vassals to admonish him, even if he does not possess the *Way*, he will never lose the empire; if a feudal prince has five vassals to admonish him, even if he does not possess the *Way*, he will not lose his kingdom; if a high official has three vassals to admonish him, even if he does not possess the *Way*, he will not lose his house; if a simple official has a friend to admonish him, he will never lose his renown; if a father has a son to admonish him, he will never sink into immorality.[6]

Of course, in spite of this reassuring ladder effect and the list's regularity, the system of remonstrance fully merits use with the person in possession of all the power, the emperor. Four func-

126

tionaries were specially appointed to give the emperor a certain type of advice: the "Assistant to the left," the "Aide to the right," the "Questioner in front," the "Support from behind." Again the model is flawless and the system hermetic: the sovereign's conduct is bound on all sides, the squaring perfect, the framing ideal. Furthermore, the description is detailed to regulate the moment of crisis in the event the views of the sovereign and his counselor diverge or the latter withdraws (see *Mencius* 4.2.3). The man of letters humbly offers his resignation, while the sovereign treats him courteously and recognizes his own inadequacy.[7] As in a well-ordered dance, the prince must accompany the counselor who is leaving him, and the latter must wait awhile on the road of departure to give the prince a chance to call him back. This ritual of resignation is the only way to distinguish the remonstrance addressed to the prince from familial remonstrance. Thus, it alone separates politics and morality, for both wife and son should address remonstrances to their husband or father, but since they form "one body with him," they cannot leave him. A comparison based on the physical codification of the "five agents," common in the rhetoric of the time, underscores the difference: the remonstrance addressed to a prince by his minister, as the latter's duty, is like the action of a blade that cuts wood; that addressed to a father by his son, out of benevolence, is like the action of a flame that allows one to bow wood. The former aims at "squaring," the second at "bending."

That this remonstrance was completely idealized is demonstrated by the importance its symbolic representation came to assume. Every aspect is given an emblem, many of which were borrowed from ritual to create the motif. Under the reign of an enlightened sovereign, according to *Ritual*, "a standard is raised to promote upright citizens, a rod is suspended from which to attach criticisms, and a drum is beaten to call for remonstrances."[8] Two functions are specially defined ritually to signify the sovereign's errors and thereby help him to correct them: a secretary, at his side, makes note of the errors committed, and an employee in the kitchen reduces the size of the dishes accordingly; if they depart even a little from this obligation, both of them are immediately put to death. Such a detailed recording of faults does not, however, contradict the concern to "avoid saying." This description is only for internal use, it is noted, to help to correct behavior. In other words, because the goal is normalization, it would be useless, if not detrimental, to display mistakes on the outside.

This principle of remonstrance is characterized, therefore, by a twofold aspect. On the one hand, it is inspired by the essential logic of Chinese thought, natural Regulation. The rectification to which remonstrance leads is conceived of as a compensation: the chef is compelled to reduce the dishes in proportion to the errors committed to reestablish equilibrium between the opposing energies of yin and yang. At the same time, because its validity is limitless, since it is at work on all levels, in the family as well as the state (according to the ancient Chinese notion of *guojia*[d]), the principle of remonstrance has a moral universality. In this connection, it finds its natural function: in Chinese thought, moral capacity is but a "continuation" in humans of the Regulation that is spontaneously at work in the world and whence reality proceeds.[9] Thus caught between the cosmological principle that inspires it and the moral demand in which it is manifested, remonstrance could never acquire a political consistency, properly speaking. For this reason, it was difficult to institutionalize; and considering Chinese history, the drawback of Confucian morality is its inability to translate into institutions. The neo-Confucians in China today are still facing this problem, for without political institutionalization, remonstrance is no more than a pure principle; it cannot affect the relationships of power and remains at the mercy of power.

The fragility of remonstrance in the face of power is all the greater because its efficacy is based on allusiveness. Remonstrance gains in being whispered or in being implied because it appeals to the collaboration of its addressee, so that he might probe its discreet appearance. For it to work, the addressee needs to play his part and be interested in lifting the veil.

Once again, the ethics of discretion in remonstrance finds authorization in Confucius. It is emphasized throughout *Analects* by a term that means the "beginning" or the "seed" of things and that, thereafter associated with the key to speech, becomes an everyday word in Chinese for criticism.[e] With our parents, Confucius states, remonstrance should remain embryonic and not be insistent (4.18). It should just barely appear indicatively and be suggestive. If our parents are not open to it, we should redouble our respect and refrain from murmuring against them. Similarly, as Confucius states a little later in *Analects* (4.26), too frequent criticism can be dangerous: addressed to the sovereign, it makes him resent us; addressed to our friends, it creates a distance between us. If the remonstrance "does not pass muster," or is not accepted, Confucius continues, one must know how to "desist," or "stop oneself," for he who embarrasses the other through criticism is "acting without consideration" and "bothers his listener." To have an effect on the other, the idea must remain instigatory, and thus inchoate, instead of insistent or imposing. Yet this concern to avoid conflict is double-edged, for this subtle, "insinuating" proposition (once again expressed through reference to the "wind"[f]), which leads the addressee indirectly "with words of gentle advice" and thereby remains "pleasing" to him, instead of confronting him head-on, only has "value," Confucius underlines, if the addressee perceives "the unfold[ing] of [the other's] aim" (the image in Chinese is of a ball of string unwound to the end): one must presume not only finesse on the criticizer's part but also goodwill (9.24).

The codification of remonstrance addressed to the sovereign in the first centuries of the empire was inspired by the principles of respect and restraint. Five modes of remonstrance were proposed, which correspond to the five virtues.[10] The first is "indicated" remonstrance, which appeals to perspicacity: one notices the sovereign's errors as they take shape and alerts him before they spread. The second is "submissive" remonstrance, which calls on human virtue: one expresses it by "conforming oneself" to the spirit of the sovereign, by "meeting him halfway" instead of offending him. The third is "observant" remonstrance, which appeals to a sense of common decency: when one sees on the prince's face that a criticism displeases him, "one takes a step backward"; if he appears happy, one "moves forward" — hence, "one advances and retreats," while respecting propriety. The fourth is "finger-pointing" remonstrance, which appeals to loyalty: it expresses the sincerity with which one comes to the aid of the prince. The last is the remonstrance that derives from a sinking feeling and calls on a sense of duty: "when a feeling of commiseration rises up in our heart of hearts," "one expresses the ills besetting the country directly"; "one resolutely agrees to sacrifice one's life for the prince," instead of desiring to "avoid dying."

In reading this list, one would think that it recognizes human freedom and that there is legitimate choice. More particularly, one might think a direct and courageous remonstrance is allowed, even if at the peril of one's life. But this typology proves a decoy; the fan opens and suddenly closes. We need not waste time with the variety of these cases, to which equal weight would be attributed, since in fact there is only one. Once again, classification leads only to an illusion of options; the codification is but a sleight of hand in the service of the ideology of submission. First of all, once this kind of activity becomes classified, it is always the "indicating" or "insinuating" (like the wind[g]) remonstrance that is held up as the Confucian option, the one preferred. Most importantly, this classification of remonstrances is immediately followed by some general remarks that supposedly serve as conclusion:

> In the service of the sovereign, one should, upon entering his employ, endeavor to demonstrate the greatest loyalty and, when one withdraws, endeavor to correct one's faults. When one is let go, not to speak ill; when one makes remonstrances, not to let them be too piercing.[h] This is why, according to *Ritual*, an inferior should not make manifest remonstrances.[i]

The variety of cases briefly envisioned lead to a single solution: a remonstrance that remains ever respectful of authority and veiled in expression. By a tightening of the vise, we are constrained to detour. As proof, we have the last sentence of this exposition, which brings us back to what we already know: the ideal remonstrance possesses its own genre; its apogee is poetry.

Since it is translated into no institution and protected by no guarantee, the freedom to address remonstrances openly is but an illusion, or rather, a trap. For example, when the recently founded empire began to stabilize, a more conciliatory emperor, Wendi of the Han, in the second century B.C., asked his civil servants to introduce him to "cultivated and virtuous people" "capable of speaking openly and making remonstrances."[11] But one of his successors, the touchy Wudi, quickly made it known in court that he would tolerate no criticism. In recent times, history repeated itself. When the Communist regime began to stabilize, President Mao in 1957 invited the intellectuals to express their views openly. But the movement of "socialist rectification" launched the following year made his blossoming of "one hundred flowers" of short duration.[12] Many were caught in this game of cat and mouse with the authorities (which depended on whether the authorities "loosened" or "tightened" their grasp[j]: the only alternative offered by the political line in China).[13]

This subduing of the men of letters at the beginning of the empire is thus rich in lessons for what follows. How can one be indirect in a state so politically censored, once the reigning power has closed itself to criticism? An entire section of the first *Dynastic History*, one not found in the later installments, gives a glimpse of the curious characters who played the role of entertainers or buffoons at court.[14] Under the cover of riddles and by resorting to enigmas, they did not set off the prince's touchiness; under the guise of amusing, they expressed a political opinion. This was the ultimate way, the historian suggests, of retaining one's independent spirit while remaining tolerated by the authorities. Hence, although these characters are apparently secondary, their cases are not anecdotal, and their portraits are sketched with sympathy. While a whole chapter of the principal Chinese work of literary reflection, *Wenxin diaolong* (fifth and sixth centuries), is also devoted to them, it is clear to the theorist of discourse that this type of indirect expression — whether relying on humor or understatement, whether funny or cryptic (these two aspects are deemed to go hand in hand) — can have major political stakes and for this reason "merit our attention."[15] Jokes can serve as a warning; the disguised expression can reprimand tyrannical behavior. In this case, the critic tells us, "even if the expression is circuitous, the meaning tends to be straightforward."[k] In other words, even if it is artful, this detour is intentional and is saved by inner rectitude.[16]

The chapter of *Dynastic History* cited earlier consists of two parts: the first, drawn up by Sima Qian, praises the courage of those in Antiquity who, pretending to amuse the prince, pointed out his errors to him. The second part, the work of a different writer, presents contemporaries who enjoyed witticisms.[17] The same shift is found in the chapter on literary theory: since the beginning of the empire, the critic explains, the expression of humor had lost its function as remonstrance and sought only comic effect; instead of aiming at moral uprightness, detour became an end in itself. It was cultivated for its pleasure alone and became a gratuitous game of conundrums and riddles.[l] Furthermore, this theorist notes in his chapter on the image that since the end of Antiquity poets have given up charging poetic motifs with political content and have used only descriptive comparisons.[18] The literary historian does not mince his words: with the advent of the empire, the Chinese "men of letters" "became soft."

This softening of the literati, the result of imperial censorship, is evident in the reinterpretation of the ancient Chinese expression that, in the classical heritage, characterizes the morality peculiar to *The Book of Songs*. The principle of the expression is ambiguous: four characters are balanced two by two, "tepid — pliable — authentic — dense."[m] External softness is balanced by inner resolve, malleability by firmness. At the beginning of the empire, the formula was interpreted as follows:

> "Tepid" means the look on the face is tepid and unctuous; "pliable" that our natural character is pliable and accommodating. Poetry indirectly expresses its remonstrances through circumlocutions, without mentioning things by name. This is why the people say that the terms "tepid — pliable — authentic — dense" characterize the lessons taught by poetry.[19]

The balance of the formula is distorted by the commentator's selectivity: only the first two terms, connoting softness, are deemed worthy of comment; the other two, suggesting inner rigor, are not commented on. Consequently, the moral lessons of poetry are limited to the indirect and agreeable nature of remonstrance. However, as Yuan Mei pointed out in the eighteenth cen-

tury, in many poems in the ancient *Book of Songs*, the author
forcefully proclaims his indignation and delivers his adversary to
"jackals and tigers" (*Book of Songs* 200). Nevertheless, even these
poems, most of the commentators believe, can be classified under
this label and derive from a common norm.[20] Later, the formulation became completely inflexible after two of its terms were
changed, and ended up: "tepid — dense — accommodating — peaceful."[n] Travestied by tradition, the ancient ideal lost its equilibrium,
shifting definitively to the side of spinelessness.

The worst aspect of the compromise between the men of letters
and the authorities, who were supposed to communicate through
innuendo, was that it became the object of a consensus: the man
of letters ended up considering the mutilation of his words normal; worse still, he adhered to this distortion and upheld it as a
value. Rare are those, indeed, over the course of Chinese history
who dared oppose the dominant ideology to denounce the danger
in this art of the poetically murmured remonstrance. The clair-
voyance displayed on this by the philosopher Wang Fuzhi in the
seventeenth century, who also resisted the Manchurian invasion
(such political engagement is surely not irrelevant), thus seems all
the more remarkable. In *The Book of Songs*, he asserts, the poems
made up entirely of imagery are the exception, for "at the beginning, the type of situation in which someone wanted to express
himself in veiled terms because he did not dare name that person
or circumstance he wanted to denounce, did not exist."[21] The
author of the song has the courage to name himself and his adversary, and it is in this manner that a criticism should be made:

> Although it is said that the moral teaching proper to poetry implies a
> sense of propriety [here we find the traditional expression: "tepid —
> pliable — authentic — dense"], all enlightened desires fear neither

Heaven nor man and proceed openly in broad daylight, without adopting the stance of weak or timid people who dare say things only in half measures.[22]

The shift is identified, once again, as dating from the imperial era. (Although there are many expressions full of imagery in a poem such as *Lisao* at the end of Antiquity, Wang Fuzhi notes, "here the poet expresses himself just as openly in many places, without censoring himself.") From that time on, the debasement of the man of letters became more and more pronounced. Hence the Song poets of the sixth and seventh centuries

> tried to do two things at once, in an attempt to procure a reputation for honesty, while fearing to put themselves in danger. They therefore used a great many allusive expressions and mounted their attacks adroitly, and yet many among them suffered for it: in showing others enough to raise their suspicions, they became implicated [in accusations] even though their intention was not ill willed.[23]

The prudent camouflaging of remonstrance, which aims to soften criticism, can turn against an author instead of protecting him. The compromise between the literati and the authorities, which one might think was balanced, proves one-sided, for as soon as the interlocutor expects insinuations, all formulations, even the most well intentioned, become suspicious, and no discourse can be innocuous. This is because the rule of the game is that insinuation should always involve the most subtle meaning, the most unspeakable or essential meaning, the true goal. Likewise, in giving himself over to obliquity, the man of letters made the authorities more touchy; he found himself the victim of his own ruse. From that point on, his position was undermined, his word mortgaged, since no one would vouch for him (not even himself). In exposing

135

himself without mercy to the infinite game of interpretations, he played the game of despotism, increasing its arbitrariness and making himself the accomplice of his own punishment. Not content to censor his speech, the authorities could always decide, as a last resort and legitimately, what he *could have* insinuated. Thus he was condemned from the start, since he had no means of opposing the authorities nor any way of defending himself.

Throughout Chinese history, many scholar-poets displeased the prince and ended their days in a far-off province or with their heads on the executioner's block. In those epochs when the authorities were less self-assured and thus more fretful, there were mass slaughters (for example, in the third century, at the establishment of the Ming, and throughout the seventeenth century). In twentieth-century China, political opposition is still often expressed in an analogous fashion, as scholars continue to play the authorities' game, more or less, and to the same effect. At the end of Maoism, foreign observers were surprised that popular resentment could find no outlet other than poetry (commemorating the death of Zhou Enlai in 1976, for example).[24] The argument at the beginning of the above-mentioned chapter on literary reflection comes up again: the "mouth" (of the people) is just as hard to "obstruct" as the course of a river.[25] Of course, the anonymous poems pinned to the flower crowns strewn over Tiananmen Square had no poetic value, but they were rich in wordplay and images hostile to the rulers. The Party, furthermore, was well aware of the stakes: the square was quickly cleaned and the repression vigorous.

The same goes for the Chinese intellectual in the twentieth century — if indeed such a figure has yet been born, if he has yet emerged from the cocoon of the literati. Do Westerners not call an intellectual someone who can assert his ideas in the face of the authorities, or at least know how to separate himself, however little, from his subordination, someone who has achieved a certain autonomy of speech and makes it known? Is he not someone who can say, "j'accuse"? Since the beginning of westernization at the end of the nineteenth century and after the great patriotic outburst of May 4, 1919, in particular, generations of Chinese have been called on to renounce indirect expression and to express themselves openly. The revolutionary slogan discovered outside the country became a lesson. The hypocrisy of detour is but an enticement, Lu Xun explains; it would have been better for Chinese rulers, who had only words of magnanimity, indulgence, humanity, and clemency on their lips, to have been "as clear and direct as Lenin: but Lenin was a Russian who said what he thought. He had greater candor than we, the Chinese."[26] But even recently, as soon as they had to confront the authorities, Chinese writers sought refuge in indirect expression, all the more since it is a recognized art form: the perversity of detour is that one can mask one's spinelessness by priding oneself on subtlety. In 1978, when Deng Xiaoping promised writers that the Party would henceforth recognize their freedom of speech and even their freedom to "constructively" criticize, certain authors, such as Bai Hua, attempted audacious, denunciatory works, such as the play *Bitter Love (Kulian)*, which evokes the fate of a painter who falls victim to the regime. After finding himself ridiculed by Party critics, Bai Hua gave in to detour and buried his political opinion beneath images of the flowers and clouds of Yunnan. For the Chinese intellectual, the temptation to protect himself with poetry remains great. But with such obliquity, dissidence is impossible.

"We did not speak so openly — it would have been too dangerous — but rather through covert hints." Many Chinese men of letters could have made this admission, and yet it does not come from them. It is from Plato, or at least is attributed to him (*Letter* 7: "legontes ouk enargōs houtōs — ainittomenoi de"). Faced with the tyrant from Syracuse, whose conduct he tried to correct through remonstrances, Plato was also led to prudence. Similarly, confronted with the absolutism of Louis XIV, Fénelon in his *Télémaque* disguised his critique of despotism beneath the features of Idomeneus. The rarity of these situations in the West matters little and in fact underscores the rift that separates public opinion in China and Europe: as a philosopher, Plato was not hindered from comparing regimes and constructing the ideal city; and in his *Lettre à Louis XIV* and *Tables de Chaulnes*, Fénelon openly denounced the kingdom's ills and the monarchy's failings. Generally, in Europe, political pamphlets were printed elsewhere and brought back into a country clandestinely (for Europe had the advantage of this *elsewhere* of cities and nations: eighteenth-century French thinkers were often in Holland); and when the protest was written in verse ("indignatio facit versus" [indignation produces poetry]), it was not so as to soften its polemical effect or lessen the charge but, on the contrary, to emphasize the satire and make it more virulent (see, for example, Victor Hugo's *Châtiments* [Chastisements]). Imagery does not disguise the critique; it makes the critique more salient.

The contrast is clear: in Europe, official censorship mainly emphasized the question of Truth and was thus religious. In China, there was never a conflict of religion (not even the anti-Buddhist measures of the years 842–845), since no one there had any conception of dogmatic truth (that is, there never was a codification of meaning defined as the truth and imposed on the conscience to ensure its salvation); since there was nothing to counterbalance the political agenda, since there was no order of value to transcend the social order, the political world was the whole horizon (the only alternative being to retreat — under the banner of Taoism or Buddhism — either as an individual or as a group). Here everything belongs to Caesar, in short: the "inquisition" was therefore political, as everything else; it was based not on articles of faith or the struggle of ideas but on opinions promulgated by the prince or the clan in power. Since the stakes were not theoretical but personal, it gave rise less to antithetical arguments than to allusive applications; it favored less the frontal, open debate than subterranean approaches and an oblique trajectory.

A change of terrain and of stakes might provide a useful comparison with the situation in China: Is there no equivalent to Chinese subtlety? Do not Westerners also know an oblique relationship — one that seeks to shelter us from societal control, involves other people, and discreetly communicates a message — on another level, one that is playful rather than political, namely, amorous relationships? It is on this level, freed from mortal conflict and the gravity of confrontation (even if people feign to want to kill themselves), that Western culture took pleasure in complicating interactions, in refining strategies. Does not desire require a certain self-censorship, an obliquity, a speaking in innuendo to allow the other to guess the meaning? The circuitousness of literary discourse is often called to the lover's aid, as in Stendhal's *Lucien Leuwen*:

> Before long, while still greatly amusing the ladies sitting near Mme de Chasteller, he ventured to hint distantly at things capable of a most tender meaning, which he would never have thought he could attempt so soon. Of course Mme de Chasteller was perfectly able to pretend not to understand these indirect remarks.[27]

Here are the inquisitive gaze of others, the social code that must be respected, a sovereign power — the beloved woman — with whom one must know how to make oneself heard without offense. Desire teaches us to be indirect, leads us to speak in hints, all with a specific goal in mind. In contrast with political confrontation, the amorous conquest cannot be stated openly; power must exert itself by concealing itself in subterfuges and beating around the bush before the declaration. In the Chinese tradition, it was common for the literati to borrow motifs from popular amorous poetry to express indirectly their grievances to the sovereign. Lucien Leuwen does exactly the opposite, but just as subtly: he insinuates his amorous complaint under a political disguise by talking about elections to the Chambers.[28]

In addressing the Lady or the prince, the scholar-poet is restricted by the rigors of love or of power, according to the ideological framework: one register veils the other and provides a means for the strategy to unfold. But in either case, the message finds a receptive ear. Until this point, we have conceived of detour only in terms of communicating meaning to a dreaded other whom one wants to seduce or at least not to offend. I will henceforth consider detour by digging deeper into the function of enunciation — in a mode not of intentional aim but of pure expression (free from ulterior motive): when the object of detour is not an implied statement, and when detour attempts not to soften or disguise its meaning but to reveal it.

CHAPTER SEVEN

Between Emotion and Landscape:

The World Is Not an Object of

Representation

What purpose does the poetic image serve? Would anyone believe that the transposition it effects between a word and an idea is merely an attempt to disguise its intention? While the Chinese tradition, from the very beginning, conceived of poetry as a form of indirection, it never confused it, as such, with the communication of political meanings too dangerous to assert openly. According to the Chinese commentators, the detours of poetic language are fundamentally justifiable, and an insidiously suggested criticism of power is but one instance of their use (although a widespread one). The logic is more general: the creation of a poetic image extends beyond the necessities imposed by censorship and finds its source in the "reason of things" (the Chinese *li*ᵃ). It is not merely that the poet "does not dare" to say something or wants to avoid saying; he cannot do otherwise.

The following statement made by Shen Deqian in the seventeenth century sums up a common point of view: when "a situation is hard to state clearly" or "a reason is difficult to express completely," "one places it in the realm of external realities and proceeds, through analogical association, to characterize it." When "emotion, in its intense profusion, tends to spread outside" and "our moods move in accordance with the world's incitement," "one borrows from external reality to introduce what one feels, so as to unburden oneself."[1] In "lodging" one's feelings in or borrowing from external realities, such linguistic circuitousness does not serve to mask experience but enables it to be expressed better — and to be described more "completely" and more intensely.

We thus are led to reimagine the modalities of poetic discourse: alongside *direct exposition* (*fu*) is the formulation by *analogy* (*bi*) and expression by *allusive incitement* (*xing*).[b] Of the three, the last, from the beginning and throughout the development of Chinese poetics, aroused the most interest. From century to century, *xing* was redefined in the attempt to sum up the essence of poetry in it. It is therefore in relation to the immediate phenomenon of *incitement*, and not from the mediated angle of intention, that we must henceforth understand how the Chinese conceived of poetic detour, as well as the profundity they found in it.

My interest in developing this analysis moves beyond the art of poetry: through it, I would like to go back to what has culturally conditioned the very relation to reality. What poetry most easily illuminates, by enacting it in language, is the relationship that consciousness forms with the world: it brings us to the source of our experience. According to the Chinese perception of the poetic phenomenon, the poet borrows from the landscape to express his inner feelings: incited by the world outside, he in turn stirs up the reader's emotions. In China, poetry arises from a relationship of incitement rather than from a method of *representation*; the world is not an object for consciousness but a partner with consciousness in a *process* of interaction. With the privileged case of poetic speech, a rift begins to emerge in the way one approaches the real, a rift I shall not cease to explore.

For this reason, I ask the reader to be patient: the Chinese theory that I retrace historically here (notably from the Han to the Song) will appear dense. But I am obliged to go through the various ways the Chinese imagined the word's power of incitement so that the return to Greek civilization at the end of the chapter can have meaning (that is, so that the Chinese concept may effectively *encounter* the Greek tradition) and to lay the foundation for the contrast with Western symbolism in the following chapter.

In the beginning, the process is altogether commonplace. The first commentary on *The Book of Songs* uses the term *allusive incitement* (*xing*) to describe the initial image of many poems that begin by evoking natural realities and then develop the human theme. There is thus a juxtaposition of two statements that unfold on different levels and that are discontinuous: the first, which might repeat itself from one stanza to the next like a refrain (often with slight variations), appears too autonomous and formulaic to function simply as the circumstantial complement of the second; at the same time, the second constitutes the main subject of the poem, which the first merely introduces. A typical example is in the first stanza of *The Book of Songs*:

> "Fair-fair," cry the ospreys
> On the island in the river.
> Lovely is this noble lady,
> Fit bride for our lord.

Many critics have noted that subjects are indirectly broached in the popular literature in many regions, "from one end to the other" of the Eurasian continent, as Jean-Pierre Diény describes it; it recalls in particular the *Natureingang* of ancient Germanic poetry. But how are we to conceive of the incitement to which this indirection corresponds? In the first phase of the commentary (in the Han era, around the first century A.D.), Chinese men of letters favored a relationship of meaning between the two parts of the stanza. Hence the ospreys harmoniously calling to each other on the island in the river were supposed to serve as an illustration of the virtue of the young woman, who was thought to represent the queen (whose marriage is celebrated by the poem): "Her vigilance is firm and her reserve deep in the image of the ospreys in their separation." Thus she can exert a beneficial influence over the entire world, since, according to Confucian logic, harmony between spouses will incite an analogous harmony in the relationships between "father and son" and "sovereign and vassal" and thus will lead to good political order. From this perspective, the initial circuitousness would seem but a simple reflection of the development that follows. But at the same time, its ability to incite is diminished: this initial image loses its function as verbal automatism and rhythmic trigger in favor of a moral interpretation. Nature thus would be used here only to celebrate the separation of the sexes.

But is it possible that the moment we search for another facet of detour, its evocative power, we are brought back, as if inexorably, to a single political perspective? In analyzing popular expression in *The Book of Songs* (at least in its first sections), the literary commentary asserts itself as an ideological enterprise aimed at making models out of these songs as well as raising the collection to the status of a classic. In interpreting the relationship between the initial image and the development of the poem, this first commentator each time highlights the dominant attribute that, couched within the introductory image, allows for the logical transition between the natural and human worlds. With another poem, which celebrates the devotion of a mother to her children and begins with the lines,

When a gentle wind from the south
Blows to the heart of those thorn-bushes

The heart of the thorn-bushes is freshened;
But our mother had only grief and care (32)

the commentator interprets the initial image as a beneficial wind favoring plant growth. The landscape with which the poem opens is thus imagined as a reflection of the situation that follows: a mother's giving herself freely to raise her children.[2]

On this basis, it becomes easy to move toward systematically interpreting the relationship between the initial image and the rest of the poem, as was done by Zheng Xuan at the beginning of the first century A.D. This first commentary, as we have already witnessed, logically points toward a political reading of the poems as praise or blame. While, from a theoretical point of view, the initial distinction between the two types of indirect expression at the beginning of the poem (no doubt based on musical modes) — analogy and allusive incitement — remains relatively confused (see Zheng Zhong: the first consists in "comparing and bringing together an exterior reality" and the second in "placing the situation one has evoked in an external reality"), the poetic detour is always interpreted, in the end, as a simple expression in imagery: the natural world is always presumed to serve as a social mirror. Hence, in the poem cited above (32), the vitalizing wind "serves as an image of the generous mother," and "the thorn-trees are like the seven children."[c] The commentary here gains in didactic clarity even if it has to postpone refining the analogies. The second poem in *The Book of Songs* begins with the following lines:

How the cloth-plant spreads
Across the midst of the valley!
Thick grow its leaves.
The oriole in its flight

Perches on that copse,
Its song full of longing.

How the cloth-plant spreads
Across the middle of the valley!
Close grow its leaves,
I cut them and steam them,
Make cloth fine and coarse.

The cloth plant is used to make cloth, and the rest of the poem is devoted to evoking women's work. One could thus consider (as was later done) this relationship enough to justify the use of a vegetal image to open the poem. But the Han commentary takes great pains to read it as a metaphor for the young woman, who, through her virtue, is supposed to deserve to be queen: the cloth plant that little by little spreads to the middle of the valley "serves as an image" for the young girl growing day by day in her parents' house, and the green of its leaves "serves as an image" for the beauty of her face. Similarly, the orioles in flight that gather in bushes "serve as an allusion" (*xing*) to the fate of the young girl, who must leave her parents to marry her lord. Even their harmonious song cannot escape this principle of analogy: it serves as an "allusion" to the woman's fate, which also resounds far and wide.

One can enter even further into this minute comparison, rummaging without restraint into the slightest details and the analogies in these images. The foliage is described as verdant and thick in the first stanza to suggest the early youth of the queen. It is described as luxuriant in the second stanza to indicate that the young girl has become ripe and must be plucked. The plant itself can be more closely inspected: since its branches that spread out daily are "like" the young girl's growing body, the brightness of the leaves serves as a "comparison" to her face. And since the cloth plant grows in one spot but spreads out elsewhere, it is "like" the fate of the young girl, who "can only be fulfilled outside," in her husband's house. Finally, the orioles' songs resound as much when they are in flight as when they are gathered in the bushes because the girl's good reputation will not change between now and when she is married.

Passed through the commentators' fine-tooth comb, the poem's initial image can be completely explained. But in carefully establishing the imagistic relationship, one loses all incitatory value. This initial image is confused with a simple comparison. Once this path was taken, there was nothing to do but try to reconcile the two requirements, the analogical value and the incitatory value; but the efforts were clumsy and succeeded only in juxtaposing the two (for an example, see Kong Yingda, under the Tang, in the sixth and seventh centuries).[3] As often happens in China, definitions were merely a chain of opinions or disparate elements that no common articulation could effectively tie together. At best, Kong Yingda distinguishes allusive incitement, proper to the initial image, from the more common mode of indirect expression in analogy by opposing the clarity of the latter to the obscurity of the former (or its "hidden" quality, which is why the commentator highlighted the latter). But where does this obscurity come from? Does this mean that these two modes of circuitous expression operate at different depths and that the logic of detour from one to the other might be modified?

To take stock of the incitatory value of poetry, we must consider the question from a different angle: the poem's initial image must be considered not in terms of its similarity to later images, but in terms of its introductory role (which was affirmed under the Song in the eleventh and twelfth centuries, notably by Zhu Xi, who marks an important turning point on this subject). In that case, the image's incitatory value is based on its ability to set affective and verbal processes in motion: the association that characterizes it is analyzed structurally rather than semantically (though the two can mirror each other): the detour here involves a phenomenon of reaction (of emotions) rather than of transposition (of ideas). The strategy behind the opening image thus becomes: "to speak of something else as a way to introduce the subject of the song."[d4] From this new vantage point, priority is given to the relationship not between images but between antecedent and consequence.

Formally at least, things become clear. The two modes of poetic detour are distinct in that, in one, the incitatory mode, which constitutes the poem's theme, is used following an initial image, whereas in the other, the analogical case, the incitatory mode is not used: in the analogical mode, "even as I speak of something external, I treat the subject in question."[5] This is equivalent to metaphor, which, when extended, corresponds to the West's rhetorical definition of allegory: saying one thing and implying another (Quintilian: "aliud dicere, aliud intellegi velle").[6] The situation is less clear, however, as soon as one comments on the diversity of the poems. In *The Book of Songs*, in fact, completely allegorical development is extremely rare, which weakens the opposition between the two modes (I will return to this point). On the other hand, the value of moral education attributed to poetry, and to its founding text, *The Book of Songs*, remains too fundamentally important to Chinese ideology for the commentator to conceive of the initial image analogically. This returns us, despite theoretical clarification, to the prior tradition, where the incitatory function tends once again to merge into semantic value. There are nonetheless a few commentators who defend this initial image from all categorical and concerted comparisons, for example, Zheng Qiao in the twelfth century and Yao Jiheng in the seventeenth century. These men were taken up by twentieth-century folklorists and formalists, starting with Marcel Granet in France and Gu Jiegang in China, who analyze this triggering of poetic discourse structurally (thereby freeing *The Book of Songs* from didacticism).

One point remains well established in the most orthodox tradition, which is represented by Zhu Xi, although it may present itself in a new and paradoxical form:

> The *analogical* mode (*bi*) consists in resorting to something in order to express something else analogically, and the subject indicated is always situated outside the discourse;
>
> the *incitatory* mode (*xing*) consists in borrowing this thing to introduce the subject, and this subject is always developed subsequently.
>
> Nonetheless, even when one is rigorous, the analogical pairing remains superficial; on the other hand, because allusive incitement is loose, it can be savored longer.[7]

The paradox is clear: metaphor, or rather its development into allegory, remains weak in spite of its implicit nature (in absentia — since we must distinguish metaphor from comparison). Its criterion for validity is irremediably petty: pertinence. In the incitatory mode, on the other hand, even though the subject of the poem is made explicit, the initial image matters in and of itself, and its relationship to the subsequent development is not predetermined (hence its slack or "loose"[e] nature): it is not molded in advance by the prescriptions of meaning; the subject comes second. Hence what it loses in transparency, it gains in savor. The formal distinction between the two figures (in terms of the relationship between antecedent and consequence) allows the relative obscurity of the incitatory motif to emerge. In this way, even if they are not generally ready to renounce all semantic value, the Chinese literati show themselves to be more conscious of the fact that the richness of this incitement stems from its *indeterminacy*.

The most interesting case, therefore, is one the commentators on *The Book of Songs* identify as the "incitatory mode without analogical relation."[f] Hence in the poem that opens with the cloth plant:

How the cloth-plant spreads
Across the midst of the valley! (2)

the Song commentator Yan Can (thirteenth century) does not read this as an image of the young queen and her fate but conceives of it as an "incitement" to women's work (the cloth plant spreading into the valley represents what she will use to make clothing: seeing the plant grow in this way, she thinks animatedly of the tasks in store for her). The same goes for the poem in which a woman longs for her husband's return, which begins with the following lines:

Deep rolls the thunder
On the sun-side of the southern hills.
Why is it, why must you always be away,
Never managing to get leave?
O my true lord,
Come back to me, come back.

Deep rolls the thunder
On the side of the southern hills.
Why is it, why must you always be away... (19)

Following an analogical reading, the Han commentator sees the growling thunder as an image of the prince's order that keeps the husband on a mission far from home: just as the thunder is heard from a distance, the sovereign's orders are heard all over the country; and just as thunder, in shaking up nature, brings spring rains, the royal command stirs up humankind and leads it into action (see the trigram *zhen* in *The Book of Changes*). For the ancient commentator, nature is never natural; it is always a reflection of imperial ideology: the subjection to the political is so strong that every image is manhandled until it reflects the moral order. For Yan Can, on the other hand, this initial image makes a great deal of sense without needing to go beyond the wife's expressing her uneasiness. Hearing the sudden growling thunder makes her think of her absent husband. This growling is not supposed to be an image but to possess a concrete value; it is described as it is perceived and has the consistency of an event erupting into existence. Since it is inexhaustible, like natural phenomena, it makes consciousness react in unison. This is why, lacking precise meaning, this initial image plays the role of an indefinite affective release — which the rest of the poem will exploit.

The association between the natural motif with which this type of poem opens and the human situation developed next involves a level of consciousness different from that on which the logical signification codified in analogy is formed: it issues from an unmediated encounter between the "I" and the world and is therefore situated on a higher level of semantic irrelevance. On this level, the "I" and the world are caught in a common vacillation. Perception is at the same time emotion; nothing is objective: there is meaning, but it cannot be codified; it is infinitely vague and diffuse. When modern poetic theorists define the phenomenon of "external coenesthesia" as an "extrinsic analogy" taking place "on the level of subjective emotional response" (the most elementary case being synesthetic correspondence as discussed by Jean Cohen), they are very close to the Chinese conception of the incitatory mode.[8] Chinese men of letters (especially after the Song) conceived of this poetic incitement as an interaction between "landscape" and "emotion" (*jing* and *qing*[g]). They were led to this by their philosophy of immanence, which understands reality in terms of polarity: everything comes into the world based on the play of opposed but correlated energies, yin and yang. A similar relationship governs the two poles of internal emotion and external landscape: "the landscape produces emotion," and "the emotion in turn engenders the landscape"; interiority borrows from the external world to express its most intimate sentiments, just as the world impregnates interiority with its affect. This "incitement" is produced "at the crossroads between consciousness and the unconscious,"[h] specifies the theorist Wang Fuzhi (seventeenth century), and this is why the distinction between what belongs to one pole or another is "nominal."[9] There is both a borrowing and a detour for the interiority expressing itself, but these operate *sponte sua*, and the indeterminacy of the exchange creates depth. In other words, there is no subject or object here; nor is there any *representation*: the outside world serves as the innermost heart's partner, and the two cooperate in a single process.

The originality of the incitatory mode, to which Chinese poetic theorists were so attached, can be summarized in this way: it produces the most immediate writing and the most indirect meaning. It combines the most lively psychological motivation with the richest symbolic expansiveness. Because of this conjunction of the indirect and the immediate, which gains indirect value through its immediacy, what was only a particular figure in *The Book of Songs* acquired the power to represent the essence of poetry.[10] This relationship, which might seem contradictory, illuminated extremely well the transmutation through which emotion is transformed into meaning and the intensity of our presence in the world is transformed into the poem's endless unfolding: in this single notion of allusive incitement, two planes are joined — the *infra-* and the *supra-*linguistic — between which the poetic process takes place.

Early on, Chinese poetic theorists insisted on the emotional character of this incitement. As opposed to the analogical mode, the incitatory mode is defined as "an expression endowed with emotion" (Zhi Yu, third century). This is why it is more immediate than the analogical: whereas the analogical "exposes" what one wishes to say "by entrusting it to external realities," the incitatory veritably "stirs" an interiority reacting to the "stimulation" of the world. Of all the attempts made over the centuries to define the various degrees of poetic motivation, this formulation by the Song commentator Li Zhongmeng has been recognized as one of the most rigorous:

> To expose the aspects of the external world in such a way as to express our inner dispositions, this is direct enunciation (*fu*); [on this level] inner feelings and aspects of the world overlap completely.
>
> To seek out certain aspects of the external world in such a way as to house our inner disposition in them, such is the analogical mode (*bi*); [on this level] internal dispositions are compared to aspects of the external world.
>
> To enter into contact with the external world in such a way as to arouse inner dispositions, such is the incitatory mode (*xing*); [on this level] aspects of the external world stir inner dispositions.[i]

In lining up so perfectly, these three modes of discourse indicate a progression, which consists of three stages or levels of poetic experience. As we move from one mode to the next, the interaction

153

between the two poles — the external world and the innermost heart — becomes more intense as the relation becomes increasingly dynamic. On this scale, we move from intentionality toward spontaneity, from deliberate action to generation. The initiative the world takes comes to determine more and more, while verbal expenditure by the consciousness becomes less and less pronounced (to "express," to "house," to "arouse"). In other words, the rhetorical gradually gives way to the poetic: the less our relationship to the world is mediated by the autonomous deployment of language, the more our poetic capacity deepens.

The indirection of the incitatory mode has already been mentioned as its principal difference from the analogical mode. We have already noted that whereas the analogical is manifest, the incitatory is obscure; one is straight, the other sinuous; one clear, the other evanescent. One of the greatest Chinese poetic theorists, Liu Xie (fifth and sixth centuries), tried to explain the difference in the following terms: while both modes are used to arouse inner feelings, in one case, we express them "rationally," using "categorical" cross-references; while in the other, we express them "by leaning on their subtle aspects."[j][11] Hence, in one case, one "speaks openly," while in the other, one "suggests indirectly," in a vague and diffuse manner (again likened to the image of the wind[k]). A Song poetic theorist, Luo Dajing, again goes so far as to conclude, in reviewing the gamut of ancient formulations:

> In poetry, nothing is superior to the incitatory mode .... Indeed, the incitatory mode consists in being moved through contact with the world, and, while the word is found here, the meaning unfolds elsewhere. It is in savoring the poem that one becomes aware of this. The theme is not exposed directly as in the direct and analogic modes of expression.

Whereas Chinese tradition usually contrasts direct exposition with the two indirect modes of expression, the analogical and the incitatory — this was in fact, we may recall, the first rift in poetic thinking — the analogical ends up being placed alongside direct expression while the incitatory is isolated as the only one that is truly indirect. In this mode, under the effects of emotion, the *here* of the word and the *there* of the meaning[1] are farthest apart: because of the intensity of the motivation, the words produce an endless beyond, which is why this incitement is also allusive.

The importance granted to allusive incitement among the modalities of poetic discourse can only be fully understood in connection with the most general Chinese conception of poetry. Clearly, this modality, though listed among others, is not one of them; it spills over discourse and refers to the origin of poetry. It illuminates the basis of the relationship between consciousness and reality. The duplicity of the notion — which makes us waver between the planes of the rhetorical and our being in the world — gives rise to the difficulty one experiences when trying to grasp it; but from this difficulty arises its interest. Many centuries before the Chinese tried to identify the modes of poetic discourse, Confucius already was treating poetry in terms of incitement: one is "incited" by *The Book of Songs*; one stays firm thanks to rites and perfects oneself through music (*Analects* 8.8; see also 17.9). *Incite* here refers to the effect poetry has on the reader: Confucius accords a primordial value to poetry (which for him was *The Book of Songs*) because it has the power to move consciousness and orient it toward goodness. Later, the same verb would be used by poetic theorists to suggest the way the world stirs consciousness, leading to the creation of a poem (see Liu Xie on the subject of *fu*, the most descriptive Chinese poetic genre). "Contemplating the world incites our inner dispositions," and

because our inner dispositions are incited by the world,
the meaning expressed cannot be but brilliant;
and because the world is contemplated through this internal
    incitement,
the words [used to evoke it] cannot be but perfect.[12]

Hence the notion of incitement can link the existential (emotional) genesis of the poem, born of the encounter with the world, with the fruition of its expression. But this poetic incitement is not simply a stirring of our affective natures. In another chapter, the same poetic theorist describes the specific conditions granting "access to incitement"[m] set:

Thus, the seasons offer in turn their overflowing profusion,
yet access to incitement gives value to the calm:
and while the spectacle of the world is so varied,
let us choose words by favoring simplicity:
then its savor can spread in all directions, never becoming
    weighted down,
while the emotion shines, ever new.[13]

The emotion only becomes effective against a backdrop of quietude; the incitement of the world reveals itself as creative only through inner availability and reflection. Through emotion and incitement, consciousness *gains access* to the aspects of the world that moved it, to make them serve as incitatory motifs capable, in turn, of moving any receptive consciousness (and offering it the pleasure of an endless savoring). Thus are implied, within a single idea, the spontaneous reaction of the consciousness raised through contact with the world and the registering, in their "worldly" aspect (in terms of wu^n), of the variations experienced within. It is therefore logical that, when expressed in language, this incitement would be selective, making its choice at the center of the confusion that stirs consciousness, just as it valorizes concision and simplicity in spite of the infinite variations from which it emerges. This makes brevity all the more fruitful in its literal inscription, its capacity to express meaning beyond words.

One cannot imagine a more universal representation of the genesis of the poem than this "Envoy," with which the same chapter concludes:

> The linking of the mountains — the undulation of the waves,
> The tangling of the trees — the fusion of the clouds:
> The eye comes and goes,
> The soul opens and receives.
> The spring warmth spreads and relaxes,
> The autumn wind threatens;
> Emotion rises — like a gift:
> Incitement is born, in response.

The only other published Western translation of this treatise renders the final notion of incitement as "inspiration" ("And the coming of inspiration as a response").[14] Indeed, the Western idea of inspiration could well represent an equivalent (in that both notions reveal the source of the poem), but I think it indicates even more the fundamental rift that separates these parallel representations. Inspiration, as it has been described since Democritus and Plato, implies a radical exteriority and describes the poem as welling up from a vertiginous and fascinating elsewhere. With incitement, the poetic process unfolds in a perfect immanence: it is even, one might say, the radicality of this immanence that creates the poem. Not only does the poetic process end with the relationship between consciousness and the world and flow from their interaction — with the interiority opening onto the land-

scape and the landscape producing emotion — but, more originally, all the elements of the world are already in a relationship of
affinity and naturally interweave their webs of attraction. The
same tension that links the consciousness and the landscape runs
through the undulation of billows and waves and makes clouds
melt into one another.

According to the Chinese, it is from this flow, which makes the
world vibrate and stirs interiority — not from the breath of inspiration, not from some divine pneuma that brings us to the limits
of ourselves — that the poetic word arises. This flux inhabits the
poem's incitatory mode, sparking a meaning above and beyond
the words. And this incitatory mode, unlike the analogical mode,
is something Western rhetoric does not have. To understand why,
we must remember the Greeks' perspective on the poetic effect.

Inspired by the gods and possessing enthusiasm, the Greek poet
became a seer. To schematize the differences, one might say that,
whereas the Chinese conceived of poetic phenomena in terms of
incitement, the Greeks conceived of poetic creation in terms of
representation. Originating in philosophy, where it was first used
to distinguish levels of being, imitation (*mimēsis*) served as a general perspective for *poiēsis*; for this reason, it was linked to the
evolution of the poetic genre in Greece, leading from the epic in
theater to a more direct representation of *muthos*. The Greek
poet's objective was to feel, to make felt, by bringing "before
one's eyes."

Bringing the play "before his [own] eyes" (*pro ommatōn*) is
what Aristotle believes the poet must first do for, and in, himself
in order to render a scene most intensely and coherently.[15] He
who sees as though he were "actually present," whether this is a
natural gift or the result of "a touch of madness," is most capable
of giving the impression of life to the thing he is describing; at the

same time, this seeing allows him to enrich his invention verbally. Such "visions" (*phantasiai*) are transferred from author to audience: "in your enthusiasm and strong feeling you seem to see what you speak of and put it before the eyes of your audience," which contributes to the "sublime."[16] In poetry, this power of visualization creates "surprise,"whereas in oratory, the speaker tries to make things obvious. Hence, when he evokes the Erinnyes, Euripides sees them himself "and all but forced his hearers to see what he imagined."[17] Quintilian takes this up in the Latin tradition: the Greek concept of *phantasiai* (*visiones* in Latin) enables us to "represent to ourselves the images of absent things to the point that we have the impression of seeing them with our own eyes standing in front of us."[18] One is thus termed "gifted with imagination" (*euphantasiōtos*) if he is "clever at representing things, words, and actions in the truest manner" (*Institutio oratoria* H. 2). And Quintilian praises Virgil's *Aeneid* for this type of vision:

His hand lets go of spindles and the weight of spun wool. . . .

"Excussi manibus radii revolutaque pensa": "In one stroke, warmth left the bones of the suffering woman," and one believed one was *seeing* Euryalus's mother overwhelmed by the news of her son's death and stricken with grief.

In fact, Quintilian tells us, the power of visualization is related to hallucination: this faculty, which allows us to dream while remaining awake and which translates into a mental disorder, is transformed in the poet's art into a power of evocation. In the Chinese tradition as well, poetic theorists celebrated the soul's capacity to close itself to all immediate and tangible presence and unfold far away (*shense*°). But they imagined it more as a possibility of flight into both space and time, allowing one to overcome physical limitations and communicate with the infinite nature of

things, or, better still, to "travel with them"ᵖ (with Lu Ji, fourth
century, and Liu Xie):[19]

> The spirit soars to the world's edges
> The soul roams the heights of the universe ... [20]

Just as Chinese painting does not depict *one* single landscape, an
imaginary or perceived spot in nature, but rather attempts each
time to render the landscape par excellence, to capture through
its brush stroke the great animation of reality (even when it depicts a simple rock or bamboo stalk), the poet described in Chinese literary treatises is seeking not to represent a given scene or
experience visually but to transcend his individuality, to open
himself to the world's infinite scope. The spirit frees itself from
the bog of sensation, breaks away from the partial nature of sight.
In opening itself to the utmost at every turn, in attaining this spiritual height, it gains access to a global and serene contemplation
that allows it to link with the depths of things, to merge with their
flight, to embrace the universe. It could not, then, be further from
the power to hallucinate, which pushes the impression of *seeing* to
the point of illusion, making us adhere to the *hic et nunc* of the
scene or object. With the Chinese, there is once again a great
partnership between the ego and the world, an interaction between internal emotion and *all* external reality (the order of *wu*),
that anticipates the evocation. It thus makes sense that under
these conditions the notion of the mental image (in the sense of
visio) remained embryonic in classical Chinese literary theory.[21] In
spite of all their attempts to reconstruct the logic of these ancient
texts along Western lines, Chinese critics today fail to demonstrate that a Chinese theory of the imagination existed, at least in
the sense in which imagination is the ability to represent images
to oneself.[22]

This power to "put before the eyes," which characterizes Greek poetry, has its own criterion: *enargeia*, the ability to make us see most clearly, meaning most directly and sensitively, that of which the text speaks (*illustratio* in Cicero and *evidentia* in Quintilian). In fact, *enargeia* is a property less of the text than of the visual image it suggests, and it is not only recommended to poets: orators and historians are praised for having "led to our sight" the object of their evocation. The author does not simply narrate, he shows; the reader-listener becomes a spectator as well, believing he is participating in the events described. In this sense, *enargeia* tends to be confused with the *energeia* that characterizes the actual and intense way the subject is rendered, the impression of life and movement it sets into play. The qualities on which the scholiasts of Homer ceaselessly insist are not those recommended by Chinese poetry.[23] Homer produces a strong impression of life because his descriptions, notably his comparisons, are the most circumstantial and "omit no detail"; they describe by emphasizing the most extreme and terrifying aspects. This is true not only for Homer when he "describes" (*eikōnographei*) the tempest but also for Sappho when she paints the symptoms of love.[24]

As discussed earlier, it is traditional (and prudent) in Chinese poetry to speak of the present by distancing it and comparing it with the past (hence a reference to the Tang dynasty is projected back to the Han). In other words, it is the opposite of the Greek poetic's concern with seeing as though one were "actually present when the events happened":[25] to evoke the past and to bring it into the present as if we were participating in the action, as if we were experiencing its urgency (Homer's *gegonota* becomes *ginomena*).[26] The *translatio temporum* thus works inversely in the two literatures, and this seems revealing in terms of aesthetic choices. In China, evocative power is accentuated through allusive distance (never constricting the event, thus leaving the field open for indirection, detour, and subtlety); whereas in Greece, the intensity of the evocation is accentuated by making the confrontation with the thing more present and thus more direct — the more pressing the description, the more it makes an impression and persuades us of its truth.

Such an opposition can be extended into the art of epithets. In referring to concrete visual details, the epithets in Greek poetry "show the thing imagined" and favor the work of the imagination (the same is true for the adjectives of color that make the descriptions more striking and participate in *eidōlopoiia*). In classical Chinese poetry (at least that of the *shi* type, which, much more than the *fu*, was the focus of poetic theory), epithets are not descriptive and even less picturesque. As we shall see later, references to "white clouds" or "green pines" are not attempts to describe the color of things; they are connotative and atmospheric. Since their value is traditionally coded and they form vast networks of association (linking colors, places, and seasons), they open up what they characterize to the principle of its function to unfold its cosmic dimension.

Just as the idea of incitement to account for the advent of the poem within Chinese tradition is privileged in poetic discourse (the incitatory mode), the principle of visualization that inspires the Greek poet in his descriptions turns up again in expression and images (*lexis*). Here we shift from the image as mental representation (*phantasia*) to the image as linguistic expression of analogy (or from the poet's placing a scene "before his eyes" to visualize it to his placing it "before the eyes" of listeners or readers as a rhetorical process). The use of images to place "before the eyes" and "create a tableau" (which in this way tends to be confused with metaphor through analogy) is a process to be favored over all others, Aristotle states, for giving an intense and picturesque quality to the description: the success of this effect is found in "all that signifies things in action" (*energounta*), as in personification. Once again, Homer is the master when he describes the passion of combat: "And the point of the spear *in its fury* drove full through his breastbone," or "stuck in the earth, still *panting* to feed on the flesh of the heroes."[27]

There remains one more essential difference between Chinese and Greek literary theory, which has to do with the field of application for these principles: whereas the incitatory mode (and even the analogical mode) was conceived of in China only in relation to poetic expression, metaphor and hypotyposis (*sub oculis subjectio*) were first defined in Greece within a rhetorical framework. Even though poets are most often cited as models (Homer, Virgil), and even though Aristotle states that comparison should be used less often in prose, since it a poetic coloration, the Greek concept of poetry remained essentially rhetorical.[28] Indeed, this is logical since it seeks to account for poetry not in terms of a process or phenomenon based in the notion of incitement as in China, but in terms of *persuasion*: the actual representation, through which poetry tries to make us believe the things described, gives us a *convincing* impression of its truth.

We have, on the one hand, the poetic incitement provided by contact with the world that spreads into the receptive consciousness and unfolds there pungently, and, on the other, the inspired vision through which the poet makes us see in order to move us, makes his evocation pathetic, and tries to captivate us. Of course, this difference in conception goes back to a difference between the poetic genres originally practiced in each culture: poetry is essentially narrative and descriptive in Greece, lyric in China. In spite of the profound mutations undergone by the poetic genre in both civilizations, the theoretical conceptions that formed on the basis of the initial genres marked the later traditions indelibly. In China, poetry continued to be considered an interaction between landscape and emotion; in the West, the poet remained a seer, or "stealer of fire."

What matters most here is not that this leads to a difference of definition of the nature of poetry but that this difference in conception touches on the poetic effect itself and thus influences how one reads a poem. In particular, that Chinese poetry is still perceived as a phenomenon of incitement and has not embraced representation, mental images, and vision modifies the thrust of the poetic motif. When the motif "sets into motion" (*dong*,[q] in Chinese; *kinein*, in Greek), it is not the same thing in the two cultures: on the one hand, there is a diffuse and overwhelming emotion like a state of mind; on the other, *pathos* and *phantasia*. This is why, as we shall see, the Chinese poetic motif unfolds as an aura of the senses, as an atmosphere, rather than symbolically. Until this point, I have considered its incitement; I will now examine its allusive value. In other words, I have just examined the circuitous logic to which the borrowing from landscape corresponds; I will now explore what this detour gives access.

CHAPTER EIGHT

Beyond the Landscape:
The Figurative Meaning Is
Not Symbolic

When the Homeric narration seemed morally unacceptable or when the literal description appeared insufficient, the Greek commentator suspected it contained other meanings (*huponoia*). These other meanings, which he surmised beneath the cloaking of what seemed no more than an image, made up its allegorical meaning, according to which one thing is said to signify another. From what in the text was a specific figure, an extended metaphor, there resulted a general mode of interpretation, *allegoresis* (allegorical exegesis), situating meaning on another level — that of the divine, the spiritual, or essences. The battles waged by the gods in *The Iliad,* which shock us by their impiety, are to be interpreted figuratively, the Homeric apologist explains: Athena's fight against Ares and Aphrodite represents the victorious struggle of wisdom over irrationality and licentiousness. Moreover, one need only play ever so little with etymologies to read the confrontation between Hermes and Leto as the defeat of discourse by oblivion. On a larger scale, the whole of *The Odyssey* is revealed as one great allegory: for Plotinus, the Ulysses who is forever trying to return home and to resist the pleasures of Circe and Calypso is an image of the soul turning away from the senses to reach the divine.

Greek allegory is thus twofold: On the one hand, it possesses a theoretical content in accord with the didactic role attributed to it, since it is always a doctrinal (natural, moral, or religious) core that one finds hidden beneath the image. On the other hand, it is based on a metaphysical split between the perceptible and the intelligible, with one reflecting the other: from the *appearance* of the image we proceed toward the *truth* of the mystery.

Here again we encounter *mimēsis*, this time used to restructure reality: the image (*eikon*) is like a copy in relation to the model or like a tangible imitation (*to mimēthen*) in relation to the ideal archetype. In other words, what Plato in *The Republic* imagined as an irremedial ontological loss can also be read — as was done with increasing frequency, especially by Plotinus — as a participation: the image always participates in its model as the mirror that reflects the latter. The (perceptible) image is therefore not the (intelligible) truth but rather leads to it; the symbolic interpretation thus becomes a moving away from the image in a process that gives it more depth by situating it on a higher plane.

That the Chinese notion of the incitatory mode (*xing*) is usually rendered as allegory therefore comes as something of a surprise.[1] Within the Chinese poetic tradition, one rarely encounters allegory; and allegorical interpretation in particular, with the split it implies, is not favored by exegetes. Greek and Chinese commentators were all fond of emphasizing figurative meanings, but they did so according to different perspectives and strategies. A fine rift thus ensues between the possible modes of interpretation, which I shall follow closely, for I expect it to reveal a great deal: it might lead us beyond simple literary problems and help us begin to glimpse another horizon of meaning. I hope in this way to verify definitively that figurative meaning cannot be conceived of independently from a certain worldview (and this is the main point: not only its ideological content but also its functioning is affected); more precisely, I hope to show that symbolism — in poetry — is not the sole mode of interpretation.

Formally, the incitatory mode should not be confused with the allegorical figure, since it proceeds through juxtaposition (a natural motif introducing a human theme), whereas allegory proceeds through substitution (the image replacing the meaning that it is intended to signify). It is therefore the analogical mode that, in *The Book of Songs*, would seem to correspond to the rhetorical conception of allegory; but rare among these poems are those that consistently develop the transposition throughout a stanza.[2]

Only one poem offers an example of true allegory, both produced and commented on as such. Or rather, its obscurity links it to the genre of enigma (*obscura allegoria*):

> When a crane cries at the Nine Swamps
> Its voice is heard in the wild.
> A fish can plunge deep into the pool
> Or rest upon the shoals.
> Pleasant is that man's garden
> Where the hardwood trees are planted;
> But beneath them, only litter...
> *There are other hills whose stones*
> *are good for grinding tools.* (184)

In this poem, carefully preserved by the anthologist (as a specimen?), one finds a taste for veiled expression and images with political undertones once used to honor princes. Through these intentionally cryptic lines, which rhyme in Chinese, court counselors prudently aired their opinions. Later, commentators tried to decode this poem as a moral allegory. That the crane cries at the marsh but his cry is heard far off in the wild means, according to Zhu Xi, that "inner authenticity cannot be masked" or, according to Yan Can, that the Sage "keeps himself hidden but his name is renowned." Similarly, that sometimes the fish plunges deep in the pool and sometimes rests on the shoals signifies that "the reason of things does not have a fixed place" or, less philosophically, that the Sage "either distances himself from others or approaches them," depending on the circumstances.[3]

Among the three hundred poems in *The Book of Songs*, this one is exceptional, especially since the Chinese tradition is wholly lacking in allegorical interpretation (or *allegoresis*, as distinct from the allegorical figure strictly speaking, as Jean Pépin has astutely remarked) — that practice, so common in Greece, in which the commentator, unsatisfied with the literal meaning of the description, interprets it on another level (which is different from the example of the preceding poem, in which a literal interpretation is not possible). Instead of interpreting the images in *The Book of Songs* in terms of generalities and essences, commentators read them politically, finding historical references: rather than look for a symbolic meaning, they perceived an allusion. As Pauline Yu has noted, what we have here is not, therefore, allegorization but "contextualization."[4] Each poem is understood by way of the specific historical situation it is supposed to represent; through this political reference, the commentary begins its analysis.[5] Thus, all the poems in the first section of the work are read not as praising feminine virtue, conceived abstractly and generally, but as referring to the virtues of Tai Si, the wife of the king Wen; on the basis of this reading, which is applied from one poem to another, each ode is understood. The first poem is supposed to deal with her mores, the second with her origins, the third with her state of mind, the fourth with her behavior toward her inferiors, the fifth (which we began to read) with her progeniture, and so on. Together, they are supposed to create a portrait of the person while extolling the beneficial influence she spread through her example, of which the kingdom's mores were a reflection. An opposite portrait is provided in the third section of the work, "Bei feng," which is read historically and seen as depicting the depraved ways into which the Wei principality, following the example of the prince Zhuang, had fallen. In spite of the spontaneity of their popular expression, these odes are readjusted to serve as a political chronicle.

Basically, Greek and Chinese commentators were faced with the same problem: how to justify a meaning that, because of an ideological shift, they judged literally insignificant if not unacceptable? How to justify an impious meaning, such as that derived from the struggles between the gods or their adulteries in *The Iliad*, or an immoral meaning, such as that in the amorous couplets in *The Book of Songs*? But whereas the Greeks sought to salvage this meaning by projecting it onto a spiritual plane, the Chinese saw a historical application in it. We remember the poem cited by a great lord to shake the obstinate refusal of a prince during a diplomatic negotiation (see chapter 4). Here I cite not the third stanza but the first:

I beg of you, Zhong Zi,
Do not climb into our homestead.
Do not break the willows we have planted.
Not that I mind about the willows,
But I am afraid of my father and mother.
Zhong Zi I dearly love;
But of what my father and mother say
Indeed I am afraid. (*Book of Songs* 76)

This stanza, which clearly refers to a young girl's resisting the pressing desires of a lover (and the Song commentators recognized this meaning), was initially read, under the Han, as the

plea allegedly addressed by the duke Zhuang of Zheng to his adviser, Ji Zhong, who had warned him of the subversive activity of
his younger brother (backed by his mother). The decoding becomes easy: "do not climb into our homestead" means do not
meddle in family matters, and "do not break the willows we have
planted" means do not commit an injustice against the younger
brother. The fourth line ("Not that I mind about the willows")
refers to this brother, who should be punished, while the end of
the stanza is an allusion to the protection the latter enjoyed from
the mother (who, consequently, prevented the duke from following his adviser's advice, as worthy as it might have been). Therefore, by identifying a historical reference, or rather by its arbitrary
attribution, the commentator saves the poem's morality: the decoded meaning is indeed "figurative,"[a] although it is not symbolic.

The way this poem was used during a diplomatic negotiation
sheds light on the origin of the tradition that produced such commentary. As we have seen, during these encounters, the princes or
their high officials did not attempt to interpret the poem cited but
tried to allow their own aspirations to appear more easily through
the poems' images, which, because of their conventionality, bore
more weight in the decision made by the other. This practice,
which fell into disuse in court life, reemerged at the time of Confucius in the private discussions between the Master and his disciples: they considered it worthwhile to "discuss" *The Book of Songs*
when they could draw from it a poem celebrating a great lord or
the beauty of a young bride, since such verses allowed them to
illustrate moral thoughts (see *Analects* 1.15 and 3.8). Not that
Confucius sought to twist the meaning of the poem in question;
rather, for him, as we have seen, the poem's effect is measured by
its capacity to incite. Not until Mencius did the desire to go back
to the original meaning begin to appear (see *Mencius* 5.1.4); yet at
the same time, in the idea of history he developed, Mencius pro-

jected onto *The Book of Songs* the same political function he later attributed to *Annals* (for the continuity he established, see *Mencius* 4.2.21). And we know how the commentators after him (see above, chapter 5) tended systematically to interpret it as praise or blame of the events reported.[6]

The tradition of commentary on *The Book of Songs* that resulted is all the more important because it was carried over to later poetic works as well, most notably *Songs of Chu* (mainly *Lisao*, attributed to Qu Yuan, fourth and third centuries B.C.). This work, however, is in every way distinct from the earlier one, so much so that it can be considered the other principal source of Chinese poetry: its inspiration is not drawn from everyday travails and events that are mentioned in brief anonymous pieces in which emotion is reserved; rather, it is characterized by grand flights of apparently shamanistic emotion, where the poet's "I" is not afraid to express itself. The harmony of the verses is completely different as well, as is the treatment of the image, since there is no incitatory mode introducing the human theme through an image drawn from nature. These works visibly belong to two very different cultures (and two different locales: the North and the South); yet literary commentators read them both as historical references with moral and political implications. The "I" that sings his dissatisfaction in *Lisao* and narrates the quest that has led him to the gates of Heaven is interpreted as being Qu Yuan himself proclaiming his disappointment in having been slandered by the court of his prince, the king Huai of Chu, and dismissed from his duties. Likewise, the various flowers and fragrant plants with which the poet decks himself or takes pleasure in cultivating, which today seem to point to a purification ritual, are supposed to "represent"[b] the virtues to which this loyal adviser remained attached in spite of his banishment.[7] Similarly, the other who ceaselessly haunts him and is implicit in a great variety of figures and symbols always refers unequivocally to the king Huai of Chu, whose merits, he complains, are not recognized; likewise, rank weeds, jealous women, whirlwinds, storm clouds, and rainbows all serve as images of, or allusions to, the backbiting advisers banished from the court.[8]

In spite of the marked discontinuity of the poem (the search for the beloved, the wandering across the sky, the abundance of supernatural and mythological elements), all the images that would appear to lend themselves to symbolic exploitation on a spiritual plane are reduced by the commentators to signifying a single and obvious political situation (so simple is its morality). All the ambiguity and richness of the symbolic disguises is decoded by reference to a given event (or rather reconstituted ad hoc: for the biographical reference is itself viewed only politically and morally). The commentator Wang Yi reads lines such as:

I slow down my horse's pace on the banks with orchids,
Dash to the plateau, stop to rest (v. 111–12)

solely as the speaker's waiting in vain for orders from the sovereign.[9] Or again, reading the following lines:

Suddenly I look behind me and shed tears,
Saddened that in Gaoqiu there is no girl. (v. 217–18)

the commentators Wang Yi and Lu Xiang take this girl to be the image of the loyal subject, while another, Zhu Xi, sees her as an analogy of the good sovereign.[10] This matters little, however, since in spite of a few less constricting interpretations by Zhu Xi and Hu Yinglin, these lines are viewed only as references to politics.

True, the social and political world constitutes a reality of another order than that of the images in these poems, images that are most often borrowed from nature; but it does not stand on a different plane. It is just as concrete and particular as they, belonging to the same type of phenomena. As such, it is opposed to any idealized or spiritual world that might mirror the sentient world and transcend it by rising to the plane of absolute being or, at least, of an atemporal and essential generality. Between any natural scene and any situation of the human world, there can be transposition but not allegory. The invisible world with which Chinese poetry deals is that of sentiment and inner feelings (*qing*), which it expresses by borrowing from visible aspects of the outside world (the landscape, or *jing* ᶜ); it is not an invisible metaphysics (conceived of as intelligible). Stated otherwise, the relationship is between the "interior" and the "exterior," "consciousness" and the "world,"ᵈ not between the thing and the idea. In China, political and moral preoccupations blocked the path to the development of spiritual meaning; and the assignment of a particular reference diverted commentators from a symbolic construction.

We have yet to ask whether this tendency toward the "asymbolic" (as Roland Barthes conceived of it) that we have noted in Chinese poetic commentary can really be interpreted as a deficiency. What I mean is: What else might be the cause of this lack? We have begun to see that while it is never interpreted symbolically, the Chinese poem unfolds allusively. The path, little explored on the one side, opens up on the other into infinity. Between the symbolic option and the allusive option, the stakes go beyond the opposition of two types of commentary and deserve further consideration: I would like, in short, to show that a poem's *allusive capacity* constitutes a possibility of meaning just as universal, fecund, and total as symbolism is for the West. By way of illustration, I shall begin with the first poem in *Seventeen Old Poems* of the Han epoch (in the first century A.D.), which was considered one

173

of the most representative works in the tradition of *The Book of Songs*:

> On and on, always on and on
> Away from you, parted by a life-parting.
> Going from one another ten thousand "li,"
> Each in a different corner of the World.
> The way between is difficult and long,
> Face to face how shall we meet again?
> The Tartar horse prefers the North wind,
> The bird from Yüeh [Yue] nests on the Southern branch.
> Since we parted the time is already long,
> Daily my clothes hang looser around my waist.
> Floating clouds obscure the white sun,
> The wandering one has quite forgotten home.
> Thinking of you has made me suddenly old,
> The months and years swiftly draw to their close.
> I'll put you out of my mind and forget for ever
> And try with all my might to eat and thrive.[11]

The commentators point out literary allusions in each line of the poem: the second line recalls a famous passage from *Songs of Chu*: "Pain! Oh Pain! parted by a parting!"; the fourth line is found almost unchanged in other poems of the time; the fifth is an almost literal borrowing from *The Book of Songs*; and for the double image of the Tartar horse (from the North) and the bird from Yue (from the South), there are at least two antecedents, one orienting the poem toward a nostalgia for the speaker's native land, the other toward a categorical attraction.[12] Similarly, the parallel between passing time and loose clothes is not new. Lastly, the image of the clouds obscuring the sun was already considered a cliché. In short, the poem frequently resorts to stock formulas and

174

dips into the well of strongly coded images. Far from using language innovatively to render his expression original and picturesque, the poet seeks to profit from the conventionality of the formulations. Just as poems from *The Book of Songs* were cited during diplomatic negotiations to prod their recipient, and were all the more effective because they were known by all and had an impersonal stock value, by relying on ancient and established formulations, this poem mobilizes its images' evocative assets on its own behalf. It evokes other, earlier echoes and resonates with all that the theme already offers in past experience and exploration. By verging on stereotype, it not only allows one to experience, once again, the the perfect appropriateness of consecrated expressions; it also sets itself apart from the arbitrariness that affects individual expression and from the precariousness that threatens isolated voices. While the Chinese poem does not rise to spiritual generalities or the principles leading to symbolic exploitation, it brings out and reactivates, from the depths of its language, the communal aspect of its subject by appealing to literary memory.

At the same time, the Chinese commentators continued to read this poem in reference to a political situation. Verbal allusion extends poetic expression beyond itself, enriching it with reminiscences; referential allusion allows the perception of a particular reading beneath the anonymous figuration. As already noted, this situation was typical: the loyal servant, object of court slander, finds himself banished. The image of the white sun obscuring the passing ("floating") clouds lends itself well to this decoding: either this sun is the good minister and the clouds his detractors (according to Li Shan), or it is the prince himself, whose judgment is obscured by bad advisers (in Liu Lang's reading). The allusion thus has to do with a complaint, veiled by the image and supposedly addressed to the sovereign. ("Thinking of you" expresses, by way of compensation, attachment: one fears the approach of old age before having had a chance to prove one's devotion.) One commentator, Zhang Qi, comes to the conclusion: "These are the words of a banished vassal. The slanderers have obscured the light; rectitude is no longer tolerated: he is justified not to dream of returning and yet cannot forget this essential aspiration to return home [to serve the prince]. He is still attached to the prince, and although the words and years pass by and it is already evening, he still makes an effort to nourish himself with the hope that the sovereign will suddenly come to his senses and recall him." A few commentators expand the reference, making it less exclusive: this poem, which expresses sincere loyalty, could also be the work of an abandoned wife or lover.

All the commentators agree that the beauty of the poem derives from its silence on the feeling elicited: the sadness is never expressed directly but emanates everywhere. This is due primarily to the effect of variation in the poem's structure. According to Lu Shiyong, "Each line corresponds to a different aspect of the emotion": the first line evokes "dejection," the second "affliction"; and the image of the loose clothes translates as a "depressive" state, while the image of the sun veiled by clouds discreetly implies a "complaint." The approach is ceaselessly modified; each successive orientation is simply sketched: to the end of the poem, the reader retains the feeling that its subject is unfolding somewhere beyond. The renewal from one couplet to the next checks any narrative or descriptive continuity that might make the poem specifically representational. At the same time, the parallelism (notably the greatly admired lines that describe the Tartar horse and the bird from Yue) induces a transverse, structural reading of the poem, which breaks the linearity of the language; the tension, finally, which carries the opposition to the extreme, reinforces this art of montage. The poem proceeds with a juxtaposition of brush strokes in which there is a play of contrasts; and its success

176

derives from the way these formulas and clichés, by combining into a whole, merge together to allow an impression to emanate through them — as an "effect":[e] thus this language, so close to convention, becomes a veritable creation.

Certain commentators explicitly describe this art of combination in terms of the relationship between the direct and the indirect[f]: the expression is direct in the description of separation, indirect in the way the separation is experienced. This indirection comes not only from the effect produced by the transposition of images, whose function is both to subdue the emotion and to spread it around (for example, as happens with the nostalgic regret in the image of the Tartar horse and the bird of Yue or the discreet bitterness in the image of the veiled sun). It derives also from the hinting nature of the signs used: the image of the clothes that become looser by the day was noted mainly for its allowing a glimpse into the speaker's state of languor. The same goes for the last line, which takes up a formula normally addressed to others but here is most often read as referring to the speaker: it expresses the deep dejection from which he is trying to emerge and that this effort can only come from within. The emotion, the subject of the poem, is always evoked obliquely: it remains contained morally and implicit verbally. (The Chinese do not separate these two merits, which is why they believe poetry has an ethical value.) This emotion remains *reserved*. But everything alludes to it.

Traditional criticism ceaselessly praised this sort of poetic expression that is both "subtle" (hinting) and "diverted,"[g] while its meaning is neither "heavy" nor "transparent."[h] This subtlety of detour is born not of a linguistic complication (it is recognized as being as simple as possible) but of an obliquity of illumination. In allowing the expressed emotion only to appear, this poem makes it inexhaustible — hence the intrinsic remainder or surplus of meaning, which gives the poem its value. This allusive value is all the richer, as Jean-Pierre Diény has observed, because the situation described remains profoundly indefinite: in reading the poem, one cannot ascertain the sex of the protagonists (nor, therefore, can one determine the role of vassal or wife); moreover, one does not know whether the subject speaking is the person traveling or the one waiting. One can interpret the poem according to either perspective, and this polyvalence contributes to its culminating impression of *vagueness*, which renders the emotion diffuse and widespread. The situation evoked, freed from exclusivity, becomes pregnant with meaning.

Yet this indefinite quality (which Chinese commentators, as we have seen, compensated for with precise political allusions) should not be confused with a generalized meaning. The nebulousness of the references, which better allows for the evanescence of the emotion (whence flows its overwhelming presence), does not have the solidity of an essence, does not lead to the development of an idea (which here might be absence or separation). No one in Chinese tradition, for example, read the image of the sun obscured by the clouds as realistically describing an element in a landscape; nor did anyone read it as a pure figure of an obstacle or distance. This poem uses an allusive structure in which the images open expansively onto the evocation of emotion without, however, converging on the level of representation to serve, above and beyond themselves, as a spiritual intuition. The role of the concrete here is to *hint* — not to lend itself to abstraction. In other words, just as it was never read descriptively or narratively, this poem was never read symbolically.

We might now begin to schematize the difference. Allusion *refers* to something that is not said but indicated obliquely: it therefore corresponds to the referentiality identified by Chinese commentators as well as to the implicit valorized by the rhetorical tradition. It can also refer either to a specific (political) situation the poet does not dare broach openly or, by breaking free from a precise reference, to a mood that is not made explicit. The poetic symbol, on the other hand, *represents* something both concrete and specific, on the basis of which it can signify an abstract or general idea. This is little developed in the Chinese tradition because, as we have seen, representation is seldom used and because, as we shall see shortly, in China it never constitutes an autonomous plane of generality.

One question deserves closer investigation: Why is the vagueness not abstract? In other words, how does the emancipation of the poem from the specificity of reference differ from its symbolic scope? Because it pushes the indeterminacy of meaning even further, and thereby gives rise to a debate on the way to interpret it, the work of a great third-century poet, Ruan Ji, provides a prime example of this. I, in fact, see no other way to pose the question than to begin to consider, practically, how a poetic text was read. The poem, with its writing and reading considered together, is a locus of language in which all linguistic experiments are pushed to the limit and all possibilities are revealed. As we come to understand why the role of Chinese poetry is not to represent — either sensibly or as an idea — we shall begin to see why the level of ideas is not considered a separate world in China. The allusive value, in remaining evasive, invites us into an experience of the mind in relation to the concrete that differs from a Westerner's experience.

Let us begin by considering the debate among Chinese poetic theorists. Yan Yanzhi, the first commentator on Ruan Ji, read him according to the tradition of an allusive and circuitous political critique: "Since he served a dynasty in chaos, he lived in constant fear of being slandered and overwhelmed by catastrophe.... This is why, in his *Songs*, each time he sighs and laments his life while expressing personal critiques, his expression is full of evasions and hidden meanings."[13] Until this point, nothing differs from what we have already seen. But Yan Yanzhi adds: "From a distance of centuries, it is difficult to fathom [the intentions] concretely. Hence I have merely roughly outlined the general thrust of his poems and touched but lightly on the implications." This warning is important but does not dispel all ambiguity, for one must ask: Is the pretext of temporal distance enough to justify one's being unable precisely to identify the political and biographical situation reflected in the poem? While referring to the classical conception of the poet as not daring openly to express his opinion (a conception linked, as such, to the tradition of the "Xiaoya" section of *The Book of Songs*), one of the first great Chinese poetic theorists, Zhong Hong (early sixth century), considers this no longer adequate. He believes that this poetic imprecision creates a specific effect and goes hand in hand with an infinite triggering of emotion: "whereas its expression remains within the tangible [things one can hear and see], its emotion projects beyond this world." This poet, moreover, "makes us forget things that are close by and petty in order to raise us into those that are open and far away."[14]

Two points in this commentary seem noteworthy and will help in distinguishing between the poetic strategy at issue here and symbolism. First, the scope of meaning is here understood according to an emotional projection, which recalls the incitement discussed earlier; but this deployment of meaning (based on concrete images in the poem) tends not to direct the reader toward another, ideal or spiritual meaning but to free the reader from too narrow or "petty" a reading of reality (this poet thus comes close to the tradition of *Zhuangzi*). Furthermore, this deployment leads us not to reconstruct the meaning on another level (passing from concrete representation to ideas or essences) but to detach ourselves from this level, which is the domain of the paltriness of things and references: under the effect of emotional incitement, phenomena communicate something beyond themselves; the vagueness attained by poetic meaning (in going beyond referential constraints) frees us from their opaque and limited presence.

This *evasiveness* of poetic meaning led to two antagonistic positions in the commentators' camp. One side preferred to interpret the poem from a single perspective of emotional *incitement* (thereby guaranteeing that the poem is not reduced to a simple verbal play but possesses the authenticity of real life) and believed they could systematically recapture, beneath the fluidity of the meaning, the political or biographical circumstances at the poem's origin (the position of Chen Hang). The other side believed that the effects of "dissemination" and "variation"[i] created by the poem's montage produced a fullness of evocation in which the most varied feelings intermingled; therefore, the poetic transposition that proceeded from the emotional incitement (*xing ji*[j]) did not provide an identifiable handle by which one might retrace its contextual origin in the poet's career and epoch. According to the second position, one did not force one's reading by seeking to identify the references at all cost. In other words, it was necessary to preserve an *allusive value* in the incitement that was *indefinite*.

The octave the poet placed at the head of his collection can be used to illustrate this debate. The musicality of this poem, however, is so limpid and thereby so pregnant that, more than any of the poems discussed so far, this one defies translation. The following is but a literal translation to give some support to my argument:

Midnight and unable to sleep:
I rise and make my zither resonate.
The sheer blind reflects the moonlight,

The limpid wind blows on my breast.
A solitary goose cries outside on the plain,
The flying bird sings in the northern forest.
To come — to go: what is there to see?
Sad thinkers — all alone — blessing the heart.

The commentary on this poem includes the two types of clarification we have already encountered.[15] On the one hand, these
lines abound in literary allusions; none of the images is new, since
here the poet is playing with clichés. On the other hand, one can
read this poem as a sequence of political allusions: midnight signifies the disorder of the time; the solitary goose is an image of the
author, who, as a loyal subject, is alone outside (since he is excluded from the court), while the flying bird refers by analogy to
the powerful minister who remains near the throne (the north of
the northern forest is the traditional position of the sovereign,
who faces south). This last image, more personally, would indicate the man at court in the process of usurping the throne, Sima
Zhao.

The poem's originality lies, however, in its indefinite nature.
First of all, the poem is untitled. From the very first words, although the insomnia making the speaker rise from bed announces
a timeworn poetic theme, the novelty lies, as Donald Holzman
has so aptly pointed out, in there being nothing here to indicate
the reasons for this insomnia (neither homesickness nor a feeling
of isolation, as in poems previously discussed).[16] This creates the
hidden, "latent" remainder of meaning:[k] although it begins by
situating the scene, the poem does not offer any explanations.[17]
The interaction between the "I" and the world in the next two
lines is also utterly discreet: because of its thinness, the curtain
(beside the bed?) both reflects the moonlight and allows it to
shine through (the word in Chinese means both). The limpid

wind ruffles the clothing on his breast and fills it with its coolness
(*jin* means, more precisely, the folds of cloth crossing in front).
Inside and outside brush against each other; their encounter is filtered. Rather than evoke an emotion, this landscape spreads its
limpidity about, and consciousness opens to its influence, makes
itself permeable. In contrast with the transparency of the elements, the birds in the subsequent two lines indicate a different
situation, one between protagonists, which was usually interpreted politically. Without even suggesting a precise application,
they imply the threat of a disorder to come. In short, the very
indeterminacy creates the image in the penultimate line of the
poem: the hesitant step leads nowhere, the view of the world
remains uncertain. Likewise, when the last line begins discreetly
to arouse feeling, it is heavy with the preceding indefinite quality,
both diffuse and invasive, like a state of mind. Wang Fuzhi (seventeenth century), one of the greatest Chinese philosophers and one
of the best commentators, said of this poem:

> If one considers this poem superficially, it is as if there were no emo-
> tion there; but in reality, beyond the words and between the lines,
> on the tips of our lashes and the corners of our mouths, the feeling
> is hidden, infinite: it can be reached by following the sonorities,
> plumbing the depths.[18]

The fleetness of the references (acknowledged by Wang Fuzhi
in "plumbing the depths") transforms the poem by heightening
the senses; the discretion with which the emotion is expressed
allows one gradually to uncover its profusion. Through the musicality, which acts as instigator here, as in Paul Verlaine, the emotion is diffused and radiates through the words. Moreover, the
images woven together in the poem like a delicate web make it
highly accessible. According to an ancient Chinese formulation

that Wang Fuzhi used with another poem by Ruan Ji, through the "distant resonance" of the meaning, the poem's words serve an analogical function, while "entrance and exit take place *sponte sua*."[1] One can both explicate specifically and remove oneself completely; one can just as well grasp the poem's references, uncovering a series of allusions, as open it up to the polyvalence of its motifs and project one's feelings onto it. No one orientation is exclusive; the poem's coherence lends itself to various points of view. This creates its *allusive structure*: because of its indeterminacy, the poetic image vibrates with an infinite number of situations and captures possible emotion from the farthest points. Hence its implicit (*hanxu*[m]) richness: it reflects the language not of an emotion but of the human capacity for emotion.[19]

For this reason, I do not think that one can confuse the allusive structure of this poem, which gives it its implicit depth, with what Holzman considers its philosophical abstraction ("However you interpret it, Juan Chi's [Ruan Ji's] poem remains abstract; his point of view, general and philosophical").[20] The *vagueness* of the poetic image does not take it to "a new plane of universality." It does not refer to any other level (which would be indicated in the commentary); its indeterminacy does not bear on a more general and essential meaning but rather makes it the vector of infinite, because indefinite, emotion. Holzman seems aware of this problem: after asserting that "all seems symbolical," he notes that this symbolism "is hardly original," consisting of clichés, and that the symbols in this type of poetry, "if they deserve that name," cannot be grasped outside the framework of each poem, since they are constantly "varying their mood." Hence he recognizes, in the end, that there is no symbolic meaning that is sufficiently stable and logical: unlike Edgar Allan Poe's raven or Charles Baudelaire's albatross, the lone wild goose in the first poem cannot be considered a symbol of freedom or desired escape.

184

Such a poetry seems symbolic because nature is never described directly for its own sake and because one is called to go
beyond the concrete character of its images. But, for all that, the
purpose is not to signify something on another level, to point
toward another (abstract and spiritual) world. On the one hand,
the figurative value of its images remains largely coded, by virtue
of the literary allusions, instead of proceeding from the nature of
the concrete itself: in this case, the image has no intrinsic value
per se; it is more conventional than inventive. On the other hand,
since it is created through incitement, as opposed to vision, and is
informed only by the interaction between landscape and emotion,
this figurative value is not established on a *pure* level of representation: unless one looks for an intention cloaked in the image and
assumes the vagueness to cover something therein (such as a political reference), the Chinese poem becomes an indefinite allusion,
whose application stretches limitlessly toward a mobility of sentiment. Thus either one decodes the image (univocally), or it
becomes elusive — like a state of mind (as we have seen, the two
are not mutually exclusive).[21] In either case, however, it does not
acquire the consistency of a symbol and does not lend itself to a
progressive apprehension of the mind. Nor do we see, in the two
levels between which it oscillates — that of (diffuse) emotion and
(concentrated) intention — what might be called a sufficiently stable and constructible level of *representativeness*.[22] The conditions
that would make it possible for it to describe an idea are thus lacking: such a poetry grows deep by making referentiality fleeting
(thereby creating the effect of vagueness that highlights its implicit dimension) and by not assuming any abstract meaning.

This lack of symbolism, for which allusiveness compensates, is
also inevitably found in theory. To be convinced of this, we have
only to consider the fate of the most original notion in Chinese

poetics, the incitatory mode (*xing*). As it breaks away from the commentary on *The Book of Songs*, in which it was the privileged category, the incitatory mode acquires a significance of another order: it designates not only the description of a natural reality that indirectly introduces the development of a human theme but also the evocative capacity of any poetic motif that is to be developed beyond words.[23] The definition then becomes: "when the text is completed, there exists a surplus of meaning"[n] (Zhong Hong). From one usage to the other, the idea of beginning remains, but the extension to which it leads changes levels: it is no longer something that makes up the body of the poem but the continuation of the beginning in the reader's mind. The deployment of the meaning it incites thus merges with the supra-linguistic dimension of the poetic process. Does this mean it becomes the equivalent of symbolism?

Clearly, the Chinese tradition sees true value in this dimension *beyond words*. Before poetry was the issue, Chinese thinkers contrasted the "proximity" of speech with the "far-reaching" quality of meaning.[24] This tension between literal exiguity and its resonance later characterized the poetic effect, for example, in Qu Yuan, the author of *Lisao*, about whom a Han commentator noted:

> His text is concise,
> his expression subtle...
> the literal declaration reduced, but what it designates vast,
> he establishes analogies up close but reveals a far-reaching
>   meaning.[25]

In this meaning, we recognize the constitutive expansion of the symbolic process. Nonetheless, it is not *based* on this but in relation to it that Chinese poetic theorists conceived of the figurative value they attributed to the incitatory mode. The distinc-

186

tion appears subtle, but it is decisive. In particular, it makes it possible to understand why Liu Xie (fifth and sixth centuries), the poetic theorist who sought more rigorously to define this figurative value, was not able to emerge from what seems a confusion:

> As for the figurative character of the incitatory mode,
> it is indirect but becomes manifest;
> the literal declaration is reduced
> but the analogical unfolding is vast.
> In the poem "Guanju," the [male and female] ernes remain
> separate:
> because this is used as a figure of the queen's virtue;
> similarly, the dove is distinguished by its chastity:
> this is why it is used as a figure of a wife's duty.
> As for this duty, only chastity is referred to,
> not the common characteristics of the bird;
> similarly, as for virtue, people value the separation of the
> sexes
> without troubling with the fact that we are talking about
> birds of prey.
> The things that clear evocation merely suggests
> are explained with notes to clarify the meaning.[26]

In this definition, only the above-mentioned formula contrasting literal exiguity with the vastness of the analogical strategy corresponds to the symbolic process, for, as stated in the beginning, the indirection of its expression keeps the incitatory mode within an allusive political critique (and the development concludes in this direction). The examples that follow reduce the symbolic signification to coded values: the poet selects images in order to retain only the relevant semantic element (chastity or the separation of the sexes) without concerning himself with the concrete nature of the images (their avian nature in this case; but in reality, it is more the commentator who makes this selection for the poet). More than functioning as symbols, these birds serve as *emblems* — in the sense in which Buffon could say that the warbler "was the emblem of inconstant love" and the turtledove of "faithful love."[27] In other words, the figurative value does not originate so much in the concrete nature of the image, as with the poetic symbol (for which one must usually depict this aspect to set off its meaning) but rather depends on codified tradition. Thus Liu Xie concludes that "notes" are necessary to "clarify" the meaning. Yet glosses explaining the values traditionally attached to an image are not necessary to interpret its symbolic bearing: the symbol is deciphered on its own basis; the representation is sufficient. Here, Liu Xie does not succeed in distinguishing the symbolic process from allusion, both literary and political. This is why he concludes that the incitatory mode disappeared with the advent of the empire (since no one dared criticize power); and this is why, although the incitatory is the privileged poetic mode, in his opinion in particular, he treats it so succinctly and devotes most of his thoughts to simple analogy.

Among the ideas that make up the foundation of Chinese thought, there is one more that might have been used to conceive of the symbol: figuration (*xiang*°). In *The Book of Changes*, it designates the ability of hexagrammatic figures, made up of solid or broken lines, to represent a situation or an idea. On this same basis, and in reaction to a later commentator's attachment to the literality of these figures, one of the great philosophers, Wang Bi (third century), defined the symbolic function for the first time in China: "based on analogical encounters, one can arrive at [symbolic] figuration [*xiang*] and, by regrouping the contents of the ideas, one can arrive at revelation" of meaning, or *zheng*.[28] It is necessary to abandon the concrete level of "figuration," this philosopher explains, to reach the "meaning" this tends to "manifest." Furthermore, at the turn of the twentieth century, the Chinese rendered the notion of symbol, which they discovered in the West, by returning to this binomial (*xiang-zheng*[p]). One cannot help but recognize that this conception of a concrete figuration tending to manifest an idea was never developed except by this thinker and that it is only from this perspective that the unfolding of poetic meaning was envisioned: this term *figuration*, used alone, served occasionally to express the idea of an image (in Wang Li, commenting on *Lisao*, v. 12, and in Jiaoran, defining *bi-xing*).

This notion of figuration gains importance at the core of poetic reflection as soon as it is integrated with the idea of incitement. A relationship is thus established not between figuration and its ability to reveal an abstract meaning (*xiang-zheng*) but between the incitement that comes from the world and the figuration of the poem, as well as between this figuration and the incitement of the reader. The perspective is one of an emotional flux that binds the world to any receptive consciousness and for which the figuration of the poem serves as intermediary. It is, notably, through the use of this binomial (incitement-figuration, *xing-xiang*[q]) that Chinese poetic theorists commented on the two poems we have just read: the incitement-figuration of the first poem is considered as transparent as a glass curtain (by Hu Ying-lin); while that of the second poem is always "fresh" and "new" (according to Fang Dongshu). This arises from the landscape being not described for its own sake but always imbued with emotion: the emotion is projected onto the landscape, which is transformed by it; or, to use another classic expression, in their encounter, landscape and emotion merge into each other. Thus incitement and figuration can no longer be distinguished. This binomial reveals the two operations to be inseparable: the poem is born of their conjunction.

189

But how does this *figuration*, when paired with *incitement*, translate in meaning? In other words, how may we characterize a strategy of meaning in images that is not symbolic — but no less infinite? Another binomial of Chinese poetics combines the notion of figuration with that of "breeze" or "mist" (*qi-xiang*: breeze figuration[r]). This dimension of meaning, which arises from poetic figuration but does not converge on an ideal level, spreads like an atmosphere. In becoming diffuse and nebulous and merging with the landscape, the incitement is transformed into a subtle influence one senses emanating from the poem's images and imbuing subjectivity. Instead of pointing toward an idea, it creates an *aura*. It is difficult, as we see, to get away from this code of exhalation: in terms of symbolic function, the notion of poetic atmosphere proves best able to express this expansion beyond words, which, although it does not lead to the horizon of generalities and essences, remains vague and pregnant and enriched by its indeterminacy. Concerning *The Book of Songs* as well as *Seventeen Old Poems*, Wang Fuzhi, the great philosopher cited earlier, states:

> The meaning is found beyond the words as well as in their wake: one bathes in them as one pleases and becomes immersed in them, and spontaneously an atmosphere is born.[29]

The image, if embellished, is that of fish in water, illustrating both the immersion of consciousness and its free expansion. As the objects mentioned melt into vapor, the consciousness bathes in the fluidity of the poetic milieu, which makes it receptive to the slightest solicitations. The mind is thus not led to see but moves as it pleases. There is therefore no symbolism to explore (as adventure); the atmosphere is born *sponte sua*: this evanescent expansion, which cannot become an object of research, occurs like a *phenomenon*. Traditionally it was rendered in the image of the emanation or vapor, as in *volatilization* (see Sikong Tu, ninth century):

> According to Dai Rongzhou, the landscape evoked by the poets is analogous to what is produced when, in the blue fields in the warmth of the sun, a vapor rises from the hidden jade: one can contemplate it but not stare at it fixedly. The figuration beyond the figuration, the landscape beyond the landscape — how can one speak of this easily?[30]

How indeed can one speak if not allusively and via the detour of an image? The beyond into which this poetic image opens has no consistency in and of itself and therefore cannot be objectified. The figuration beyond figuration is not a representation unfolding on a spiritual level but a figuration freed from any reductive reality (see *Laozi* 41: "the great image has no form"[s]; and see below, chapter 12): it is a figuration that no longer figures in an individual and thus self-contained way but rather becomes vague and diffuse, charges itself with emotion and spreads it about. The world beyond the landscape is not a symbolic landscape but a landscape rendered evasive, which, by this means, becomes suggestive. Moreover, this world that is "born beyond figuration"[t] (Liu Yuxi, eighth to ninth century) is not another world but this world — the only world — distilled of opacity and made available for enjoyment. This enlargement of the figurative meaning, therefore, leads to nothing but its own emptying. It evacuates all that is too specific in figuration in order to make it infinitely allusive. This is why Chinese poetic theorists believed that, whereas direct expression was "full," indirect expression (and poetic expression, or *bi xing*) was "empty"[u] (in the most general sense of the term and not only in the poetic tradition devoted to suggesting the void, in the style of Zen [Chan]; see Wu Qiao).[31] But since it is "empty," this indirect expression is all the more "alive." It is in these terms

that Chinese poetics took stock of the originality of the incitatory
mode (Chen Ting-zhuo, nineteenth century):

> It is difficult to say what the incitatory mode is. If the transposition
> effected by the image is not deep or the meaning it establishes is not
> dense, one cannot speak of the incitatory mode. If there is depth and
> density but the image is univocal or the meaning forced, one still
> cannot speak of the incitatory mode. We see the incitatory mode
> when intentionality is present before the brush and there is a spiri-
> tual dimension beyond the words, when its expression is both most
> empty and most alive, most hidden and most overflowing in its pro-
> fusion, when it seems distant yet at the same time close by, when it
> can be interpreted as an image as well as dispense with such inter-
> pretation, and when, through its variations, it envelops us — all of this
> leading to a fullness of emotion.[32]

In the final analysis, what permits poetic indirection to express
emotional intensity is that it liberates meaning from all exclusivity. The poetic meaning is both image and nonimage, near
and far. The world that characterizes it is that of non-duality:
of the totality of possibilities, not of the absolute. In other words,
the unfolding of the poetic image opens it to all perspectives by
going beyond their differences; and this complete availability of
meaning, to which poetic incitement gives access, constitutes its
allusiveness.

Unlike the symbol, which invites us to explore an ideal meaning beyond the concrete, this allusive value does not lend itself to
the mind's intuition: it is "savored" (*wei*^{v}). After Zhong Hong first
noted the surplus of meaning in the incitatory mode, the idea of
savor was adopted, and it is from this perspective, we remember,
that we were best able to distinguish the incitatory mode in *The
Book of Songs* from simple analogy. Even when rigorous, the latter

remains "superficial"; while the "slack" and "spacious" nature of the incitatory allows the "savor" to "be prolonged." Only savoring can correspond to this endless exhalation of the poetic image, by taking possession of its diffuse and residual nature. It is therefore the appropriate mode of assimilation: by prolonged contact with the materiality of the poem — through rereading and memorization — and its progressive distillation in the consciousness. "Mastication," "dissolution," "imbibing" — such are the metaphors used in Chinese to indicate poetic reading.[33] The expansion of meaning is not experienced as a spiritual discovery, allowing us to see the invisible, opening up the horizon to us. It is an osmosis operating through the continuous exchange between the poetic milieu and interiority. "Figuration beyond figuration," "landscape beyond landscape," or "savor beyond savor": these expressions are interchangeable. Just as figuration beyond figuration is not another figuration, savor beyond savor is not another savor: it is the savor that, being distilled, goes beyond initial specificity and that, as it expands, becomes enriched with all possible suggestions.

In following these points of difference, a rift begins to take shape. One might say, in short, that since the motivation for poetic indirection oscillates between emotional incitement and insidious intention, the indirection does not stabilize in China in the goal of figuration; and since the meaning of its emblematic value, based on allusions, expands infinitely like an atmosphere, it is not used to represent an idea beyond words. Chinese poetry describes neither ideas nor essences; it is neither mimetic (and in this way picturesque) nor symbolic. It is allusive, through specific application — or imprecise: in thus becoming indefinitely extensive, its allusive value conveys the depth of, but does not explain, emotion. This characteristic points to a difference in perspectives: Chinese poetry is allusive because the Chinese consider the relationship between the spoken and the unspoken and valorize the implicit, whereas the Greeks developed representativity (in which the implicit is but a result).[34]

This is why even if we play allusive incitement off the opposition between symbol and allegory, which for the West led to romanticism — in reaction to the classical theory of representation in which the symbol stands on its own (it "is") and does not signify — we realize that the Chinese idea eludes us still.[35] One might think that it is similar to the symbol because it is less transparent than allegory; because it is less rational as well, more immediate and spontaneous; because it is more indirect, in short, and its richness is inexhaustible.[36] But unlike the symbol, it does not give us access to another level — whatever name we might give it: the general, the abstract, or the spiritual.

Suddenly we are faced with this essential question, which is nevertheless impossible to articulate: Why was the level of theory and essences not formed in China? To attempt to answer this, I must appeal to philosophy.

CHAPTER NINE

From the Master to the Disciple:

The Proposition Is Only an Indication

The question becomes: What allows the symbol to represent an idea, point in its direction, or hint at it? Even in its romantic conception, when the symbol was celebrated in the West for itself (or as an end in itself, as intransitive), its power came from its ability to subsume the diversity of the concrete. In other words, the symbol gathers (*sumballei*) a multiplicity of perceptible aspects into itself to grant us access to their essences beyond. Essentially, the symbol, when it is an image, reveals itself to be parallel to the induction that leads to a general theoretical definition. Through the figurative, it tends toward the invisible, or spirit, world, which, thanks to it, discovers its own infinity.

This inductive process, leading to the understanding of essences, was not favored in the writings of ancient Chinese wisdom. As Confucius's *Analects,* documented by his disciples in *Lunyu*, demonstrates, this wisdom never sought to define *general* ideas, even on a moral level, and did not attempt to create a science, even one of virtue.[1] It *constructs* nothing theoretically, nor does it reveal anything mystically. Its intention is not to direct our behavior from the outside, by shaping it to the teachings of a doctrine, but to favor its adaptation in relation to a circumstance. This wisdom guides us toward an ever more intimate reconciliation with what each situation and occasion expects from us in order to create a proper balance. And it does so in an eminently variable way and without imposing a model. In this way, it enhances our experience of the coherence that is constantly at work in this incessant variation and makes its renewal possible. And this is what, definitively, is revealed as Heaven.

The stated concern of this wisdom is therefore not knowledge, with an eye toward truth, but the regulation of conduct — which makes the Regulation of the world possible. Also, far from pretending to describe the real, to reproduce the great articulation of things abstractly, the Confucian utterance, passed from the Master to the disciple and relating to the circumstance, can only be an indication. But in reacting specifically to the moment, it simultaneously opens onto the infiniteness of the course of things. From an angle and based on the slightest detail, it indirectly illuminates something that could not be defined generally: the essential immanence of things. This is why its virtue lies not in unfolding as *logos* but in being indicative.

We should therefore begin by fully assessing something that might otherwise appear merely a rhetorical commonplace: this topos of all morals according to which the important thing is not to speak but to act. By passing through this opposition (*xing-yan*[a]; compare in Greek *ergo-logo*), coming up against it once again, the Confucian utterance renders the truism profound; banality, constantly broached but never developed, says the essential. Not that Confucius condemns speech on principle, but he remains "careful" with it (1.14). Since everyone knows that speech tends to overlap behavior, one should be "cautious" and "slow" with it (see the notions of *na* [4.24] and *ren*[b] [12.3]). Ideally, speech remains in the background (14.21 and 14.29); he who simply is aware of it is already on the moral track.

"Fine words," on the other hand, distance us from speech (1.3 and 5.24), since words exist "simply" to "convey" (15.40). This cuts short not only the pleasures of eloquence but also the beginnings of a philosophy of language. Yet this commonplace, which might seem irreparably flat — and from which one cannot imagine what reflexive advantage might be gained — also rewards examination. Through it, we begin to notice that the richness of the Confucian lesson comes from its refusal of originality, from its not seeking to make itself conspicuous in its ideas. Its profundity lies in its formulating the obvious. In speech, as we know, "specious words confound virtue" (15.26). This is why Confucius was at war with "glib talkers,"[c] those eager in his time to test the unsuspected powers of discourse. He adamantly refused to be one of them, even though he seized every occasion to draw the princes to virtue (14.34). Nonetheless, the judgment he cast on those who exploited the resources of rhetoric is not without ambiguity: while rhetoric often arouses resentment in others, which he thereby judges harmful to its user (5.4), he was also forced to recognize that it had become difficult, in his troubled time, to survive without it (6.14), since the artifice of language protects one's viewpoints.

One can easily understand why glibness should be distanced — *vir linguosus, homo loquax* — and why it constitutes a political danger (15.10 and 17.18). But is the ability to debate an issue, to formulate an argument, also an obstacle to reflection? When Confucius finds it inappropriate for a certain administrative position to be entrusted to a young person, his disciple argues in principle: direct contact with the world of commerce is also an education, and it is not through books alone that one can study (11.24). Confucius turns his back on this discussion, claiming to detest such glibness: "It is on this account that I hate your glib-tongued people" (11.24). His disciple must try to understand what makes his conduct inappropriate in the present situation rather than try to defend himself through generalities. Even worse than resorting to generalities, he has tried to exploit a contradiction in the Master's words in an attempt to refute them. Instead of taking advantage of the lesson, the commentators note, he immerses himself in the polemic. But at the same time, it is the very idea of discussion that must be renounced. Barely glimpsed through the filter of pro and con, the path of dialogue is definitively barred.

By remaining in seclusion, by avoiding all artifice, speech becomes "reliable" and inspires adhesion (xin^d): the confidence it instills not only establishes a relationship between friends (1.4.7), but it is also essential in politics. Such confidence enables the government to make itself obeyed without giving orders; it simply teaches by example (13.1). Inversely, as soon as the relationship is not reliable, nothing is viable: confidence, Confucius states, is like the "cross-bar" that yokes the oxen to a carriage, allowing it to advance (2.22); it is on such a seemingly insignificant piece that everything in society depends.

The sinological tradition usually renders this term as *sincerity*, which is ambiguous in relation to what Confucius had in mind: the point is not that man says what he thinks but that he does what he says; Confucius reproaches speech not for lacking candor but for being fraudulent. In other words, his concern is not that speech should reflect consciousness but that it should not be contradicted by acts; it need be not truthful but effective. Conduct — as Confucius knew from experience — is the only security (5.9). At the same time, he does not acknowledge the problem of lying, which the Greeks only began to imagine (so much was man rendered passive by science; in Plato's *Lesser Hippias*, see involuntary versus deliberate lying) and which the Christians, by developing the sentiment of guilt, later rendered unfathomable (for the demonic pleasure that can be had in it, see Augustine, *libido fall-*

198

endi).[2] For Confucius, speech remains a tool, without a subjective dimension. Hence he need not preoccupy himself with splitting discourse into appearance and truth.

Let us review the facts. It is advisable to refrain from speech not only to be more able to keep one's word but also so that one's words will be more effective. Although these are analects between the Master and his disciples, all Confucian teachings are based on the principle of the Master's minimal intervention. Not that he wants to enclose himself in the silence so dear to mystics and worship the ineffable: he speaks as little as possible out of pedagogical concern in order to allow the other to discover by himself.

Two successive passages in *Analects* show the extent to which the Master is oriented in this direction (7.7 and 7.8). At first, he explains, his teachings are open to everyone: whoever comes to him with the slightest ritual gift attests to his goodwill and has never been sent away. Yet he also warns: if the other does not display a real desire to understand, he will not "open up" his spirit; if the other does not ardently try to speak, he will not "show" it to him with his words. "Open up," "show": such phrases, notes the commentator Hu Guang, imply a "releasing." Only when the listener's spirit is ready does the Master enlighten it through the anticipated instruction. Then few words suffice; rather than cheapen his words in profusion, the Master prefers a simple pointing. But since this indication encounters the listener's maximum receptiveness, because he is motivated, it is decisive, unblocking what had prevented him from advancing.

The Master's words intervene only at the last minute, when the disciple's spirit is receptive; they are minimal, as opposed to expansive, so that the other can make them as much his own as possible. Indeed, Confucius states, "When I have presented one corner of a subject to any one, and he cannot from it learn the other three, I do not repeat my lesson" (7.8). It is therefore up to the disciple to continue on his own; the instruction is as good as his ability to put it to use. The ancient treatise on education that is part of *Ritual* (13–15) does not contradict this. Just as a good singer helps others to continue in unison, a good educator helps others to pursue their own abilities: "He leads the students without forcing them, pushes them forward without constraining them, opens the path without leading them to its end" so that their spirits remain "calm" and "at ease" and they "understand" by themselves. These carefully balanced formulas afford a glimpse of the free "play"[e] given to the student on his "quest"; the Master points him in the right direction but lets him find his own way; he "subtly" gives a "hint" (*wei*[f]: indicatively), notes one commentator; in short, he indicates the way. The student must find the rest of the path. This method is active, we might conclude, but such is the price the word must pay to be effective. Here we find what constitutes the worth of the word, be it poetic or reflexive, within the Chinese tradition: its ability to incite and its allusive dimension. To be effective, words must remain inchoate, must merely begin to say; their richness comes from their implicitness.

There are passages in *Analects* that act out this indirect pedagogy. When a disciple asks Confucius to teach him husbandry and then gardening, Confucius denies him flatly (13.4); then, after the disciple has left, he explains to the others that these fields are irrelevant to morality (which alone assures confidence in a country and thereby favors wealth). He does not explain himself openly when his disciple is there, note some commentators, because Confucius realizes that the disciple, incapable of further questioning him, is not up to the task of "finding the other messages" his refusal was beginning to indicate and thereby profiting from his lesson. Confucius justifies his refusal only after the fact with the idea that his words will later come to the attention of this disciple, who will then understand their true meaning: in distilling his lessons, from the laconic refusal to the explanation given it, the Master designs a progressive path that allows the disciple to understand. The same two-part lesson occurs when Confucius is addressed by a disciple who favors shortening the period of mourning (17.21); since he notes that the disciple holds his own opinions in too high a regard and is satisfied with his own reasoning, Confucius deems it useless to try to persuade him or to argue with him. It is better to begin by letting it slide in such a way that his lesson, which would have been in vain in an immediate and frontal refutation, has a chance of reaching his student through a long process of maturation, carried by rumor or rebound.

If the other is not in the habit of saying "What shall I think of this? What shall I think of this?" Confucius states almost petulantly, "I can indeed do nothing with him!" (15.15) This requirement inversely implies another. While the Master's concern is to intervene only at the appropriate moment, it is also never to miss an opportunity: "When a man may be spoken with, not to speak to him is to err in reference to the man. When a man may not be spoken with, to speak to him is to err in reference to our words. The wise err neither in regard to their man nor to their words" (15.7). As we shall verify later, all Confucian wisdom in this sense issues from the possibility represented by the art of conforming to circumstance in order to exploit the opportunity it presents.

As for the disciples, they measure their progress by their ability to apply the Master's lessons by themselves. When one of them interprets the Master's thoughts with a citation from *The Book of Songs*, Confucius sighs and says, "With one like Ts'ze [Zigong], I can begin to talk about the odes. I told him one point, and he knew its proper sequence" (1.15). But when Zigong compares himself with the Master's favorite, Yan Hui, he can well evaluate their differences: "Yan Hui hears one point and knows all about the subject; I hear one point and know a second" (5.8). The first statement indicates that Yan Hui can develop the lesson to the end; therefore, the slightest indication bears fruit in him, with nothing left unexploited. The second statement indicates that when Zigong learns something, he can then complete it, thereby remaining limited by a successive progress, which is flatly deductive, without rising to universality. But this is also what justifies the Master in continuing to be in dialogue with him, guiding him step-by-step, whereas with the better disciple, the assimilation of the slightest indication is so complete that it suppresses the dialogue.

This is why one day Confucius can say, with a trace of malice, that his best disciple gives him "no assistance" (11.3): indeed, does he not deprive Confucius of the incitement that a less talented disciple, such as Zigong (3.8), offers by his repeated questions? Confucius enjoys pushing the paradox even further: since this most cherished disciple never needs to raise an objection — so great is his ability to draw as much as possible from what is said to him, which consequently he cannot help but adhere to — he can appear "stupid" (2.9). However, on a closer look, this apparently passive reaction to speech reflects a spirit that is "never flagging" (9.19), attesting to the fact that this speech has attained full efficacy, not in arousing a return to speech but in transforming it into silence. The ideal of Confucian speech is not to promote dialogue (by a direct confrontation of consciousnesses) but to imitate nature's indirect manner of operation: it is comparable, Fan Shi explains, to the "rain falling," which, without anyone noticing how, makes everything "grow."

The value of speech is thus measured by what it produces through its opportune intervention. The value comes from the influence it exerts, through its force of impact, rather than through what is said. This, to some extent, begins to put into question the Western notion of speech truth. "To tell, as we go along, what we have heard along the way, is to cast away our virtue" (17.14). This is the case even if what one has just heard within oneself is excellent, for then one is just "hawking," the Chan Masters would later say, without having had time to assimilate. Confucius is especially suspicious of recited lessons, as he states explicitly about one of his most passionate disciples: "When Tse-lu [Zilu] had heard anything, if he had not yet succeeded in carrying it into practice, he was only afraid lest he should hear *something else*" (5.13). It is vain to accumulate arguments, just as it is dangerous to attach oneself to any formulation, however correct it might be. One day, after the Master has praised the endurance of a disciple with a verse from *The Book of Songs*, this disciple recites the verse alone (9.26). Confucius reproaches him gently; one cannot stop there. As a maxim, this formula becomes an impediment; it no longer renews itself. In other words, any formulation is but temporary; none suffices in and of itself. Hence the relevance of a word comes from its adaptation; it is a matter less of content than of occasion.

What haunts Confucius, consequently, is not the failure to say something but for his words to have no effect. The problem with words is their sterility, which arises from their uselessness when they have missed their mark. This danger can be measured in words of injunction, which should possess the most efficacy: "When a prince's personal conduct is correct, his government is effective without the issuing of orders. If his personal conduct is not correct, he may issue orders, but they will not be followed" (13.6). What, indeed, does it mean to follow words of a formal order (Confucius asks elsewhere)? One cannot fail to obey; but it is "reforming the conduct because of them which is valuable" (9.23). On the other hand, Confucius continues, if the admonition remains discreet, one cannot help but find this "pleasing," although "it is unfolding their aim which is valuable." Here we have returned, through the expedient of pedagogy, to the principle of reading discussed earlier: what counts is not words, strictly speaking, but what they set into motion, their beyond.

An image helps to summarize this ideal of words: the teachings of Confucius are like a bell used by Heaven to alert the people (3.24). The image, which became commonplace (it is found, notably, in the treatise on education in *Ritual* [18] is of a wooden hammer that, as in Chinese gongs, would strike the metallic wall from without. "Heaven would employ Confucius," observes James Legge in his note to *Analects* 3.24, "to proclaim the truth and right." But on reading the image more closely, we see that it is different from what Westerners, such as the English commentator paraphrased here, project onto it, because of cultural tradition: the gong warns but does not *articulate*; it is not a mouthpiece through which truth can be "proclaimed." In China, the Master speaks less than he indicates; he does not deliver a message but rather draws attention and incites people to reflection; and the resonant power in the striking of the hammer on the bronze bespeaks the depths of this incitement.

Hegel, when he discovered Confucius, was disappointed. How great the distance between the prestigious reputation surrounding the memory of the Sage and what one reads in him! One finds only "sound, honest morality, nothing more"; there is no "profound speculative probing" and still less "hypothesis" (or "theory"). In his opinion, "We have nothing to gain from his teachings." Although Confucius has a certain amount of "practical and worldly wisdom," Hegel feels it is "as well expressed and better, in every place and among every people," such as in Cicero's *De officiis*.[3] Hegel took what should have been read as points indicating the route of a progression for general and abstract (in a negative sense) formulations, worthy in their platitude of the wisdom of nations. The Confucian proposition, as we have begun to see, is the opposite of watered-down: its value is *indicative*.

At first glance, it is true, one is disconcerted by Confucius's theoretical inconsistency: "The Master said, 'If a man in the morning, hear the right way, he may die in the evening without regret!' (4.8). That is it, the aphorism is closed. "One would fain recognize in such sentences," writes Legge in his commentary on these verses, "a vague apprehension of some higher truth than Chinese sages have been able to propound" (see also, for example, *Analects* 6.17). One is just as disappointed when Confucius broaches fundamental questions, such as benevolence and knowledge (that is, perspicacity):

> Fan Ch'ih [Fan Chi] asked about benevolence. The Master said, "It is to love *all* men." He asked about knowledge. The Master said, "It is to know *all* men." Fan Ch'ih [Fan Chi] did not immediately understand *these answers*. The Master said, "Employ the upright and put aside all the crooked; — in this way the crooked can be made to be upright." (12.22)

In spite of its appearing meaningless (so little is conceptualized, so little is argued), this response guides us toward an infinite depth of reflection. The disciple "did not immediately understand" because in his eyes, as in ours, the love of men implies a universal principle, whereas knowledge (and one should read this as the knowledge of men and therefore the possibility of employing them) leads to a choice among men and therefore to a discrimination: Is there, then, a contradiction between these two virtues, even though they are supposed to form a pair? Confucius's implicit response, "Employ the upright and put aside all the crooked," is the product of a discriminating knowledge; but its result, "in this way the crooked can be made to be upright," brings us back to the universality of a benevolence whose love embraces all.

This laconic response, which is enough to resolve the contradiction (between loving and knowing) that threatens morality, can lend itself to a more refined, and therefore increasingly broad, interpretation; we find this in the gradual way the disciples understand it, which is presented afterward. When he relates the Master's words, the first disciple sees only an answer concerning knowledge (of men); while his listener rightly perceives that it treats two questions at once and that its richness comes from this double play: it was enough for the ancient kings to have chosen one good minister, he notes, for all those devoid of virtue to disappear. Nonetheless, the exegete Huang Kan notes that even this interpretation is insufficient: this disciple rightly saw that a just knowledge of men allowed for the employment of the best and made evil disappear, but he did not properly take into account another aspect of benevolence underlying Confucius's response — its capacity to transform evil into good (under the influence of the exemplary, "the crooked can be made to be upright"). A Song philosopher, Cheng Yi, one of the most subtle readers of *Analects*, comments more generally: "Although it seems close and superficial, nothing in its contents prevents a remark of this sort from going the whole way; ... it is not the same for the remarks of the others; when they treat things that are near, they forsake the things that are far away, and when they treat the things that are far away, they misunderstand the things that are near."

"Near," "far away": the opposition is familiar (since I spoke earlier of the poetic "far away"), but what exactly does this *far away* of meaning signify? It is not precisely a distance created by abstraction (forsaking concrete particularity) but one created by the path of meditation, by the possible *prolonging* of this reflection (through its implicitness): in short, a response as simple as

Confucius's would contain infinite possible deployments.

The richness of the Confucian remark comes from its *scope*. Most often Confucius gives only easily accessible indications, such as, in politics, "reverent attention," "sincerity," and "the employment of people at the proper seasons" (see *Analects* 1.5), but elementary indications include "communication in every direction"[g]: taken to the extreme, they contain the ideal of any government. The choice therefore comes down to a revealing sign, in an apparently "minute" account,[h] or an anecdote that indicates a circumstance (see *Analects* 7.31): "The Master angled, — but did not use a net. He shot, — but not at birds perching" (7.26). This detail alone allows a glimpse at the nature of human benevolence, the fundamental solidarity that unites all beings: "Seeing how the Sage treated animals, one can understand how he treated men," a commentator states. "If he acted in this way for little things, one can imagine how he acted for larger ones" (see also *Analects* 6.12 and 6.13). In other words, the concrete biographical circumstance opens onto a meaning for the whole. To clarify: the relationship at stake takes us, by a simple, progressive extension, from a reduced, local aspect to an implicit global dimension without a change in level, such as between the concrete (visible) and the abstract (intelligible), and without, consequently, representativeness. This is why this remark is *indicative* rather than symbolic. One is not, therefore, surprised that commentators treat it in the same terms as were previously used for poetry: this type of remark is meant to be not understood but "savored,"[i] by steeping oneself in it (see the commentary on *Analects* 6.9 and 7.31); this gives access not to an idea but to an "atmosphere"[j] (see the commentary on *Analects* 5.25). Wisdom, in fact, is not conceivable through an idea; rather, it emanates in a diffuse, all-embracing fashion, starting from the slightest aspect of the Sage's personality.

This proposition, whose value comes from its ability to expand into the spirit it solicits, discreetly bars all speculation. When one of his disciples questions him on politics, the foremost issue debated in schools, Confucius merely responds, "Go before the people *with your example*, and be laborious in their affairs"; when asked if he can give "further instruction," Confucius simply adds, "Be not weary" (13.1). One can imagine that the disciple wants to hear from the Master's lips some brilliant exposition on how to govern men, but Confucius is wary of satisfying this expectation, for politics, like everything else, is a matter of personal invest-ment — from which discourse, as soon as it takes on importance, causes us to stray. This is why Confucius chooses laconic expressions, which force one to return to his remarks and give food for thought; at the same time, they give play to obliquity. Confucius is questioned successively on three political personalities (14.10): about the first, who is also his disciple, he says, "a kind man," a way, the commentators explain, of discreetly offering a counter-point to the image of severity attached to this figure; about the second, a great officer of Chu who had demonstrated loyalty to his prince but had dissuaded him from employing Confucius, he answers, "That man! That man!" another clever way, the commentator explains, of "discharging him"; about the third — a great minister in the past whose morality was questionable but whose memory is defended by Confucius because of the historical role he played — Confucius answers, "For him, the city of Pien [Bian], with three hundred families, was taken from the chief of the Po [Bo] family, who did not utter a murmuring word, though, to the end of his life, he had only coarse rice to eat" (14.10). About the minister himself, Confucius remains silent. One can deduce the minister's merit from the way he, stripped of his position, accepted his fate.[4]

This oblique presentation of thought plays a determining role in philosophical debate:

Someone said, "What do you say concerning the principle that injury should be recompensed with kindness?" The Master said, "With what then will you recompense kindness? Recompense injury with justice, and recompense kindness with kindness." (14.36)

The position represented by the initial question is that of the Taoists (see *Laozi* 63): by its unreserved radical nature and the — indiscriminate — generosity to which it bears witness, it appears at first to attain a moral absolute, which should remain unquestioned. Confucius surpasses this by returning to a position that seems much more common and lacking in heroism. But in treating injury with justice, not revenge, one stops the spread of injury; at the same time, in responding differently to kindness and injury, one maintains two distinct levels, which is essential to morality. Instead of yielding to the facility of extremism, this remark brings us back to the requirements of adaptation and equilibrium. This is why, while it is "clear, simple, and concise," one commentator explains, the "indicated meaning" is to imagine "indirectly and from different sides."[k] This is comparable to "the great process of the world," whose "simplicity" and "facility" of direction represent a manifestation (of immanence) to us, whose "subtlety," however, "knows no bounds." This apparently simple remark, which relies on no theoretical method (neither refutation nor demonstration), is open to endless exploitation from every possible angle: it is as inexhaustible as nature itself.

Furthermore, instead of abstractly constructing an opposition, especially one on morality — the "superior" versus the "mean"[l] man — Confucius engages in delicate separations: he operates on the basis of small divisions through which differences begin to emerge in order to allow the split to grow of its own accord. "The superior man is affable, but not adulatory; the mean man is adulatory, but not affable" (13.23): the latter lacks the courage to differentiate himself from others and at the same time enters into conflict with them since he looks out for his interests alone; the former, by contrast, is predisposed to enter into harmonious relations with others because he is internally defined by an uncompromising personal standard. In other words, similitude is played against harmony: a single nuance that can be plumbed indefinitely is enough to illuminate obliquely the universal opposition. Other reversals that reflect neither paradox nor enigma are "The superior man is easy to serve and difficult to please" (13.25): he is easy to serve because he engages every other man according to his ability, while he can only be pleased by a respect for morality. And "The mean man is difficult to serve but easy to please"; that is, he is difficult to serve because he demands everything from others, while he cares not what means are used to please him. Their differences as a whole are gleaned from their surroundings: "The superior man is satisfied and composed; the mean man is always full of distress" (7.36).

One type of concise statement, devoid of all logical articulation, best sums up the virtues of the Confucian proposition: the list. In *Analects*, the simple list works like an aphorism, constituting an autonomous and complete development on a par with the anecdote, saying, or dialogue:

> The subjects on which the Master did not talk were — extraordinary things, feats of strength, disorder and spiritual beings. (7.20)

Not only does the list suffice, through its enumeration, to direct thought (or, in this case, to divert it), but also it requires probing the implicit: the ordering it effects remains to be justified and hence unfolds like an adventure of the mind. At the heart of this process, the two median terms, strength and disorder, interpret each other through contiguity, the second accentuating the third,

whereas the first and the fourth respond to each other from a distance. From the third to the last, the gap is difficult to bridge (to
the point that one translator, A. Cheng, thought it necessary to
reorder the sequence: "The Master never spoke of the extraordinary or spirits, of brute force or unnatural acts" [p. 65]). As we
can imagine, enumerating the things about which the Master did
not talk allows the things privileged by his words to become more
apparent. The first term immediately creates a line of demarcation (although this term remains ambiguous): Confucius would
treat the mundane rather than the extraordinary, would prefer to
elucidate banality than allow himself to be seduced by the glim-
mer of the marvelous. The next two terms specify that the thrust
of the Confucian proposition is regulation (as an ordinary principle), in rejecting what is most openly opposed to it, the shows of
strength that lead to disorder. The last term, then, instead of continuing in this vein, bifurcates thought and points it in another
direction, that of the supernatural; instead of closing the list, it
opens it into the realm of mystery. In short, a tension we thought
had been eased reemerges and culminates in this reversal. While
violence, as an extreme expression of strength, is categorically
rejected as a subject worthy of speech, the commentator indicates
that the spirit world, as a force of the invisible, is to be approached
with caution — because, in this case, our speech might be unworthy. While continuing the progression of the preceding terms, this
one is their counterpoint, indeed presented as a direct opposite;
and the proposition takes shape within this *interval*.

   That the rubric does not offer homogeneity — and instead of
remaining flat and in continuous alignment, the series ruptures
and turns — should not lead us to imagine that the procedure lacks
a system (or that it is whimsical, representative of the irrationality
Westerners so easily attribute to Easterners). Evident here in
miniature is the originality of the Confucian method: instead of

setting up a general theoretical point of view that might embrace diversity under the ordering gaze of reason, the Confucian proposition follows an *itinerary* logic; instead of leading up to a panorama, it *marks out* a circuit. Through turns and detours, it affords the most insights possible.

A question arises: Does not the implicit richness of the Confucian proposition derive, in part, from the Master's authority rather than from its style? As tenuous as the style might be, one would credit a proposition with infinite meaning as soon as one knew it came from the Master ("The Master says..."). *Analects*, which is not completely homogenous, furnishes a point of comparison on this matter. Book 16, for example, belongs to another compilation (one much less well established and made in Qi, not in Lu: the disciple says not "the Master" but "Confucius"). In some of the first remarks collected in this section, Confucius renounces lapidary expression and indirect criticism in order to give a lesson in politics; most of the rest consists of lists that, unlike the preceding list, are limited to flat cataloging (such as the three types of advantageous friends and the three types of injurious friends; the three types of advantageous enjoyment and the three types of injurious enjoyment).[5] In losing its power to indicate, the Confucian proposition becomes catechism.

The problem is the same as that of any orthodoxy, but it is considerably heightened because the originality of Confucian thought comes precisely from its lack of doctrine. At what cost is a wisdom of personal regulation — whose subtlety derives from its representing no fixed position but never ceasing to adapt itself to the situation at hand — transformed into a dominant ideology, as was the fate of Confucianism under the Han before the advent of Christianity? Clearly, its success was its downfall. The loss was twofold, for the following aspects go together: first, the apothegm later attributed to Confucius loses its inchoate value, which operates obliquely, in order to become an exhaustive exposition; second, the Sage's moral lesson loses its characteristic antidogmatism, only to founder in formal recommendations.[6] The propositions become both explicit and rigid, thematic and organized. Using showy language and reducing the stakes, these remarks seek not to incite but to illustrate. Either they indulge in picturesque, if not puerile, detail, which immediately assumes a hagiographic value, or the images described are mechanical — and the moral stereotyped. The Confucian openness is therefore transformed into its opposite: the codification of moralism. In short, the art of conforming oneself to what a circumstance demands in order to embrace its unfolding (thus implying the absence of established principles) gives way to the inertia of conformism. This is borne out by the other collection of Confucian propositions, which are supposed to complete *Analects* (but which no doubt represent merely something in the style of a third-century text), *Kongzi jiayu*:[7] the text assumes the guise of a review, while the terms developed in series are so many conventional rubrics; the prescription is not only explicit but quibbling; not only does it leave no room for thought, it sermonizes.[8]

Chinese men of letters were aware of this loss, at least to literature: "After the death of Confucius, the subtle proposition was not continued."[9] They also analyzed the structure of the analects to determine the elements of Confucian originality by comparing them with the same episodes related by historians (as Chen Kui of the Song did in *Wenzi zhuyi*).[10] The formulation of Confucius's analects can be both more "simple" and more "ordered" to accentuate the density of meaning, just as they can "relax" and spread themselves out to allow this meaning more completely to be glimpsed. They neither "drain" meaning, through a desire to be "complete," nor break the "concentration" necessary to being "concise." The indicated meaning is found in this delicate equilibrium (for equilibrium is always the most effective), which allows the analects to point rather than to display — to begin to say, while giving the most room possible to the unsaid. This is why they can *remain* indications without straying into the insignificance of anecdotes or the abstractions of moralism.

The brief form of the analects has counterparts within the Greek tradition: the *maxim*, whose general prescription is addressed to everyone, and the *anecdote*, which relates a curious little event and therefore is of limited scope.[11] What the Confucian proposition has in common with the maxim, which enjoyed a rich tradition at the dawn of Greek philosophy (from the councils addressed by the first poets to the sayings of the Seven Sages praised by Plato, as well as the *sumbola* and the *akousmata* of Pythagoras), is a density that commands attention, a "psychagogical" and stimulating aspect prized by the Stoics, and an at-hand (*procheirotaton*) character, which allows it to be kept at one's fingertips as a guide for conduct. But the Confucian proposition does not have the maxim's gnomic character, which puts it on the same level as first truths and common sense and makes it, like the adage, an ideological stereotype (unless the maxim lacks an initiatory or esoteric value — which the Confucian remark also lacks). There is a rupture in the maxim form during the seventeenth century in Europe from the impersonal maxim, in which the author is the mouthpiece of a truth, to the critical, incisive, and ironic maxim (in France, with La Rochefoucauld). Whereas earlier maxims repeat the *doxa*, later maxims put it into question or at least subtly undermine its foundations. The Confucian proposition shares the maxim's brevity, which tends to make the mind of the listener or reader more active. Both of them, in fact, have the virtue of incompleteness that gives more food for thought by simply beginning to say and, through its dispersion, thwarts dogmatism. The

Confucian propositions are also *semina dicendi*, and people have noted in them the same literary qualities celebrated by Western humanists: the *varietas* (*ordo confusior*) that exalts discontinuity and the *obscuritas* that, through ellipsis or metaphor, is not immediately clear. But the Confucian proposition does not have the mark of a witty phrase, or the conceit of wit, that made the fortune of the modern aphorism; nor does it cultivate paradox, tending rather to illuminate an original and personal vision.

By its circumstantiality, the Confucian remark is thus closer to the ancient *chrie*. At least the genres correspond: the question-answer format, the possibility of action, the particularization of the interlocutor or the occasion, the possible use of the apothegm in a short account or brief dialogue. Confucius's analects hence recall the much more recent an agenre, which, long after a person's death, transmits to posterity biographical facts or witticisms, fragments of thoughts or conversations, that give one a better sense of the person and his conduct. The oral or pseudo-oral nature of these accounts preserves an impression of life and spontaneity, which pleases the reader — and infatuated him in France in the classical centuries. Just as one speaks of *Ménagiana* for the collections of Monsieur Ménage or *Huetiana* for those of Monsieur Huet, one can speak of *Confuciana*. But the ancient *chrie* is limited to the common sermon, usually addressed to children, or served as exercises of *grammaticus*; and as prolix as it might have been, the ana genre remained minor in European literature. These "spiritual stews" were saved by the remarkable nature of their circumstance or their representativeness. We expect truth not from them but from the account in Revelation or from theoretical discourse.

Basically, what makes the Confucian remark, which is neither maxim nor anecdote, incompatible with this protean genre of *brevitas* is that it dissolves the fundamental opposition between

the particular and the general. This tidy remark, lacking in theoretical pretensions, neither is initiatory (*sermo humilis, exilis*) nor
in the margin of another discourse, that of truth or essences. This
is why the slightest detour in it can reveal something essential and
how the little event it describes can be indicative of the totality.

In a paragraph of *Analects*, the Master's favorite disciple presents
his lesson in the following terms:

> Yen Yüan [Yan Hui], *in admiration of the Master's doctrines*, sighed and
> said, "I looked up to them, and they *seemed to become* more high; I
> tried to penetrate them, and they *seemed to become* more firm; I
> looked at them before me, and they *seemed to be* behind.
>
> "The Master, by orderly method, skillfully leads men on. He
> enlarged my mind with learning, and taught me the restraints of
> propriety.
>
> "When I wish to give over the *study of his doctrines*, I cannot
> do so, and having exerted all my ability, there seems to be something
> to stand right before me; but though I wish to follow and *lay hold of
> it*, I really find no way to do so." (9.10)

Critics have noted, in particular, the disciple's lost character:
something in the Master's teachings ever eludes him, even though
he sees that, basically, this is not at all obscure (for, in a certain
way, this "stand[s] right before [him]"); this quest from which he
cannot escape, however much he might want to, keeps him in suspense. Meno, by the same token, admits to his perplexity in front
of Socrates; he loses his composure and feels "benumbed," for
Socrates in his dialogues never ceases to provoke, like a "gadfly"
about town, the souls of his fellow citizens (*Apology* 30E; *Meno*
80C). Each finds himself disarmed by the Master's incitement.

Is Confucius, then, a Chinese Socrates? Sinologists have long

216

claimed as much. Each of them, in fact, belongs to the last age of oral tradition, when wisdom still sprung from the freshness of dialogue and was not couched in books; and we know of their conversations only what was recorded by their disciples. Their interests are of the same order, bearing on conduct and moral experience. Just as Confucius keeps a prudent distance from cosmological or religious speculations, Socrates, according to Cicero's formula, "drew philosophy away from the hidden secrets of nature" in order to apply it to the duties of everyday life.[12]

One can take the comparison even further. Each of them admits his ignorance and does not claim to possess a doctrine (see *Analects* 2.17 and 9.7); they are wary of speeches and speak as little as possible. At the same time, each is characterized by assiduous zeal in forming disciples and helping them to advance (see *Analects* 7.18). While recognizing that they are not repositories of wisdom, they are aware in their inner hearts of having been given a vocation that is beyond their control (from Heaven or the daimon), which gives them confidence in the face of their contemporaries: Confucius when threatened at Kuang and Socrates before the tribunals (see *Analects* 9.5). Finally, while respecting established religious practices, they both seem to aspire to a more internal religion, discovered in their own moral experiences (see *Analects* 7.34).

People have also called Confucius ironic, which completes the parallel with Socrates — but is he? Certainly he talks "in sport" (17.4), to the point of insisting on his remarks and smiling at his disciples (5.6). This playfulness is one of the characteristics most noted by modern scholars, for example, Vincent Y.C. Shih and Christoph Harbsmeier, in reaction to the canonization of the Master.[13] Confucius does not, however, appear to adopt an adversarial position, as Socrates often does to push his interlocutor into developing it, thereby countering and exposing its incoherence and inanity (the situation of *aporia*). The following brief remark, read closely, will demonstrate the difference:

> Ts'ze-kung [Zigong] was *in the habit* of comparing men together. The Master said, "Ts'ze [Zigong] must have reached a high pitch of excellence! Now, I have not leisure *for this.*" (14.34)

While Western translators deem this remark ironic, believing that Confucius pretends to praise his disciple the better to denounce his pretension ("Ts'ze [Zigong] must have reached a high pitch of excellence!"), a Chinese commentator interprets it as an indirect strategy: "Howevei much we wish to make comparing men's merits and faults a practice that allows us to plumb the depths of things, devoting ourselves too exclusively to it distracts our minds and makes us lose our guiding principles. This is why Confucius praises his disciple, but in a questioning mode, then disparages himself in such a way as severely to reprimand this conduct." Another commentator adds: "When the Sage criticizes someone, his words are not pressing, but he nonetheless reaches his mark better than he could by any other means." Here once more is the Chinese ideal of an allusive and circuitous criticism that reaches the other more effectively by not "squeezing" him too tightly. While it was necessary to split the proposition to account for its initially apparent contradictory aspect, the Chinese commentator worked it between two successive moments of the process — which recalls the logic of detour — and not within the heart of the discourse, by juxtaposing appearance and reality.[14]

That Confucius's remarks are not split into appearance and reality recalls the mode of poetic commentary in China, which deliberately rejects allegory. As F. W. J. Schelling pointed out about ancient mythology, irony and allegory are closely allied, since they both use dissimulation (such as *pseudologia*), which asks to be exposed. By the same token, they lead consciousness toward another reality. Socrates is ironic so that his interlocutor can go beyond the appearances of his false knowledge and aspire to truth; he feigns naïveté and plays the child ("eirōneuomenos kai paizōn" [*Symposium* 216E]), but in the manner of the Silenus boxes, whose exteriors were too crude and ridiculous not to lead one to suspect what might be inside. Kierkegaard, when interpreting Socratic irony, showed how, through derision, it foreshadows a higher order, whose mark it bears as if inside it. Under the guise of an absurd simulation, the nocturnal transition toward another sphere, rich in other values, is being prepared, a sphere to which access is gained only through continuous progress. Irony becomes a purifying treatment that prepares its recipient for conversion.

The figure of conversion that dominated Greek philosophy's sense of its role is absent from the Confucian teachings. Confucius does not invite his disciples to turn their backs to the shadows in the cave in order to ascend to the light. Since his comments lack duplicity, they do not open up to allow a glimpse of any true beauty beneath a misleading and crude exterior. Everything, in short, leads toward this fundamental difference from Greek philosophy: the objective of the Confucian remark is not truth, which is why it cannot be developed dialectically (and why Confucian thought is lost as soon as it is transformed into discourse, since it has nothing to show). Instead, the Confucian remark strives toward an adaptation not between spirit and thing but between conduct and situation (such as "occasion-position,"[m] as it proceeds from the course of things). I have been suggesting the reason behind this desired adaptation in passing, with a word taken from the margins of philosophical works yet directly related to the idea of process: the object of the Confucian proposition, which still preoccupies Chinese philosophy, is *regulation* (as the process whereby an organism maintains its equilibrium by adapting to circumstances).[15] But this object, in fact, is not an object, which is why it eludes the disciple.

When Confucius mocks himself, it is not to set a trap for his interlocutor but to make him measure his distance from this demand for regulation in order to underline an excess or a flaw.[16] And when his favorite disciple claims to be confused by the lesson, it is not because he suddenly sees an opinion to which he might have adhered, and which henceforth would appear illusory to him, dissolve (the experience of Meno). What constantly eludes him, according to the commentators Zhang Shi and Hu Guang, is the delicate "balancing"[n] that never ceases to vary (to adapt itself to the moving course of things) but that alone allows conduct to keep its constancy and never to deviate (and whose model is the course of the heavens). The disciple says that this is "before" him and that suddenly it is "behind" him because he never goes far enough or goes too far; on the other hand, by ceaselessly offsetting one with the other — the broadening of the spirit effected by literature with the checking of conduct imposed by rites — the Master guides him. Far, then, from setting itself up in any other place, the commentators specify, this regulation, which is infinite in scope ("I looked up to them, and they *seemed to become* more high"), presents itself, in the final analysis, as evidence of an immanence ("I tried to penetrate them, and they *seemed to become* more firm"). At the same time, it eludes the grasp, since regulation, in its supreme stage, takes place *sponte sua* through continuous adaptation, without being the object of application and without being assignable to a single "place" or "being."[o]

What disconcerts Confucius's disciple, in short, is not the disturbing mobility of the dialectic urging him to aspire to an essential identity but that the desired equilibrium can only be maintained through a continuous evolution and thus can never be *identified*. This is why the path of the Confucian lesson is subtle, and rejects the rupture that irony would provoke, while converting consciousness from the moving world of experience toward the plane of the in itself and the general. The Master leads his disciple continuously and "progressively."[P] It remains for us to consider this plane of the in itself and the general, whose advent in Greece was marked by Socratic maieutics, and, continuing with Confucius, why Chinese philosophy dispensed with this plane.

CHAPTER TEN

There Is No Plane of Essences, or

Why Detour Is Access

Early on, the Western philosophical tradition agreed on the nature of Socrates' contribution. As Aristotle, the first historian of the subject, said on several occasions, there are two things with which Socrates can be credited: inductive reasoning and universal definitions. Induction (*epagōgē*) is the progression from the particular to the general: by considering a variety of examples, the mind apprehends the common characteristic that makes them a unique type. Definition, as the true *logos*, is the collection of these general characteristics expressing the essence of a thing, its *ousia*. That which, by deriding our opinions, causes us to sense Socratic irony and to which a dialectic attempts to give voice is this in itselfness, whose criterion is universality (implying noncontradiction), the sole ground of science.[1]

Agreement has also been reached on the origin of this criterion. Although inductive reasoning had been used before him, Socrates was the first to recognize its importance and make systematic use of it. His task was twofold: to go beyond the naive dogmatism of the physicians, who claimed immediate access to universality and the ability to say everything about the world but whose inner contradictions revealed the arbitrariness of their assertions; and to confront the skeptical relativism of the sophists, with Protagoras in their lead, who reduced the measure of truth to what it seemed to each individual. Socrates' solution was to use dialogue to go from the particularity and contingency of experience to the acknowledged universality of a form of ultimate knowledge independent of the individual: questioned about courage, piety, and wisdom, Socrates put the opinions of both groups to the test in an attempt to identify the nature of virtue in the form of the idea, one and coherent (*nen te eidos*) and consequently immutable.

All this is so well known, or rather so familiar, that one has the impression of reciting it. Socrates' contribution to Western philosophy is so well integrated that no one is surprised by it; indeed, it is so conflated with the ascendancy of reason that we are unable to see our bias. The approach can be criticized, but the criterion of universality itself has hardly ever been questioned. How far did Nietzsche go? Even when the universality of a definition is called into question, one still depends on universality as such. By contrast, the situation with Confucius, as described in *Analects*, is completely different: when he is asked about virtue, Confucius does not even try to define it.

While Plato has Socrates say about the definition of knowledge (the object of definition par excellence), "Our answer might be quite short and simple," we also learn that, lacking all definition, "we are going an interminable way round" ("perierchetai aperanton hodon" [*Theaetetus* 147C]).[2] We must therefore either choose the convenience of definition, which, with its use of abstraction, allows us to reach the essence of a thing, or be doomed to an interminable circuit or detour. With Confucius, Chinese thought sets out along this unending detour. However, the globality to which it refers should not be confused with the generality to which Socratic definition leads. Another kind of universality is at work here, one that is immanent in the least word of the Sage;

and this is why this detour can be, at the same time, a form of access.

Despite the differences between Greek and Chinese conceptions, the initial question addressed was of the same order:

> Hsien [Yuan Xian] asked what was shameful. The Master said, "When good government prevails in a State, *to be thinking only of salary*; and, when bad government prevails, *to be thinking, in the same way, only of salary*; — this is shameful." (14.1)

The salary referred to here is the payment received for carrying out a responsibility for the prince. According to one ancient commentator, He Yan, Confucius's answer means: while in a well-run country it is proper to occupy a post and to receive a salary, in a poorly run country it is a matter of shame to do so. The most classical commentator of all, Zhu Xi, interprets Confucius's words differently, seeing several, progressively deeper levels in them: while it is understandable to all that it is shameful to think of one's salary in an ill-governed country, Confucius is trying to help his disciple see that it is equally shameful to think only of one's salary in a well-governed country. In any case, it is clear that, in response to the question about the shameful, Confucius seeks neither to construct a definition nor to inquire into the validity of the term, conceived of as a generality; nor, however, does he merely give his disciple an example of a shameful act — for this would maintain the relationship of a particular to a general case (where the example illustrates an abstract truth). Confucius's answer should instead be read as an "indication" signaling a course of reflection (see the commentary of Cheng Yi on *Analects* 14.2[a]). Earlier commentators conceived of this course differently (their readings, however, are not mutually exclusive: there are several possible paths), which they pursued for a greater or shorter distance. But the important thing, Zhu Xi explains, is that the Master's answer "marshaled" the disciple's "aspirations," "by causing him to become aware of the way in which he might progress."

That Confucius's chief concern is not with definition, whose criterion is universality, can be confirmed by considering the variety of answers that he gives to the same question, for example, on the subject of filial piety (and the compilers of *Analects* were careful to group these answers together, 2.5–8). When questioned by a great nobleman, Confucius confines himself to a laconic principle, defining filial piety as "not being disobedient," which he later explains in terms of the need to fulfill ritual obligations (this obvious principle contains an ad hominem application: the great nobleman might be tempted to oppose the prince by usurping certain rituals reserved for the prince alone); by contrast, when the nobleman's son asks the same question, Confucius answers by taking the young man's point of view: "Parents are anxious lest their children should be sick"; when, finally, his disciples question him, Confucius takes inner responsibility much more into account (his tone, too, becomes more vehement): to the one whose love for his parents has become overly familiar, Confucius insists on the need for "reverence"; to the one who is so intent and serious about serving his parents that he forgets to be affable, Confucius speaks of the importance of the "countenance" he presents to them. However, his answering each one differently should not be mistaken for relativism; in other words, although not adopting Socratic generality, Confucius does not take the position of a Protagoras (because, for Confucius, point of view is not synonymous with truth). Confucius, the commentator Cheng Yi concludes, "provides his interlocutor with the amount of information appropriate to the level he has reached: thus the difference in his utterances." The first answer was more distant (and at the same time

226

subtle), the second more restrained, the last two simultaneously more personal and moral (analogous examples can be found in *Analects* 12.14 and 13.17 on political administration and 13.20 on being entitled to be called an officer). In sum, Confucius adapts to each case, taking into account differing capacities (6.19); or, more exactly, since the idea of adaptation still implies the relation between the particular and general, we might say that in the case of filial piety Confucius performs a variation (in the musical sense of the term). As Cheng Yi says, "The Sage's word is transformed in relation to the person to whom it is addressed"[b3] (12.22): that is, it *becomes* other according to each person's need. Confucius's word is this continuous *modulation*, which corresponds exactly to what is required to attain global regulation.

Confucius's overriding concern with control and regulation can lead him to give contrary answers to the same question. In one of the analects (11.21), a disciple asks whether he should immediately put into practice what he has just learned: Confucius tells him to consult with his parents first . Then a second disciple asks the same question: Confucius tells him to put it into practice immediately. Understandably, his interlocutors are perplexed by this apparent contradiction. Confucius explains: the second one is retiring and slow; therefore, he urged him forward. The first has more than his share of energy; therefore, he restrained him. Thus we can see that Confucius tries to maintain a delicate equilibrium between surplus and deficit, which is entirely determined by the situation: regulation is based not on a preestablished principle that transcends the course of events but on a purely indicative relationship whose coherence is immanent (that of the Chinese word *li*, as opposed to *logos* as reason). Thus instead of tending toward an abstract definition that ultimately subsumes the difference between individual cases, Confucian discourse evolves; the appropriateness it seeks, which gives it precision, is not between the particular and the general but between an utterance and its occasion (this, as we have seen, is the source of power for incitation). Ultimately, Confucius does not pose the problem of definition because he is not seeking to extract a stable — and therefore ideal — entity, separable from becoming: he does not inquire into the essence of things because he conceives of the real not in terms of being (as opposed to becoming) but as a process (whose nature is to be regulated). Socrates, on the other hand, to escape from the impasse created by a nascent ontology, assumes the necessity of definition (even if its ontological dimension is not made explicit until Plato).

This opposition is demonstrated well by Confucian tautology, the flip side of Socratic definition. Far from being flawed logic, tautology constitutes the ideal form in which to express regulation. When the duke Ching of Qi questions Confucius about governance, he simply says: "*There is government* when the prince is prince, and the minister is minister; when the father is father, and the son is son"[c] (12.11). Posed here is the question par excellence, and it comes up in a most solemn circumstance (with a great prince as interlocutor). In Confucius's answer, the predicate, by simply repeating the subject, says nothing more — and nothing less — than this subject. That the predicate obviously corresponds to the subject — because it is it, and the expression unfolds seamlessly from one end to the other — signifies that, up and down the social hierarchy, each person coincides exactly with the position demanded of him (as prince or vassal, father or son). As a result, the entire system (in this case, the social system) has a regulatory order (which, of course, applies to ideology as well: the idea being that it is better for each to embrace his condition to the best of his ability than to try to change it; regulation, not surprisingly, is the opposite of revolution). Whereas the predicate of definition, constructed beyond the bounds of the subject, leads to a complete inventory of generalities, the predicate of Confucian tautology, by not going beyond its subject, expresses the Master's meaning most precisely: this is the art of conforming, without excess or deficit, made possible by the spontaneous adaptation of behavior to a situation (which the immediacy of the tautological expression perfectly captures; in definition, by contrast, the adaptation is constructed). Thus tautology bears not a weak but a strong meaning — indeed, from the Confucian perspective, the strongest possible. Its aim is not to establish an identity, as with definition (which, moreover, is reached via essence), but to test a congruence. (The aim here is not, as it is with definition, to make theory possible: it is — and this is the fundamental purpose of Chinese thought — to disclose the obvious.)

Tautology, along with its above-described basic virtue, provides another useful service, based on its requirement of contextual suitability. We know from history that Confucius's interlocutor in this discussion is a bad prince. But he is nevertheless a prince. Thus by resorting to tautology, which says nothing, the speaker runs no risk: he can be accused of neither daring nor lèse-majesté. At the same time, by proclaiming the obvious, tautology can be used opportunely, as a kind of screen, to express oblique meanings. The commentator notes that this prince had not taken proper care to name an heir (he therefore was not fulfilling his role as prince and father) and that his minister was currently usurping his power (and was thus not acting as a good vassal). As we know from history, this minister killed his prince, the worst possible form of deregulation in government. Under the cover of tautology, Confucius thus launches an indirect — and consequently more incisive — criticism. By saying nothing, tautology leaves more to the understanding and increases the allusive power of speech.

Very similar to tautology, and taking as few risks, is the truism.

The truism, in its refusal to construct a generality, is as distinct from the maxim as tautology is from definition. Once again, the occasion is solemn and the question an important one: the duke Ding asks if there is a single saying, the application of which would assure the prosperity of the nation (13.15). Confucius begins by expressing skepticism about this genre of maxim in general and then, as a last resort, offers the following: "To be a prince is difficult; to be a minister is not easy." Instead of constructing a political principle, Confucius chooses a formula totally devoid of theoretical content: his platitude merely underscores the requirement contained in each of its terms. This is why, in response to a question from a disciple about what he would do first if the ruler of Wei were to call him to help run the government, Confucius answers (much to the surprise of his interlocutor), "Rectify names" (13.3), because names codify functions and this codification makes adaptation of behavior possible. The problem Confucius poses here is thus not the logical one of designation but the political one of regulation; he is concerned not with the abstract meaning of the word but with its prescriptive content. Once words cease to correspond to the things they are supposed to indicate — such as when one continues to say "cornered vessel" about a vessel that is no longer cornered (6.23)[4] — the roles of both are confused (the preceding discourse also allows for an oblique reading: the ruler of Wei is a son who is no longer a son because he has become his father's rival). Thus the inflation of words coincides with the usurping of positions (see *Analects* 13.14). The decadence that Confucius complains about is the result of a disorder at the heart of language: words no longer respect their normative content, and the joy of tautology is lost.

In theory, definition is characterized by a splitting in two (the concrete from the abstract, the particular from the idea); strategically, it is characterized by a frontal approach of which definition is the object. However, even intuition, which is at the center of Confucian discourse and, as such, characterizes the Master's teaching, is never conceived of as a generality. Indeed, on the meaning of *the human* (ren[d], the virtue of humanness; however, more than a virtue in the narrow sense of the term, *ren* designates the awareness of a fundamental solidarity among all beings), Confucius begins by telling his favorite disciple that it consists in "subdu[ing] one's self and return[ing] to propriety"; he tells another, less gifted disciple (thus the need to be more explicit) that when in public he should "*behave to everyone* as if [he] were receiving a great guest" and "employ the people as if [he] were assisting at a great sacrifice"; resorting to humor to frustrate the expectations of a third disciple, he says, "The man of perfect [*ren*] is cautious and slow in his speech" (12.1–3).[5] Confucius varies his response depending on the level and quality of his interlocutor, but he always speaks indirectly. In his third answer, one commentator remarks, the end by which Confucius pictures the question is particularly narrow; nevertheless, the reserve he recommends — to counter the other's proclivity to hold forth — proves enough of a guide to lead him to an understanding of a fundamental requirement. The same holds for all the answers Confucius offers on this subject to the same interlocutor (Fan Chi 6.20, 12.22, 13.19): they are so many "corners," hammered into one point or another, to make access to the essential possible.

In the absence of definition argumentation becomes impossible. Thus, on the question of humanness (a question into which the disciples never tire of inquiring), Confucius's concern is neither to create an idea out of it nor to prove its validity; instead, by maintaining constant proximity to this question, Confucian discourse implies an ever deeper measure of its importance. Through the twists and turns of the word, and no matter how elliptical the discourse, this intuition begins to take definite shape. Thus what justifies the modulation of Confucian discourse is not solely its relation to the immediate interlocutor: in all cases, only by an oblique approach can an understanding of the essential be obtained. At the beginning of the fourth book of *Analects,* the first seven statements, all of which deal with human virtue, lack any context. They are just so many intuitive insights that no general statement could possibly summarize:

> 1. The Master said, "It is [human] manners which constitute the excellence of a neighborhood. If a man, in selecting a residence, does not fix on one where such prevail, how can he be wise?"
> 2. The Master said, "Those who are without [humanness] cannot abide long either in a condition of poverty and hardship or in a condition of enjoyment. The human rest in [*ren*]; the wise desire [*ren*]."
> 3. The Master said, "It is only the *truly* [human] man who can love, or who can hate, others."
> 4. The Master said, "If the will be set on [*ren*], there will be no practice of wickedness." (4.1–4)

As with any fragmentary utterance, these statements are not integrated into an overall structure — indeed, the separate statements barely relate to one another. What gives them originality and force is that, as strongly accentuated as maxims, they nevertheless are open-ended; from one to the next, each uses a particular point to make what is only a partial statement. The first takes up the meaning of the human from the modest point of view of conditioning and habitat, which are a function of the milieu in which one lives (for the Chinese, morality is above all a matter of local environment); at the same time, there is an undercurrent of the theme of complementarity, linking solidarity, which is derived from a feeling for the human, to the necessity of choice (in this instance, a place to live), which corresponds to being wise. However, already in the second statement, this complementarity is transformed as it becomes part of an indirect hierarchy: while the man who has an adequate sense of the human lives appropriately, the wise man conceives of appropriate behavior in terms of intention. Gravitating naturally toward universal love, this sense of the human can potentially result in a lazy-minded indifferentiation, that is, an insipid unanimity. This is the source of the somewhat aggressive reminder in the third statement: it is not only necessary to love others, it is also necessary — because one loves — to dislike those who, by the evil they have committed, deserve to be disliked. This theme, although echoed in the subsequent statement, is presented in a somewhat amended form, rejecting the codification of good versus evil, since it could hinder moral progress: once the sense of humanness is authentically experienced, it dispenses with proscriptions by conceiving of ethical life exclusively in positive terms. Taken together, each statement orients consciousness in a somewhat different direction — but always in order to say the same thing — and none of them is conclusive: each relies on the other, both by intersection and complementarity, rectifying what each one of them individually, if interpreted univocally, might seem to present as fixed or limiting.

Rather than being conceived of as a fixed notion, the sense of humanness is thus thought of as a dimension, one that, in the existence of each of us and through our relationship with others, reveals morality. Moreover, through morality, human beings communicate with the very foundation of reality. Through immediate experience of the radical solidarity of all living things, even the smallest, we attain an intuition of the coherence that is constantly at work in the great course of things: the human being comes to realize what is Heaven (there is thus no longer the separation of morality and metaphysics into distinct entities: the moral sensibility by itself illuminates the domain of the first philosophy). This is why Confucius can simultaneously speak of the meaning of humanness as both the thing closest to us and an inaccessible ideal:

> The Master said, "Is [humanness] a thing remote? I wish to be [human] and lo! [humanness] is at hand." (7.29)

> The Master said: "The sage and the man of perfect [humanness]; — how dare I *rank myself with them?*" (7.33)

This is why he can give a concrete and positive definition of the quality of humanity (see *Analects* 17.6) as easily as he can renounce the very possibility of discussing it and become evasive (see *Analects* 5.4, 5.7, 14.2, 14.5). In its endless capacity to be deepened, the meaning of humanness makes communication possible between the most ordinary moral behavior and absolute wisdom (see Zhu Xi's commentary on 6.28[e]). The unlimited extensity of the term goes hand in hand with the infinite progress of morality. However, to define is, in the first instance, to delimit (compare the Greek word *orizesthai*), to mark the borders that separate, like two fields, one type from another. Confucius can thus not so much define the meaning of humanness as indicate in what "direction" it must be searched[f] (6.28) and how to "approach" it (13.27).

As a consequence of this fluidity, there can be nothing surprising about the following statement in *Analects*:

> The subjects of which the Master seldom spoke were — profitableness, and also the appointments *of Heaven*, and perfect virtue [humanness]. (9.1)

234

This is the most grammatically correct reading of the text (which cannot be suspected of being corrupt). The majority of commentators — including the greatest, such as Cheng Yi and Zhu Xi — understood it and accepted it without demur. Later, however, several scholars, judging the formula unacceptable, tried to force the text into a totally contrary reading: either by correcting it — the philologist's final gambit — in this case by replacing "seldom"g with its opposite (thus: "Confucius spoke frequently about profit, destiny, and humanness"), or by offering a reading that is even more strained, taking "and also" as a verbal construction (thus Pierre Ryckmans: "The Master seldom spoke of profit. He celebrated the divine will and humanity").[6] James Legge, who resigned himself to following the orthodox reading, nevertheless remarked that there was something absurd in saying that the Master "rarely spoke" about human virtue when it was the central theme of his teaching.

This philological point thus calls for a philosophical investigation. One of the first such investigations, and a modern one, by Yang Bojun, attempted to resolve this *aporia* by taking a scrupulously mathematical approach: among the numerous — more than a hundred — references to the meaning of humanness in *Analects*, a large proportion result not from the Master's initiative but in response to questions posed by his disciples. Since this was an essential matter of investigation, anything said by the Master on the subject was carefully preserved. Nevertheless, Yang Bojun concludes, in light of everything that Confucius said during his life, he indeed rarely spoke about human virtue. Classical commentators were little concerned with this kind of calculation: their reading of the text was a result of a more general understanding of Confucius. We know that one value of the Confucian list is its tendency to produce inner tensions and discrepancies rather than a bland homogeneity: Confucius, the ancient com-

mentators explain, rarely spoke of profitableness because, by limiting people to individual self-interest, profit diverts them from
morality. He spoke rarely of the appointments *of Heaven* because
its nature is so subtle that it is virtually impossible to grasp.
Finally, he had little to say about perfect virtue or the meaning of
humanness because the "path to it is so broad" (few are those who
reach it; see Han Yu and Li Ao) that all Confucius might say about
it would represent only a fraction of its real dimensions. One
commentator, Zhang Shi, justifies saying that the Master "rarely
spoke" by noting that he did not approach these questions explicitly, "pointing with his finger."[h] And another, Hu Guang, says:
"The Master gives various answers on the meaning of humanness.
When it is said that he 'rarely spoke' about it, this is because he
spoke only of the 'direction' that allows it to be sought; as for the
meaning of humanness in itself, he says nothing." In other words,
the Master does nothing more than begin to speak; or, as previously noted, his discourse on this subject is merely indicative.

To speak seldomly, as many commentators have remarked, is
quite different from not speaking at all. In fact, the Master was
explicit about those subjects of which he would not speak ("The
subjects on which the Master did not talk were — extraordinary
things, feats of strength, disorder and spiritual beings" [7.20]) because they lead either to deregulation or are beyond human understanding. By contrast, according to the Song reading, another list
details what the Master was "currently"[i] studying and how these
texts influenced his lessons: *The Book of Songs, The Book of Historical Documents*, and the observation of protocol (7.17). Between
these poles of speech and silence, a third possibility appears: that
in which words are rarely employed or their use is intentionally
restricted. Discourse here refrains from touching on subjects of
egotistic interest and remains silent about the invisible (destiny
and spiritual beings); as for the essential (which the meaning of

236

humanness reveals), Confucian discourse speaks of it rarely because it can only be approached obliquely.

This is why one of Confucius's disciples — Zigong, undoubtedly one of the most "theoretically" inclined among them — can say, "The Master's *personal* displays of *his principles* and *ordinary* descriptions of them may be heard. His discourses about *man's* nature, and the way of Heaven, cannot be heard" (5.12). As tradition later made explicit, the way of Heaven is the great rule of the course of things, which, because it does not deviate, is continuously renewed; and the way of Heaven is what is incarnated in human nature, in each individual, as the spontaneous injunction of conscience. Moreover, in this dimension of experience, the meaning of humanness and human virtue is revealed to us, and ever more deeply, by making us conscious, through moral sensitivity, of the fundamental solidarity that links our existence to the existence of others and thus to the overall coherence in which we all participate (see Confucius: "At fifty, I knew the decrees of Heaven" [2.4]). By the same token, the gap underscored by the disciple between what "may be heard" and what "cannot be heard" from the Master does not refer to two separate spheres of the Master's teaching, as if there were something esoteric in it; rather, it refers to the double dimension, whether implicit or explicit, in the same teaching (which, by its every subject, can only be one: the universal requirement of regulation). This is why Confucius warns his disciples:

> The Master said, "Do you think, my disciples, that I have any concealments? I conceal nothing from you. There is nothing which I do that is not shown to you, my disciples; — that is my way." (7.23)

According to his own words, the originality of Confucius's teaching is that it entails no mystery, boasts of no secret. As one commentator notes, while Confucius may not explicitly name the regulatory order of the things he intuits, in the least of his words and the smallest of his gestures there is implicitly a "perfect teaching." While he seldom speaks of the foundation of things, even while never ceasing to be concerned about it (since, in relation to what can be said about it, this foundation remains an inexhaustible subject), he does not cease, through everything he does, to make it manifest.

In sum, the less he speaks, the more he shows. Ultimately, in fact, direct and indirect forms of communication are reversed: while appearing indirect from the point of view of a definition-centered discourse (because it leads us on an endless detour of modulation), the indicating word is more direct than any possible definition. This is because, regardless of the angle of intervention, the indicating word always allows everything in a statement to be seen: it reveals the bottomless depths of things instead of passing through the mediation of a theoretical construction (which, in comparison, would seem endless). Hence this passing to the limit: "I would prefer not speaking," Confucius says one day (17.19). And when Zigong, who remains attached to the theoretical content of the word, worries that he will no longer leave anything to "record," the Master explains: "Does Heaven speak? The four seasons pursue their courses, and all things are *continuously* being produced, *but* does Heaven say anything?" Heaven does not need to speak to reveal itself: the regulatory principle that characterizes it is revealed in the least appearance of things. In the same way, all the Sage's wisdom is revealed in the smallest element of his behavior: there is thus no more reason to expect a message (revelation) from Heaven than to expect lessons from the Master. They have nothing more to communicate than the regulation they incarnate. However, because this regulation is continuously revealed everywhere and at all times, we are always overwhelmed

by it and thus incapable of isolating it in order to become conscious of it. Indeed, nothing is more difficult to grasp than the
globality of the obvious. Thus once it succeeds in illuminating its
source and connects us to the totality (of Heaven and the Sage),
the smallest detail attains a strategic importance: Confucian discourse does not attempt to transcend the particular through definition (by raising it to its universal essence through abstraction)
but, by treating it as an indication, allows for a glimpse of its
source of immanence.

It can now be seen why regulation, which constitutes the foundation of Confucian teaching, cannot be the object of religious
revelation: from the point of view of both Heaven and the Sage,
the coherence on which it depends is totally immanent; it corresponds to nature. It is also understandable why it cannot be the
object of any definition: to harmonize with the ever-changing
course of things (which is the source of its constant equilibrium),
it is in an unending process of change and can thus not be delim-
ited by a formulation with a fixed and definitive content. By contrast, the smallest detail lets us catch a glimpse of it. This is why
a statement of the following kind, which on the surface might
appear banal (or be misunderstood as having a merely psychological interest), expresses it:

> The Master was mild, and yet dignified; majestic, and yet not fierce;
> respectful, and yet easy. (7.37)

The three statements pivot around the same word, "yet," which is
an "empty word" (er^j), implying both opposition and simultaneity. In the first and third clauses, it sets off two opposed qualities;
in the second, it allows the named quality to remain at its opti-
mum without succumbing to excess. Also, in each case, it is the

same meaning that is extended; or rather, it is not so much a meaning as an effect of balance, constantly renewed: each formulation does not progress in relation to the one that precedes it; nor does it repeat it — it varies it. And none of the formulations are conclusive. From one to the other, there is a continuous shifting; equal distance is maintained as the formulations gravitate around a single center — the Sage's equilibrium. This equilibrium is apparent in every aspect of his behavior, including what he says and what he establishes ("rituals and music"); and the palpable harmony that results from it (*wen-zhang*^{k}) reveals the foundation of the real (this bottomless depth from which everything springs). In Chinese terms, it illuminates the way of Heaven (the Tao), which — because it never deviates — endlessly pursues its course and renews life.

Conversely, the danger of any *deviation* — in causing us to tip in one direction or another — is that it puts us out of phase with the course of things. In causing us to sink into a particular orientation, which renders us partial (resulting in our adopting a single character trait or opinion), it obstructs our ability to evolve (and this barrier is bad because it goes against the very nature of the real, which is to be in process). The following statement indicates this point of view:

> There were four things from which the Master was entirely free. He had no foregone conclusions, no arbitrary pre-determinations, no obstinacy and no egotism. (9.4)

Once again we must be on guard against psychologizing these terms or reducing their range by a moralizing interpretation. I do not believe that this quote is saying that the Master was full of "empty ideas" (*yi*^{l}) or "unfounded ideas" (which, as far as I can see, is obvious), although it has recently been translated that way:

THERE IS NO PLANE OF ESSENCES

rather, it is that he has no ideas at all; that is, he approaches the real without any definite aim or preconceived notions. Furthermore, there are no "shoulds"[m] incumbent on him; he acknowledges no categorical necessities that predetermine his behavior: this can be seen in Confucius's refusal to share the intransigence on principles of his disciple Zilu (see *Analects* 17.5 and 17.7). By prejudging the course of things, this arbitrary predetermination leads to the stagnation inherent in habit and fixation: if this "obstinacy" (gu^n) is a failing, and perhaps the only real one, it is a case not of our being tempted by evil (Chinese thought is free of all demonism) but of our letting ourselves be trapped in privileging one orientation over all others and being unable to go beyond it. Finally, it is not that Confucius is without "egoism" ($wu\ wo^o$); rather, because he rejects ready-made opinions and established imperatives, he is linked to no position, and nothing can particularize his personality. Moreover, commentators have noted how this kind of statement forms a logical chain: ordinarily, the preconceived idea gives rise to a projection of imperatives, which force us to adopt a certain position that ultimately constitutes our individual "I"; this "I" then gives birth to ideas, and the cycle continues. This is the vicious circle of individuality. By not privileging anything in advance and by refusing all prejudice, the Sage is able to give free rein to the power of immanence and to identify himself, through it, with nature: this is why in him the regulation of behavior is spontaneous and why he can remain at ease even when grave.

The only fixed rules of wisdom are to be without fixed rules — this is why there is no rule but regulation — and to maintain one's complete availability (see *Analects* 14.41). For the Sage, this availability remains in force even when it is judged, from the outside, as a form of opportunism (see *Analects* 14.34) and even when others have nothing good to say about him (9.2; compare 8.19) or nothing to say about him at all (7.18). He is without character and without quality, because what is not individuated cannot be named. Other wise men fall into mutually exclusive categories: they either stand by their integrity or display tolerance; they either take refuge in their ideal or accept compromise; they either withdraw from the world in disgust or collude with it. By contrast, Confucius is aware of being opposed to them all precisely because he is *without position* and "can" therefore take either position,[p] depending on the situation (18.8). Nor will he ever, out of habit, be cruel or lax. According to the terms of the alternative among which all educated Chinese must choose, Confucius is as ready "when called to office, to undertake its duties," as he is "when not so called, to lie retired" (7.10); he sets his mind neither on nor against anything in advance (4.10). He educates himself wherever he is: when in the company of worthy men, he thinks of equaling them; when with the worthless, he turns inward, toward himself (4.17 and 7.21). This is why his personality is unfettered, his mind undogmatic, and he himself undefinable.

Here is the progress along the path of wisdom: there are those with whom one can "study" but with whom it is not possible to pursue the "way"; there are those with whom one can pursue the way but with whom it is not possible to get "established"; finally, there are those with whom one can become established but who are unable to "weigh *occurring events*"[q] (9.30). This becoming established, or stability, which alone allows a person to find his or her foundation and acquire consistency, must itself be overcome: as Confucius states, the ultimate stage of moral education is reached when one is capable of assessing a circumstance and being renewed through it (which Mencius will make explicit [7.2.25[r]]). Instead of hardening in a fixed attitude, true plenitude opens to becoming.

Two consequences flow from this view of wisdom and the discourse that expresses it. On the one hand, since it preaches a form

of adaptability that allows for no immobility and requires that circumstance be the ultimate determinant, Confucian thought rejects, on principle, any search for definition (which could only be
the search for the identical through the difference of moments
and situations). Confucian thought therefore leads to no truth;
there is no quality that it can abstract as essence to be constituted
as generality. At the same time, because it refuses to isolate itself
in a particular determination, remains ever open to various possibilities, and — by its impartiality — encompasses all positions, this
wisdom is characterized by nonexclusivity. The originality of
Confucius is that he is nonsectarian. His sole true singularity is
that he is without singularity. In other words, the perfect operation of this regulatory principle causes Confucius to coincide with
the immanence at work in the real; this is why the Sage ultimately
merges with Heaven (in Chinese thought, the transcendence of
Heaven in relation to man does not proceed from an exterior
source: it is but the totalization of the immanent in the world).
Rather than striving for *generality*, Confucian thinking insists on
globality.

Of all Confucius's statements, this is the most important. The
Master, finally, will explain everything:

> The Master said: "Shan [Shen], my doctrine is that of an all-
> pervading unity." The disciple Tsang [Zeng] replied, "Yes."
> The Master went out, and the *other* disciples asked, saying, "What do
> his words mean?" Tsang [Zeng] said, "The doctrine of our Master is
> to be true to the principles of our nature and the benevolent exercise
> of them to others, — this and nothing more." (4.15)

As we can see, the Master, in fact, says nothing (that is, nothing in particular). Yet it is precisely in saying nothing in particular

243

that he says what needs to be said and abides within globality. There is another passage in *Analects* in which this idea of a pervasive unity at the heart of the Master's teaching is again expressed, this time about knowledge; however, the disciple Confucius addresses is unable immediately to grasp his meaning, which occurs almost beyond language, as Master Zeng shows (15.2). Thus we have two examples of Confucius's offering, for the intuition of his disciples, the key to his teaching. But what kind of unity is he speaking of? Not a unity achieved through abstraction but, as he says, one that proceeds through "threading"[s] (the image is of the thread used to tie together ancient Chinese money). In other words, the purpose of this unity is not to subsume the various aspects of things by collecting them in a single category but to allow them to communicate from within. When Master Zeng, to enlighten the others, speaks of "be[ing] true to the principles of our nature" and "the benevolent exercise of them to others," it is not — as has often been misunderstood — to give this unity an approximate moral content; instead, as the commentator Hu Guang notes, he uses these statements to illustrate two opposing terms (one about oneself, the other about others), both of which are pervaded by the same necessity. What we learn is that, instead of remaining isolated, the various "ends" by which we approach the Master's teachings are internally linked because they refer to the same principle. The gloss on this point, because of its conceptual value, needs to be examined closely: "The Sage's consciousness has an overall coherence," which does not form a totality, "from which the harmony of the whole proceeds" "through its adaptation to all situations," or "from all angles"; but its "applicability is different in each case."[t] Thus, regardless of the angle from which the Master's teaching comes, we always discover this (same) globality. Envisaging the relationship from the other side, we can also say that, while continually modifying his discourse and particularizing the object, modulating it in relation to his interlocutor and the occasion, Confucius essentially says nothing particular or different. Instead, there is always this regulation, incarnated in the variation of his words, which is the way of Heaven.

A formula found in the ancient *Book of Changes* summarizes this intuition well (it could also have been used as an epigraph to this book):

> Words are twisted but reach the center
> Things are both flaunted and hidden.[u7]

As this kind of formulation invites us to do, let us take this obvious parallelism and tie together the two ends of the phrase: only a circuitous use of the word, by its very variety, can hit the bull's-eye, revealing that which constantly conceals the obvious. What justifies this detour, the commentator explains, is that "everything is in transformation" and that "there is no possible (stereotypical) model":[v] the real can therefore not be thought of via definite forms, in other words, by abstracting an essence. As formulated by Chinese thought, the opposition is not between two levels of the real, that of being and becoming or sensible appearance and truth, but, as the commentator says, between the unending flaunting of things, which, as such, is distinct, and the "eminently subtle internal coherence" that makes this process possible.[w] The logic of this process can thus be conceived of not by using a fixed — and therefore isolable — formula but only by taking into account its sequence. And this is precisely what occurs in *The Book of Changes*, by making use of the mechanism appropriate to it.[8] It defines the course of things not according to a single model but through its *variations*, and thus necessarily "at an angle" (*qu*[x]), by passing through one or another of the figures embodying its phases (the series of trigrams or hexagrams changing into each other); at the same time, each diagram, such as it appears at the moment of choice, gives us a cutaway view of the totality of immanence at work in this process.

Between *detour* and *center,* we find the empty word *er,*[y] "at the same time as." I believe this means that detour leads to the bull's-eye but not only as an outcome; more essentially, it must express the simultaneity of opposites (as in the expression quoted above, where revealing and concealing occur simultaneously): while always in the process of taking a detour — since the figures are constantly changing into each other, constituting what in Greek terms would be called the idea of the process, or *eidos* — one is also always on target, whatever the envisaged figure, and one embraces the process in its totality. Equally, the circuit on which the evolving discourse of *Analects* takes us constantly reveals the overall necessity of regulation (which forms the center of the real — as it does of wisdom). Regulation, remember, can only be conceived of globally. In other words, since there is no split between the indication (the concrete) and what it reveals (the abstract) — and it in this way differs, as I have shown, from the symbol in imagery and the definition in theory — through its localized details, this discourse, which is always indicative, keeps us in the totality it is trying to express. There is thus simultaneously detour and access: detour by the multiple angles of entry, which form an endless circuit; and access, as each angle, by raising a "corner," reveals the overall *coherence* that is globality (see *Analects* 7.8).

Just as the poetic word in Chinese culture can be read as an allusion (most often an insidious one) and in this way remain evasive in order to suggest the infinity of a state of the soul (or, what is the same thing, an all-encompassing atmosphere), the word of the Sage is simultaneously global and modulated (its variety being a function of a different approach or interlocutor). When, among the various answers he gives to the question of filial piety, Confucius

THERE IS NO PLANE OF ESSENCES

replies, "not being disobedient" (2.5) to a great nobleman, he certainly is sending an ad hominem warning; nevertheless, the commentator Zhu Xi explains, "the Sage's word is global, and it is as though it were spoken not only in regard to great noblemen" (who had a tendency in Lu to usurp princely power). "This is why," Zhu Xi adds, "it is surely the word of the Sage."[z] By the same token, he notes elsewhere, although the Sage gives different answers to different questioners about the meaning of humanness, including what may appear to be a joke to his last interlocutor (see *Analects* 12.3), his word "is never different at the outset."[aa] This is so because each of his words "gets to the bottom of all meanings"[bb] and because the Sage "does not have two statements at the outset"[cc] (Cheng Yi, commentary on 13.19).

This "at the outset" is important. While the word as definition strives for universality, the word as indication proceeds from universality. In the one case, universality constitutes the aim (telos), in the other, the source. Socratic generality or Confucian globality: definition, on the one hand, modulation, on the other; their differing strategies are based on this difference of modes of universality.[9] Generality can be defined, globality cannot. Instead, one becomes aware of, realizes. Definition causes one to know, modulation brings about realization.[10] But what does *realize* imply beyond a simple form of knowing? Perhaps we should extend the question to answer it: What is it that makes such an act of realization indispensable, how does it condition access to wisdom, and what is the process by which it comes about? To answer this, we must envisage the experience from the other side, that is, from the disciple's standpoint; and to do so, we must proceed from Confucius to Mencius, his principal successor in the eyes of tradition.

<label>247</label>

Chapter Eleven

Advancing Toward Maturation:

The Leap of Realization

We must proceed with caution. The danger in pursuing this type of comparison is that one might immobilize the opposition, allowing the noted contrast to develop into a difference of principle while losing sight of the complexity of the phenomena imagined. This cannot but occur when one abandons the concrete plane on which these phenomena are situated: in this case, that of the strategies of meaning and the various effects that can be drawn from them. The danger, in short, is that one might limit the Chinese to the absolute role of the other, and thereby form a simplistic, ideologically questionable vision of a difference in spirit or mentality. We find this in regard to the indirect. Plato, whom Westerners so easily consider one of the great representatives of the Western theoretical tradition, warns of the "indicative" nature of his remarks (I take the term directly from him). Only a few, he states in *Letter 7*, "are capable of discovering the truth for themselves," "with a little guidance" (*dia smikras endeixeōs*) (341E); as for the others, it would be vain, even improper, to try to transmit the sublimity of such lessons to them.[1] And, in fact, a number of commentators — notably, René Schaerer and Alexandre Koyré — draw our attention in this direction. They are keen to demonstrate that Platonic dialogue possesses a subtle organization that, through the effects of pause and contrast, suggests other relations; hence, they maintain, it should be considered a "system of allusions" to a thought "that is situated beyond the here and now," which the reader must discover. Even in Plato, the great master of the Western *logos*, "it is not only the overall conclusions, but the entire concatenation of ideas that most often eludes direct expression."[2]

Letter 7, which appears recognizably in the hand of Plato, actually sketches a general theory of the indirect. Of the various means to knowledge described, including names, definitions, and representations, none is satisfying: each lacks firmness, or stability (*to-bebaion*), to articulate the constant in-itself nature of things; at the same time, when couched in written words, each is too fixed and rigid to seize the indefinitely moving aspect of things. Only after "rubbing" these means to knowledge "laboriously" against each other can consciousness progressively raise itself to the level of science. The latter, consequently, cannot transmit itself as such; a personal experience is necessary. What "preoccupies" it, Plato concludes, and that to which it "applies itself" is impossible to put into words, as is the case with other objects of knowledge: "Acquaintance with it must come rather after a long period of attendance on instruction in the subject itself and of close companionship, when, suddenly, like a blaze kindled by a leaping spark, it is generated in the soul and at once becomes self-sustaining" (341C–D).

A long period of "close companionship" (*sunousia*, initially through assiduous contact with the Master), then a sudden spark of light — as if through a "leaping spark" (*apo puros pedesantos*): we find these two successive phrases and their images used by Mencius to describe access to wisdom. People often compare Mencius with Plato for the role he played in the Chinese tradition: Mencius, Confucius's successor, in the fourth century B.C., would have been in a position analogous to Plato's in regard to Socrates (see Chad Hansen's work on the possibilities of this parallel).[3] But how far can we take this comparison? What appears merely a digression in Plato (with an apologetic design) in the late and marginal text of *Letter 7* (so late and marginal that its authenticity was long questioned, by, for example, Hermanus Thomas Karsten and Constantin Ritter) is found at the heart of Mencius. What we find here is more than a difference of accent or proportion; such a dissymmetry entails a change in perspective. In short, though real and undeniable, this coincidence allows us better to measure the difference — the path that is merely sketched in the one is broadly exploited in the other. This *possibility* of the indirect, which is not completely foreign to Platonism, though the dialectical enterprise of Platonism necessarily turned the philosopher's gaze away from it, or at least led him not to pursue it further, which, however, does not signify a lack on his part, serves the Chinese as a common intuition and underpinning of thought. With Mencius, it emerges from its obviousness to be more closely considered. Hence reading Mencius offers an opportunity better to understand how wisdom is separated from philosophy. In witnessing the birth of philosophical dispute in his time, he ostensibly attempts, using the resources of the indirect, to break free from it.

The Chinese tend to think of the process of apprenticeship as a *maturation* (rather than as an intellection). For Mencius, this idea of maturation is much more than a simple image: he uses the motif of maturation to account for the hidden advancement by which an internal progress takes place, the result of which appears to have been attained indirectly. Early on, the question posed involves the workings of morality (*Mencius* 2.1.2).[4] He who wishes to nurture his moral personality, Mencius states, should not expect to achieve this end by incidental acts of righteousness, for morality is not a place one can "attack" from the outside,[a] through a successful operation; rather, it is the fruit of a long "accumulation."[b] The phenomenon is of the order of a continuous growth and not of a taking, which remains adventitious and presupposes something external. In other words, it cannot be touched like an object. It is impossible to lay hold of it; one must allow it to happen by giving it time to unfold. Hence the double recommendation, whose rigorous formulation should be studied closely, on which Mencius insists: in regard to everything one wants to learn, it is necessary to "take care of things" but without striving to arrive "directly" at one's goal (zheng[c]).[5] Furthermore, Mencius states, one should neither "forsake" it, by being unconcerned, nor "help" it to grow, by forcing its development.

One should apply oneself assiduously *and* restrain oneself from "anticipating" the result (see Zhu Xi[d]), give oneself over to the task while allowing the process to follow its natural course, obey its rhythm. Through the fecund tension of this twofold process, Mencius expresses something that everyone feels acutely but that is difficult to explain: the need for personal involvement combined with openness (in regard to the process) if one is to progress and the need for an apprenticeship to be diligent and natural, both exacting and easygoing. Mencius illustrates this idea by a now-famous apologue. A man of Song was grieved that his young plants were not growing quickly enough and began to pull at them to force them to grow. On returning home, he told his family of all the pains he had taken; when his children ran to the field, they saw that the plants had all withered. "There are few in the world *who do not deal with their passion-nature as if* they were assisting the corn to grow," concludes Mencius (2.1.2). In general, people either are negligent, deem all effort useless, and neglect to weed their corn, or they assist it to grow, like the man who pulled out his plants.

252

We see the meaning of the image of growth here. Progress is based on an individual's thinking—not in terms of action (either autonomous or voluntary) but in terms of transformation (both discrete and widespread): even when transformation takes place within ourselves, even when the apprenticeship is concentrated, the evolution set into play depends on factors other than those we anticipated, and it surpasses our initiatives. In many respects, this process is not visible to us. Although it lacks the spectacular quality of action, which is striking in its immediacy, it alone is efficacious. All progress takes place in silence. Hence it would be an "error" "directly to assist" an event,[e] notes the commentator Zhu Xi; it would be as much of an error to lose interest in the process. In other words, intervention can only be indirect, but it must be timely. It consists in favoring the process through propitious conditioning (such as weeding a plant) without, however, attempting to determine its course or to project one's expectations onto it (such as by pulling on it). Help, in short, is too direct and too manipulative; one cannot help a plant to grow, but one can—and indeed one should—help it to flourish through attentive care.

Another image used to express the naturalness of the phenomenon is flowing water. It is an image favored by Mencius, as by all ancient Chinese thinkers (see *Mencius* 7.1.24 and 4.2.18). "Flowing water is a thing which does not proceed till it has filled the hollows *in its course*," Mencius states, just as the "student who has set his mind on the doctrines *of the sage*, does not advance to them but by completing one lesson after another" without attempting to learn other things. The ability to penetrate with the mind is the result of accumulation and passage, progressing little by little. "When one has enough [clarity] on a given point," says one commentator, "he proceeds to the next passage."[f] It is therefore impossible to skip stages and force comprehension. But once it has filled a hollow, water overflows into itself and continues, carried on by its own momentum: similarly, based on the things that have become clear to us through effort, the light we have acquired spreads and communicates through our spirits, *sponte sua*.

A Tang emperor charged a music Master to help one of his musicians make progress. Let him leave his instrument, replied the Master, and go far away. When he returns, I will instruct him. This is what experience teaches us, fundamentally, in any apprenticeship. We struggle for a long time to play our scales, and then one day, without our being aware of it, the fingers become more supple, our playing becomes less awkward, and it starts to come to us; or the lesson learned with difficulty the evening before appears easy and clear the next morning. It took continuous and patient effort, but we have the impression that progress has been made unbeknownst to us, by its own efficacity, set into play by the process. The sudden ease we acquire does not appear a direct result of this interior process; we experience it as coming from elsewhere — outside our control — not from some mythic elsewhere, such as the Western concept of inspiration puts into play, but from that other resource beyond our intentions and efforts, represented by the inherent logic of the process under way. It is as if we were carried along by its unfolding. This "comes to us," as they say; in other words, a transformation takes place during an apprenticeship (maturation) that one could not have foreseen and that only becomes possible if one allows oneself to be directed by it — while at the same time one makes an effort — to allow it to do its work. Chinese thought emphasized what *comes* in this way because it strove to express the idea of immanence. And the Master's remarks are but indications because he also counts on their spontaneous unfolding: their power to incite is fundamental, as is our perseverance, but (theng) access to wisdom occurs by itself.

This idea of accessing wisdom through indirect influence and natural unfolding, rather than through speech, is at the forefront of the five modes of teaching listed in *Mencius* (7.1.40). The first way a superior man effects his teaching, in fact, is comparable to the transformation that takes place "like seasonable rain." "With vegetation," the commentator notes, "once he has sown the seed and unearthed the plants, man has completed his efforts and the transformation can only take place of its own accord; what is missing is the beneficial impregnation of the rain or dew; when this shower takes place, the transformation is hastened. The subtlety of the process of teaching is of the same order" (such is the ideal represented in the teachings of Confucius, according to Yan Hui and Master Zeng. Next in this typology, according to Mencius, come the cases in which a Master perfects the virtue of a disciple, some of whose talents he assists in developing. It is not until the fourth case that teaching takes place through "inquiries he answers": this case corresponds to the situation of the less talented disciples (such as Fan Chi with Confucius and Wan Zhang in *Mencius*). The fifth case is set apart from the others: in the absence of a direct transmission of wisdom, the disciple attempts to perfect himself by helping himself with the things reported by others in the past; this is Mencius's situation, more than a century later, in relation to Confucius (see *Mencius* 4.2.22).

Teaching therefore functions as a beneficial factor favoring full development and not by virtue of a message or explanation: it works by a diffuse and discrete absorption, effected through osmosis, as from a propitious environment. Speech proves of the same order as action (such as pulling out the corn); neither one can make corn grow. There is consequently no room in this pedagogy for dialectics or even the rhetorical effort of persuasion. And yet the ancient Chinese also engaged in the art of debate (especially after the fourth century B.C. and during the third century).

255

The followers of Mozi, in particular, developed, outside the sphere of letters, techniques of argumentation that endeavored to convince; they sought to defend their principles through rational debate. As opposed to the Confucians, they were interested in science as well as logic and even technique (and their social origin was different, too: no doubt they came from the world of artisans instead of the courts of princes). They used precise definitions, shaped alternatives, and rigorously codified the relationships among ideas. Their dialogues are impersonal, since, in their eyes, the validity of an idea should be independent of the person articulating it and the listener; through philosophical dispute (embodied in the concept $bian^h$), they strove for a certitude abstracted from all context and atemporal. Here, at last, we find ourselves close to the Greek idea of truth.

But their endeavor was not continued. Not until the beginning of the twentieth century, after their encounter with Western thought, did the Chinese become interested in logical formalization. Yet by then, it had been so covered up by classical tradition that the texts treating it survive only in fragments (which have been admirably reconstructed by A.C. Graham). One cannot understand such an occultation without taking into account the reluctance of scholars faced with this other possible orientation. Certainly Mencius was aware of the newly formed demands of philosophical discussion, and in this way, his oeuvre differs from that of Confucius, but he does everything in his power to subsume it. To a disciple who informs Mencius of his reputation for being "fond of disputing," Mencius replies, "Indeed, I am not fond of dispution, but I am compelled to do it" (3.2.9). There follows a comprehensive justification presenting the first tableau of a history of Chinese civilization. This civilization is marked, Mencius explains, by alternating periods of order and disorder. In the time of the first kings, water flooded the world, and men were reduced

to a precarious condition; thus Yu was charged with digging chan-
nels to conduct the waters of the seas and with forcing the wild
animals to the confines. With the disappearance of the first kings,
the ancient wisdom fell into decline, and the princes thought only
of their pleasures and made the earth unlivable once more. From
this came the necessity for a new return to order, marked by the
advent of Zhou, who punished the evil princes and drove away the
dangers. Then, yet again, the world fell into decay, and immoral-
ity abounded: "perverse speaking" and "oppressive deeds" reappeared; there were "ministers who murdered their sovereigns"
and "sons who murdered their fathers." Confucius, "afraid" of the
situation, composed *Spring and Autumn Annals* (in an attempt to
reform the world). Then the princes gave free rein to their lusts,
unemployed scholars indulged in unreasonable discussions, and
evil reigned. All spoke falsely and contrarily and filled the world
with their debates; on the one hand, the Mohists (the followers of
Mozi) propounded a general altruism at odds with filial devotion,
while others (the followers of Yang Zhu) propounded "each one
for himself," which did not acknowledge the claims of the sovereign. What can Mencius do, in turn "afraid" by such a situation,
except claim, "If the principles of Yang [Yang Zhu] and Mo [Mozi]
be not stopped and the principles of Confucius not set forth, then
those perverse speakings will delude the people, and stop up *the
path* of benevolence and righteousness"?

During the course of this development, Mencius's deftness lies
in his placing himself alongside the Sages who intervene periodically in the world to restore order; he thereby situates himself on
a level completely other than that of his adversaries at the heart of
philosophical debate. His work is presented merely as one of regulation that has become his responsibility by necessity, without his
having to take a personal stance or defend an idea. There is even
an internal logic, he says, that naturally leads from unorthodox

ideas to the scholar's position and thus makes discussion on the scholar's part superfluous: "Those who are fleeing from *the errors of* Mo [Mozi] [general altruism] naturally turn to Yang [Yang Zhu], and those who are fleeing from *the errors of* Yang [Yang Zhu] [unconditional egoism] naturally turn to orthodoxy. When they so turn, they should at once and simply be received. Those who nowadays dispute with the followers of Yang [Yang Zhu] and Mo [Mozi] do so as if they were pursuing a stray pig, the leg of which, after they have got it to enter the pen, they proceed to tie" (7.2.26). In other words, any discussion is excessive: there is a necessity inherent to the evolution of a person that leads him to balance extremes; and this process of maturation, in itself, becomes complete.

By avoiding discussion, Mencius basically dispenses with the treatment of truth. Rather than formulate a theory, he reconfigures the debate according to an ensemble of positions — the adequacy of his own becoming sufficiently manifest in his placing himself at the center, the point where counterbalancing takes place and immanence occurs. By virtue of this fact, and rather than relying on argumentation, which tries to prove something, his discourse proceeds indirectly, through an effect of montage; instead of furnishing an explicit refutation, it operates obliquely, letting its proposition fall into place like a mechanism. Proof of this may be found in the way one is supposed to read the long history of civilization that serves to justify him. The montage effect consists, first of all, in a simple alignment. Lined up one after another, the epochs of order and disorder create a sense of alternation that, given the current crisis, implies the necessity of renewal. Without this needing to be proved, the role Mencius attributes to himself is integrated into the logic of the whole, which suffices to indicate its merit: Mencius is "afraid," as was Confucius before him; he routs out disorder, as did the ancient kings before him. Certainly the nature of the disorder has changed; it has become more and more ideological, but the necessity of intervention remains. It is even ineluctable.

Mencius, moreover, has no need of a conclusion. The parallel perspective is enough to show, through the superposition with which it culminates, not only that Mencius intervenes by the same claim as the previous Sages but also, by going backward (and through the play of canonical citations, no. 12), that these Sages, in his place, would have rebuffed the unorthodox doctrines that were causing people to forget filial loyalty and respect for the sovereign (the errors of the followers of Yang Zhu and Mozi). Through the sheer force of comparison, the ancient sovereigns thus vouch for his authority. Mencius's position is also bolstered by an opposition of registers: confronted with the proliferation of theories and, consequently, of controversies, Mencius makes one forget that he is using words by assimilating himself to the task, renewed epoch after epoch, of restoring the world. In particular, he proceeds from a deft reconfiguration of roles. How else are we to accept that the reestablishment of order to which he aspires, in the epoch of philosophical disputes, is analogous to the reformation of the world at the time of the flood? To assure this transition, Mencius has Confucius, his great precursor, play a pivotal role. Surprisingly, Confucius is presented merely as "author" (of *Spring and Autumn Annals*; see above, chapter 5), in such a way, clearly, as to prefigure Mencius's role as scholar (Mencius earlier notes that it was as an author that Confucius would have wished to be judged for better or worse; therefore, it is normal that, as a scholar, Mencius will be misunderstood and criticized). It was during Confucius's time, indeed, that disorder allegedly tipped from the natural to the ideological and spread to discourse. Confucius's intervention would lead to a complete reversal. We are told at first that Confucius, "afraid," drew up the annals; later, when the annals were completed, it was the others who were "afraid": from this simple comparison, we glean that Confucius's intervention on the literary level was as efficacious as the previous remakings of the world. How not to deduce that it would be the same for the works of Mencius, since he has taken up the torch?[6]

Another essential reconfiguration is found in the positions of the altruists (Mozi) and the egoists (Yang Zhu), who are presented as antagonists sharing the same extremism. Not only are they forced together as counterparts (this especially undermines Yang Zhu, a theorist of individualism and the first to articulate the naturalness of tendencies who either inspired or, at the very least, influenced Mencius); but this very conjoining simultaneously razes the polemical field and self-destructs (since all of these discourses, Mencius says, refer back to one or the other of these positions): by the contradictions it illuminates, this coupling leads the positions to cancel each other out (like so many deviations). All this montage, in short, and without it being explicitly stated, leads to the idea that Mencius's words, in fact, are not mere words, that Mencius is not a wrangler but a Sage. This culminates in the idea that Mencius is both in the philosophical arena and outside it: while the others spout nonsense, arguing for and against, he proceeds with the regulation of the world. There is neither initiative here (which might make his intervention appear arbitrary) nor a personal point of view (which might render his position partial): he is merely reacting to the state of things, yet, in introducing nothing in particular into them, he coincides with the immanent logic that leads to their resolution.

Greek literature also knew this art of montage. Pindar's odes, such as *Olympian II*, reveal a general signification set apart from their mere composition (see the analyses of Gilbert Norwood and Aimé Puech). In *Agamemnon*, Aeschylus does not judge the prince directly, but in his handling of contrasts, pauses, and reminders, he nonetheless makes his case before the spectator. There remains, however, a manifest difference, which stems from Mencius's openly assuming the position of philosopher and *thereby* participating in the theoretical debate. In not sufficiently taking into account this method (because they expected Mencius's argumentation to be explicit), many Western sinologists have articulated disappointment in his work, deeming him "an unoriginal thinker." His method of presentation, stripped of convincing reasoning, is considered limited to moralistic banalities. The Chinese tradition has nevertheless made him, especially in the last millennium, one of its principal sources of inspiration. Do we therefore need to learn how to read him?

I shall begin with the simplest example:

> When Ch'î [Qi] was suffering from famine, Ch'an Tsin [Chen Zhen] said *to Mencius*, "The people are all thinking that you, Master, will again ask the granary of the T'ang [Tang] be opened for them. I apprehend you will not do so a second time." *Mencius* said, "To do it would be to act like Fang Fû [Feng Fu]. There was a man of that name in Tsin [Jin], famous for his skill in seizing tigers. Afterwards he became a scholar of reputation, and going once out to the wild country, he found the people all in pursuit of a tiger. The tiger took refuge in a corner of a hill, where no one dared to attack him, but when they saw Fang Fû [Feng Fu], they ran and met him. Fang Fû [Feng Fu] *immediately* bared his arms, and descended from the carriage. The multitude were pleased with him, but those who were scholars laughed at him." (7.2.23)

The episode is self-contained. In rolling up his sleeves to attack the tiger, as the crowd urged him, Feng Fu returned to his first condition, departing from his new aspirations. Yet this apologue is not a fable (attempting to teach a general lesson): it is related by Mencius in response to a precise question — and in an urgent situation. Without commenting directly, Mencius implies his refusal to intervene again with the prince. It is up to his interlocutor to glean through the imagery the reasons justifying his retreat: the changes that might have occurred in his relations with the prince, by which his course of action is modified, as well as what reserve or liberty he might thereafter retain. Beneath the elegance of the response — which frees Mencius from an obligation without implicating the sovereign who is his host — we can glean a political reflection that deserves closer attention (see the commentary by Wang Fuzhi). That the public granaries were opened once, to grant an exceptional request, constitutes a humanitarian measure that is praiseworthy. But this could never be reenacted, because doing so would be a form of political management. If penury recurs, it is because production is poorly organized, taxes excessive, and the reserves insufficient; the goals of power have remained shortsighted and the country ill governed. Beyond this analysis, Mencius places us on guard: a true man of politics does not try to play the providential figure, even if this is expected by the crowd; he mistrusts the exceptional and the spectacular. In other words, good politics is not a matter of prowess, for if it were, it would ceaselessly renew itself — which is impossible. The mark of good politics is discretion; the more efficient it is, the less it allows itself to be seen — and thus to be praised. It would never, therefore, seek to cause a sensation or create an event. In this way, it is identified with the regulation of the world, in which immanence, continuously at work, passes unnoticed.

Instead of *explaining* (that is, making a theoretical point) that there exists a unity of wisdom, despite differences of time and place, that assures the continuity of civilization, the Master says:

Shun was an Eastern barbarian, he was born in Chu Feng [Zhufeng], moved to Fu Hsua [Fuxia], and died in Ming T'iao [Mingtiao]. King Wen was a Western barbarian; he was born in Ch'i Chou [Qizhou] and died in Pi Ying [Biying]. Their native places were over a thousand *li* apart, and there were a thousand years between them. Yet when they had their way in the Central Kingdom, their actions matched like the two halves of a tally. The standards of the two sages, one earlier and one later, were identical. (4.2.1)

The example is elementary but demonstrative. Through parallel presentation — in other words, lining up the two cases face-to-face — the demonstration takes effect: the maximum separation in space and time (East/West; before/after) enables comparison, and the unity becomes clear. There is no logical coordination (or syntactic conjunction); it is the correctness of the pairing, and the rigorousness of the framing, that serves as proof. This text is demonstrative not by constructing reasoning but *by arranging the elements*. *Mencius* often functions in this way, through a system of examples. Instead of forming a concept, it codifies a situation, making it typical; instead of listing reasons, it sets up opposing positions, whose values are placed in correlation. In short, instead of explaining an argument, it functions as *purview*.

One of the most delicate questions in Mencius's political thought involves the relationship between the prince and the scholar. When he is asked what principle governs his refusal to visit the princes, Mencius begins to cite examples from the past. In former times, unless in his employ, one did not approach a prince (the implication is that one waited to be called on). This leads to simplistic images of a man climbing over his wall to avoid his prince and a man bolting his door and not admitting him. Such an attitude, taken to this extreme, is exaggerated, Mencius recognizes. There follows an examination of a particular case from the

263

life of Confucius. A great lord who wanted to summon Confucius to see him but without disturbing the rules of etiquette watched and sent him a present when Confucius was not home. The latter was therefore forced to go thank him, and he likewise chose a moment when the other was not home. Lastly, there are citations that picturesquely demonstrate the moral cost of flattery. "By considering these *remarks*," concludes Mencius, "the *spirit* which the superior man nourishes may be known" (3.2.7).

Mencius thus does not directly answer the question put to him, nor does he say anything about himself (although his own conduct is being questioned); yet he implicitly defines his position through a succession of sketches (in which only others are mentioned). Through juxtaposition and difference, they form a system that constructs the answer. Mencius begins by leaning on past customs, a valid apriority, although he shows that a rule made from this can lead to excess; next he gives a specific example of balanced conduct, guaranteed by the personality of the Sage, which shows the importance of strategy (compare the strategy Mencius develops for himself in *Mencius* 2.2.2). He then completes the picture by indicating, through value judgments, the inverse excess of the initial reserve. The response as a whole seeks to strike a balance between narrow-mindedness and complacency, intransigence and dishonor. Yet such an equilibrium, always dependent on circumstances, cannot be defined and can only be appreciated according to the situation. Mencius sets out a series of cases rather than prescribe a certain type of behavior; the survey developed in the paragraph lets us feel its balance.

Since it ceaselessly changes according to the situation, the *golden mean* cannot be codified. This constantly central position, a veritable adaption that, as such, can never be immobilized (since it never ceases to embrace the renewal of things), cannot be transformed into truth. Following Confucius, Mencius imagines the profoundness of this. Let us return to the antagonism between the altruists and the egoists as construed by Mencius (7.1.26). Between the position of Yang Zhu, who would not be open to "plucking out a single hair" to benefit the whole kingdom, and that of Mozi, who was ready to sacrifice himself "from the crown to the heel" for it, the position of Zimo, in keeping to the center, would appear closer to the golden mean. But in fact, Mencius warns, "holding" to the center means not attaching oneself to it (the double meaning of zhi[i]) for doing so would immobilize it fatally. "Holding it without leaving room for different circumstances" (wu quan[j]) "becomes like their holding their one point": "it takes up one point and disregards one hundred others," and this does "injury" to the "way of right principle." In other words, the golden mean has nothing in common with the half measure (aurea mediocritas: what is needed is not too much); depending on the situation, it can correspond to one extreme or another (it can mean to "become resolutely engaged" as well as to "withdraw," according to the terms of the Chinese alternative, but it cannot waver).[7] Constant adaptation is therefore only possible through variation, through continuous balancing (regulation), and this is why no generalizations can be formed of any principles.

This refusal to theorize when constructing an argument is found even in the most elaborate debate in Mencius (6.1.1–6). The question asked is manifestly philosophical, since it bears on human nature and the status, inherent or not, of morality. In short, the speakers confront each other to defend their ideas. The dialogue begins as follows:

The philosopher Kâo [Gaozi] said, "Man's nature is like a ch'î [qi] willow, and righteousness is like a cup or a bowl. The fashioning of benevolence and righteousness out of man's nature is like the making of cups and bowls from the ch'î [qi] willow."

Mencius replied, "Can you, leaving untouched the nature of the willow, make with it cups and bowls? You must do violence and injury to the willow, before you can make cups and bowls with it. If you must do violence and injury to the willow in order to make cups and bowls with it, *on your principles* you must in the same way do violence and injury to humanity in order to fashion from it benevolence and righteousness! Your words, alas! would certainly lead all men on to reckon benevolence and righteousness to be calamities." (6.1.1)

A second movement is developed following a second analogy. Human nature, says the speaker to Mencius, is like whirling water: if an outlet is opened for it to the east, it flows to the east, and if an outlet is opened for it to the west, it flows to the west; human nature is as indifferent to good and evil as water is indifferent to east or west. Mencius takes up the comparison using his own terms. While the water is indeed indifferent to east or west, it is not so in relation to high and low: human nature tends toward good, just as water seeks low ground. Certainly water can be made to move upward, but this is contrary to its nature; when man is made to do what is not good, his nature has been treated likewise. The rest of the debate also uses analogies — but what can analogies prove? — and no other logical operation clarifies the discussion, such as a general definition of what is meant by *nature* (or by *internal* and *external* in it) or even a distinction between the subjective and the objective (compare the ambiguous meaning of *yue*[k] in *Mencius* 4.4) or between quality and essence, genus and species (compare *Mencius* 3). Furthermore, the opposing remarks do not really counter each other: the points where they diverge are not explained. The countering argument is reversed but without an examination to identify its erroneous aspects. Elsewhere in the first paragraph, for example, Mencius shows the dangers of the opposing argument in terms of its consequences without refuting it. There is no continuity between sequences: new images appear, other aspects are imagined without the demonstration progressing and without Mencius, who always has the last word, trying to draw a general advantage from the ground already gained. Lacking analysis and sequence, deduction and confrontation, the dialogue is philosophical in appearance only. In any case, it is not dialectical.

Two contrasting opinions are held by sinologists on this. Some, in an attempt to save the philosophical reputation of *Mencius*, have tried to uncover hidden links in it and to defend the analogical "method" in the name of the standards of the time (the path taken by D.C. Lau and, after him, A.C. Graham).[8] Others point out the invalidity of *Mencius* in terms of logic (Arthur Waley, for example, and more recently, Chad Hansen).[9] But I think it is appropriate to begin by asking about the purpose and objective of the supposed debate in *Mencius* (the question has already been posed by I.A. Richards).[10] No doubt these analogies are not intended to demonstrate; but in illustrating a point of view, they provide food for thought. Their goal is not to prove a truth but to *try out different positions*. According to one of the best Chinese commentators, Wang Fuzhi, Mencius "follows his interlocutor's remarks in order to poke holes in them, without ever showing him the essential — in order to apprise him of it," "for, according to the way the superior man treats an unorthodox opinion, when he has set into motion a series of distinctions and has then passed through a set of *aporiae*, that is enough."[11] Mencius merely parries — until his interlocutor has spent himself. But the essential comes into play beyond the discussion; it lies in the process of maturation, outside the confrontation.[12]

Is it possible for Mencius ever to engage directly in a controversy and make his position explicit? In the following, we have a Mohist, who, through the intermediary of a disciple, sought an interview with the Master. Mencius begins evasively, offering excuses: "I indeed wish to see him, but at present I am still unwell. When I am better, I will myself go and see him. He need not come here *again*" (3.1.5). But the other returns, and Mencius grants his request: "Today I am able to see him. But if I do not correct his errors, the *true* principles will not be fully evident." To "correct his errors,"[l] according to the ancient commentator Zhao Qi, means "to attack his adversary in expressing himself directly;"[m] according to a more orthodox commentator, Zhu Xi, it means "to express himself completely in order to correct the other."[n] Is Mencius, then, putting his trust in the power of discourse (and renouncing detour)? In fact, the way he then justifies his decision leads us to reconsider what he expects from such a discussion. Mencius has heard that his interlocutor is a Mohist. Contrary to the tendencies of the time, one of the principles most dear to the Mohists was nonparticipation in sumptuous funerals for one's parents. This fellow, like any good Mohist, therefore must purpose to reform the world on this point, because of his values. But did he not bury his parents sumptuously — and therefore contradict his principles? Mencius has noticed a gap in his interlocutor's position, and this is why he decides to speak to him. Given the insistence the Mohist placed on seeing him, as well as the inconsistency of his conduct and thus the impasse in his militancy, in which he finds himself cornered, Mencius is aware that he is prepared to abandon his position. Therefore, he has no need to convince him or elaborate fastidiously any arguments; the fruit is ripe and ready to fall. Once again, in the process of inner maturation, the role reserved for speech is minimal intervention.[13]

The inverse case exists as well. Mencius refuses to act as Master to an interlocutor not ready to hear him. After complaining of his natural inability to mend his ways, the son of a princely house tells

Mencius of his plan to ask the prince who is Mencius's host for lodging so that he can listen to his lessons. "The way of truth," Mencius replies, "is like a great road. It is not difficult to know it. The evil is only that men will not seek it. Go home and search for it, and you will have abundance of teachers" (6.2.2). By concerning himself with lodging, notes one commentator, this princely son, who is not sufficiently "invested," betrays too little passion; furthermore, his facile grievances about his ineptitude indicate that he has not yet renounced his passivity or realized that everything depends on effective conduct — man being what he makes of himself. It is useless, under these circumstances, to listen to a Master: he is still too far away, in his personal itinerary, to be able to profit from it.

An illustrious precedent of this refusal to teach is in Confucius's *Analects*:

> Zû Pei [Ru Bei] wished to see Confucius, but Confucius declined, on the ground of being sick, to see him. When the bearer of this message went out at the door, (the master) took his lute and sang to it, in order that Pei [Bei] might hear him. (17.20)

We might be shocked that the Master uses such a strategy (or that his disciples considered it worthy of reporting). Proof is given, in any case, that speech is free from the duty of sincerity; nor is it ironic (for Confucius is not pretending). Yet his demonstration gains force from its indirection. Rhetoric also strives toward manipulation, but here manipulation takes place through a refusal of discourse: in staging his ostensible refusal to speak to him, Confucius invites his interlocutor to look into himself. The process is sufficiently classic for Mencius to desire to make a principle out of it: "There are many arts in teaching. I refuse, as inconsistent with my character, to teach a man, but I am only thereby still teaching him" (6.2.16).

269

Engaging in controversy only to diffuse it or abruptly sending away the petitioner so that he might look into himself — these are examples of not counting on speech to operate as instruction and in this way disappointing the listener's expectations so as to favor his awakening. The seeds of the procedures that Chan Buddhism (Zen in Japan), after the eighth century in China, made so spectacular by their disconcerting aspect are already found in *Mencius*. *Mencius* can even illuminate the logic of these procedures — although Westerners continue to see them through the lens of a fascinating exoticism. Could one have gone from the progressive and linear dialogues of the primitive Chan, imported from India, to the disruptive forms of exchange popularized by the classic Chan had the latter not been quietly fraught with the anti-discursive (but thereby highly concentrated) intention found very early in the scholarly tradition? The Chan Master always answers with an aside, a cry, by striking a stick, or by simply walking away: so many "blows," as in a game, that pierce the infinite cloth of language; so many "towers" to shake the faith; so many oblique routes to unfetter consciousness.[14] As we have seen, the question comes not from the idea that the truth is ineffable but from the idea that one loses adaptability as soon as one becomes attached to the truth. The Master's remarks are always merely an *incitement*. We have yet to understand, to return to *Mencius*, how this incitement is used to spark the consciousness to realization.

How, based on the advancement of maturation, whose progression to some extent escapes volition, can realization occur deep within consciousness if not by bursting open like a sudden result, in apparent rupture with the preceding continuity — as if by a leap? The image, as noted, is found incidentally in Plato "like a blaze kindled by a leaping spark." It is also found at the core of one paragraph in *Mencius* to account for access to wisdom.

A disciple complains of the arduousness of Mencius's teaching: "Lofty are your principles and admirable, but *to learn them* may well be likened to ascending the heavens, — something which cannot be reached. Why not *adapt your teachings so as to* cause learners to consider them attainable, and so daily exert themselves!" (7.1.41) Mencius first answers by defending his demands: if someone is a poor workman, a great craftsman will not alter or put aside the marking line; by the same token, if someone is a poor marksman, a good archer will not modify his own drawing of the bow. In other words, it is not a question of lowering the way to bring it within the reach of others; it is up to them to gain access to it. Next he continues with this image of drawing the bow, a common one in ancient China, and in *Mencius* in particular, to evoke the apprenticeship to wisdom (see *Mencius* 2.1.7 and 6.1.20): "The superior man draws [the bow], without releasing [the arrow]. As if by a leap,° he follows the path of equilibrium and holds fast to it. Those who are able follow him" (7.1.41).[15]

The path of wisdom, we are told once more, is equilibrium and regulation (which manifests constancy through variation: this is why the superior man is not attached to it, like an object, but rather holds himself to it firmly, as to a path). The image of drawing the bow is significant because it emphasizes the importance of *positioning*: if the relative positions of the shot are in all aspects correct, what follows (attaining the goal) occurs *sponte sua*. The commentator Zhu Xi is specific on this point:

As if in a leap: as if in a leap [this] surges forth. Following what was said before about the tension in the bow. This signifies that to instruct others, the superior man transmits the method of learning to them but does not inform them of the subtlety needed to reach [the result], just as the archer draws the bow but does not discharge the arrow. Yet the thing he does not tell them, already, as if by a leap, is manifested before them.

The paradox is merely apparent: the Master demonstrates how to prepare oneself, not how to succeed; but from the complete balancing of conditions, there "already" surges the "subtlety" of "attainment" — which is impossible to communicate (see *Mencius* 7.2.5). The "already" is important because it balances out the initial reserve (p. 252). In regard to everything one wants to learn, we were told, it is necessary to apply oneself assiduously, without, however, striving to arrive directly at the goal (by trying to help). One cannot, in fact, anticipate a result until one has completely espoused the frame of mind required by the apprenticeship and thus conformed to the rhythm of its unfolding. But because, coinciding with the spontaneity of the process, one no longer anticipates a result (which one does not even think of as a goal), this result comes when least expected and immediately imposes its reality on us. Its advent precedes our consciousness of it, hence the "already"; it proceeds directly from the process set into motion, hence its surging unexpectedly in our consciousness. But the rupture implied by this leap of the surge does not occur within the process of apprenticeship — there is no intrusion from the outside to wait for, since this process follows an internal logic — thus there is only a rupture in our consciousness of its unfolding. In fact, the opposite is true: because this process of apprenticeship continuously follows its course and therefore we remain invested in it (hence its efficacy) and because we can never be completely conscious of this continuity (which is illuminated only through the attention of our efforts), its benefit surprises us. In reality, the thing that surges forth in a leap is but the fruit of immanence at work in the process set into motion.

Zhu Xi concludes:

> The paragraph shows that the path has its own defining principles, just as teaching has a fixed method: this can be neither raised nor lowered; words cannot show it, silence cannot hide it.

What strikes us immediately and can be neither forced nor modified, neither shown nor hidden, is the efficacy of immanence; the thing to which we suddenly gain access is already there, surging from its presence. If the immanence at work immediately asserts itself, both in nature and within ourselves, it follows that, because it continuously operates on all levels – and thus never defines itself and never recedes or juts out – it eludes our consciousness: what is the most difficult to realize, as we already know, is *evidence* (be it of regulation in *Mencius* or of the nature of Buddha). Words cannot show it, silence cannot hide it.[p] It is as indifferent to one as to the other, neither one has a hold on it nor can cleave to it. As Roland Barthes has noted about Zen and haiku, "There is a moment when language ceases (a moment obtained by dint of many exercises)," but it is not a question of "halting language at a heavy, full, profound, mysterious silence"; "what is posited must develop neither in discourse nor in the end of discourse."[16] What is posited is *matte*. Further along, he says that what gives access to Zen (and what the haiku designates simply) is "*It's that, it's thus,... it's so*," or better still, "merely saying: *that!*" It is the *that* which suddenly surges up in front of the student to whom the Master has transmitted the method of learning (but not the subtlety with which to attain it);[17] it is the *that* which Confucius ceaselessly exposes to his disciples, through the smallest aspect of his bearing (his *wen-zhang*[q]) – which he does not try to hide or claim to show them.[18]

Words do not show it, silence does not hide it. We recall Heracleitus on the subject of Apollo the Oblique: "The lord whose oracle is in Delphi neither declares nor conceals" (*oute legei oute kruptei*) (frag. 39 [93]).[19] But Heracleitus does not keep to this double denial: the Master of Delphi "neither declares nor conceals" but "shows by a sign" (*alla semainei*). One may interpret the saying as a justification of Heraclitean discourse (according to Nietzsche, Heracleitus the Obscure wanted his formulas to be interpreted "as oracular sentences"), or as oracular and sacred words (guiding without guidance, revealing without designating; see Jean Bollack and Heinz Wismann), or as a paradigm of all metaphysical discourse (according to Aram Frenkian, speech can only *suggest* "the most intimate essence of the world").[20] Inversely, one may consider that here Heracleitus distances himself from words of revelation and by counterstroke affirms the originality of philosophical discourse (which says things without leaving them in the ambiguous semidarkness of religion; see Marcel Conche). But the Heracleitean formula seeks to surpass the antinomy between speech and silence, rather than suspend it or spell it out (such as when speech cannot show and silence cannot hide). As suggested by the reference to the god of Delphi, this sign emerging between speech and silence is in part tied to transcendence; it mediates between the visible and the invisible. As such, it calls for the interpretive work of hermeneutics. How does one *say* the Truth (as soon as one speaks about Truth, as the Greek thinkers did)? "Language is not enough to seize the Truth that transcends it," writes Eric Weil about Heracleitus's fragment. "One can only, in fact, 'signify' Truth but can speak of all the rest."[21] In spite of their proliferation within the Chinese tradition, the commentaries have not set themselves up as hermeneutics. Instead of *interpreting*, they elucidate. It is not on the basis of transcendence, as we have begun to see, that the Chinese discourse unfolds; it does not hold Truth as a horizon. This remains to be proved even among Taoists, who, as early as Antiquity, conceived of the absolute of the way, the Tao.

CHAPTER TWELVE

The Great Image Has No Shape,

or How to Indicate the Ineffable

The strategy of the indirect is immediately called into play when faced with the absolute. Discourse is characterized by naming: in linking, it renders dependent. What we want is to express something that escapes all characterization, is free from all relationships. We wish to express the one — whereas discourse is multiple. In this case, we have no other recourse than to work discourse inversely, making it deviate from its usual functioning: in turning discourse against itself, in a detour from its claim to saying things, we gain access to something that infinitely surpasses the order of things. It is not of the order of consciousness but of the order of the ineffable and of what is usually called mystery.

Among the Greeks, the first hypothesis in *Parmenides* created a rift in the functioning of *logos*, which until then had been considered competent. Philosophy had begun, according to Emile Bréhier, by admitting, "as sole criteria of reality," those "positive characters" capable of entering as "elements in a definition."[1] Being was therefore in a position to be stated, and discourse was not a source of concern. But what *if*, hypothetically, before even conceiving of the one that is, one conceived of only the one one, the one "purely and simply one"? One cannot say whether this being is whole or in parts (being one, it is not multiple; thus there

275

are no parts, and, having no parts, it cannot form a whole); nor can one say whether it has limits or shape; nor whether it is self or other than self; nor whether it is same or other. From it, one successively derives mobility and immobility, similarity and dissimilarity, equality and inequality, and, finally, time itself — since it is neither younger nor older. In the final analysis, one cannot really say that this being "is," since being itself is refused it. The trap laid by discourse closes in around it, thereby stripping the One of all possible characterizations; we logically become deprived of all definition, including its very name.

Carried away by this dizzying negation, discourse closes itself off to any way out; in forbidding itself each statement, it goes to the brink of its own destruction. But this dead end, soon abandoned in dialogue, would prove to have promise. It was exploited by Neoplatonism to conceive of the first One from which reality proceeds. For Plotinus, this divine One, absolutely pure of any position, is the unique principle of everything, to the extent that it is beyond all statement: "all-transcending," superior even to essence, without shape or form, it is the nonbeing at the origin of being, both absolute and undifferentiated (*Enneads* 5.3.13).[2] Later philosophers pushed even further along the path of negation, radicalizing its exigencies: this unique principle can no longer be identified even with the Father of the intelligible triad (as in Porphyry) nor be posited as the "unique and ineffable cause," with which transcendence is emphasized (as in Proclus); this absolute ineffable can only be attained through the negation of that which alone remained unrepudiated in the Platonic hypothesis — the negation of the one itself (Damascius).

In his first hypothesis, it is neither nameable nor definable (*Parmenides* 142A). Plato had already concluded "No name could identify it," continues Plotinus. To say it is above even the most divine mind and not "a thing among things," according to the

Plotinian formula, is not to say it is this or that, to say its name, but to designate it to ourselves "in our own feeble way" (*Enneads* 5.3.13), or according to our own conventions, as Damascius would later say. Our words and writings are thus, at best, ways of "urging toward it" (*Enneads* 6.9.4). While we have no choice but to resort to language every effort is made to go beyond language and awaken us to contemplation. In saying that it is "ineffable" (*arreton, aporeton*), in recognizing that it is "unknowable darkness," we experience the overturning of our discourse and are condemned to "march in the void" (Damascius, *Premiers principes* 1.4). Hence we stop "on the threshold of the sanctuary," able only to arouse "suspicion" (*huponoia*), by giving an "indication" (*endeixis*). The only alternative to silence would be to "indicate" it, by using discourse in a "bastard" mode, and thereby oppose its legitimacy (Damascius reworking *Timaeus*).

One might expect to find the same ideas among the Chinese, at least with the Tao thinkers, or Taoists. In the famous aphorisms of *Laozi* (generally attributed to Laozi, who lived a little before Confucius, but more probably originating in antitraditionalist milieus in the fourth century B.C.; see D.C. Lau), it is also a question of a completely "undifferentiated" one (*pante adiakriton* with Damascius, *hun*[a] with Laozi), which cannot be "named" and which precedes all reality; although it lacks "characterization," "shape," and individuated reality, all beings "proceed" from it (in Greek, *ex autou panta*; in Chinese, *wan wu you zhi yi cheng*[b]). "Empty" and "indistinct," it plunges us into "unrecognizable darkness."[c] The Platonic "severing" through which one rises to meet it (*aphairesis-remotio*) (see Meister Eckhart's *Von Abgeschiedenheit)* is matched by the "diminution upon diminution" ("diminish and yet again") of *Laozi*. And, on both sides, this extreme reduction coincides with the greatest "integration," for the one has resolved the whole in its own simplicity and "has become the all."

In saying how "marvelous"[d] he finds this nonbeing from which everything issues, Laozi reminds us of Plotinus ("That awesome prior, The Unity, is not a being" [*Enneads* 6.9.5]). And, like Plotinus, the first great Chinese philosopher to comment on *Laozi*, Wang Bi, privileged this nonbeing[e] as the principle of reality. Furthermore, Plotinus and Wang Bi were contemporaries, living in the third century A.D., at the end of an empire (the Roman and the Han, respectively); both confronted the disarray born of political dislocation and threats of invasion. Hence they both strove to accommodate to the philosophical traditions of their respective Antiquities a new rise of religious aspirations, which in both cases, at least in part, originated elsewhere: from far-off oriental traditions outside Hellenism for Plotinus; from Buddhism, which was at the time penetrating China, for Wang Bi.[3]

Thus one speaks of neo-Taoist mysticism (the study of the *xuan xue*[f] mysteries) just as one speaks of the mystical thought of the Neoplatonists. It is true that at this stage all the traditions of thought appear to converge: Might this be due to man's lack of imagination in the face of mystery? Or to the equal inability of all languages to say the ineffable? Or because the aspiration to the unconditioned One would lead to an eclipse of the various conditionings — including cultural conditioning? But could such a tidy label establish a bridge between these conditions? In reading the aphorisms in *Laozi*, and Wang Bi's commentaries on them, we are led to question more than the universality of this mysticism.[4] Certainly, when confronted with the absolute, all discourse is forced to make detours and not always as a last resort. We have yet to verify whether the indirect strategies used to approach the ineffable — in both China and Greece — are in fact the same.

Let us begin by exploring the possibilities of parallel. "In this case the being — insofar as we can use the word," says Plotinus about

278

the infinite and secret One, "is knowable only by its sequents." The One, or God, "has no quality since no shape, even shape Intellectual; He holds no relationship but exists in and for Himself before anything is" (*Enneads* 7.8.11). One cannot help being struck by the analogy between these lines and the following lines from *Laozi*:

> There is a thing confusedly formed,
> Born before heaven and earth,
> Silent and void,
> It stands alone and does not change,
> Goes round and does not weary.
> It is capable of being the mother of the world.
> I know not its name,
> So I style it "the way."
> I give it the makeshift name of "the great."[5] (25)

To refer to this primary Oneness, it seems indeed that there is hardly any choice. The Taoist vision draws on the same logical determinations perfected by the Neoplatonists (and their ideas help me to express it): we see first its undifferentiated nature as well as its anteriority in the world's procession; second, the stripping away that leads to its oneness, its independence, and its emptiness; and lastly, its universality and constancy, which nothing can disrupt. To the Father of Plotinus's theology corresponds the mother of Taoism. It is also logical that *Laozi* recognizes its ineffable nature: calling it Tao, "the way," is a convention and only in a "makeshift" fashion does this word characterize it.

Because it is "constant" (32), because it is "concealed" (41), the Tao is nameless yet remains the locus of *Laozi*. In fact, the first aphorism in the collection begins with the constancy of the Tao, at least in Wang Bi's reading (the lines, because of their indeterminacy, lend themselves to very different interpretations; see the

modern and more philosophical interpretations by Peter Boodberg
and Chad Hansen):[6]

> The way that can be spoken of
> Is not the constant way;
> The name that can be named
> Is not the constant name. (1)

The Tao that can be spoken of, the name that can be named, explains Wang Bi, merely designates realities or specific situations
and has nothing to do with the sole order of the perceptible and
the concrete:[g] they cannot express the constancy through which
reality lasts. But here we do not have a difference of levels, such as
between the being, the sensitive, and the intelligible, and herein
lies, in my opinion, the difference between the Chinese and Greek
traditions (chang,[h] furthermore, means constant, durable, ordinary, not eternal, as it has often been translated; see nos. 52 and
55). Indeed, the canonical text continues:

> The nameless was the beginning of heaven and earth;
> The named was the mother of the myriad creatures.

"All concrete existence has a starting point in the undifferentiated," Wang Bi continues. But instead of separating the two levels
of being, the difference introduced within the real operates between two stages. Again we quit Greek ontology for the Chinese
conception of the process of the real: here we have the stage in
which "concrete actualization has not yet taken place" — and
where naming is therefore not yet possible — the starting point
for all beings. After this original stage, there follows another, that
of actualization and characterization, in which naming becomes
possible: the stage of "giv[ing] life," "nurs[ing]," "bring[ing] to

fruition and maturity," according to the terms of *Laozi* (51) — the stage, in short, in which the Tao ceaselessly serves as the mother of all beings.

That we are dealing with the same reality through these two moments, and that therefore there is no metaphysical rupture between the phenomenal and its foundation, is confirmed in the way *Laozi*'s next two formulas complement each other (again according to Wang Bi):

Hence always rid yourself of desires in order to observe its secrets;
But always allow yourself to have desires in order to observe its manifestations.

Through the absence of desire, in making a void within oneself, one can regain the undifferentiated stage from which all beings proceed, the most subtle level of reality; in embracing the innate tendency of desire, which, as such, corresponds to the natural inclination of beings, one can follow the process of the real to its completion in its ultimate manifestations. In other words, the Tao, which is the totality of the process, is both things at once (Mou Zongsan is correct to insist on this point): it is both the undifferentiated source from which everything proceeds (like the confused source from which reality emerges) and the concrete actualization culminating in each characterized individuation (this is why through each reality one gains direct access to the Tao that gave it existence).[7] Thus the Tao is both the beginning and the culmination (this is why the motif of the mother can encompass both aspects; see nos. 25 and 52). There are not two levels of reality but rather an upstream and a downstream. It is, on the one hand, the stock (unitary and buried), and, on the other, the branches spreading out their different guises for all to see.

I must therefore renounce the possibility of rendering the two opposing Chinese terms[i] with the categorical opposition of being and nonbeing, as has often been done in a projecting of Western ontology onto it. These two terms, while opposite, are also strictly correlated: each stage leads into the other, "produc[ing] each other," and they are two sides of the same process (2). I shall therefore render them in terms of process as *individuation* and *disindividuation*; and I shall say that we have, on the one hand, *harmonizing individuation* (*wu*), and, on the other, *differentiating actualization* (*you*). The term that complements the phenomenal concretization and specification of things proceeds not from a stripping down through abstraction (via the edification of an intelligible world into the realm of the general and leading to the nonbeing of the One) but from a *voiding* (of things that are both specific and concrete; or, better still — to retain the process aspect of reality — of things that present themselves both as specification and concretization). Such a voiding takes reality outside the reification that would otherwise bog it down; not only is this dimension the source of the other, as a condition of its renewal (for it is on the basis of the lack of differentiation of the void that new individuations are possible); but it also manifests itself continuously through it by "operating."[j] It is from the undifferentiated source that the most minute actualization ceaselessly draws its momentum. "Everything that manifests itself as beneficial in actualized reality," continues Wang Bi, "must have recourse to the undifferentiated source in order to function." In other words, the things I experience as a specific benefit are always only possible in relation to the fundamental undifferentiation — otherwise known as the foundation of emptiness.[k] In the stage of actualization, in fact, the real becomes rigid, choked; when, on the other hand, it opens itself up to the dimension of the void, the blockages dissolve, and it can "communicate"[l] once more (see Wang Bi's commentary on no. 14). In other words, the extent to which it returns to the un-differentiated represents the extent to which the real frees itself from the exclusions and fossilizations that shackle it; instead of becoming bogged down in things, it remains flowing and diffuse. The images in *Laozi* that attempt to translate this efficacy in terms of an *emptying* (11) are famous: the emptiness left in the middle of the hub that allows the spokes to converge and, conse-quently, the wheel to turn; the emptiness left by the potter in the middle of the clay that allows the pot to contain something; and the cutting of doors and windows in a wall that makes a room hab-itable. In one way or another, nothingness is always necessary for *use*. This is why in emptying fullness I give fullness its full mean-ing. Therefore, all use and functioning are but momentary mani-festations of an efficacy that remains fundamentally unconditioned and ceaselessly crosses the whole of reality. This efficacy of the *void*, as we have seen, is a *fundamental immanence*. In all determi-nate usage, at the actualized stage of things, what is captured in a specific mode is this immanence.

This emptying of constraints constitutes the primary intuition in *Laozi*. Its perspective on this is no more theoretical than practi-cal (such a distinction has no meaning). The Tao, as a way *by which one proceeds*, does not lead to a distinction between the rule of conduct (especially in politics) and the process by which all of existence ceaselessly renews itself. Thus, because its fundamental lack of differentiation is open to anything and everything — and not in a creationist mode — the Tao is thought of as "engendering" reality (see Wang Bi's commentary on the end of no. 10) or as the mother of efficacy. All concerted "action," on the other hand, as well as all individual "attachment,"[m] is just focused activity creat-ing obstacles to its unfolding. Let us not be mistaken: Taoist "nonaction"[n] is the opposite of renunciation and passivity, yet undeniably, as soon as I act, I leave "nonacting" aside and find

283

myself defeated; if I "attach" myself, I am condemned to "lose" (29). Therefore, the more I act or make a conscious effort (and this is especially true of the prince), the more this interference has disastrous consequences. The Taoist sage rigorously reacts against all the complications that go hand in hand with the development of so-called civilization: the more taboos and prohibitions, the poorer the country; the more laws, the more lawbreakers (57). Virtues are but so many fixations that, by their differences, attest to the loss of original harmony (18). To return to the Tao (to the "basis" or "root" [16], as *Laozi* recommends) is therefore to free one's activity from all impediments to natural inclinations: to renounce the perspective of accumulation that characterizes learning (48) and to return to fundamental simplicity, which, because it has neither distinctions nor limits, allows everything to function naturally.

The renunciation of speech should be understood from this perspective. If one who "knows" "does not speak" (56), it is because he "relies solely on natural inclination" and allows himself to be carried along by the spontaneity of things (Wang Bi); and if, on the other hand, one who "speaks" "does not know," it is because as soon as one speaks one inevitably begins to "create problems." To speak is to favor this and forsake that and thereby to oppose reality to itself: to enter into the partiality of rifts, to attach oneself to a distinctive feature, to exploit something artificially. Renouncing speech, on the other hand, dissolves all constraints (which are always relative) and allows the fundamental lack of differentiation (by which everything communicates) to return and makes it possible to find harmony again. The sage, we read, "soften[s] the glare," "untangle[s] the knots." Silence is preferable to speech because, first of all — and logically — it is more effective; this is why *Laozi* recommends a "teaching that uses no words" (2–43). Teaching by words limits us to focus on the outcome of things (which allows for the perception of desire); it situates us in the last moment of actualization, codified and rigid, in which shell upon shell is formed, thus thwarting our effort. It is but a great expenditure (of rhetoric) for little gain. On the other hand, through his silence, the sage teaches us to renounce artificial oppositions, to rid ourselves of prejudices; he returns to the initial stage in which, since nothing individual has yet been actualized, everything remains permeable to its influence. His silence is an incarnation of emptiness, whose inexhaustible effect it possesses. A tangible manifestation of the Tao, silence is like the undifferentiated source of speech.

The paradox of any mention of the ineffable is well known: I can say nothing about it, and yet I speak to you of it. It has also been noted that the Neoplatonic philosophers tried to resolve this contradiction: this first One is not considered accessible to science since "in knowing, soul or mind abandons its unity; it cannot remain simple: knowing is taking account of things; that accounting is multiple." Yet it is accessible through a "supreme" presence: thus although I can say nothing about it, I can at least show the way that leads to its contemplation (*Enneads* 6.9.4). And Damascius continues: our soul has the divination of what it cannot say; since it cannot "give birth," it "stimulates" its "unspeakable gestations" (*Premiers principes* 1.3). As for Laozi, he tries to resolve the issue by opening up an opposition within language itself: I cannot name the Tao since any name is a characterization and the Tao is uncharacterized. The only possibility is thus to *indicate* it (I borrow the term from the Neoplatonists) by always only beginning to say, without ever allowing the meaning to go all the way (toward its actualization), which encloses it in characterization. The task, in short, is to suspend the tendency of all discourse to specify: to *disindividuate* the words and keep speech upstream

— in a stage anterior to the differentiation of meaning that might bring us closer to the lack of differentiation of things.

The opening stanza of *Laozi*, which we have begun to read, closes with the following lines:

> These two are the same
> But diverge in name as they issue forth.
> Being the same they are called mysteries
> Mystery upon mystery —
> The gateway of manifold secrets.

These "two" indicate the beginning and the completion, the upstream and the downstream, the lack of differentiation from which everything proceeds and the specific actualization to which this process leads. We also know that while these two stages are opposites, they communicate and are bound together: the lack of differentiation is not a sterile void since it is the origin and efficacy is manifested through it; specific actualization is never trapped in its specificity but remains open to the lack of differentiation, finally returning to it. Since the main characteristic of a name is to designate a difference, this common source, on which reality rests and from which the ability of the real to renew itself emanates, cannot be named. This *bottomless depth* can merely be "indicated"° by a term shown to have no end. Thus this term is considered the opposite of a term (which restricts meaning). "One cannot merely confine oneself to the mysterious character," notes Wang Bi. Even this term "mysterious," the most likely to signify the impossibility of a characterization, threatens to trap us in its own characterization and close us within its bounds. Hence its redoubling thwarts this trap: "mystery upon mystery." Through this repetition, the term is kept open beyond itself, exceeding its bounds.

286

This opposition gave rise to a more general construction in *Laozi zhilüe*:

> The denomination determines an object, whereas the indication follows that which one wants to say; the denomination is born of the object, and the indication originates with the subject.
>
> This is why when one broaches that according to which there is no reality without issue, one indicates it as tao; and when one is searching for that from which arises all that is indefinitely formed, one indicates it as "mystery."

Neither of these terms is applicable *as such* (no more so than the other terms that appear so often in *Laozi*: "deep," "great," "subtle," "indistinct." Whatever the terms used, in fact:

> Naming originates from an objective characterization, indication comes from a subjective approach. The name does not arise from a void, nor does the indication come from it either. Hence the name greatly misses the intended meaning, and the indication does not succeed in saying it fully. This is why, in indicating it as mysterious, one says "mystery upon mystery."[8]

Naming and *indicating* are both insufficient to express the Tao: naming, because it operates through objective characterization, whereas the Tao is formless and can never be considered an object; and indication, the result of an attempt at communication, because it is marked with subjectivity, whereas the Tao overflows any individual understanding or intentionality. Each, therefore, is affected by a certain fullness and is not capable of expressing the essential emptiness (of the unconditioned). Nevertheless, the insufficiencies of these two words are not equal: on the one hand, since a certain "portion" of it is necessarily separated from meaning,[p] the naming term cannot speak of the two things at once and thereby precludes the possibility of their coexistence (their common source); it can thus be used to characterize specific actualizations but remains fundamentally inadequate to speak of the Tao. On the other hand, since it necessarily retains a dependent quality, the indicating term cannot completely express meaning; it never goes all the way (since what it says is infinite) and therefore always begins to say, remaining inchoate. The dilemma is clear: in characterizing the meaning, naming loses it; while indicating can merely point to it. If one wishes to keep the meaning in its initial stage, to avoid its sinking into specification, one cannot hope at the same time to express it completely. Nonetheless, whereas in the first case the harm is irreparable, in the second one can always try to fix it. To write (in order to say the Tao of things) is thus essentially an undertaking that consists in separating speech from the characterization of words, all the while trying further to express what their mere indication leaves incomplete.

Laozi speaks explicitly of this principle. We remember that naming the Tao "the great" (25) is only "makeshift," for it has been called great, continues Wang Bi, only because one has chosen, from among all possible interpretations, to call it great. But great is not opposed to small here: the Tao is no greater than it is small (34); since it is nothing, it enters into things that have no crevices (see no. 43). If I attach to it the idea of greatness, this immediately refers me to a certain meaning, and I enter into the logic of discourse as characterization and subsequently miss its undifferentiated aspect. This is why *Laozi* continues:

I give it the makeshift name of "the great."
Being, it is further described as receding,
Receding, it is described as far away,
Being far away, it is described as turning back. (25)

The indication "receding" *detaches* us from the idea of greatness as implying rigidity and specification. It cuts short the individuation of meaning. In changing the terms in quick succession,
the stanza focuses on the differences beginning to emerge among
them and thereby keeps them open. Similarly, the Tao is not limited to a simple receding but spreads in all directions, which is
why it says "far away"; by the same token, it does not isolate itself
in the term "far away," which is why it immediately says "turning
back." Through this sliding from one term to another, each is
liberated from its tendency to characterize, and the semantics
remains at its initial stage without bogging down in any particular
content. The concepts change in quick succession, keeping the
meaning transitory. Here is a characteristic that we have already
underscored in the words of Confucius: the Sage's remarks are
continuously modified and never come to a standstill. Instead of
always attempting to speak of truth more intimately (by trying to
grasp the identity of its object more precisely), this *transformation*
is the equivalent of its objective: through it, at any given moment,
it avoids foundering in attachment, and thus partiality, and is able
to maintain itself in *globality* (which in this case is that of the undifferentiated; see no. 49).

Only the proposition's capacity for *variation* conveys the inexhaustible renewal of the Tao. Wang Bi draws up a rule for reading
Laozi, which we should keep in mind. If one tries to reach the text
through specific philological analysis or tries to interpret each chapter separately, one misses the meaning of the work, for it does not
say one thing in one place and another thing in another; the meaning is never *individuated*.[9] If, however, one approaches the text
with a *global* reading, one gains access to it without difficulty.

This first One cannot be imagined in any particular form, since it
is indeterminate and one. "Neither round nor straight," concludes

the first hypothesis of *Parmenides*, since both would have parts and be many" (137E).[10] "Absolutely One, it has never known measure and stands outside number" (neither *schēma* nor *morphē*), continues Plotinus. "You may not hope to see it with mortal eyes, nor in any way that would be imagined by those who make sense the test of reality and so annul the supremely real" (*Enneads* 5.5.11).

"Shape that has no shape," "image that is without substance,"[q] *Laozi* also describes it. This negation of shape is also a recognition of the invisible:

What cannot be seen is called evanescent;
What cannot be heard is called rarefied;
What cannot be touched is called minute.
These three cannot be fathomed,
And so they are confused and looked upon as one. (14)

There is thus an invisible ("without shape or image" and "without sound or echo," Wang Bi insists, which, as such, escapes the "senses"), although in the two cultures, this invisibility is not of the same order. In fact, this is where the difference is again manifest. The invisible (or the inaudible or the intangible) in *Laozi* appears as such only by way of the undifferentiated, according to the conception of a reality in process. It is the result of a reabsorption of the sensible, or a voiding of the concrete, and does not constitute another level, such as another world, accessible to other eyes, as in Greek thought. This invisible is indeed beyond the visible but as an extension of it; it is of the order of the evanescent and not the unintelligible (*noēton*). It escapes us because of its fineness ("minute," "subtle," says *Laozi*), but this does not imply an ontological rift; it transcends the sensible through its infinite capacity for transformation (it can "go in any direction" and "communicate through everything," Wang Bi specifies, since

290

it knows no obstacle of concretization), but it does not *hyposta-tize*. This invisible is rather the *diffuse basis* of the visible from which the latter ceaselessly actualizes itself. In short, this invisible lacks metaphysical consistency. Hence one is not surprised that between China and Greece, the way of making the visible indicate it is so very different.

Let us reread more closely the two Chinese expressions cited above: the text says not that the undifferentiated is without shape but that it is a "shape that has no shape"; not that no sensible image can be made of it but that it is an image "without sub-stance." Shape is denied but *from within the shape*; the sensible is surpassed *but not left behind*. *Laozi* reworks this elsewhere in a for-mula that seems significant of the totality of its thought: "The great image has no shape"ʳ (51). As soon as the shape takes shape, Wang Bi explains, "there is a split, and as soon as there is a split, there is exclusion"; it becomes one and not another. "Hence, as soon as the image is actualized, it no longer is the great image." The great image, that is, the image that contains all images (in the manner of the Tao) and manifests the source of things, is an *un-imaged* image, but it is not abstract (it does not refer to the level of essences): it has simply liberated its character of image from any anecdotal or specific aspect of its content; by retaining the indis-tinct, it remains open to plenitude.

The result of this is an original dialectic that can be seen as parallel to Western ontology. I have never seen it expressed more clearly than in the following passage from *Laozi zhilüe*:

> If the image actualizes itself in a concrete shape, it is no longer the great image; furthermore, if sonority is actualized in a sound pro-duced, it is no longer the great sonority.
>
> But if there is not a variety of images actualized, the great image has nothing within which to unfold; and if the various notes of the

291

scale are not produced, the great sonority has nothing within which to manifest itself.

Hence, it is when a variety of images is actualized, but nothing concrete exercises a supremacy, that the great image unfolds; and it is when the various notes of the scale are produced, but consciousness does not fix on it, that the great sonority manifests itself.[11]

The great image, therefore, does not exist apart from specific images (to develop on another level); nor does it shut itself within their limitations (with these specific images imposing their individuated character as the only reality); rather, it unfolds *through them to infinity*. In other words, the great image is never anything other than a specific image, but nothing specific affects it: nothing concrete imposes any law on it; in it, consciousness is not annihilated by anything. Reality remains sensitive to it but is no longer rigid (reified and codified); what it contains of the sensible does not lead to limitations. The concrete, in short, does not obstruct it but opens to other possibilities; instead of representing something individual and defined, it allows the undifferentiated dimension to pass through its individual characteristics, animating and unifying them. Thus consciousness, evolving freely in it, does not get bogged down in literalness; nor does it need to decipher another, spiritual meaning in it (as is the case when the image is allegorical). What pertains to the image pertains to the phenomenon in general (and this reflection plays on the double meaning of *xiang*, image and phenomenon). For the Chinese, transcendence does not lead to any world other than ours, the only one (as phenomenal world); but the phenomenal is also freed from any restrictive, exclusive, constraining, or monopolizing aspects. It calls for detachment, but without this leading to a conversion (attaching us to a reality of another order).

This should allow us to understand better why Chinese literature has never privileged symbolism (and instead has privileged the diffuse *aura* of a motif or person, an atmosphere). It is not symbolic because it has nothing else to represent (that is, on another plane, such as the intelligible or essences); and this is why, as allusive writing, it lends itself so well to a specific interpretation (political in particular) yet remains indefinitely allusive (in other words, one can just as easily enter into the reference as detach oneself from it completely; see the end of chapter 8 above). What it implies is well defined without being limited to this definition; one can give it a particular application, but it is not exclusive, and other applications are also possible. The Tao, *Laozi* states, "resembles nothing"⁵ (67), for if it resembled something, it would soon become small and would thereby lose its greatness — the greatness of the great image. At the same time, *Laozi* states not that it resembles nothing but that the world *says* it resembles nothing: this recognizes that it does not a priori exclude itself from the order of resemblance and tangibility; rather, its resemblance escapes us, remaining indistinct and shadowy.

In pointing to the undifferentiated source of the Tao, the role of the image is therefore not to call on the sensible to converge above it (as seen in the images in *Laozi* from which one might expect a symbolic unfolding — such as mother, the valley, or the nurse, which never organize into an ideal structure) but to stimulate the void that animates the sensible world to pass through it: to express through the individual the disindividuation in which it is rooted and to make the plenitude it contains manifest through the indistinct. This is why *Laozi* expresses reality in relation to *presence-absence*, in terms of the full, the indistinct, and the evanescent. Instead of making its object more present, a comparison might efface it and make it ungraspable; in suspending the characterizing function of discourse, it checks the risk of ontological signification:

Deep, it is like the ancestor of the myriad creatures.
[…]
Darkly visible, it only seems as if it were there.
[…]
It images the forefather of God. (4)

This "like" connotes uncertainty and plunges us into the indistinct. Like the "makeshift" name of the Tao as great, it is described in a "makeshift" way.[t] Or rather, it is *not described*, for the point is nothing less than to use the sensible against itself, with the aim not of representing but of de-representing:

Tentative, as if fording a river in winter,
Hesitant, as if in fear of his neighbors. (15)

The image here is worked to the reverse of its imaging power: it is used to characterize that which cannot be characterized, to express palpably the absence of palpable signs. The tentative or hesitant air of the sage embodying the Tao is certainly not meant to be understood psychologically; it translates the voiding of all specific traits. About the man tentative at the edge of the frozen river, Wang Bi explains, we have no idea if he will attempt to ford it or not; nothing in his face betrays his feelings. One cannot know in what direction he who is hesitant and in fear of his neighbors will turn; there is no indication suggesting his intention. The images that follow are along the same lines:

Formal like a guest;
Falling apart like thawing ice;
Thick as an uncarved block;
Vacant like a valley;
Murky like muddy water. (15)

By evoking a mode of specific indeterminacy, each image brings us to the very limits of the sensible, both upstream and downstream from it: whether it has not yet unfolded (the guest, the uncarved block) or is in the process of dissolving (the thawing ice, the vacant valley), it is contained in the undifferentiated space that tends to reabsorb it. Through their variation (for it is always a matter of variation), these images keep us as far as possible from the seen or the distinct, in a realm where the concrete is discreet and everything merges in harmony. They are used to paint the unpaintable.

Two registers thus stand in opposition, in the guise of a portrait: one characterizes the salient stage of actualization, the other, the more retiring stage of disindividuation (20). Others are "joyous," as if partaking in a feast; I alone am "inactive" and reveal no "sign," "like a baby that has not yet learned to smile" (or "listless as though with no home to go back to"); or again, the multitude "have more than enough," while I alone "seem to be in want"; the others are "clear," while I alone am "blank."[12] The alertness of others is contrasted with the speaker's "muddled" state; their purpose is contrasted with his "uncouth" manner. In the face of the multitude who show themselves and are active, the undifferentiated source of the Tao can only express itself unexpressively: as dull, effaced, and spent. This negative connotation is an invitation to return to a moment prior to the differentiation in which our energy is consumed. It brings out from the depths the "raw" and "fundamental"[u] stage — as opposed to the luxurious and the picturesque — a stage stripped of features and signs that does not allow itself to be consumed. This is the stage of the true greatness, in the sense of the great image, in which nothing is defined or opposed and everything communicates without obstacle to infinity:

[...] calm like the sea;
like a high wind that never ceases. (20)

For expressing in sensible terms the undifferentiated source of things, no mode is better suited than *blandness*, the stage in which no particular flavor comes forth to overpower others, where everything remains confused. On the other hand, while this leads to the very limits of the sensible, to the place where the sensible is grasped the moment it escapes us, blandness also belongs to the realm of the sensible. It is similar in this way to the great image:

The way in its passage through the mouth is without
    flavor.
It cannot be seen,
It cannot be heard,
Yet it cannot be exhausted by use. (35)

As opposed to music or food, which "induce the wayfarer to stop," blandness is not seductive. The same is true for the Tao, explains Wang Bi. It passes unnoticed: "One might say it reaches no goal"; but this is why "one cannot reach its end." This alone is why it can say what has no end. This motif of blandness illuminates another formula of *Laozi,* according to Wang Bi: "To use words but rarely / Is to be natural" (23). "Words that lack flavor and do not appear to be worth listening to," he explains, "are the perfect expression for the spontaneity of things"[v] — which I call their source of immanence. "Much speech," on the other hand, "leads inevitably to silence" (5). The more words are bland and discreet (and the less they try to create an effect), the better they convey the depths of the real.

Another oblique approach to the ineffable is the reversal of discourse and negation — the path of paradox and *apophasis*. Either I hollow out the image — to make the sensible express what is not sensible, as we saw in the preceding case — or I subtract qualities to signify not their abolition but their surpassing. The second possibility was established in the Greek tradition by the hypothesis in *Parmenides*, which was exploited by the Neoplatonists and adopted by theology. What is denied to Him, wrote Saint Thomas Aquinas, is not so because it is lacking but because he "superexceeds" it. *Laozi* is familiar with this use of negation: when it states that "Heaven and earth are not ruthless" or that "the sage is not ruthless" (5), we are dealing, according to Mou Zongsan (commenting on Wang Bi commenting on *Laozi*), not with an "affirmation," as in an "assertion" (which would be contradictable), but with an "indication" (that Heaven and earth, or the sage, are beyond the "partiality" that keeps us). The negation of a quality is an invitation to transcend the opposition within which it is caught (ruthless/not ruthless); and we gain access to a higher, inexpressible level in which exclusion is abolished.

Laozi uses another mode of negation that is much more original, to the point of being untranslatable:

Do that which consists of taking no action;
pursue that which is not meddlesome;
savor that which has no flavor. (63)

In this case, the negation refers not to the predicate, as is always the case in the Greek tradition established in *Parmenides* (it is neither this nor that), but to the direct object of the verb. The difference is essential for its philosophical ramifications. In this case, the activity indicated by the verb is conserved; only its object is withdrawn. This signifies that the sage embodying the Tao continues

297

to act and to savor; but he does not submit to the pressure of the objects of acting and savoring (and everything partial and limited that the latter always implies: one occupation or flavor to the exclusion of another). His doing or savoring are no longer determined; they unfold without exclusion. The Taoist sage neither forsakes the world of experience and sensibility nor lets himself become engulfed in it. Likewise, when the strategist is advised to "march forward when there is no road" (or "roll up one's sleeves when there is no arm," "drag one's adversary by force when there is no adversary," and "take up arms when there are no arms" [69]), it is not to make him disengage himself from the conflict but so that he will maintain the conflict on a level prior to its actualization where it cannot constrain him, allowing him to operate without effort or limitation. Just as the great image is an image liberated from its particular character as image while remaining an image, and just as blandness abolishes the pronounced and limited nature of flavor while remaining sensible, the actionless action of the sage or the Tao is not the negation of its efficacy but its complete fruition — since it is not conditioned and mingles with the capacity of immanence.

Taken further (to the negation of negation or the negation of the one), the process of *apophasis* leads to a "complete reversal of discourse and thought" (*peritropē* in Damascius). This is also characteristic of *Laozi*. For example, the second part of the collection begins:

> A man of the highest virtue does not keep to virtue and that is why he has virtue. A man of the lowest virtue never strays from virtue and that is why he is without virtue. (38)

The value of paradox is well recognized: "Straightforward words seem paradoxical" (78), for example, "In the world there is nothing more submissive and weak than water. Yet for attacking that

298

which is hard and strong nothing can surpass it." To have access to the Tao, consequently, is to be able to perceive the true capacity in that which appears negative, in order to profit from it (41; see also nos. 36 and 43). Hence, once again, the parallel that at first presented itself is condemned to remain formal, or at least is not allowed to go any further, for the reversal achieved by Greek philosophy is logical and proceeds from *aporia*: this "complete reversal of discourse and thought" is simply the "demonstration" "imagined" by us and of which we speak (*Premiers Principes* 1.8).[13] As for what we glean from religious revelation, this is based on faith in another world and another life: "Blessed be *ye* poor; for yours is the kingdom of God" (Luke 6.20). Like the reversal promised by religious revelation, the reversal in *Laozi* is based not on reasoning but on the conduct of man and his destiny; like religious reversal, it can be the object of others' misunderstanding, to the point of inciting their mockery (if the "worst" students did not laugh when they heard about the way, the Tao "would be unworthy of being the way" [41]). But unlike religious reversal, the reversal in *Laozi* is not expected in another life; it is supposed to be realized in immediate experience, and the reward on which it rests is spontaneous. It is by "tak[ing] upon himself the calamity of the state" that one "is called a king worthy of dominion over the entire empire" (78) (or, as stated again in the last lines of *Laozi*, "Having bestowed all he has on others, he has yet more" [81]) not because one expects a reward from Heaven for this willful humbling but because he who humbles himself rises in the eyes of others, since he no longer elicits jealousy. Furthermore, by putting his person last, the sage is most sure to come out first (7): not because he has made a vow of humility but because he who shows modesty rises all the higher. The benefit reckoned on is earthly (since ancient China lacked the concept of a heaven), and the sense of reversal is not mystical but *strategic*.

In fact, one cannot understand the logic of reversal praised in *Laozi* (and in the other schools of Chinese Antiquity) without integrating it into its proper perspective: The search for efficacy (first of all in politics). But just what is this *effect*, properly speaking, and how is it produced? The Chinese point of view — of a reality in process — can illuminate things on this score, for if there is to be an effect, there must be a development; and for there to be a development, it must occur at a stage prior to the situation. It is therefore vain to produce an effect, to situate oneself on the same plane as this effect (for this is always more or less forced and therefore precarious and limited). It would be more effective to act in such a way that this effect, established beforehand, would be led to unfold by itself naturally, through simple immanence — brought about by the situation alone and thereby avoiding the risk of finding an obstacle or limitation in it. The effect's efficacy is thus directly proportionate to the propensity on which it rests; and this propensity is all the stronger the greater the necessity for reward. This is why the Taoist sage intervenes in a sense contrary to the desired effect: he who wants to "shrink" (someone or something) must first "stretch" it; to "have a thing weakened," one "must first strengthen it," to "have a thing laid aside," one must "first set it up" (36). Wang Bi illustrates how the subtlety of this intuition plays itself out in politics: he who wants to rid himself of a tyrant must draw support from the inherent course of things, which, as such, will lead the tyrant to destroy himself rather than take up arms to punish him. In the Chinese vision, the reward that leads to reversal is not conceived of as a recompense (accorded by transcendence), as in religious vision, but rests on the principle of an immanent regulation (and we see to what point this can be taken: waiting for this regulation exempts us from revolution).

This conception of an effect *unfolding through immanence* brings us to the heart of the question of the indirect and can illuminate it from within. It relates to the strategic point of view from which we started. It is advantageous to intervene in a situation not when the confrontation is actualized, in other words, directly, but at a stage prior to its evolution, "before symptoms develop" when it is all the more "easy" to manage (64). Intentionally seeking the effect from the start, in the stage when its features are sensible and definitive, renders it artificial and scattered. This is why it could be indicated about morality that the most virtuous man "does not keep to virtue," which is why "he has virtue" (38). (The sage has all the more virtue when he does not strive for virtue, and it emanates from him as a result, whereas the man who never "strays" from virtue, ceaselessly repeating virtuous gestures, remains "without virtue" [39].) It is by freeing it from its concrete aspect, by allowing it to unfold by itself, that the effect becomes truly effective. And this concept applies to art as well: "great perfection seems chipped," just as "great skill seems awkward" and "great fullness seems empty" (45). Not only does true eloquence mock eloquence, that is, all the characteristics associated with eloquence; but above all, in steering clear of the characteristics of eloquence, it allows us more fully to measure its true effect. In this domain as well, one can say that "the effect cannot be obtained directly as such" but must be "situated constantly on the level of the mother of the effect" (Wang Bi's commentary on no. 28), the undifferentiated source from which this effect will emerge (see the excellent commentary of Wang Bi on no. 39: one does not "attain purity through pure works" but by going back to the prior time of the original one; see also the conclusion of *Laozi zhilüe*). An effect is only perceptible if we have been made sensitive to it in its advent, if we can espouse the necessity that leads to it and experience it in its unfolding. If, on the other hand, it imposes itself on us from the start, we are immediately saturated by it. The effect is only sensible *as it is being actualized*; all completely actualized — or static — effect is already lapsed.

Thus both distance and detour are justified in a single stroke: distance, because only in taking a distance from the desired effect can one make its lack felt and allow it naturally to occur and because only in giving free rein to the effect, instead of sticking close to it, does one render its unfolding possible; detour, because the one refers to the other and in itself implies its reversal, leading to a return, and because the source of the effect is opposed to its sensible manifestations. Through detour, we see the effect emerging from the void or contrast, and, having returned to its advent, we embrace its development.

At the outset, the problem appeared the same. Apropos of the ineffable from which everything proceeds, Plotinus and Wang Bi, the Neoplatonist and the neo-Taoist, logically resort to the same type of paradox.[14] Plotinus: "The One is all things and no one of them; the source of all things is not all things, and yet it is all things in a transcendental sense — all things, so to speak, having run back to it: or, more correctly, not all as yet are within it, they will be" (*Enneads* 5.2.1). And Wang Bi: "If we want to say that it exists, we see no concrete shape; if we want to say that it does not exist, all existing things issue from it" (chapter 6; see also chapter 13).

Nevertheless, in these statements, and in spite of the similarities in their articulation, we notice something more global that distinguishes the two (what Michel Foucault calls "heterotopia"). It is not that what they say is different, but, although each perspective might confirm the other, they do not correspond. Thus although parallels can be drawn, because they have different axes, these statements do not say the same thing. This offers us the occasion to recognize that, on a subject so apparently universal as mysticism, thought remains attached to its cultural horizon.

Among the Greeks, contemplation of the One passes obligatorily through predication (*kategorein*; even if it is to refuse any predicate to the One), and this predication is developed on the basis of categories (which correspond in principle to the various cases of Indo-European languages), which can be found in the hypothesis in *Parmenides* and at the center of Aristotle's *organon*.[15] Furthermore, the search for this primal One remains dominated by the preoccupation with an intelligible essence (even if this situates the One beyond the intelligible). Even when it is inhabited by a religious restlessness, as with Plotinus, it remains turned toward theory. Among the Chinese, the preoccupation is with the efficacy at work in the course of things (in politics first and foremost). It is by having "in [his] hold the great image" — that is, by separating himself from the stage of arbitrary exclusions — that the prince enables the whole world to "come" to him and spread peace (no. 35). Since it is simply the way by which one is supposed to proceed, the Tao does not lend itself to theoretical constructions; it is not the object of either contemplation or love. Even a philosopher such as Wang Bi, who was one of the most tempted by speculation in all of Chinese history (speculation on the one, the principle, perhaps under the foreign influence of Buddhism; see his commentaries on nos. 42 and 47), retains this perspective. One does not see him cross the threshold that would lead to metaphysics.[16]

Just what is this threshold? To emerge from the impasse to which it is led by the impossibility of predication in relation to the One, Greek thought proceeds to a doubling of planes. To escape the contradiction of the One and the multitude (for if the One is purely one, how can it enter into relations with the multiple?), Plotinus doubles the one into a first One, pure and true, toward which we must "leap," and a second one, on a lower level, transposable into a series with numbers. Similarly, to escape the contradiction between the all and the principle of the all (if the principle of the all is above the all, the all destroys itself, and if the principle is part of the all, it destroys itself as principle), Damascius doubles the first One into the One itself and devises a term above it and even more abstract than it, which is not one but nothing, the ineffable. Greek thought emerges from the impossibility of predication by creating new hypostases behind reality, which make it rise all the higher in transcendence.

It is precisely this doubling of planes, through successive abstractions, that Chinese thought lacks. This is why, in the final analysis, the detour of the image aimed at expressing the ineffable appears so differently in the two traditions. In Plotinus, as in all theology based on *apophasis, analogy* is the proportional application of what we know about the lesser levels of being and thought to the otherwise unknowable One: "failing more suitable terms, we apply it to the lesser terms brought over from lesser things and so tell it as best we may" (*Enneads* 6.8.8).[17] We have seen that, in *Laozi*, the image is not used to effect a transfer of attributes of an inferior order to another that surpasses it; to return us to the undifferentiated, it uses the sensible to render the sensible insensible. It aims not to illuminate from below an infinitely superior reality, but to make felt from within, through contrast with the salient aspect of things, the dimension of the void running through these things and enabling them to function.

Thus the great image does not refer to a reality other than its own individual and concrete reality; but, in detaching us from a particular character, it allows us to see the limitations and exclusivity of the individual and the concrete. It does not give us access to a hypostasis higher than it, but it liberates us from being bogged down. It gives us access to things that unfold spontaneously, as sources of immanence, in nature. It remains for us to ask: If it is not access to *something else*, just what is this access, and how does it come about?

CHAPTER THIRTEEN

"Net" and "Fish," or

How to Gain Access to Nature

Western hermeneutics is constructed on the following opposition: on the one hand, imaged figuration offered to sight; and on the other, the spiritual sense hidden beneath it. To bind them together, another image comes to the fore, that of the veil or cloak. These are conveyed in trammels, the envelope, or covering (*involumentum, integumentum, involucrum*); beneath the exterior of the literal expression lies a mystery to be uncovered. The commentator's role is to unveil: to undress the lesson, be it philosophical or theological; to remove the fabulous mantle that hides it from the eyes of the everyday and display it in its authentic nudity.

This sheathing of the image cannot fail to be ambiguous, for it hides the better to uncover; and the veil is there only to be raised. It is necessary both to move through it and to detach oneself from it; its screen is there to be crossed. While it attracts us with its imagery, it charges us to look beyond it. Reality lies behind it, accessible to other eyes. Even the *other* that allegory tends to signify here becomes the Other par excellence — the other world and the other life. The envelope of the concrete figuration is intended to be relinquished, as must be that of the body in order to reach the soul: going beyond the envelope of the sensible — images or the flesh — and shifting our gaze are the conditions required for the attainment of truth.

During the last centuries of Antiquity, it became commonplace to recognize the utility of detour in expression as consisting
in the use of myth or allegory: as an affirmation of the need for
going beyond, which alone allows access to the things we cannot
apprehend otherwise — the invisible and the divine. The myths of
Isis and Osiris, Plutarch says — and as barbarous as they appear to
us, it is not just a matter of vain poetic imagination — are comparable to a rainbow, which reflects the sun and covers itself in iri-
descent colors when the sun hides behind the clouds. Because of
its indirectness, the myth can act as an intermediary for everything
that "human frailty cannot clearly grasp." Through its very discretion, it is halfway between clear discourse and enigma, a "more
suitable interpreter" (Maxime de Tyr). Among the Christians,
Clement of Alexandria made the symbolic genre (*to sumbolikon
eidos*[1]) the principle of all religious expression.[2] He demonstrates
its importance both among Greek poets and philosophers and
in the Bible: the allegory of the one goes hand in hand with the
typology of the others; Apollo is called Loxias (the Oblique), just
as the god of the psalmist "opens his mouth in parables." He also
sets forth the various advantages of the symbolic genre. In occult-
ing the message, the veil of symbolic figuration arouses our desire
to cross this obstacle to find truth: it makes us reach further
toward it and, through the exertion of the quest, makes us experience it as our own. At the same time, the ambiguity inherent in
the image creates an inexhaustible wealth of meaning that better
suits the profound nature of the divine: it also ennobles the meaning like fruits that "show through the water" or shapes that
embellish the veils covering them "by only allowing them to be
divined." In short, the symbol protects religious truth from the
incomprehension of the vulgar by limiting access to it. Only an
indirect expression, in short, would confer respect on the majesty
of the mystery.

This motif of the veil woven by myth and symbol and cloaking the mystery has become a commonplace of Western exegesis. We are no doubt unaware of the way it underlies the horizon of meaning in the West, so familiar have we become with it through an abundant tradition, from Greek allegory to the patristics, in spite of their internal polemics. I have not found the equivalent in the Chinese tradition of commentary. The Chinese tradition does use another image, however, to indicate the necessity of going beyond literal meaning to gain access to ineffable intuition, the net and the fish (or the snare and the hare):

> Nets exist for catching fish; once a fish is caught, the net is forgotten. Traps exist for catching rabbits; once a rabbit is caught, the trap is forgotten. Words exist for expressing ideas; once the ideas are expressed, the words are forgotten. I would like to find someone who forgets words and have a talk with him![3]

This image concludes a chapter of *Zhuangzi,* which is usually cited beside *Laozi* as the other great text of philosophical Taoism; its author (at least for the first chapters) lived in the fourth century B.C. During the revival of Taoism in the third century A.D., *Zhuangzi* was recirculated by Wang Bi, the most important commentator on *Laozi,* to formulate the ascending relationship that moves from speech to figuration and from figuration to ideas (with the intention of serving as an exegesis on *The Book of Changes*).[4] As with the veil, this image indicates that speech and figuration must be forsaken, while at the same time they serve as go-betweens; and, as in the exegeses of Greek and Christian allegories, the meaning lies, according to the commentator Cheng Xuanying, in the most profound "principle" of things, the source of "mystery."[a] Just as in Western exegesis all that cannot be understood literally is interpreted allegorically, *Zhuangzi* itself would be only a net or a trap, and he who remains attached to it, Wang Fuzhi warns, is condemned to stray from the right path.[5]

But can the analogy be taken any further? In spite of these apparent similarities, we suspect that the image of the net (or the trap) does not completely coincide with that of the veil (or the covering). Something resists their likening and modifies from within our grasping the meaning and the relationship at stake. This thread is tenuous, but it should allow us to go much further: to understand the rift that appears so discreetly in metaphors, we must imagine what might globally condition the perspectives of interpretation in both cultures. My aim is to probe the original reasons that indirect expression was favored to express mystery in both China and Greece. In other words (to pull away from the Greeks), I wonder if Chinese thought also resorted to myth. And if it did not use it in the same way, what were the consequences? I strongly suspect that if the strategy of detour differs, that to which it gives access must also be different.

The net represents words, the fish meaning. We have, on the one hand, the instrument of language, and, on the other, that which we want to express. The rift opened up between them by the image tends to demonstrate, later in *Zhuangzi*, the inability of language to communicate. The theme, as it is expressed there, might seem among the most commonplace. But it is rooted in a reflection that is much more original, which is found at the beginning of the work and denounces language as the origin of our straying. Instead of revealing the Tao, it "hides" it (far from voluntary, this hiding represents a congenital defect); in its very principle, language makes us miss reality. The strategy of discourse must consequently be all the more delicate to put into effect, and the necessity of detour all the more urgent to work around these difficulties, as the critique of language at the end of Chinese

Antiquity (notably under the influence of sophists of the school of names) was pushed even further.

On the inability of speech to communicate, one anecdote suffices. A duke is reading in his hall, a wheelwright is working below in the courtyard. The latter puts down his tools and goes upstairs to ask the duke what he is reading. The duke replies, "I'm reading the word of the sages." "Where are these sages?" asks the wheelwright (feigning naïveté). "They are long dead," replies the duke. "Then what you are reading is nothing but their dregs!" Called on to explain, he illustrates his point based on his own experience: when working on a wheel, if he eases up on the pace, although more pleasant, the work is less well executed; if he works too furiously, he gets tired, and the results are just as unsatisfactory. The subtle in-between, which reflects not only the "hand" but also the "spirit," "cannot be expressed in words" and cannot be passed on, even from father to son (an idea similar to that in *Mencius* 7.2.5, though without the humor).[6]

Even in manual work, the wheelwright demonstrates, there is something beyond speech. Since its domain is "the visible," speech cannot reach the "inner dimension," which leads us to divide reality into different areas.[7] There are things that cannot be expressed but can be imagined that represent the "end" of things; and there is a beyond, which one cannot even imagine, since it does not belong to the order of things. Things that cannot be "divided" and things that cannot be "embraced" make up two infinities, each of which no longer belongs to the domain of "actualization."[b] Through speech, and then through thought, we can attain the "delimitation of things" "locally." But the "immensity" of reality escapes us.[c8]

From this perspective, language nevertheless retains its pertinence, however reduced that might be. But the critique to which it is subjected does not merely circumscribe its domain in this way. Here it is not a matter, as I suggested in the beginning, only of the most exterior, and basically secondary, aspect of its process. The real escapes language, or rather, and more serious still, language hides reality, because language immediately posits us inside the unilaterality of a point of view. I say this as opposed to that, I see things this way as opposed to that way. As soon as we speak, we are closed inside a partiality that makes us miss the essential communal dimension of things. The characteristic of language is to mark differences, that of discourse is to use language to state an opinion, whereas lack of differentiation characterizes the Tao of reality.

But where does this unilaterality come from? As soon as our mind takes shape, we read in the second chapter of *Zhuangzi* (the heart of the work), it inevitably adopts a certain form, consisting of a particular point of view, at least momentarily, simply because it is this and not that. This is what *Zhuangzi* calls, in an expression whose subtlety it exploits, "set-mindedness."[d] Just as our bodies, once they are born, no longer transform themselves until their extinction, our set-mindedness makes up a particular fixation; and inasmuch as it is more or less set in one way and not in another, it is limited by this individuality. Here it is not a question of our taking one position or another or of prejudice; rather, it is merely a question of the logical response to any *event*. All that becomes actualized, by occurring in a certain way, simultaneously deprives itself of all other possibilities. Any event will therefore always be merely a small event compared with the unconditioned plenitude of the Tao. The opposition "for" and "against"[e] in things we support and those we oppose is simply the result of this phenomenon. Basically, *Zhuangzi* here measures the ordinary deficit praised in Confucius (the Master is without privileged "ideas," predetermined "necessity," specific "position," or particular "I"; see *Analects* 9.4). In other words, the ideal is a consciousness that is always in the process of becoming but *never is fixed* and thereby

remains open to the totality of possibilities instead of immobilizing itself in a point of view. This immobilization of point of view
is responsible for philosophical disputes in which each side sees
only one aspect of things, for instance, the literati opposing the
Mohists and each side affirming what its opponent denies. The
only issue is "clear vision,"[f] which, in the context of this development, signifies going beyond any unilateral perception: when the
things as well as the discourse elicited by them are placed "on the
same level," without partiality or interest (the notion of qi[g]; see
the title of the second chapter of *Zhuangzi*). Everything, including
the notion of a point of view, disappears, since all points of view
are equally contained therein. Clear vision is this global vision.[9]

Once again, *globality*, conceived of as an absence of partiality,
appears on the horizon of Chinese thought. It is the point of
view that is no longer one that prefigures — yet never completely
explicitly — all wisdom. This is why Chinese thought operates
through a reduction of exclusives (of perspectives) and not through
an abstraction of essences (and this is why, of course, it is based on
harmony). One can read this concern in a phrase as simple as the
following (in the same passage): "Our words are not just hot air."
Many have tried to interpret the phrase, and Western commentators understand it today as follows: speech is not merely the
blowing of air; since it expresses something, it means something.
Chinese commentators have usually understood it in a completely
different way: speech differs from the wind because it comes from
a fixed point of view, which is thus rendered particular, whereas
the wind never ceases to blow everything in its path indiscrimi-
nately. Whereas we speak from the point of view of set-mindedness, which immobilizes us in a certain position, the wind is not
set: always *in flux*, it varies in all areas of its rustlings. This brings
us back to the theme of natural music with which the second
chapter of *Zhuangzi* so magnificently opens: the most varied

sounds are contained equally in the wind, without exclusion, and all are stimulated at the same time.

Everything else is human perspective. For everything, there is both a this and a that; there is one standpoint, and there is another: we may not see things from the standpoint of that, but we do see them from the standpoint of this. But in fact, since these standpoints coexist, one should concur with the specialists in names, such as Hui Shi, that one cannot exist without the other and that they are interdependent. They therefore condition each other because *one is the other*. This is why the sage, rather than depending on one side to the detriment of the other, which would condemn him to an arbitrary position, contemplates reality naturally, by following nature's lead. To leave behind a unilaterality in which there is always a this as opposed to a that, in which each aspect counters another: such is the "pivot of the Tao." And when this pivot positions itself "in the center of the circle" (the vicious circle described around the endless train of this and that), one can respond inexhaustibly to all aspects of things without having to compare and contrast them. One can inexhaustibly make use of for and against without becoming bound by them. The main characteristic of the pivot, in fact, is to pivot ceaselessly, in one direction or another, depending on the circumstances.

We see the problem posed by language at this point. As opposed to the global vision, in which all question of angle has disappeared, as soon as we speak, we have what is right and what is wrong, what is this way and what is not. The use of language never ceases to pit reality against itself; in walling us in with factitious oppositions, language causes us to lose sight of the fundamental unity that, by making it constantly communicate within itself, allows it to exist. Another famous apologue in the second chapter of *Zhuangzi* mocks this illusion of differences. A keeper of monkeys distributes acorns to them, promising: "Three acorns in the morning and four in the evening." The monkeys become angry. "All right," replies the keeper, "you will get four in the morning and three in the evening." And the monkeys are satisfied. Wisdom consists in preventing oneself from falling into this trap: rather than set differences, which are artificial, into play and thereby attempt to prove his originality (through his point of view), the sage follows the "flow of things"ʰ and its evolutions. This is what *Zhuangzi* calls "respecting natural harmony,"ⁱ or "walking two roads."ʲ It is only in walking on both one *and* the other side, without allowing one to obscure the other from sight, that one is able to emerge from the unilaterality of point of view.

The loss of wisdom corresponds to the loss of this global vision in which nothing is excluded. *Zhuangzi* makes us descend into it by degrees:

> In the beginning, our forefathers attained the heights of knowledge. What was this knowledge? They considered that nothing existed. This was perfect and complete knowledge, to which nothing could be added.
>
> The next phase was to think that things did exist but without boundaries. The phase after that was to think that there were boundaries but with no judgment of for and against. With the opposition of for and against, the Tao was lost; and with the loss of the Tao, preferences came into being.[10]

People often have assumed that in undermining so completely the foundations of differences, *Zhuangzi* is a work of relativism. I do not, however, believe this is well founded, since, in the global vision, any notion of relativity dissolves, and each thing is seen from its own angle, which corresponds to the logic of its deployment. It is language that confines us to relativity, for, in the absence of common criteria, everything is a matter of mutually

313

exclusive perspectives, none of which is better grounded than the others: nothing is greater than the tip of a hair, just as a large mountain is small. With this in mind, how can one thesis be opposed to its opposite? In the dialectical game of for and against (and certain thinkers, at the end of Antiquity, became masters at this), no thesis can resist its infinite reversal. Imagine that there is a "beginning [of the world]." But how can there be a beginning of a beginning? One might answer, "There is not as yet any beginning of the beginning." But why is there not a beginning of the non-beginning of the beginning? In the final analysis, "I do not know whether I have said something or nothing."[11] As we see, the more we continue in this direction, the more speech is destroyed.

From this point on, the impasse is total: the Tao has never been divided, whereas language does not offer the least bit of constancy. Although, to take a stance, men have established demarcations and hierarchies, they have been unable to mask the fact that at the heart of all divisions lies the indivisible, just as at the heart of all disagreements lies the unspoken. Hence, while they engage in discussions to impose one point of view over others, the thinkers of the "hundred schools" each time lose sight of the other aspect of things. We return to the paradox of *Laozi*: true discussion "does not speak."

But silence would be merely an inverse obstinacy and therefore no better. The issue, then, is to consider the heart of language: to invent a speech that can baffle its condition as language and break its mold; a speech that frees itself from the factitious oppositions we usually project onto language and thereby lifts us outside the unilaterality of point of view; a speech that is not blocked in any direction but articulates the eternal transition of things, which one can pour into but never fill, just as one may empty it, but it is never empty. The pivot of the Tao has already made its demands; it is only in never ceasing to pivot, in order to

314

embrace reality from all angles, that it can follow the spontaneous movement of things and grant us access to the natural.

Since the limitations of language close us into the unilaterality of a single point of view, whereas the Tao is "boundless,"[k] we must seek to go beyond speech. Since its demarcations are factitious and hide the depths of reality, speech must be rendered extravagant. In short, for language to emerge from the relativism to which it is condemned, it must be opened to disproportion. *Zhuangzi* begins with the following lines:

> In the northern ocean lives a fish named Kun. It is I do not know how many thousand *li* long. It can change into a bird called Peng, whose back is I do not know how many thousand *li* long. When it takes flight, its wings are like the clouds in the sky. Gliding on the movement of the sea, it flies to the southern ocean. The southern ocean is the heavenly pool. [12]

From the beginning, everything is arranged to open up the boundaries that mark the limits of things and, using this as a basis, to detach us from the oppositions on which this specification rests. Disproportion (through the gigantism of the beings evoked) breaks the bounds of ordinary measurements; transformation (of the fish into a bird) checks the individuation of species; migration (from the depths of the oceans to the heights of the sky, from the northern ocean to the southern one) reabsorbs the distance between the poles. This figure of the *fish-bird* works in the opposite direction from that in which language leads us. Whereas language ceaselessly breaks reality into pieces, opposing its different aspects, this image ties reality together: the species are no longer confined by their specificity, the horizons are no longer separate from each other.

For discourse to stop hiding the source of things, it must be removed from its norm; to liberate it from its hidden arbitrariness, it must be made conspicuously strange. In the first chapter of *Zhuangzi*, this progressive *overflowing* is commented on by the author and becomes more explicit every step of the way. In the second sequence in the chapter, a sage addresses another sage:

> I was listening to the words of Jieyu, who uses big words that lack substance, going on and on but never coming to the point. I was stupefied by his words, which are as boundless as the Milky Way. Irrelevant and excessive, they are not related to human experience.[13]

Strange phrases follow: "Far away on a mountain called Gushe, there live holy men whose skin is like snow and who are as sensitive as virgins. They do not eat the five grains but live off wind and dew; mounting the clouds, yoking dragons, they travel beyond the four seas. The simple concentration of their spirits is enough to cure diseases and make crops ripen." The narrator concludes, "Now, I think this is preposterous, and I do not believe it."

As in the preceding case, this figuration systematically baffles established demarcations: it is clear that the holy men escape their human specification and go beyond our world. All the rifts with which language covers reality are suspended for them: they are both this and that, one does not even know if the things people say about them are possible or not. If one analyzes the virtue attributed to them more closely, one realizes that it derives from their capacity to cross through genres and bind them together. This is why it is said that when their spirits are concentrated, vitality reigns to its full extent, people are healed and the crops mature (in China, spirit is conceived of as the capacity to circulate through reality). In short, as the narrator's interlocutor notes, their efficacy comes from their unifying "all the variety of which

316

reality is made." They embody reality's capacity to communicate the source of itself, which permits it to exist.

Remember, this episode is introduced by remarks that judge it as discourse: "big," "lack substance," "going on and on but never coming to the point" (that is, losing touch with reality), and "boundless."[l] Its vastness is what makes it "preposterous."[m] In the episode that follows, this vastness, which goes beyond all norms, is compared with the thrust of *Zhuangzi* itself. It is noteworthy that the person who criticizes it is a sophist of the school of names, Hui Shi, who made Zhuangzi sensitive to the relativism of names.[14] He broaches it through the following anecdote:

> The king of Wei gave me the seeds of a gigantic gourd. When I planted them, they produced enormous fruits whose walls were not thick enough to hold liquid; if cut into sections to make containers, they were too flat to hold anything. What an empty vastness! Since they were useless, I smashed them to bits.[15]

Zhuangzi was well aware of the allusion to his own book (the commentator attests to this), but he chose to respond indirectly in turn. There was a man from Song, he recounts, who made a salve to prevent hands from chapping; for generations, his family's occupation had been to bleach silk. When a stranger heard about the recipe for the salve, he offered him one hundred gold pieces. The family, overjoyed to gain in one morning more money than it had earned for generations, urged him to sell it. The buyer was then entrusted with a fleet in winter and, after winning a victory thanks to this salve, received a vast estate from the king. The moral is clear: the same salve that helped one side merely to bleach silk allowed another to gain the highest reward. Next Zhuangzi adjusts his remarks to the image brought up by his inter-locutor: the gigantic gourd, which he complained he had not been able to make into containers. Why, asks Zhuangzi, did he not think of tying it to himself like a buoy to "float down the rivers and lakes"?

Since the dialogue is limited to this exchange of ideas, it can only be made intelligible by exploiting their contrast. The idea of cutting the gourd to make it into containers goes back, in the eyes of Hui Shi, to the particular content of denominations. Since it is too huge and exceeds the norm, and therefore has no bounds within which to contain anything, Zhuangzi's remarks cannot fill this use appropriately. Therefore, Zhuangzi is careful not to refute the critique. First of all, to understand it, one must radically change perspectives. What could be more effective in discourse than the simple substitution of images? The buoy that allows one to float on water links up with a free circulation through the real. Instead of serving as a particular container, this gourd transformed into a buoy allows one to drift about, carried along by the waves. It uncovers a completely different use for us, which, like it, is of another magnitude (compare also the benefit of the estate with that of bleaching silk): this useless vastness enables us to emerge from the specification of things (codified by language) and evolve in accordance with them.

While in this case, the critique of discourse typical of Zhuangzi was still approached indirectly and remained allusive, in the episode that closes the chapter, it is treated frontally; and while in the preceding episode, it is a matter simply of demonstrating how to "use the useless," here the point is to show more radically how it is that "through uselessness" one may "use the useless" (Wang Fuzhi's phrase). Here we see the idea pushed to an extreme point of explicitness; and it is again Hui Shi who initiates the discussion:

> "Where I live, there is a big tree called the tree of Heaven. Its trunk
> is so knotted and swollen, it cannot be measured with chalk lines and

ink; its branches so twisted they cannot be measured with compass and square. It grows on the side of the road, but no carpenter gives it a second glance. Your words are big and useless like this tree, which everyone ignores."

Zhuangzi replied, "Have you ever seen a weasel? It lies in wait for its prey, then leaps right or left, up or down, until it falls into a trap or is caught in a snare. And then there is the yak, as large as the clouds in the sky. As big as it is, it cannot catch even a mouse. You have a big tree and disparage its uselessness. Why not plant it in the middle of nowhere, in a plain stretching to infinity. Then you can wander at will and be idle next to it, roaming freely away from it and resting at its feet. It would not be cut down prematurely nor would it be disturbed. How can its uselessness bother you?"

The sophist Hui Shi seems here to reproach the Taoist Zhuangzi for attempting to invent a use for language that brings it out of its functional relativity, for in this bundle of images that concludes the chapter, we see confirmed the opposition sketched in the beginning. The tree whose trunk is too gnarled and whose branches too twisted to correspond to established norms (set by chalk, ink, square, and compass) recalls the inadequate and outsize proposition concerning the pure spirits on Mount Gushe, which consequently appears unreliable. The weasel that jumps from one side to the other to seize its prey brings us back to the specified, utilitarian adaptation to which speech commonly lays claim. The yak, whose gigantism reminds us of the bird Peng of the first lines of the text, illustrates the lack of adaptation that goes hand in hand with excess and vastness. Just as in the preceding case the containers were too awkward to hold anything, here the yak is incapable of taking possession of things individually. Through successive leaps, which grid space, the weasel mimes the utilitarian way one usually attempts to seize reality through language. This is precisely the activity of demarcation, which is basically illusory, that Zhuangzi, in opening his book, proposes to undo. In going beyond the frontiers imposed by words, in no longer squaring with the recognized norms of things, his propositions give us access to another dimension: existence, disengaged from functional specifications, becomes available again; one can evolve in it freely — to eternity (see the title of Zhuangzi's second chapter). In bringing the world out of factitious demarcations, the evasive proposition of *Zhuangzi* gives it over to bliss.

Zhuangzi calls for a conversion of our way of seeing (exclusively in terms of vision). This is why he can be ironic (as preparatory to this rupture; as opposed to the Confucian proposition, in which the progress toward regulation is continuous). This is also why his words can be misunderstood (by those who remain "blind" and "deaf" and mock the episode on Mount Gushe).[16] At the beginning of the chapter, the powerful flight of the immense Peng high up in the sky meets with the mockery of a cicada and a young dove: "Suddenly we take flight, and when we come upon an elm or sappanwood tree, we alight; sometimes we simply fall to the ground before reaching it. Why fly so high up in the sky to go to the South?" In the air and on the land, the powerful flight of the one is opposed to the satisfied flutterings of the others; whereas one soars higher and higher, the others remain earthbound. "What do these two know?" asks the narrator. The disproportion of scales makes the two perspectives unmeasurable: Zhuangzi has responded in advance to those who might judge his propositions by the measure of common adaptability.

I must, however, confess that this reading is not the most orthodox. Many Chinese commentators (from Guo Xiang in the third century to Wang Fuzhi in the seventeenth century) have considered that, in spite of the extreme differences of size, the bird Peng and the young dove can be put on the same plane: if

each is satisfied with his lot and conforms to his nature, the capacity for fulfillment is the same, and one does not prevail over the
other.[17] Rather than read into the story a rupture caused by disproportion, they see a just proportion of scale: a large bird needs
large spaces, yet a cage suffices for a young dove. Rather than read
it as an aspiration toward going beyond the limits, they see a traditional equilibrium in it. No doubt the enterprise of going beyond the limits (of language first of all), which *Zhuangzi* appears
to imply, was difficult to reconcile with a literary ideology attached to the ideal of regulation: each should be satisfied with his
lot and cooperate in the common good by remaining in his place.
I wonder if Zhuangzi, like Qu Yuan (see p. 171) whom he resembles in many ways (linguistic characteristics and the culture of the
South; shamanistic inspiration; the taste for myth and the bizarre;
the fabulating role of the image; themes of flight into the heavens
and carefree wanderings; and so on), was completely accepted by
the Chinese tradition. Certainly the exceptional "magnificence"
of their genius was celebrated and people were inspired by their
"luxuriant" imaginations, but they were continuously read according to criteria and requirements external to their works (for Qu
Yuan, the rules of writing from *The Book of Songs*; for *Zhuangzi*,
the moral of equilibrium). In the country of the center, any excess
is forced to return to harmony.

Western commentators (notably Robert Allinson) have underscored the writing methods in *Zhuangzi* that aimed at checking
the demarcating function of language, thereby lifting discourse
out of the partiality of a point of view.[18] For example, by frequently resorting to an alternative logical interrogation in which
two propositions appear equally possible, *Zhuangzi* brings us out
of the unilaterality of positions. "Did I really speak? Have I ever
really spoken?" As soon as both statements seem equally valid,

taking a stance no longer seems legitimate. The opposition of for and against becomes outworn; our "thetic" reason is suspended. This effect is heightened by what we today perceive as mythic elements in *Zhuangzi* (along the lines of the holy spirits on Mount Gushe): not only does the fabulous nature of myth remove us from the perspective of the ordinary (that of the young dove), but what it recounts is both admissible and not admissible. Hence the opposition between true and false is paralyzed. Furthermore, the metaphors and comparisons, so common in *Zhuangzi*, overwhelm the specification of things: through the transfer it puts into play, metaphor binds reality to its own interior and shows us the angle from which what was distinctly perceived blends together; it brings us out of univocal determinations and reveals a common aspect through difference. In opening up our understanding of things, all these detours of speech connect us to the course of reality, in which nothing is excluded. Things that were opposed find themselves on the same plane; things that were contrasted become equivalent. The same is true for the figure of the prodigious or the monstrous (not only the fish-bird of the first lines but also all the lame, humpbacked, and crippled beings, without lips or eyes, which commentators on *Zhuangzi* have interpreted), which, by blurring boundaries or violating the norm, puts the unilaterality of judgment into question.

From one angle or another, the goal is to open up *points of view* to rejoin *vision*; to return from exclusive perspectives to *globality* — that of the Tao — in which all are equally possible. The vastness and the extravagance of *Zhuangzi* have no other aim. As proof, we have only to read some lines from the last chapter, in which all the tendencies similar and dissimilar to those of a Taoist are reviewed:

With empty and far-off remarks
words infinitely vast, expressions without beginning or end;

322

he lets himself wander at a moment's whim without falling
   into partiality
and refrains from considering things from a unilateral
   point of view.[19]

The following is henceforth established: the excess of discourse,
which makes it seem so confusing, is aimed at bringing it out of
the unilateral point of view.[n] "He judged the world too muddy
and bogged down," the text continues, "to be able to address it
rigorously." In the presentation of this meandering and apparently
absurd discourse, one might find the traditional justification for
words of revelation: when man cannot hope to have direct access
to transcendence, the extravagance of discourse constrains him to
quit his point of view and turn his gaze to that which goes beyond
it. For someone like Origen, impossibilities in the literal course of
events that disrupt reading, such as incoherences, signs of anthro-
pomorphism, and incongruous metaphors, are so many signs inviting us to search for a meaning on another plane — theological
or spiritual. "Stare secundum litteram nullo modo potest": it is
necessary, in allegorizing the passage, to seek a higher intelligence.
Thus, when the psalm, in recounting the crossing of the Jordan by
the Jews, describes a river that turns in its bed and mountains that
leap, Saint Augustine perceives a sign of the "mysterious signification" of the event.

   This is precisely where the rift reappears. The overflowing
propositions of *Zhuangzi* lead to the reabsorption of arbitrary demarcations and thereby return to the limitless aspect of the Tao.
Moreover, the text's elusive allure brings us back to the indistinct-
ness of reality in its undifferentiated source ("vague, indistinct,
and without particular form,"[o] it is noted later in the text). But,
in rupturing with the manifestation of things, its extravagance
does not lead to the interpretation of meaning on another level —

either spiritual or theological. On the contrary, in the development that follows, the absence of any gap between the discourse of *Zhuangzi* and the course of the world is emphasized. While "evolving all alone together with the spirit of the heavens and the earth," it never takes a distance from particular individuals; while avoiding for and against, it continues to "cohabit the ordinary world" (or rather, in becoming free from for and against, it becomes truly able to abandon itself to the flow of things; see Guo Xiang). The idea of *even though* predominates in the passage: even though prodigious, Zhuangzi's book addresses the "meanderings of beings" without "harming" them; even though he returns to the source of reality and plumbs its depths in such a way that he evolves on a par with the "creator," he remains in accord with the transformation that arises in all things, aware of their individuality.

Here, once again, is an essential difference from the Western tradition (and there is quite a tradition here); indeed, I have never ceased progressively to revolve around this difference in the course of this book. *Zhuangzi* invites us to shift our perspectives but not in order to lead us into another reality (that is, a reality of another order, either ontological or theological, which might represent the intelligible or the divine). It aims to detach us from the limitations and oppositions in which we contain reality. In other words, the heights it invites us to reach lead to the emancipation of experience — not to a belief in another world. The gesture of going beyond suffices; and transcendence is not objectified into a Truth. And if Zhuangzi comes the closest in Chinese Antiquity to the Western aspiration to a sense of the beyond, such a beyond assumes no theoretical consistency for him.

This is illuminated for strategies of meaning by the parallel images of the *net* and the *veil*. The image of the net is purely instrumental: when a meaning has been reached, the figuration can be forgotten. The image of the veil, on the other hand, implies a doubling between appearance and reality. The veil hides what it covers; hence it is necessary to reject the veil to attain reality. The going beyond, in this case, is transformed into an uncovering; and the tension between the two levels stimulates the quest. "Quae plus latent, plus placent": the more hidden, the more pleasing. Even when he pursues, like Zhuangzi, the image of the hunt as a metaphor of the quest for meaning, Clement of Alexandria insists on the intensity that the difficulty encountered confers on the activity: "Just as the passionate hunter loves to scout, search for, track and unleash his dogs before taking his prey, truth is indeed sweet when won by long search and hard labor."[20] In Western exegesis, this tension was even exploited to enhance the rift between the two planes and heighten the transcendence of the meaning expressed. The intelligible and the divine come forth all the more when called on to contradict the sensible. Whereas with Zhuangzi, the figure of the abnormal, even the monstrous, merely destroys the traces by which normality affirms itself and thereby paralyzes the specifications of language to rejoin us to the undifferentiated source of things, with the Greeks, the symbolism of monstrosity was interpreted *as the underside* of figuration. One gains access to transcendence in turning away from its image. The most indecent myths about the gods, Proclus states (the wars on Olympus, adulteries, castrations), best remind us of their supereminence. By their unnaturalness, they show "what exceeds nature in the gods; through anti-reason [they show] what is more divine than all reason; through objects presented to our eyes as ugly, [they show] what transcends all partial beauty in simplicity."[21] The extravagance of figuration tends, on the one hand, to reabsorb the exclusions within the heart of the real, and, on the other hand, to maximize the essential rupture — between the natural and the supernatural — on which the idea of reality is based.

It is time to reformulate the question: If there is no *other plane* to which the detour of speech grants access, how can it operate and where might it lead us? Of all ancient Chinese works, *Zhuangzi* is today considered to make the most use of myth and symbols. But how conscious is the text itself — as well as the commentary on it — of such workings? In other words, how did it perceive its strategy? One of the last chapters of *Zhuangzi*, immediately following the image of the net, can illuminate this point.[22] According to the commentator Wang Fuzhi, in this movement from one chapter to another, there is something that serves as a preface to the work as a whole and might constitute the pivot of its interpretation: after passing judgment on language, Zhuangzi describes how he envisions escaping the difficulty and avoiding being reduced to silence.

Three types of detour are imagined successively. The first is "supposed"[p] words, whose figuration is "borrowed from outside." This imaged transposition occupies nine-tenths of discourse, or, according to the early interpretation of Guo Xiang, people believe it to be nine-tenths. As an example, commentators cite the episode of the holy men on Mount Gushe. This episode corresponds to something we interpret, based on the Greek tradition, as a reworking of myth or allegory. We are therefore surprised at the justification given: "a father cannot intervene on behalf of his son." A father should not praise his son; "it is better for someone else to do so in his stead." There follows a more general psychological justification that reworks the now familiar leitmotiv: everyone approves of the things similar to his way of thinking and disapproves of people who differ. Of the things that should correspond to the functioning of myth, *Zhuangzi* says nothing more (or rather, it states laconically, in the conclusive passage cited previously, that these "words found elsewhere" are used "to deploy"). There is not the slightest reflection on the relationship between

the figuration and the message it might contain or on the revelation it should produce. The justification of the imaged figuration
is reduced to what seems the principal preoccupation of *Zhuangzi*: to escape from the partiality of speech. The transposition of
words merely plays a role of intervention — between persons —
that increases credibility.

The commentary says little more. The argument, taken from
Zhuangzi itself, is always that the figuration must be "put aside"
to attain the meaning. Hence in the episode of the holy men on
Mount Gushe, there would indeed be a consciousness of a "global
image"q and, consequently, no need to wonder as to a historical
point of view (according to Guo Xiang and Cheng Xuanying).[23]
But the overflowing of experience that gives rise to this myth
does not lead to the discovery of another order of things. There is
indeed "projection beyond the limits of our world" and "going
beyond what can be seen and understood," but the only function
of this going beyond is to evoke the "unfathomable depths" of the
sovereign's virtue. The fabulous dimension has no other effect,
just as the passage has no limit; it serves merely as the hyper-
bolization of the political. The horizon, as far away as it has been
pushed, does not open onto another reality. No other level — such
as the spiritual — is proposed according to which this "myth"
could be interpreted.

Hence, when a modern critic such as Robert Allinson sees
in the giant fish with which *Zhuangzi* opens a symbol of the
"subject-reader" or interprets its diving to the waters' depths as
the image of our "epistemological starting point," I believe he
openly breaks with Chinese tradition.[24] This does not mean that
he does not have the right to read *Zhuangzi* in this way, but his
interpretation reveals the perspective of Western exegesis. His
reading not only sets itself apart from the Chinese commentary
but fails to respond to the conditions that make this commentary

possible. We remember the story of the salve for chapped hands that allowed a clever stranger to win a naval battle and receive a vast estate. Allinson proposes to interpret this salve not in a material sense but as a spiritual remedy. The "message" is therefore "on a higher plane," that the "brain can be used for a higher purpose." One can see very well, however, that this spiritual plane serving to interpret the message allegorically is introduced by the exegetist. His reading seems more Neoplatonic than Chinese.

The second mode of discourse proposed by Zhuangzi is "respected"[r] words. Here the quote is used as detour, since these words have already been said by elders. Again Zhuangzi does not welcome them at first (remember the wheelwright's estimation of the "dregs" of the ancients). What creates the value of these words is less their authority than their recurrence (the same is true for the village adages; see the chapter "Zeyang"). Hence, in the first chapter, Zhuangzi reports two other versions of the story of the bird-fish, one from the legends of the country of Qi and the other from the conversation of an ancient king. These successive references give more weight to the proposed figuration (these two types of detour, figuration and citation, the commentator recognizes, often merge). In both figuration and citation, the objective is the same, to bring words out of their partiality: in this case, their individuality is done away with by melding them with an already-known voice.

It is to the third form of detour that Zhuangzi grants the most interest. (I am surprised that modern commentators interested in the theory of language in Zhuangzi, such as A.C. Graham and Chad Hansen, have not paid more attention to it.)[25] To illustrate this form of detour, Zhuangzi uses a receptacle, an image that intrigued the ancient Chinese[s] (and was used by several schools): this container tips when it is full and stands up when empty — that is, it rocks according to the situation and does not stay in the same position.[26] We can see how evocative this image is when applied to discourse: the words it illustrates are ideal words because they do not have a fixed position but oscillate as much in one direction as another, following reality. Hence it is said that in their natural outpouring they harmonize through the "natural limit." Or again, in "pouring from one side or the other," granting favor to no one position in advance and therefore conforming to the inclination of things, they "go to the very end" of their process.

Once again, the value of words arises from their capacity for *continuous variation,* and only words that vary can express *globality* (which here coincides with the natural limit or going to the very end of the span of reality). Since they spread out indifferently from one position to another in uninterrupted flux, they represent the words of vision in which nothing is excluded. Many expressions we have encountered convey this idea: the "pivot of the Tao," in ceaselessly pivoting in its groove in the first chapter, "harmonizes" with the requirements of a situation "without ever being in default"; the art of "arguing without words," and thereby avoiding the trap of the limitations of language, allows one to "pour without filling" and to "void without emptying," thus remaining in transition, never moving definitively to either side. Or yet again, the words of Zhuangzi are praised for their ability to "wander" at each "moment" without falling into "partiality."[t] A laconic expression most completely sums up this idea: "accordingly — is all."[u] In the most obvious way, these words that never cease to vary in order to harmonize with the course of things, and that never stop in any given position, take a stance against *set-mindedness*, which is limited by a particular perspective, as we saw in the beginning of the critique of language. Whereas set-mindedness shuts itself into a proposition, which excludes the opposite thesis, becoming for this and against that, words in continuous variation remain completely open: since the mind does not impose itself, it uses for and against freely, depending on the circumstance. In short, the words that can express reality are supple (ductile) enough to embrace all developments, because they do not follow any set principle.

These *fluctuating words*, which constantly evolve, correspond to the critique of language with which we began. Even though we do not speak, "agreement is not affected by words."ᵛ But the agreement found naturally in things "is not itself in agreement with language." This is why language opposes the acceptable and the unacceptable, making that which is appear, as well as that which is not. Only fluctuating words can escape this danger, for in ceaselessly modulating themselves, these words always coincide with the acceptability of things without encountering the opposite; they constantly respect their "because this is the way it is" without countering with that which is not. Their variability, which nothing reduces a priori, enables them to consider each thing and thereby correspond to the logic of its unfolding. No longer is anything "not so" or "unacceptable."ʷ Fluctuating words thus correspond to the spontaneity of things, the global *vision* containing, without exclusion, all viewpoints. Hence they can embrace the flowering of the real in its entirety, for they are not content to put reality back into a "natural agreement," which the use of language makes us leave behind. Instead, they merge this "natural agreement" with the "natural limit,"ˣ Zhuangzi adds in conclusion: in each time following the point of view appropriate to each individual reality, and thus not erecting differences or preferences between points of view, fluctuating words begin and end in each moment like an unbroken circle.

"Aside from these figured words and respected words," says the commentator Wang Fuzhi — that is, aside from images and citations — "everything that emerges between them that is subtle or forms detours in the analysis" (or the discussion) is a *fluctuat-*

*ing word.*ʸ²⁷ Although we easily understand how the imaged figuration or the citation constitutes a detour in language, this might seem less obvious for this third genre of expression. A phrase from the above-mentioned passage of *Zhuangzi* can illuminate this point — in spite of its paradoxical aspect: since words say nothing, one can speak and say nothing,ᶻ just as one can remain silent and say a great deal. According to Wang Fuzhi, by remaining silent, these words do not get bogged down in anything, whereas if they speak, nothing remains hidden. Fluctuating words are precisely those that remain silent because they do not isolate one aspect of things to the detriment of others, in the way ordinary speech treats a theme or subject from a particular angle. At the same time, fluctuating words remain silent because, without directly broaching any particular thing, they never cease to refer to a subject imagined from a particular angle. We see here the philosophical creation of the allusive value of speech: it concerns without saying and implies without broaching. This is why Wang Fuzhi can say, "The figured words and the citations, just like everything that is not figured or cited, is all one": "All is fluctuating words" and can go to the end of things. Figurations and citations, as well as their absence, are but modalities of a more general program. Only if one does not claim to speak specifically (that is, in an exclusive and fixating fashion), with the meaning thereby unfolding indefinitely on its own, can one effectively speak of reality.

Above, I have had to make a choice in translation, and I must now assess the consequences. In translating *heavens* as *nature*, the *heavenly agreement* becomes the *natural agreement*, and the *limits of Heaven* becomes *natural limits*. In fact, at the end of Chinese Antiquity, especially for Zhuangzi, the heavens were nothing more than the coexistence of all the spontaneous unfoldings. Earlier I noted that Zhuangzi says it was enough not to "pronounce" on any particular aspect — which defines the sage — to be able to contemplate reality from the "level of Heaven"[aa]: that is, to embrace all the particular points of view, according to which beings ceaselessly unfold for themselves, in his global vision.[28] Hence the heavens of *Zhuangzi* conform quite closely to what we call *nature*; and one can better understand why the detour put into effect by fluctuating words simultaneously *gives access*. This detour does not grant access to something else, such as a sense of a beyond on another level — a metaphysical or religious conception of the heavens — as the allegorization in Greek myths or biblical tales does. Words need only overflow the limitations of language, no longer approaching the real in a compartmentalized and arrested way — in short, they need only ceaselessly be an allusive variation to allow us to rejoin the spontaneous coexistence of things and to give us access to the natural. In reabsorbing the exclusive points of view created by language, and therefore in liberating us from the partiality of its usage, words bring us up to the heavens as a horizon of the real.

Everything designates this allusive variation the ideal writing — that which can totally express reality. To verify this, we must close the circle by returning briefly to literary expression.

CHAPTER FOURTEEN

The Clouds and the Moon

Is it possible to imagine an *ars poetica* on these foundations? In other words, can we conceive of the detour as norm and indirection as the object of a precept, and then recommend them to the writer? Let us move from description to prescription, from commentary on texts to the rules of writing. On allusion, Chinese criticism long remained allusive itself, emphasizing its importance without explaining it. The allusive, it is not hard to imagine, resists theory — even as it, in a sense, renders it useless. To call attention to it is enough; to treat it heavy-handedly tends to destroy it. One finds nevertheless that Chinese criticism (especially starting with the Ming dynasty, fourteenth to seventeenth centuries) became gradually more preoccupied with rules and methods (*fa*ᵃ); it sought to codify its art technically. Whence arose a new concern for explaining allusion and breaking down its effect. A poetic theorist of the seventeenth century, Jin Shengtan (1610–1661), for example, was not content, yet again, to point to the inexhaustible richness of indirectness; he endeavored meticulously to analyze how the detour was supposed to function and what its extent was to be. In one stroke, he provides us with an opportunity for verification and retrospectively throws more light on the elliptical notations of the ancient authors.

The text most representative of this art of detour at the heart

333

of ancient literature, which might thus serve as a model for writers, was, in his eyes, the main commentary of *Spring and Autumn Annals* (*Zuozhuan*; see chapter 5 above). But rather than treat this great text of Antiquity directly, he develops his analysis — as compelled by detour — on the basis of a much more recent work belonging not to the noble genres of classical literature — poetry, philosophy, history — but to opera, namely, *The Western Room* (*Xixiangji*), which was composed around 1300. Still, he shows that even a popular work such as *The Western Room* (heretofore judged unworthy of commentary), and a theatrical work to boot (and thus more given to representation, it would seem), rigorously obeys this quasi-unique principle of literary writing.

Let us start with the rules that codify the necessity for indirectness and hold it up as a strategy. The literary text is more "successful," says Jin Shengtan, when, "as our gaze is turned away to that side, our hand writes on this side."[b1] "And if there comes a moment when our gaze should turn to this side, then our hand must write on that side." "If one does not grasp this principle, and if, when our gaze is turned to this side, our hand also writes on this side, then all is exhausted." "This side," "that side," here the eye, there the hand. Let us attempt to translate these oppositions into a theory. The first rule of writing supposedly concerns the distance necessary between the aim of the text and the subject it nominally treats (it is, therefore, not a distance taken from language, as with poetic discourse in the West, but a distance taken from the subject). The author, in short, must not directly write (the hand) what he initially has in view (the eye): he must write *alongside*. From this displacement, which is intentionally arranged, arises the effect of depth in literary development, for if the text were to stick to its point, the reader would have nothing to search for and interest would be canceled out.

From the distance taken, the possibility of a return emerges — making the distance traveled a detour. This sole precept supposedly accounts for literary development as a whole. Or rather, literary development is said to be nothing more than the uninterrupted renewal of this principle. "The most successful thing in literature," Jin Shengtan continues, is, "when our gaze is turned to one side, not to assume writing on this side but to get as far from it as possible and, on this basis, to come back, by meandering, to the point of approaching it and then stopping;[c] then to take our distance again as much as possible to get a new start, and then to come back again meandering to the point of approaching it and stopping once again" (16). By its very principle, a technique of this sort is repetitive, and this is why the written text is nothing but a continuous variation, without any possible conclusion. Jin Shengtan sums up the advantages of this path in the following terms: "If one changes the point of departure repeatedly, if one takes as much distance as possible from the subject each time in order to return to it, by meandering, to the point of approaching it and then stopping, one never flatly copies what one has in view, and one allows others to cast a glance beyond the text and see for themselves." Thus the subject must be broached by a sequence of distancings that constitute so many indirect expedients for getting close to it; and the text, in its development, is made up only of the uninterrupted concatenation of these meanderings. At the very point of touching on the topic, the writer always stops. The essential, to be essential, must remain implicit, because, in the end, it is avoided, and all these paths never cease to move toward it.

From this derives the fundamental rule of this art of writing. One can never fully explain what one wishes to say except by pointing toward it — and not because of mysticism but for purely technical reasons (reasons of literary *economy*). To write well is to graze the surface while never ceasing to come back to it (indeed,

335

in order never to cease coming back to it). What one broaches is rich with all the tension that leads up to it; it becomes fascinating by the interest that it never stops capturing. "Literature is most successful," resumes Jin Shengtan for the third time, when, "first fixing one's attention on a point, one turns the paintbrush all around this point while letting it evolve continuously in one direction or another, without ever abandoning its object nor crowding it too closely"[d] (17). In other words, one must neither stick to what one wants to say nor lose sight of it — neither "quit" it nor "attach" oneself to it, according to the Buddhist formulation. These contrary requirements define the ideal distance — what I call the allusive distance. This distance maintains the tension while giving free rein to the capacity for evolution; it concentrates attention on its object without immobilizing it as an object: by eluding the grasp, the object preserves its animation, continuously exceeding what one says about it, constantly taking wing. The author, in sum, must never cease to revolve around the "that" which he has in view ("that," the veritable stakes, a Buddhist expression[e]). An image gives a precise sense of this notion:

> This entirely resembles the lion that rolls the ball at the circus. It is only the ball that matters, but it allows the lion to use all of his agility. In an instant, everyone in the arena watching the lion is dazzled. But the lion is not directly concerned: the people stare at the lion, but he stares at the ball. What is thus whirling around is the lion, but what makes him whirl around in every direction is always the ball. (17)

So methodically developed, the analogy is easy to follow down to its finer details: the lion's uninterrupted pirouettes around the ball are comparable to a paintbrush's swirls around a subject. And just as the lion never ceases to spin around the ball without taking hold of it, so the text never ceases to whirl around its subject without exhausting it. But since it never lets itself be directly apprehended, the subject is continuously dazzling: the reader is drawn by the meandering development without entirely distinguishing the intention that is guiding him. If what the writer wants to say never ceases to motivate him to say it, everything he says and everything that presents itself to the reader retains movement and intensity only by what he lets elude his grasp while he is pursuing it.

Since we are dealing here with technical rules, it is easy to give examples. I will begin with an example of distancing. Even though he has in mind the lightning bolt that will ultimately strike his hero, the author of *The Western Room* begins by having the hero describe at great length the temple in which he is strolling, as well as the courtyard, kitchens, pagodas, and pavilions (scene 1). The author's gaze is turned to one side (the amorous event), but his hand writes on the other side (the stroll in the temple). Also, the entire scene prior to the apparition is written in "empty words" that suggest the fulgurant momentousness of the event. It is equally easy to show that the subject is animated by its eluding description and giving rise to detour: the figure of the beloved is scarcely broached head-on, while the paintbrush later swirls at greater length around her — to evoke her indirectly. We also are dealing with a "living" character, Jin Shengtan explains, whereas "if one had described her face, her encrusted jewelry, her eyebrows, and her hair curling over her temples," "one would have had a plaster statue."

One principle, to which Jin Shengtan returns, guides this reflection on the art of writing: all face-to-face confrontation with the object must be avoided. "I maintain that literary development must situate itself before the theme it evokes or else follow it. But, facing the theme itself, there must be no development"

337

(25–26). Or further, the text must "float" around its subject (like a banner around its staff [f]) — which, when faced, becomes too precise and thus the portrait of a "dead man." To guard against this danger, Jin Shengtan resorts to the following ancient anecdote: a man has stolen the precious sword of an acquaintance by imitating his handwriting to perfection; to avenge himself, the other paints on the front door of the house that the thief has just built at great expense a highly accurate portrait of the latter's dead father — complete with hat and ceremonial vestments reproduced down to the slightest folds. On seeing this perfect rendering, the thief's son is petrified and does not dare enter the house. Indeed, he will never inhabit it.[2]

Through this literary allusion, one fleetingly glimpses a meaning that, when unearthed, becomes considerable. By endeavoring to paint an object, the effort of representing stifles it, making it unlivable, as the house became in this example. In aiming at resemblance, this face-to-face confrontation becomes petrifying, canceling out the space for the movement and life of things and thus all possibility of evoking them, whereas by floating around its subject, the text never ceases to animate it. Thus we have arrived at the furthest point of a mimetic conception that aims to describe the *in itselfness* of things (because it believes in it): by taking a distance from the object, detour offers the means for a possible first step toward approaching it; it rescues us from the inhibition of a face-to-face confrontation and a sterilizing engulfment. It opens onto a multitude of itineraries, creates the conditions for a further deepening, and valorizes the possibilities of an approach.

Perhaps the most surprising thing is that Jin Shengtan chose to demonstrate the necessity of detour by means of the theater (or rather, the opera, a genre that came late to China), for it is precisely through the theater that the Greek tradition conceived of the principle of imitation (*mimēsis*: that of "men who are doing something," *prattontes* [*Poetics* 2.48A1]). Is not the stage the place of representation par excellence, the place where one makes people "see" by putting the thing "before [the] eyes" (*pro omma-tōn*) of the public? (*Poetics* 17.55A22). The commentator on Homer and the tragedians lets us appreciate the "living" quality of the characters by praising the "clarity" with which their sentiments are depicted and by which they impose themselves on us (according to the common coupling *energeia-enargeia*; see chapter 7 above). And if the play contains anything unstated, it is not for the sake of any allusive distance. Just when Ajax "addresses" his "last word" to the audience:

> Henceforth I speak to those in Hades' house! (v. 865)[3]

the commentator explains that we are to understand (*huponoein*) that he is throwing himself onto his sword to kill himself. Yet this understanding involves only the action being physically performed on the stage; it does not concern the subject itself—the signification of *muthos*, the truth of the characters.

Conversely, Jin Shengtan establishes a general hierarchy of writers to comment on the dialogue occurring on stage between characters — on the basis of their allusive abilities (*The Western Room* 1.2):

> If one takes an overall view of the literature of all ages, there are writers whose paintbrush never reaches their subject; there are those whose paintbrush always reaches their subject; and there are those, finally, who before using their paintbrush, after using their paintbrush, and when they do not use their paintbrush at all always reach their subject.[4]

Those who do not reach their subject might make as many strokes of the brush as they will, but they shall never reach it. It would be better, one suspects, if they refrained from writing. Those whose paintbrush reaches their subject do so with each new stroke they make; they succeed as many times as they use their brush. Yet this success remains limited to its moment and must forever be repeated. As for those who "before using their paintbrush, after using their paintbrush," and even "when they do not use their paintbrush at all," always reach their subject: "where their consciousness cannot go, their paintbrush has already gone," and "where their paintbrush cannot go, their consciousness has already gone." Between "consciousness" and the "paintbrush," the complementarity in these writers becomes total: what the one attains, the other has no need to attain; they may therefore supplement each other. Moreover, the implicit is everywhere present, and the blanks in the text are full of meaning. It is up to the reader to know how to fathom them. Only those who are "capable" of reading these works "actually read them"; "the others might read them all they want, they never will have read them." This latter category of writers brings us back to the precepts expounded earlier: when the text is "before the text," "after the text," and "around the text" and does not coincide flatly with it. As such, it has as its model the *Zuozhuan* commentary on the ancient annals and can be found in Mencius as well as *Zhuangzi*, the Confucian and the Taoist. It is also represented perfectly in *The Western Room*.

But from a technical point of view, which is henceforth our own, what makes up this (unwritten) "text" "before" or "after" the text, which is always overflowing the text? To celebrate the value of this implicitness, Chinese criticism becomes explicit for once and analyzes it in detail. After he has fleetingly glimpsed the young woman, Jin Shengtan continues, the young man visiting the temple never stops thinking of her. But how to approach her,

THE CLOUDS AND THE MOON

secluded as she is with her mother in the remote recesses of their apartments? The young man must have reflected unceasingly before arriving at this solution: to ask the monk who had him visit the temple to rent him a room in this enclosure. The monk, of course, agrees to do so, and Jin Shengtan imagines that the young man spends the night evaluating his chances of success and that the next morning, having given the matter too much thought, he is increasingly restless. All of a sudden, when he encounters the monk, he approaches him with these hardly suitable words — and without the slightest diplomacy:

> If you do not come to my aid, I shall vow a deadly hatred to you, monk Facong!

This approach is far too abrupt, Jin Shengtan remarks. (The proof is in the monk's astonishment and his demanding an explanation.) Nevertheless, this surprising proposition, once analyzed, conveys all the young man's nocturnal worries and sums up, in its brevity, his long interior monologue. If the young man had said, as would have been more logical, "I have come to rent a room, and I ask you respectfully, monk Facong, to oblige. Please help me!" then "we would have had before us only the young man of the morning" and not the one of the night before, whose bad sleep and alarm we are able to imagine. A simple reversal in the order of the propositions would have made their expression more normal but stripped them of implication. The paintbrush would only have reached its subject by individual strokes, whereas this abrupt approach contains, in a single stroke, all the prior deliberation. It is good example of the "text before the text."

This art of indirect presentation is something with which Western audiences are familiar. Think, for example, of the famous "Yes..." ("Yes, it's Agamemnon..."; "Yes, I've come into his temple...") with which the classical tragedies begin *ex abrupto* and which logically implies a preceding event (as if the action had begun without us — one need only think of the first words of Racine's *Phèdre*, which convey that the protagonist's suffering is at its peak). The difference seems to me to derive from the consciousness the critics have of it. Since he comments on the theater as part of the literary tradition, which is attached to allusiveness, Jin Shengtan emphasizes this indirectness: indeed, he makes it the basis of his commentary. Such indirectness, which can be found in other cultures as well, is theorized by the Chinese. At the same time, the Chinese tradition rarely comments on theater as theater (but rather in the same way it comments on historical or philosophical prose and poetry). That theater *represents* an action (on the stage in front of an audience) has scarcely attracted its attention. In the West, by contrast, this relationship of representation born of the theater is the basis of the general conception of creation (*poiesis*); and by imitating nature, which stands before him, the poet makes it an *object* that he must paint persuasively and true to life. Whence his lesser interest in allusiveness.

One might also imagine a different beginning — not abrupt but meandering, not implying that action has already begun but introducing its subject very gradually. Such a beginning is typical, in the eyes of Chinese literary criticism, and is the subject of detailed commentary. Jin Shengtan calls it "the technique of the moon passing by way of the detours of the gallery"ᵍ (see *The Western Room* 2.1). On a quiet spring night, a young woman unable to sleep raises the curtain on her window and waits for the moon. The moon rises in the east, fresh and pure, but its brightness must first touch the edge of the roof, then pass to the columns in the gallery, to the balustrade, and then gradually cross the threshold of the balcony and come up to the window before it can reach the

Lady. Because she remains at the window, it is inevitable that the moon will eventually brighten it. But it is also necessary that, before reaching her, the moon move progressively from the roof edge to the columns, to the threshold, and finally to the window —a "continuously meandering" path "alternating shadow and light," "now hidden, now uncovered," and giving access along the way ("before brightening the Lady") to an "entirely different world."[h] This world, as it moves along this path through turns and detours, reveals itself to be infinitely "profound" and "subtle" (*miao* — a term without equivalent in English, meaning at once mysterious, wondrous, and naturally successful).

Let us transpose the scene onto literary procedures. The example given is the moment when, in the same play, the young woman begins to admit her love to herself. She begins her monologue by describing the melancholy of late spring, when the petals fall; she laments her loose-fitting garments (a classic sign of despondency due to absence); and finally she declares her lack of interest in the outside world:

> Why bother still to lean against the balustrade
> To see the clouds pass by on the horizon!

Then suddenly, with the help of an initial opposition ("the feeling linked to spring is brief" — "the silk of the willows grows longer"), another opposition slips in surreptitiously, evoking "a man far away," "separated by the flowers," while "the far reaches of the sky" seem "so close" in comparison. Yet no sooner does this allusion to her love emerge than it is carefully hidden. The young woman then complains of the cold in her feather bed, of the fire that could never warm her. Next comes a new allusion to the "beautiful verses" sung the previous night by the young man — whom she refrains from naming but regrets being unable to "approach." And then, at once, a new detour: she voices her inability to keep still, the impossibility of falling asleep. Finally, she invokes her beloved, whose image "never leaves her."

Here, according to Jin Shengtan, all the art lies in the "meandering concatenation" by which the theme gradually appears. From the beginning of the scene, the young woman is full of love, just as the Lady was at the window waiting for the moon from the start of night. And just as the moon was eventually *supposed* to shed its light on the Lady, the young woman cannot fail to declare her feelings. Yet the young heroine is too pure and reserved to express this inclination from the start. Her avowal needs this alternation of shadow and light, of allusions that are increasingly direct but always followed by meanderings. Jin Shengtan is far from acknowledging the intrusion of desire and avoids interpreting the less apparently transparent motives (cold, insomnia) *directly* erotically (for perhaps they are more transparent, in terms of desire, than the moments of timid declaration). On the other hand, he carefully analyzes, formally and technically, the "degrees" of "detour," the arabesque of the text.[i]

Jin Shengtan analyzes the technique of indirect introduction in poetry as well. A poem describing a royal temple fallen to ruin begins with the following lines:

> At the bend in the stream — the wind in the pines [stretches] far,
> Rats slip by — [under] ancient tiles.
> I know not what king owns this temple...
>
> (Du Fu, "The Jade Flower Palace")

Rather than describe a "landscape," the first two lines are a "narrative"; that is, they mark the stages of a gradual unfolding. In a good example of Chinese micro-interpretation, Jin Shengtan sees

344

not one scene in these lines but four.[5] Scene 1: "The stream turns, and the walker turns with it"; scene 2: "If the stream had not turned, the wind in the pines would not have been heard; but, as it turns, one suddenly hears the wind"; scene 3: "Because of the wind, one looks at the pines, and, because of the pines, one sees rats"; scene 4: "Looking at the rats, one sees them slipping by; and the tiles appear where they slip by." These tiles lead to the ruined temple. From one stage to the next, there is a natural concatenation, and the subject is gradually introduced. A less skillful poet, Jin Shengtan concludes, would have described the temple in the very first line, "by exclamation." But the meandering path along which these four scenes[j] successively take us has yet another, entirely different effect: even though the temple has not yet been mentioned, we have already *become* sensitive to its state of abandon.

The meandering is therefore not gratuitous; it gives us access to a world that we could never reach directly on our own. But why resort to the notion of a world (*jing*,[k] originally a Buddhist term) that is more than a described landscape? To what hidden richness would it lead that might not be discovered directly? Fortunately, the observation here is so meticulous that it avoids the vague effusions often used to compensate for technical literary analysis. It underscores, once again, the importance of process. The value of detour lies in its capacity for *unfolding*. By deploying a succession of phases — like the succession of scenes here — it gradually *opens up* reality; and the continuous concatenation to which it gives rise enables us, by accompanying it, to immerse ourselves in it: not to seize hold of it all at once, as direct expression purports to do, but gradually to become imbued with it, to establish a relationship with it, to embrace its development, to enter into its inner depths and vitality and thereby experience its at-once infinitely diffuse and all-encompassing nature as atmo-

345

sphere (here, one of desolation) and globality (as opposed to generality). A scene-landscape is described, yet we *enter* a world; this requires a path. It is detour that *gives access*.

Yet how to conceive of this access? Clearly, the path to which detour gives rise does not lead to access as its result (as if at the end of the road, there were a door to be opened to see what is behind it): rather, it effects this access through this unfolding (see above where the moon introduces us *along its way* to an "entirely different world" — "before brightening the Lady"). The outcome starts at the beginning: in other words, the very notion of outcome loses its meaning. The infinite beyond is not promised *after* — as something one is moving toward — but is rendered possible by the initial distancing and becomes the recipient of the process. Stated otherwise, this access is not of the same order as the end (telos); it does not separate reality into levels of being or divide it into different planes. In short, it has no metaphysical function. This detour, as we have seen, is *simultaneously* an access (which is only a paradox from a teleological point of view, such as Westerners have inherited from the Greeks, but which the Chinese do not share). This is confirmed in the following images, which introduce a poem the Chinese poetic theorist Sikong Tu (ninth century) has consecrated to literary "meandering"[1] — such, in fact is its title:

> Climbing mount Taihang:
> The azure vegetation surrounds the meandering path.
> A halo of vapor: from the jade flowing [in streams]
> The scent of flowers rises to infinity...[6]

The ascension is not oriented to the vast landscape promised at the summit; rather, the surrounding vegetation draws in the horizon: it envelops in its depth the road that winds along the slope.

Similarly, one does not ask where the stream that winds at the bottom of the valley leads; yet it is from its meandering that the vapor rises in a halo (granting it the profound reflection of the jade), that the scent of flowers spreads to infinity. Vegetation, halo, scent — one diffuse globality unites these images; and the alternation through which this path takes us gives us access to the depth:

> One thinks [it] departed but already [it] returns;
> [It] seems secret but is not hidden.

Because of the meandering unfolding that occurs through it, reality reveals itself not smoothly — as in a panorama — but in a *state of transition*. Its withdrawal makes its resurgence possible, and both allow us to discover it. Because a certified presence, by exposing it flatly, would breathe on the surface, and a definitive absence, by cutting us off from it, would conceal it forever in its mystery, it introduces us *naturally* into its innermost recess by withdrawing in order to return, that is, by reappearing at a different end as soon as we think it is retreating — all the while preserving this intimacy (as expressed through the secret) without rendering it obscure (hidden) and without requiring a leap to reach it (while passing to the level of the invisible). The *variation* engendered by detour indeed unveils a world, but it is not another world: it unveils this world — the only world — which now has become inexhaustible.

This is the *world* concretized in the Chinese garden. The affinity between text and garden has long been recognized: "Tending a garden is like composing a poem or any other literary text: the meandering of the path must be methodically arranged"[m] (Qian Meixi).[7] But how does one enter a Chinese garden (which is usually separated from the outside world by a wall)? Starting with the door, a system of partitioning is established, multiplying steps and moldings, presenting successions of courtyards and alcoves — sometimes sheltered, sometimes open-skied: by forming partitions, so many distancings and screens make this entry circuitous and gradual. The same principle of detour can be found in the unfolding of the promenade: paths ascend and descend artificial mountains, bridges zigzag across pools of water, galleries wind between the pavilions they link together. But this zigzagging is not, of course, an end in itself (see what Shen Fu [eighteenth century] says about this in chapter 2 of *Accounts of a Fugitive Life*). By its alternation, evident in both contrast and multiple points of view, it opposes the sterile uniformity of the straight line; that is, it varies as much as possible our relationship to the landscape — and thereby makes it *ambient*. It never stops letting us discover: "In the middle of a vast space, to have only a small horizon; in the middle of a small space, to see a broad horizon; in the middle of emptiness, fullness; in the middle of fullness, emptiness; now hidden, now uncovered, now easily perceptible, now profoundly concealed." Through the bipolarity of opposition and correlation, the world never ceases to proceed through continuous interaction. By never ceasing to evolve from one pole to the other, the circuitousness of detour makes it possible to counteract the apparent immobility in which things are isolated: it leads us to follow the real in the tension of its constant advent.

This garden leads nowhere: its lanes run only into themselves. No perspective dominates any other or is given preference; but at each meandering, the landscape is endlessly renewed. We may therefore say of the Chinese garden what we already have said of the Chinese literary text. Like the circuitous path of textual meaning, the garden promenade is an unfolding; it functions through the landscape's gradual permeation in us (while it frees us from the world outside), and, as such, it is without end. This prome-

348

THE CLOUDS AND THE MOON

nade is a *continual access* (to harmony, nature, emotion). Moreover, the intertwinings in the enclosure of this space make the
walker always feel that other paths might just as well have been
taken — like the reader who knows that other, possible readings
remain and that he can never see the meaning to its end. Reading
and walking join together in the sentiment of inexhaustibility.
Because of the detours of its paths, the garden never runs dry
under our gaze. One might say it forever possesses a remainder
or surplus of landscape (just as one might speak of a surplus of
sound, meaning, or taste). Each aspect corresponds to others;
what one sees there alludes to what one does not see; it shares,
with the written text, the profundity of the implicit.

Let us now shift from the unfolding of the garden to that of the
landscape on a scroll. The tradition in painting is not to treat the
subject directly. When, for a competition, painters were asked to
paint a mountain monastery or an inn in the forest, most often
they depicted neither an inn nor a monastery but, for example, a
monk carrying water drawn from a nearby stream, with the temple visible in the distance, or a sign above the trees signaling the
presence of the inn in the middle of the woods. A monastery is
always much more than its few buildings; its reality far exceeds
them. Likewise, the hospitality promised by an inn is more perceptible when the inn seems lost in the immensity of the landscape. Approached head-on, these subjects evoke nothing. But by
distancing oneself from them, one may *take their measurement* —
which proves infinite. Once again, detour alone makes a return
possible: the itinerary it implies, a return to the subject, is the
occasion for deepening it and becoming permeated with it.

  Like the writer's hand (in relation to his aim), the painter's
hand paints "alongside." The same expression, indeed, is valid for
both: the paintbrush is held "slantwise."[n] Far from immobilizing

us in front of the subject and forcing it on us (to the point where, in our saturation, we can no longer see it), they reveal it by its relative absence. One example from Western Antiquity is famous: "Having to represent the sacrifice of Iphigenia, Timanthes painted Calchas as sad, Ulysses as even sadder, and made Menelaus as afflicted as art could possibly make him. Having exhausted all the signs of emotion, no longer knowing how properly to render the father's expression, he covered his head and left it to the viewers to imagine him as they wished." In what it refrains from representing, painting exceeds representation and invites us to go beyond it. Nevertheless, with this example, we remain within the framework of rhetoric: development and *climax* (with a final, supreme conclusion: still teleology). Further proof is that this example long served as the favorite theme of rhetoricians (Cicero, *De oratore* 74; Quintilian, *Institutio oratoria* 2.13). To bring the representation to its culmination, the painter-orator, counting on the accumulated intensity, finishes his work with dotted lines. Yet we remain within the order of the more or less — of litotes.

When Qiu Ying paints the return of a Chinese princess to the court (*Return of Cai Wenji*, a classical subject), he abstains from representing the character that is his subject — to the point that we do not even know where she is in the painting. Is she lying down, perhaps, in the heavy, ox-drawn carriage following the troop of horsemen in the background? Or in that other carriage, barely visible behind the rock? Or somewhere else? But the camels whose heads are sticking out are enough to let us understand that the cortege is coming from very far away, while the troop's high spirits and the animated landscape with its proud summits let us share in the emotion sparked by the event (while the tension of the cortege and the detours of the route highlight its importance). The more one contemplates the painting, the more one sees this return unfold and the more this return unearths a world. Instead of looking for "the thing itself" or "man himself" (the quest for *in itselfness*), instead of imposing on our senses the "undeniable spectacle" (as a function of the fundamental association of *persuasion* and *truth*),[8] as European painting of the same epoch tends to do, Chinese painting, by means of detour, makes its subject evasive. Not treated specifically in any place, the subject subtly invades the scene.

This manner of painting *alongside* a subject was summed up in a formulation that has since become current in the language of painters and from there has passed into literary criticism: "painting the clouds to evoke the moon?"[o] (*painting* here means, according to the Chinese technique, painting in washes by wetting parts of the paper so as to highlight all additions of ink or color). Jin Shengtan comments on it as follows:

> Have you ever thought about the technique of "painting the clouds to evoke the moon"? One wishes to paint the moon, but the moon cannot be painted; that is why one paints the clouds. But when one paints the clouds, our interest does not turn to the clouds, and it is not turned to the clouds because it is turned to the moon. Nevertheless, our interest must turn to the clouds. If one makes the slightest mistake on the clouds, they will turn out either too heavy or too light, which is a defect clouds can have; and if there is a defect in the clouds, there will also be a defect in the moon. If, with the clouds, one was able to avoid too much heaviness or lightness, but due to an infinitesimal lapse of attention, the wetting of the paper left the slightest trace, like a speck of dust, then there is a defect in the clouds; and if there is a defect in the clouds, there is also a defect in the moon. But if one was able to avoid giving too much heaviness and too much lightness and there is not the slightest trace of wetting, like a speck of dust, then when one contemplates these clouds, one will have the impression they exist, but, when one wishes to grasp them,

one will have the impression they are unreal; when one approaches them, it will be as though they are no longer there, and when one blows on them, they will seem to move. Such clouds are perfectly executed. When visitors come to see these perfectly executed clouds the next day, they will all cry out: "The moon is so beautiful!" And there will be no exclamation on the subject of clouds. While this may be very unfair to the pains the painter has taken and not give due respect to his perplexity when, the previous night, he was painting the clouds, is it not true, if one seeks to fathom the painter's profound sentiment, that he was entirely turned to the moon and not at all to the clouds? (*The Western Room* 1.1)

We find this procedure demonstrated throughout the opera commented on by Jin Shengtan. When the young hero comes on the scene, he describes his aspirations but not his own character. Nevertheless, the majestic tableau he paints of the Yellow River landscapes gives a sufficient glimpse of the nobility of his sentiments. More importantly, all the interest of the opera is concentrated on the young woman, though she is so sublime that one could never hope to paint her portrait. Unable to describe her, the author begins by depicting the young man who will fall in love with her. Yet this portrait must offer nothing that is too heavy or too light and must not be sullied by the slightest "speck of dust"; only thus can it let the ideal embodied by the man's partner shine through.

There is thus an ineffable element — the moon, the beloved woman — and so a recourse to indirectness. Yet what indirectly evokes perfection, so difficult to express, belongs to the same plane as perfection: the young man in relation to the woman, the clouds in relation to the moon. The one stands *alongside* the other: to reach the one you must go through the other — whence the need for detour. There is therefore no double level as in symbolism — the perceptible and the invisible, the concrete being and its essence (such as a bird and freedom or the sun in the perceptible world and the good in the world of ideas). This leads me to reformulate more precisely the question we have already encountered — which clearly contains nothing paradoxical: How may this *alongside* lead toward a beyond? Or, to revive an earlier expression: Why does allusive distance, in creating a gap with the object it evokes, open the way to the transcendence of this object?

CHAPTER FIFTEEN

The Allusive Distance

If it is to be taken any further, the question of allusive distance demands consideration on two fronts. On the one hand, Chinese criticism ceaselessly recommends that we not press the subject by squeezing it too closely. This is because the *loose* ("slack"[a])[1] relationship that the text entertains allows for a certain play that enables it to evolve freely. At the same time, because the meaning is not imposed, it unfolds of its own accord. The formula is among the most classical: "Whereas the text makes turns and detours at whim, the meaning comes all by itself"[b] (Lü Donglai, speaking of *Spring and Autumn Annals*, the model text).[2] The Chinese man of letters, not being a voluntarist, does not require a meaning; he makes himself available (furthermore, the quest for meaning as an end in itself, the West's great modern phantasm, was never his concern). While remaining "preoccupied," to use Mencius's expression, he waits for it to *mature* within him. "Do not rush it, do not force it": here we see the value, central to the Chinese (of all schools), of things that come "without having to act" or, rather, intervene, that is, without demonstrating activity (*wu wei*[c]), the *sponte sua*. Like any event, meaning is not about action (interpretation as deliberate activity: the hermeneutic enterprise) but about *process* (the unfolding of which falls to the commentator to further through his work). What valorizes detour, in short, is that by baffling any injunction of meaning (both immediate and imperative) through the rift it provokes, it "leaves the field open"[d] to becoming and respects the possibility of immanence.

On the other hand, this question makes us think about reality. When we ask why it is through absence (which is relative and efficient) that presence manifests itself or why distance from the subject allows us better to penetrate it — in short, why it is that detour leads to discovery — we scarcely find in the Western theoretical arsenal an adequate response, or at least one that we had foreseen. Of course this experience is fundamentally familiar (and not only in texts: also in human relationships?). And this leads me to reformulate the question in contrast with Greek philosophy: How would we grasp the real (I cannot find a word less marked by Western theoretical preoccupations) if we did not approach it *in itself* (separate, identical, ideal), that is, if we no longer conceived of it in relation to being? As soon as we leave ontology behind, as the Chinese have led us to do, the answer is illuminated in the following way: *frontally*, in the fullness of things. To function, fullness needs emptiness; empty and full "interact,"[e] as we say today (and this is also the exact Chinese term); they are completely correlative. Also, without *emptiness, fullness* becomes inert, opaque. With the strategy of detour, fullness, in intervening into emptiness by the rift between them, is allowed to function properly; in integrating emptiness into its trajectory, fullness is allowed to radiate. This is why the allusive distance renders the reality it addresses evanescently and invasively (as aura, halo, or atmosphere) but without defining it or representing it (the two processes go hand in hand, as with the Greeks) — that is, without considering its identity: it renders its *pregnancy* (conforming to the Chinese notion of transformation) and not its essence (which opposes being and appearance).

356

On the subject of emptiness among the Chinese, one encounters naive wonders and fantasies (equivalent to Western fantasies of nothingness). Yet the question remains: How can distance be allusive? To illuminate this, I shall again follow Jin Shengtan (seventeenth century), though I shall return to the privileged terrain of poetry (his commentary on Du Fu, the great poet of the eighth century).

Let us begin by returning to the opposition between the landscape as world and the landscape as stage (according to the Chinese homonyms *jǐng* and *jìng*[f]). Jin Shengtan uses a series of contrasts to convey their difference: what the stage evokes is "boisterous," what the world evokes is "calm"; what the stage evokes is "near," what the world evokes is "far off"; the stage is found under the noses of "superficial people," the world "at the depths of the gazes of profound people."[3] But the stage and the world refer to the same landscape, the difference coming from the way it is apprehended. This play of oppositions thus leads to a reformulation of the question in terms of the experiences of consciousness (Chinese criticism is essentially phenomenological): How can the allusive distance, which enables detour, make us pass from the landscape as *stage* to the landscape as *world* — that is, how can it make us go beyond the boisterous aspect that immediately monopolizes us to help us reach the far-off that inhabits it and its serene harmony?

The first poem that Jin Shengtan comments on illustrates such an interrogation through the thematic rift that separates its development from its title: "A Visit to the Fengxian Temple in Longmen." This title is typical: it announces a walk taken one day to this temple and leads us to expect its description. The octave begins as follows:

Already, afterward, the monastery I visited,
And now, moreover, I spend the night in the world that is its
   own:
From the hidden valley a secret concert is born;
The moon shining through the forest: it spreads shadows of
   light.

The poem begins with the words "already" and "moreover,"
which usually function to conclude one point and introduce
something else. Furthermore, the landscape described at the
poem's beginning is a night landscape, not a daytime landscape as
the title suggests. How to explain this discrepancy? Should one
infer that the poet wrote an earlier poem that was not preserved?
The commentator, continually troubled by this philological question, suddenly finds an answer whose obviousness is striking but
also of another order. It is a *poetic* answer: "One day I was there
with nothing to do, and suddenly I understood!" Of course, the
poet could have written the poem at the moment of his visit, but
then he would not have been able to reach this world of the "hidden valley" and the "moon shining through the forest." Such a
poem would not have touched us, and it would have been "as if
it had not been written." To return to the critical set of ideas: by
day, the poet would have depicted the *stage*; by night, he evokes
a *world*.

What makes up this world? Imprinted in the depths of the
night are the artificial oppositions that distinguish the landscape
by day and would serve to describe it. Here it is evoked, however,
in a way that is both "vague" and "detached,"ᵍ for in these two
lines, Jin Shengtan adds, "one does not really know if it is sonorous
or calm, light or dark, if this is due to the wind or the moon, if one
experiences fear or contentment." The harmony of the concert
rising from the valley is so subtle that it escapes the senses (1.3; a

way to interpret *ling*[h]); the landscape is made up of both shadow and light (1.4). It is a *fluid* landscape, "about which one is aware, in the depths of one's consciousness and out of the corner of one's eye, that its world really is this way." In spite of its tangible indeterminacy, or rather because of it, this world is intensely present. The vagueness of night opens this landscape to non-duality, drawing it away from the rigid contours within which it was bound. In other words, it reinstates the *fullness* of this landscape into the *emptiness* that makes it emanate. To reuse a term: it evokes this landscape in all its *pregnancy*.

This is how one can measure the benefit derived from the rift between the title of the poem and its development. It creates an allusive distance that allows one to go beyond the superficial and engrossing (salient or boisterous) things that the landscape by day, as stage, presents. At the same time, Jin Shengtan notes, it liberates poetic inventiveness, stripping away all frozen formulations — commonplaces and stereotypes — usually used in this type of visit. Yet it does involve a visit, as indicated by the title of the poem, but one distilled, in the depths of the past night, of any inferred convention. "Alas," Jin Shengtan concludes, "if by a miracle one could compose such a poem today, one would not fail to correct the title to read, 'Night Passed at the Fengxian Temple.'" But then, by the suppression of the rift between the poem and its title, the poem would be descriptive (of a stage at night), not allusive (like a day visit deepening during the night). The discourse would coincide with its object (meaning it would have an object), just as the poem would coincide with its title, and one would not have seen, and told of, the *fullness* of things: with all distance abolished, the dimension of the world would be impossible.

That this *becoming world* of the landscape is what this poem evokes is confirmed in the last two lines of the octave:

359

About to wake up, I hear the morning bell,
It makes man — through unfolding — profoundly realize.

This gaining of awareness, Jin Shengtan notes, should not be understood in the strictly religious (Buddhist) sense of awakening, as has often been done. It corresponds more radically to the "Where am I?" that assails us certain mornings when the spirit has barely emerged from its confusion and one cannot remember where one is. "I am in the Fengxian temple," the poet remembers as he hears the bell ringing. But he understands this profoundly; he realizes it. After the previous day's visit has been distilled by the night, in the morning the poet finds reality in full flight (in unfolding): the landscape of the visit reappears (and the poem harks back to its title), but, because of the distance created, what the landscape contains proves inexhaustible (whereas during his visit, Jin Shengtan notes, "it was not this way"). The poem, brought back to its title, has become fully allusive.

Has one ever systematically looked into the relationship between a poem and its title in Western poetry? In the Chinese tradition, as we see, this relationship is fully exploited. The title of the poem, in noting precise circumstances, referentially and prosaically furnishes all the narrative elements, based on which the development of the poem, in drawing away from the title, can propose a poetic variation.[4] This relationship between title and poem therefore constitutes a privileged device for engendering allusive distance. In the preceding case, Jin Shengtan notes, the development of the poem "assists" the title by completing it.[5] But there are other possible relationships between title and poem that allow one to conceive of allusive distance in terms of typology.

Let us first consider the counterpart to the first case, in which the "title assists the poem." Here is a title that notes circumstances with a great deal of pomp and detail. This poem, Jin Shengtan explains, was composed on the occasion of a "new promenade on the outskirts of the inspector Zheng's lake, following the invitation of the director of the Yu ministry's nephew, Wenchao, the grandson of the director of studies, Cui Yu, and the son of the director of the ministry."[6] In classical fashion and according to conventional themes, the poem describes this boat outing: the secret charm of the landscape, the high waters of spring, the drunkenness of the participants. But from the accumulation of details in the title emerges a critical intention that conveys negativity throughout the poem (which, without the title, we would never suspect). This occurs through the type of interpretation with which we are already familiar (the one established in relation to *Spring and Autumn Annals* to signify praise or blame; see chapter 5 above). While the title precisely cites the most distant relatives, by giving both their personal names and their functions at the court — which ostensibly marks its esteem for them — the poet mentions only the function of his host's father and says nothing about this host himself. This intentional gaping hole in the title makes it quite clear just how little consideration the poet grants his host and how bored he is at having to leave "once again" for an outing on the lake. Thus the apparently conventional, and thereby anodyne, lines of the poem, such as, "The banquet has lasted a long time, and we have set off again on the lake," discreetly convey, with obligatory politeness but all the more maliciously, that the poet accepts this invitation with a heavy heart and is eager to see it end. "If one is not aware," Jin Shengtan concludes, "one might think the poet is painting a landscape here; but those who savor the intention behind the composition of this title well understand that there is, in reality, no landscape to paint." On the periphery of the poem's development, the title projects a shadow onto it that immediately renders it suspicious (at the same time, the poem is irreproachable and can be offered to the guests). Certainly, this is a rare case, and this reading is that of only one commentator (he offers a different reading afterward). But this interpretation is used to illustrate a typical case in which it is by the detour of the title, in relation to the development of the poem, that the poet slips a critical allusion into his verses.

The inverse case exists as well: instead of the title undermining the anodyne theme of the poem to make it insidious, the title can camouflage, beneath a convention, something developed in the poem that would otherwise appear too openly critical — and therefore dangerous to its author. For example, in the sign poem (*poème affiche*) "Climbing the Tower on the Ramparts of Yanzhou," one of Du Fu's first poems, the theme indicated by the title could not be more classical, and one expects a description of a landscape.[7] The poem is indeed about a landscape, but the panorama that unfolds is nevertheless disturbing: above, "clouds float," joining the two edges of the vast horizon; below, the flat "moor" spreads out as far as the eye can see. There is nothing stable here, nothing promising, to catch the eye and sustain interest. The floating clouds are the emblematic, very coded sign of human inconstancy, and the moor is indicative of the world of abandon. In next referring to the vestiges of ancient dynasties, the poet suggests that the situation in the present reign has become critical. Furthermore, in indicating at the beginning of the poem that this is the "first time" he has discovered this horizon and by noting at the end that, faced with this landscape, he is the "only one" to tarry, plunged as he is in "perplexity," he implies that the political situation is all the more serious because people are unaware of it. "The whole poem," Jin Shengtan resumes, "is a deploring of the present times; had the poet not used the pretext of 'climbing up the tower,' he could not have avoided too forceful a critique; this is why he cloaked the poem with this title." Its title, in short, serves as a cover (but not the cover of allegory: this landscape does not signify something else; its perception — which is real — is discreetly inflected). Fortified by its title, the poem can unfold its critiques under cover, since it declares in advance that it will keep them implicit.

In this case, Jin Shengtan notes, the title "does not correspond at all to the poem." Between the title and the poem, the deepest possible rift is drawn; unlike the displaced title that assists the poem (or the title that serves as detour), this title displays its distance from the development of the poem. It remains to be seen how the allusive distance comes about when it is, in an extreme case, "the poem that does not correspond at all to its title." In my opinion, this last example is the most interesting, because we go from a particular insinuation, where the meaning is masked, to a much more general question about the capacity of evocation: How can one speak of the *source* of things — or grasp their ultimate reality? The title of this poem is "On the River, While the Waters Unfold as if on the Sea — Simple Sketch."[8] In this octave, nothing describes the grandiose spectacle of this inundation. In the first part of the poem, the poet merely indicates that he no longer has a taste for fine verses that create sensation, which he strove to achieve as a young man. As he grows older, he is content to follow his inspiration, and even the most classical images — birds or rivers at the arrival of spring — no longer necessarily touch him. At the end of the poem, he goes back to the great masters of landscape poetry, whom he would have liked to call on to evoke the landscape. Only two lines have anything to do with water: the "balustrades" "recently added" allow fishing lines to be hung, and an "anciently assembled" "raft" takes the place of a fishing boat. But nothing in these images illustrates the vast waterscape announced as subject. The thematic relationship is clear but not specific. The images maintain a *loose* relationship with the theme, a *fluid* link, that does not tend to impose a meaning. On the other hand, the renewal of the course of things to which the poet alludes (the old age that "leaves"; the spring that "comes"), although it has no thematic relationship with the waterscape, should be read, according to Jin Shengtan, as that which makes us "become aware" of such a landscape and whose effect can evoke it. Everything begins again ad infinitum like the river's waters. It is therefore not in "finding meaning"[i] that the poem expresses reality in full but in opening itself to this great renewal of things, in renouncing rigid codifications, in welcoming it on its own terms. What inspires us at the heart of this landscape is that it goes beyond the dual oppositions that arbitrarily reduce our apprehension of it (the Buddhist theme par excellence, Jin Shengtan notes, but more largely shared). One can most completely express reality by freely enjoying the lines — "as it comes."

As great as the poet's talent might be, Jin Shengtan specifies, he could never completely render the unfolding of the river's waters stretching out toward infinity like a sea: neither the "incessant renewal of the river's course" nor the "limitless horizon of the earth." Furthermore, at the very beginning of the poem, the poet warns that he has renounced "fine verses" that seek to create an impression on the reader; similarly, at the end of the poem, he leaves to others the art of painting a landscape. Hence this poem, as its title indicates, can be but a brief evocation composed in a few strokes. Nonetheless, Jin Shengtan concludes, what no description of the river or sea could ever fully attain, even by force, this vague sketch succeeds in doing.

Poetic success therefore comes, once again, only through the relationship between the title and the poem. "That with this title we have this poem, now there is a feat!" "There is no word in these eight lines that refers directly to the title, and, at the same time, when one reads this poem, one immediately understands that this title alone could introduce it." Between the title and the poem, there is both distance and allusive richness — which is all the greater since the relationship between them is not imposed but unfolds *sponte sua*. The way it is commented on here, this poem is not without echoes of the fluctuating words of the Taoist thinker (see chapter 13 above): like the container that has no set position but when full tends to tip and when empty tends to stand up, the lines of the poem remain open to the suggestion of the title. Imposing nothing of themselves, they can inexhaustibly lend themselves to it. As we know, only fluctuating words, in suspending the specifying function of language and in never ceasing to open themselves to the will of things, express the bottom of things. Here the reclusive nature of the poem in relation to its title sets into motion a detachment that does not bear the weight of a theme but allows itself to be manifested everywhere.

I would like to end with the following theme, which is classical in China: How to express the loneliness experienced when one is far from loved ones? According to a tradition that goes back to the origins of Chinese poetry, rather than directly express sentiment, it is better to express this loneliness by reversing the perspective, that is, to begin with the sentiments that these relatives must be experiencing. This technique is known as "opposite"[j] evocation: one imagines a relationship from the other point of view (which is to say from the other pole; again we see the Chinese polarity in which the one correlates to the other and implicitly refers to it). In *The Book of Songs*, a soldier leaving for a far-off expedition climbs a mountain and turns toward his paternal home (110). He describes only what his father, mother, and older brother must be saying about him and his long absence; he does not mention his own homesickness. The commentator's justification is one of the most common, having become something of a truism: "If he expressed it, the feeling would become superficial."[9] Or again: "Recording how one thinks about one's relatives could never match the depths of consciousness that occur when one thinks of how one's relatives think about oneself."[10] "Even if one recounts the words of how one's relatives feel about oneself," these words "house," and therefore express, "one's own consciousness."[11] In moving away from one's own position, in expressing it through another's position, one implies one's own experience. This process comes neither from a desire for objectification nor from a game of mirrors but takes advantage of the distance that alone makes it possible to *envision* something. Or again, by creating a distance from definition-representation — here through the opposite point of view — the detour gives breathing space to the evocation: the feelings expressed (those of the relatives) become deeper as they allude to one's own feelings, which remain implicit.

Another poem by Du Fu, "Yue ye [Moonlit Night]," takes this technique to its extreme:[12]

> This moonlit night in Fuzhou:
> My wife is alone in contemplating it.
> Far away I think of my small children.
> They cannot know this in thinking of
>   Chang'an (or that she dreams of Chang'an).
> In the perfumed atmosphere the halo of her chignon is damp,
> Beneath the clear limpidity her arms of jade are icy.
> When, at last, as we press against each other on the empty
>   casement,
> Coupled — will the traces of our shining tears dry?

This poem was written during the great rebellion that shook China in the middle of the eighth century. After having settled his family in Fuzhou, in the western province of Shanxi, the poet (a functionary) left to rejoin the side loyal to the emperor; captured on the way by rebel forces, he was kept prisoner in the capital, Chang'an, which the rebels were occupying. This poem is supposed to express the loneliness its author experienced one night in contemplating the moon in Chang'an and thinking of his loved ones far away in the town of Fuzhou. Yet nothing refers directly to his emotion. The poem begins by expressing it from the opposite end: his wife is alone this night in the far-off town of Fuzhou, contemplating the moon; and his feeling of solitude is reinforced in the next two lines by the indication that their children, who are with her, are too young to understand what their mother (or their father) feels when thinking of Chang'an. The next couplet expresses, in this nighttime setting from which the poet is absent, the delicate fusion of the woman and the landscape: her chignon that perfumes the air around her, while the night's vapors penetrate it with dampness; her arms that, beneath the moonlight, have the sheen and freshness of jade. But the couplet does more: that the chignon has become damp and the air perfumed, that in the coolness of the night her arms have become icy, indicates that she has been contemplating the moon for a long time — thinking of her absent husband, she waits and cannot sleep. The last lines describe the long-awaited moment: when they meet again (when?) and the traces of the tears they have shed will begin to dry. The last lines, in fact, reproduce the gradual process of their obliteration: "traces" — "shining" — "tears" — "dry."

Chinese commentators admired the subtle art with which the poet expresses his feeling by addressing it from a distance. "There is no brush stroke that is not a detour,"[k] states Shi Buhua. "Sentiment and situation, evoked indirectly, are completely rendered"[l] (Du Yi). "The more relaxed it is, the more poignant it is"[m] (Du Yi), meaning, the more relaxed the relationship between the text and its theme, the more this theme becomes absorbed. The first detour (ll. 1–2): the feeling of solitude is expressed from the perspective of the other side (of the relationship), not that of the man in Chang'an (thinking of his wife) but that of the woman in Fuzhou (thinking of him). The second detour (ll. 3–4): his wife's feeling of solitude is expressed through his children's lack of awareness of this, since they are too young to share it. The third detour (ll. 5–6): the length of the solitary contemplation is suggested through its effects (the damp chignon, the icy arms); at the same time, the discreet charm of the scene makes one aware of the absence (the description of the wife is both intimate and reserved: we are at the edge of convention, but we go beyond it subtly). The fourth detour (ll. 7–8): the present moment of solitude is rendered from the perspective of the opposite moment — the joy of reunion (which, however, echoes the pain of the present separation — the tears — so difficult to forget). One presence bathes these expressions of absence in its luminosity, illuminating the twists and turns that bind them — the moon: only the moon can contemplate the separated spouses at the same time (the moon is traditionally linked in China to the theme of separation); it illuminates the central vision of the woman and her "arms of jade," and its light, when the couple at last contemplate it together, will shine on their tears.

This poem best attains "through detour" the "implicit richness of feeling"[n] (Wang Fuzhi).[13] This sentiment, as we have seen, is always expressed *as absence* in relation to what is said; it is that (infinite) *emptiness* within the fullness of the text. To express his emotion, not only does the poet not mention it, but he uses no psychological notation — no term here names the feeling — and the poem does not attempt to *identify* the experience it evokes; it exploits no symbolic motif (to deploy the infinity of meaning on another plane). This feeling is rendered indicatively, which keeps us in the order of phenomena (such as expressing the duration of the wait through the chilling), or according to values already encoded in the poetic tradition (moon, tears). But if the entire effect of the poem rests on a single strategy of detour, this is more than a technique, or, if this technique can be used to such an extent, it implies a conception of reality that differs from the Western view. The poem's subject is treated outside its subject matter because there is no subject in itself, there is no *in itself* of things; or one can be evoked through the other because one already is the other, and the real is essentially correlated. So many deviations from Western tradition are tied together and never cease to appear or to have consequences for meaning. To conclude, we must return to them.

CONCLUSION

Detour or Split?

Detour-access: To what, finally, does this detour through China give us access? It is, of course, the longest of detours, indeed a detour without end: one never stops learning Chinese, discovering new texts, reading new commentaries. Yet from the very start, I expect the possibility of a return. The subject of this book is also its manner of procedure.

I expect that this detour through China will open up a perspective: the ability to question ourselves from the outside. I know well that Western philosophy has never ceased renewing its inquiry, that each philosopher comes to say no to his predecessor, and that criticism, in all fields of thought, has always been the dynamic of its history. Nevertheless, however taken it might be with surpassing itself, Western philosophy never questions itself except from within. However radical it may wish to be, this criticism is always relatively integrated, remaining within the limits of an implicit understanding from which certain positions may emerge. There is always that *on the basis of which* we question ourselves, which, for that very reason, we cannot question. Even the most brilliant debates have an undercurrent of connivance. Proof of this lies in those common stakes born of Greek thought (being and freedom), which Westerners have never abandoned — but which China has never known.

We cannot escape this situation: there must be an elsewhere if we are to be able to step back. With it, our view of the question can be more global; most importantly, one may go back into what conditioned it, plumb its most recondite corners — envisage it more radically. Following the coherence of the subtle proposition traditional in China, we begin to perceive from without the source of our own speech. As seen from China, the articulation of myth and discourse (*muthos/logos*), such as it was conceived in Greece, *again becomes* surprising. We know that *logos*, as reasoned discourse deployed by philosophy, took shape from the inspired narratives (*muthos*) of the ancient poets (poets, sages, and soothsayers). It slowly emerged from that source and eventually asserted itself against it. At the same time, as soon as *logos* (at once reason and definition) can no longer give an account, as soon as it falters or weakens in the face of mystery, then myth takes over and extends the interpretation of the world into the fabular mode (whether it is believed or not). In Plato, when the work of dialectics is exhausted, myth relieves it; on a larger scale, when the discourse of knowledge, whether scientific or philosophical, admits its limitation, the discourse of belief replaces it.

In China, this ambiguous relationship between discourse and myth, in which the one rivals the other while coming to terms with it, which breaks the word in two, but in order to acknowledge the domain of each, does not exist. Nor does Chinese thought render the world in a fabular mode in any of its great narratives; nor does it rely completely on the word's power of argumentation; nor does it appeal to faith or liken the reason of things to their definition. More generally, through its reserved stance toward the word and its attachment to the unsaid, the Chinese tradition makes us aware of what we already know but never fully assess: the Western confidence, which has existed since Antiquity, in the power of speaking and explaining, which has served as the foundation for the most important thing the West has produced — the organization of democracy and justice (the court, the assembly), which merges with the work of philosophy. Thought and discourse are the same thing, says Plato (*Sophist* 263E), for thought is dialogue, internal and "voiceless"; Confucius, on the other hand, speaks of "the silent treasuring up of knowledge," in a formula the Chinese have never stopped using (*Analects* 7.2). Plato even ended up transforming religion into theology; in China, by contrast, what is surprising is the lack of dogmas, and since there is no *credo*, there have never been wars of religion. Finally, when the Western tradition takes cognizance of the ineffable (in relation to the divine), it is God who speaks; the tradition resorts to the discourse of revelation (by drawing from an Eastern, originally Hebrew, source). In China, Heaven does not speak, or, more precisely, as Confucius says, "Does Heaven say anything?" (*Analects* 7.19).

In China, skepticism about the word's power to explain led to a belief in the word's subtlety; the unsaid moves onto the same level as discourse as it becomes *allusive*. Such, at least, is the notion that to me seems best to represent the difference here. How does one express a phenomenon that one discovers outside one's own culture if not by deriving a particular notion from this culture and then working the phenomenon according to this new angle — in such a way as to extrovert it gradually and thereby make it signify something other than what it originally seemed to render? For Westerners, allusion is a rhetorical figure among others that, as Pierre Fontanier remarks, "consists in letting us sense the relationship of a stated thing to an unstated thing, the notion of which is awakened by this very relationship."[1] In the context of China, at the end of the route, we see that allusion has another possible use. It can express the dependence of the stated vis-à-vis the unstated and legitimate the word by its implicit dimension.

373

While statement limits meaning and makes it sterile, allusiveness keeps the word open as to its deployment and makes it pregnant with meaning.

Delving into the split — since it is by means of a split that one is beginning to think here — means exposing oneself to the objections of both sides. How far, indeed, can one push cultural generalizations before they become illusions or are undermined by too many exceptions? I am not claiming that Western culture has not known the richness of the implicit; but I do not think implicitness, at least before recent times (since the poetic revolution of the late nineteenth century — above all Mallarmé — did perhaps bring us a bit closer), is this culture's most affirmed value of the word, whereas this has traditionally been the case in China with the notion of *hanxu*.[a] Witness psychoanalysis, which through its effort to speak or to make others speak (and the result it expects from this explicitness) seems quite revealing of the Western confidence in the transformative power of the word. (Will psychoanalysis, thus far shunned in China, ever take root there?)[2] On the other hand, we have seen that certain Chinese thinkers in late Antiquity took pleasure in exposition through argument: the Mohists expatiate, while Zhuangzi, even while preaching the renunciation of the word, debates with sophists. All the same, this taste for disputation, which went hand in hand with the rise of the schools, knew no tomorrow. And although so positive a mind as Wang Chong (in the second century A.D.) might defend the clarity of discourse, his own prose is unpopular.

I have noted throughout this book that the value of allusion cannot be understood apart from an intellectual bias — which brings us back to our own bias. In an attempt to extend the split further, I would even say that whereas for the Greeks myth or discourse seeks to explain, for the Chinese the word tends to elucidate. Rather than reveal, it aims to indicate. While the Greeks

374

demonstrate the truth (the truth of representation or of the basis
of an argument), the Chinese indicate the way by which to proceed
(the Tao of natural and social regulation). In sum, for the Greeks,
discourse has an object, which one attempts to surround as closely
as possible, whereas the Chinese recommend that the word be
slackened because the proposition is all the more subtle if it only
lets one have a glimpse. This is the essential point: through its evasiveness, the proposition plays into the hands of immanence.

The notion of allusion has two aspects: the importance of the
unsaid in relation to the said and the relevance of the relationship
between the two. The figure, we say, lets us feel the relationship;
in the allusion, the said awakens the idea of what is not said. Yet
we wonder what makes this link possible — allowing us to feel this
relationship so that the implicit idea is awakened. Once again, one
will understand the nature of the allusive relationship if one compares it with the symbolic function: while the latter rests on a
representative relationship (such as the flame representing love),
allusion rests on a relationship of correlation. (According to the
Chinese formula, I show you the mulberry bush, but the target is
the sophora. When the poems about Tiananmen Square praised
Yang Kaihui, Mao's prior wife, the point was not to allude to a
symbol of revolutionary heroism or love of one's country but to
refer to Jiang Qing, his last wife, who in fact was being criticized.)
With allusion, the motivation is not internal, as it is with the
symbol; at the same time, the relationship is not entirely external
either, for then there would be no motivation for the allusion.
Though the one never represents the other, it nevertheless implies
it, refers to it, makes one think of it. It is here that we see once
again how modes of thought influence modes of expression.
Indeed, it seems to me that the Greeks favored the mimetic relationship (particularly between the perceptible and the idea) and

were scarcely interested in the correlation of things (think of the difficulty Plato encounters in *The Sophist*) and that the opposite is true for the Chinese. Rather than exploit representation (to reach one level through another: the spiritual world through the physical), the Chinese based their vision of the world on correlation. Thus they favored allusive meaning over symbolic expression.

Indeed, most generally, Chinese thought is relational. Not only are all of its terms paired, each with its counterpart; but from this interdependence, each gains its consistency. And this is true in their view of nature as well as of society. Chinese cosmology rests entirely on interaction (between the poles of sky and earth, yin and yang, and so on). As Joseph Needham pointed out, the Chinese noticed, very early on, the influence of the moon on the tides; rather than being taken as primary, constitutive elements, as in Greek physics, the five agents (*wu xing*) of the Chinese system convey modes of compensation and substitution at the core of reality. From an anthropological point of view, only through the five social relationships (*wu lun*: father-son, lord-vassal, husband-wife, and so on) can the individual attain morality. Nothing can be considered separately; things exist only by virtue of their interrelationship. This is reflected in expression (I am usually suspicious of this sort of projection, but this time it seems incontestable): what Westerners translate as *thing* (an individualizing notion) means *east-west* in Chinese; and what Westerners translate as *landscape* (a unitary term) means *mountains-waters* in Chinese.

One thing cannot be conceived of without the other because the one is already the other; that is, it is latently present in it and necessarily refers back to it. Thus the said refers to the unsaid, the text to its context (the situation to which one refers or the intertext), just as the visible refers to the invisible to which it is correlated — and just as the world, for the Chinese, is a permanent exchange between the latent and the manifest. The word oscillates between the poles of the implicit and the explicit. The most successful Chinese writing has even made correlation a principle: in parallel expression, so current in China, each part of the paired expression is understood through the other. One must, as they say, "cross the text to see the meaning."[b] This is why a detour of meaning, for the Chinese, has nothing surreptitious about it, since, when I say the one, the other is implied, and when I say the other, I make the listener think more deeply about the first. And this is why detour *in itself* gives access.

The correlative structure of the Chinese world finds its opposite in isolation *in itself,* that isolation in principle and essence that seems characteristic of Greek thought. To retrace this in itselfness implies splitting reality — relinquishing the plane of phenomena to reach the plane of the intelligible or the divine (of ontology and theology), the abstract plane elaborated by definition or the spiritual one that the symbol tends to represent. This means not that Chinese thought has never known abstraction but that its abstraction has never established a status as essence; nor does it mean that it has not known symbolism but that its symbolism has not served to explore another world. Indeed, there is no plane or world in Chinese thought other than that of process (of the order of the way: the Tao) and that of the capacity that lets it operate (*de*). This is why the separation between the "this" of the word and the "over-there" of meaning,[c] as the commentators analyze it in reference to allusive incitement (Luo Dajing; see chapter 4 above) or to annals writing (Liu Xizai; see chapter 5 above), never takes on a metaphysical dimension. The beyond to which the subtle proposition opens up may be of another order (for example, from the natural to the social), but it is not transcendent.

There would seem, therefore, two ways to present our vision of things: *detour,* where one thing refers to another and communicates with it, since they form a pair and are interrelated; and *split*, where everything refers to itself but on another plane, which it imitates and which informs it and from which it derives its reality. Modern ideology (particularly that from Nietzsche) stresses above all, for a culture born of Greek idealism, the construction of a form-essence and the invention of a model. This super-world of theory has devalued the Western world; this transcendent outside has cut us off from phenomena. In short, our metaphysical bias seems to have impoverished our experience. But perhaps we have lost sight of the advantage of such intelligibility; perhaps we have not even realized all that depends on it. This super-world has enabled Westerners to conceive of the ideal; the Western invention of the soul and God has made it possible to experience the sublime (indeed, this notion of the ideal has no equivalent in Chinese: *lixiang*,[d] which serves as its translation, literally means the thought of *li*, that is, of the regulating principle of things). Moreover, this transcendent exterior has enabled Westerners to conceive of freedom — including freedom in the city (the Chinese conceive of natural spontaneity, in the sense of *sponte sua* — that which comes through immanence).

This difference in the conception of the world appears in politics as well. The figure of the intellectual could not have developed in the West if there had not been this plane of the model and the ideal, which transcends power relationships and which the Western intellectual has made his domain. The Chinese man of letters feels uncomfortable making himself into an intellectual because he does not have this ideal world to lean on when confronting the political sphere (since nature, to which Taoist thought gives him access, only offers him a chance for escape or withdrawal). Caught in this purely mundane vision of reality, he resorts to evasions in the face of power and finds room to maneuver only in subtlety. This room to maneuver is precarious, since at best it is the result of a compromise that is forever subject to revision at the whims of the prince or the Party. It can never be an autonomous territory, can never serve as the basis for an assertion of the rights of the mind. *In the name of what*, therefore, can the Chinese man of letters break free from the forces of power, affirm his positions, and thus speak openly? This is a question that is still being asked in China, one that makes dissidence more difficult.

There is also, therefore, a benefit in saying things as directly as possible, of speaking as straightforwardly as possible, of wanting to get as close to the truth as possible. I say "as possible" because we are dealing with an extreme, and therefore an ideal, point. If there is fecundity in the evasive and the implicit — on which I have dwelled at length here — there is also a fascination in wishing to speak from the *closest* point. Alongside the subtlety of detour, there is the jubilation of being explicit. That, at least, is what I have experienced over the course of this book. In seeking to make explicit what most eluded the outside observer that I was, I have found the *possibility* of the allusive — a quantity never fixed.

Notes

CHAPTER ONE: "HE'S CHINESE," "IT'S ALL CHINESE TO ME"

1. Arthur Smith, *Chinese Characteristics* (New York: Fleming H. Revell Company, 1894), p. 63. All references to this text are from this edition and will be referred to by page number.

2. Even during the celebration of the birthday of the great writer Lu Xun, people inevitably ended up speaking of the critique of Deng; see *Hongqi*, September 1976.

3. This is understood all the better if one remembers that the weakness of the Gang of Four stemmed from, among other things, their lack of military support; hence it was logical for them to try to correct this weakness by assuring their control of armed forces.

4. Thus Yao Wenyuan, who worked on the student paper *Xuexi yu pipan* at Fudan University in Shanghai before taking up the same themes in *Hongqi*, which he edited. Another example of a link between a provincial and a central organ is the *Peking Journal* and the *People's Daily*, which is edited in Peking but more official than the *Peking Journal* (see spring 1979).

5. Especially since the advances made on the Soviet side were a way for Peking to express its dissatisfaction with the American signers of the SALT agreements.

6. See, especially, *People's Daily,* August 4, 1978.

7. A study of the evidentiary value of the photographs that appeared in the

official press was undertaken by Roderick Macfarquhar for the period preceding the Cultural Revolution; see *China Quarterly* 46 (1971), pp. 289ff.

8. Will the economic opening of China, following its relative political opening, lead the Chinese to change their mode of *output* and consider indirection superfluous? This would be an occasion to verify the relationship — which we can only imagine today — between the following two modes of productivity: direct communication and capitalism.

9. Lucian W. Pye, "Communication and Political Culture," Conference on Communication and Cultural Exchange in China, January 3–7, 1978, East-West Center, Honolulu, Hawaii; see also, Alan P.L. Liu, *Communication and National Integration in Communist China* (Berkeley: University of California Press, 1971), and Frederick T.C. Yu, *Mass Persuasion in Communist China* (New York: Frederick A. Praeger, 1964).

10. The importance granted to indirect expression in China has often been noted by the greatest Western sinologists; see Bernhard Karlgren, *Sound and Symbol in Chinese* (Reprint, Hong Kong: Hong Kong University Press, 1962), p. 83; and Marcel Granet, *La pensée chinoise* (Reprint, Paris: Albin Michel, 1968), pp. 53ff. But the phenomenon has never, to my knowledge, fostered a comprehensive study.

CHAPTER TWO: FRONTAL VERSUS OBLIQUE ATTACK

1. "Mou gong pian," in *Sunzi bingfa*.

2. "Xing pian," in *Sunzi bingfa*.

3. "Mou gong pian," in *Sunzi bingfa*.

4. "Jun zheng pian" and "Jiu di pian," in *Sunzi bingfa*.

5. "Shi pian," in *Sunzi bingfa*.

6. "Qizheng," in *Sun Bin bingfa*.

7. *Ibid.*

8. Formula by the Tang emperor Taizong cited in the commentary on "Shi pian," in *Sunzi bingfa*.

9. "Qizheng," in *Sun Bin bingfa*.

10. "Shi pian," in *Sunzi bingfa*.

11. *Ibid.*

12. In *Laozi* (see below, ch. 12), the oblique attack alone summarizes the military arts: "Govern the state by being straightforward; wage war by being [oblique]" (*Tao Te Ching*, trans. D.C. Lau [Hong Kong: Chinese University Press, 1982, no. 57]).

13. Mao Zedong, "Problems of Strategy in Guerilla War Against Japan," in *Selected Works of Mao Tse-Tung* (Peking: Foreign Languages Press, 1965), vol. 2, p. 79). Edgar Snow mentions elsewhere, anecdotally, that Mao was influenced by his mother, who liked the politics of indirect attack.

14. Victor Davis Hanson, *Le modèle occidental de la guerre*, trans. Alain Billault (Paris: Belles Lettres, 1990).

15. Polybius, *The Histories*, trans. W.R. Paton (Cambridge, MA: Harvard University Press, 1976), 13.3.

16. Xenophon, *Hellenica*, in *Hellenica, Books VI and VII; Anabases, Books I–III*, trans. Carleton Lewis Brownson Loeb Classical Library (London: Heinemann, 1921), 6.5.

17. Marcel Detienne and Jean-Pierre Vernant, *Les ruses de l'intelligence: La mētis des Grecs* (Paris: Flammarion, 1974), p. 9.

18. In *Knowing Words; Wisdom and Cunning in the Classical Traditions of China and Greece* (Ithaca, NY: Cornell University Press, 1992), Lisa Raphals has tried to apply Detienne and Vernant's research to the Chinese domain: she shows the Greek *mētis* to correspond to the Chinese *zhi*, the notion of which has been developed since Antiquity and is found at play in the great novels. This projection of one field onto another never takes into account the *possible* originality of the other field. The most buried cultural stances — which are likewise the most pregnant — escape this type of parallel; if one does not treat what might be the internal coherence of this other field, in order to structure its differences (but without making them absolute), everything will always seem *more or less the same.*

19. On this subject, see the interesting study *Espionage and Treason* by André Gerolymatos (Amsterdam: Gieben, 1986).

20. Marcel Detienne, "La phalange: Problèmes et controverses," in *Pro-*

blèmes de la guerre en Grèce ancienne, ed. Jean-Pierre Vernant (Paris: Ecole des Hautes Etudes en Sciences Sociales, 1968).

21. Diogenes Laertius, 9.51.

22. Clement of Alexandria, *Stromata*, 6.65.

23. Jacqueline de Romilly, *Histoire et raison chez Thucydide* (Paris: Belles Lettres, 1956), pp. 180ff.

24. *Ibid.*, p. 225.

25. Thucydides, *The Peloponnesian War*, 2.87, trans. Rex Warner (New York: Penguin, 1954), p. 181.

26. De Romilly, *Histoire et raison chez Thucydide*, p. 227.

27. *Ibid.*, p. 226.

28. Likewise, in Chinese military strategy, the oblique attack can be renewed through a frontal attack, suddenly and openly, to surprise and disorient the enemy. By playing correlatively with the indirect, the most direct expression, which might seem to contradict the subtlety of indirection, becomes a new way to act obliquely toward the other and to keep the initiative.

29. Liang Shiqiu [Qiu Lang, pseud.], *Ma ren de yishu* (New York: Fleming H. Revell Company, 1894).

30. Smith, *Chinese Characteristics*, p. 71.

31. Liang Shiqiu, *Ma ren de yishu*.

Chapter Three: Under the Cover of the Image

1. On this subject, I refer to the study, now a classic, by Jean Pépin, *Mythe et allégorie: Les origines greques et les contestations judéo-chrétiennes* (Reprint, Paris: Etudes Augustiniennes, 1976).

2. Western translators (notably James Legge and Arthur Waley) have often considered the Chinese reading of *The Book of Songs* allegorical. But this is mistaken, in my opinion, and on this subject I recommend Pauline Yu, *The Reading of Imagery in the Chinese Poetic Tradition* (Princeton, NJ: Princeton University Press, 1987), pp. 46ff.

3. See Shen Deqian, *Shuoshi zuiyu* (China: Qing Qianlong, 1761–95), no. 17.

4. *The Book of Songs*, trans. Arthur Waley (New York: Grove Press, 1966).

All references to this work are taken from this edition and will be indicated by song number in parentheses.

5. Shen Deqian, *Shuoshi zuiyu*, no. 17.

6. Dong Lailü, cited in Su Wenzhuo (So Man Jock), *Shuoshi zuiyu quanping* (Hong Kong: Zhihao yinshua gongsi, 1978), p. 46, n. i.

7. Séraphin Couvreur, *Cheu King* (Taichung: Kuangchi Press, 1967), p. 112.

8. Yan Can, *Shiqi.*

9. Shen Deqian, *Shuoshi zuiyu*, no. 20; see Su Wenzhuo, p. 50.

10. Shen Deqian, *Shuoshi zuiyu*, no. 21; see Su Wenzhuo, p. 52.

11. *Confucian Analects*, in *The Chinese Classics*, trans. James Legge (Taipei: SMC Publishing, 1994). All references to this work are taken from this edition and will be cited by number in parentheses.

12. "Taishigong zixu," in *Shiji*. For more detail on these references, see my book *La valeur allusive* (Paris: Ecole Française d'Extrême-Orient, 1985), pp. 93ff.

13. Plutarch, *Sur les oracles de la Pythie* (Paris: Belles Lettres, 1937), no. 26.

14. "Yu Li shi er Bai tong xun Fan shi yin ju"; see the commentary of Jin Shengtan, *Du shi jie* (Shanghai: Shanghai guji chubanshe), p. 12.

15. Du Fu, "Ai wang sun," ll. 1–2; see Jin Shengtan, *Du shi jie*, p. 41.

16. Bo Juyi, "Letter to Yuan Zhen."

17. The famous murals—*dazibao*—of contemporary China are inspired by this tradition. Moreover, today, Chinese thinkers believe that herein lies the future of Chinese democracy.

18. Song Wan, "Chang Gu ji zhu xu"; on this subject, see my article "Naissance de l'imagination: Essai de problématique au travers de la réflexion littéraire de la Chine et de l'Occident," *Extrême-Orient, Extrême-Occident* 7 (1985), pp. 50ff.

19. Yao Wenxie, "Chang Gu shi zhu xu."

CHAPTER FOUR: QUOTATIONS AS PROXY

1. Lao Xiaoyu, *Chunqiu shihua*, ch. 1; this chapter by the Qing scholar is devoted to the practice of *fu shi* and was my main source on this subject.

2. Du Yu, *Chunqiu Zuozhuan jijie* (Shanghai: Shanghai renmin chubanshe, 1977), vol. 3, p. 1057.

3. Lao Xiaoyu, *Chunqiu shihua*, ch. 1.

4. In French, *motif* and *motive* are the same word. — TRANS.

5. Marcel Granet, *La civilisation chinoise* (Reprint, Paris: Albin Michel, 1968), pp. 320ff.; and *La pensée chinoise* (Reprint, Paris: Albin Michel, 1968), p. 60.

6. Lao Xiaoyu, *Chunqiu shihua*, ch. 1.

7. See the brief analysis by Luo Genze, *Zhongguo wenxue piping shi*, p. 37.

8. Lao Xiaoyu, *Chunqiu shihua*, ch. 1.

9. *Ibid.*

10. Du Yu, *Chunqiu Zuozhuan jijie*, p. 965.

11. Lao Xiaoyu, *Chunqiu shihua*, ch. 1.

12. "Yiwenzhi," in *Hanshu*.

13. Granet, *La pensée chinoise*, p. 36.

CHAPTER FIVE: INSINUATING AND AVOIDING TO SAY

1. *The Works of Mencius*, in *The Chinese Classics*, trans. James Legge (Taipei: SMC Publishing, 1991). All references to this work are taken from this edition and will be cited by book, unless otherwise stated.

2. James Legge, "Prolegomena," in "The Ch'un Ts'ew with the Tso Chuen," in *The Chinese Classics*, vol. 5.

3. Edouard Chavannes, *Mémoires historiques de Se-Ma Ts'ien* (Paris: Maisonneuve, 1967–1969), p. 146.

4. While *Zuozhuan*, which recounts the indicated events, tends to unfold in keeping with the line of the reigns, *Gongyang*, which generally limits itself to revealing the intention supposedly expressed in the events, tends to become more laconic (see, for example, the Xiang *gong* reign, which has been commented on very little).

5. Legge, "The Ch'un Ts'ew with the Tso Chuen."

6. It even happens that the same mention is justified differently by the commentators. Hence the indication "In the spring, the Southern Gate was repaired

again" (Xi *gong*, twentieth year) is interpreted differently by *Zuozhuan* and *Gongyang*. For *Zuozhuan*, this critique has to do with inconvenience (since such things should be done only in the spring); for *Gongyang*, it has to do with abandoning standards of the past.

7. An example of this sort is found in *Lunyu*, bk. 11, p. 13.

8. The model for the principle of variable geometry is found in *The Book of Changes* and seems one of the most original aspects of Chinese thought (yet one of the most difficult to justify); see my study *Figures de l'immanence: Pour une lecture philosophique du* Yiking (Paris: Grasset, 1993), pp. 88ff. and 238ff. in particular.

We might also wonder whether a commentary such as *Gongyang* possesses an overall unity and/or a unifying principle — since the disparate nature of the rules of interpretation might also come simply from the diversity of the commentators participating in the work or taking over for each other within this school.

9. The commentator's concern for precision can even lead him to modify his criteria. Apropos the mention "In autumn, a palace away from home was constructed for the king's daughter" (Zhuang *gong*, first year), *Gongyang* comments, "Why mention this fact? To criticize it. What is being criticized? The construction conforms to ritual, but the fact that it is done away from home does not." (For the same type of example, see Zhuang *gong*, twenty-fifth year: a sacrifice is mentioned at the altar of the sun gods and at the capital's gate; the sites are included, *Gongyang* states, because the first site is correct while the second is not.)

10. These examples are used to characterize the chronicle's writing in "Zong jing," in *Wenxin diaolong*.

11. Legge, "The Ch'un Ts'ew with the Tso Chuen."

12. It is true that the subject of the story was not the prince of Lu, from the point of view of the person writing the chronicle. I note, moreover, that *Guliang* thinks it is good to change criteria in this regard and discovers an indication of violent death in the fact that the personal name of the prince, which normally is not mentioned during his lifetime, is used during the particular circumstance in which the death occurred (see also Xiang *gong*, twenty-fifth year).

13. Jacqueline de Romilly, *Histoire et raison chez Thucydide* (Paris: Belles Lettres, 1956), pp. 64ff.

14. "What is important is not that Julien Sorel, after he has learned that he has been betrayed by Madame de Rénal, travels to Verrières and tries to kill her. It is that silence, that dreamlike journey, that thoughtless certainty, and that eternal resolution which follows the news. But there is no passage where these things are said. There is no need for 'Julien thought,' or 'Julien wished.' In order to express then, Stendhal had only to slip into being, to enter into a monologue with Julien, making objects, obstacles, means, and hazards flash before our eyes with the speed of the journey. He had only to decide to relate the journey in three pages instead of ten, and to be silent about something rather than say such and such." In Marcel Merleau-Ponty, *The Prose of the World*, trans. John O'Neil (Evanston, IL: Northeastern University Press, 1973), p. 88.

15. The commentary by Du Yu raises them to the level of definitive formulas (see Qian Zhongshu, *Guanchuipian*, vol. 1, p. 161); and the notional status they acquired in *Wenxin diaolong*, ch. 2 and 3, can be verified.

16. Sima Qian, *Shiji*, ch. 117.

17. See the study by Xu Fuguan, *Liang Han sixiang shi* [The history of thought under the Han] (Taipei: Xuesheng shuju), vol. 3, pp. 416ff.

18. See the various occurrences in chapter 130 of Sima Qian, *Shiji,* and in the "Letter to Ren An"; this interesting modification of the meaning of the expression was noted by Burton Watson and analyzed in a study by Paula Varsano (to be published by the University of Montreal).

19. Poem by Han Yu, commented on by Wu Qiao, *Weilu shihua*, ch. 1.

20. *Wenxin diaolong*, ch. 2.

21. On the distribution of this ritual fire among those who wanted to honor the emperor, see Donald Holzman: "At the capital, a ritual fire, produced by very archaic means at the imperial palace, was distributed to the high officials who brought it home with torches" (Une fête chez Su Shih à Huang Chou en 1082," *Etudes Sing in memoriam Etienne Balazs* [Paris: Ecole des Hautes Etudes en Sciences Sociales, 1980], p. 128); see also "The Cold Food Festival in Early Medieval China," *Harvard Journal of Asiatic Studies* 46, no. 1 (June 1986), pp. 51ff.

CHAPTER SIX: THE IMPOSSIBILITY OF DISSIDENCE

1. *Confucian Analects*, in *The Chinese Classics*, trans. James Legge (Taipei: SMC Publishing, 1994). All references to this work are taken from this edition and will be cited by number in parentheses.

2. In *Analects* 15.6, one finds the same overcoming of an intransigence through the superior ability to adapt oneself over time. This idea is similar to the one developed in *The Book of Changes*: the good man is inflexible deep down (see the trigram *qian*), while accommodating the outside world (trigram *kun*); see the hexagram *tai*.

3. Xu Fuguan, *Liang Han sixiang shi* [The history of thought under the Han] (Taipei: Xuesheng shuju), vol. 1, pp. 102ff. and 281ff.

4. *Zuozhuan*, Huan *gong*, second year.

5. *Ibid.*, Huan *gong*, thirteenth year.

6. *Xiaojing*, which is taken up again in chapter 12 of *Bohutong*, is devoted to remonstrance and serves as a basic reference on this subject.

7. This principle of resignation, after three unsuccessful attempts by the writer, already was codified in *Gongyang* (Zhuang *gong*, twenty-fourth year).

8. *Dadai liji*, 3.3B; reprinted in *Bohutong*, ch. 12.

9. As is this formula, on which *Great Commentary on the Book of Changes* is based: "The alternation of yin and yang is what is called the 'way' (from which reality proceeds); to continue this is (human) well-being."

10. *Bohutong*, ch. 12; and "Bianzheng," in *Kongzi jiayu*.

11. See Yves Hervouet, *Un Poète de cour sous les Han: Sseu-ma Siang-jou* (Paris: Bibliothèque de l'Institut des Hautes Etudes Chinoises, 1964), vol. 19, p. 11.

12. After 1942, in *Interventions into the Discussions on Art and Literature in Yenan*, Mao called on writers to renounce the insidious and circuitous expression that characterized the art of the great Lu Xun. But at the same time, he began his systematic purges against intellectuals who dared come out against him (such as Wang Shiwei). On the literary opposition in contemporary China, see Merle Goldman, *Literary Dissent in Communist China* (Cambridge, MA: Harvard University Press, 1967). Yet did these Chinese writers' contestation, which was at

times so courageous, succeed in forming true dissidence — in opening up a new path? The question remains unanswered.

13. For example, Jean Pasqualini, who became a "prisoner of Mao," complained openly to his jailers. Misfortune caught up with him. His cell mates, better informed, refrained from such naïveté.

14. *Shiji*, ch. 126; see the interesting study by Timoteus Pokora, "Ironical Critics at Ancient Chinese Courts," *Oriens Extremus* (July 1973), pp. 49ff.

15. "Xieyin," in *Wenxin diaolong*.

16. To be "straight" on the inside and "curved" outside, to preserve one's integrity while respecting hierarchy — such is the compromise idealized by the Chinese tradition, whose utopian character *Zhuangzi* takes pleasure in denouncing (see the beginning of chapter 4): face-to-face with the despot, he who begins by obeying never ends by debasing himself, and, inversely, he who makes remonstrances is fatally condemned.

17. The best representative of the first category is Shun Yukun, at the court of Wei; however, the remarkable Dongfang Shuo, who lived under the reign of Wudi, marks the transition from one mode to the other.

18. "Bixing," in *Wenxin diaolong*.

19. "Jing jie," in *Liji zhengyi*.

20. See Shen Deqian, *Shishuo zuiyu*, nn. 17 and 30; Su Wenzhuo, *Shuoshi zuiyo quanping* (Hong Kong: Zhihao yinshua gongsi, 1978), pp. 47 and 70.

21. Wang Fuzhi, *Jiangzhai shihua*, ed. Dai Hongsen (Peking: Renmin wenxue chubanshe, 1981), vol. 2, no. 37, p. 127.

22. *Ibid.*

23. *Ibid.*

24. *Tian' an men shi chao* [Poems dedicated to Tiananmen Square], ed. Tong Huaizhou (Peking: Renmin wenxue chubanshe, 1978). See also David S.G. Goodman, *Beijing Street Voices: The Poetry and Politics of China's Democracy Movement* (London: Marion Boyars, 1981); unfortunately, Goodman does not analyze the allusive dimension of these poems.

25. "Xieyin," in *Wenxin diaolong*.

26. Lu Xun, "In Celebration of the Recapture of Shanghai and Nankin,"

April 10, 1927 (essay discovered in 1975 at Sun Yatsen University of Canton);
see *Luxun: Pamphlets et libelles,* presented and trans. Michelle Loi (Paris: Maspero,
1977), pp. 121ff.

27. Stendhal, *Lucien Leuwen,* trans. H.L.R. Edwards (Harmondsworth, UK:
Penguin, 1991), ch. 17, p. 162.

28. "He saw Mlle Bérard open her little eyes as wide as she could.

"'Good,' he thought, 'she thinks I'm talking politics, and is anxious to make
her report.'

"'I could never plead *in the Chamber* the causes that stir me most deeply.
Away from the rostrum, I'd be tormented by the depth of the feelings that fired
my soul; but on opening my mouth before that supreme and, even more, severe
judge I tremble to displease, I could only say to him: "You see how troubled I am,
you so fill my heart that it hasn't even the strength to reveal itself to your eyes."'

"Mme de Chasteller had begun listening with pleasure, but towards the end
of this speech she was scared of Mlle Bérard; Leuwen's remarks seemed to her
far too transparent. She hastened to break in" (*Ibid.,* ch. 24, p. 199).

CHAPTER SEVEN: BETWEEN EMOTION AND LANDSCAPE

1. Shen Deqian, *Shuoshi zuiyu,* no. 2; see Su Wenzhuo, *Shuoshi zuiyu quan-ping* (Hong Kong: Zhihao yinshua gongsi, 1978), p. 8.

2. Whereas the image (incitement: *xing*) at the beginning of two poems is
almost the same, which well defines its clichéd character and prosodic function,
the interpretation given of it varies: the semantic selection set into motion
through the formulaic expression accommodates itself to each particular case. To
pursue the theme of the wind:

Zip, zip the valley wind,

Bringing darkness, bringing rain...

In this poem (35), whose subject is the grievances of a woman rejected by her
husband, the initial image of the valley wind is supposed to evoke the harmony
of the energies of yin and yang. "When the energies of yin and yang are in harmony," notes the commentator, "the wind in the valley rises; when the husband
and wife are in harmony, the family is formed; and when the family is formed,

heirs are born." One also finds this image of the valley wind at the beginning of poem 201:

Zip, zip the valley wind,

Nothing but wind rain...

This time the poem evokes the grievances of a friend who complains of being abandoned, and the initial image is read as the expression of interdependence: "Wind and rain come together; friends need each other."

3. "The incitement with an allusive value (*xing*) serves," according to Zheng Zhong, "to situate the event evoked in external reality." From there, this poetic mode consists in inciting/initiating: in choosing an image and developing an analogy in it, one incites or initiates its interiority. Each time the poet uses natural, animal, or vegetal elements to express what he wants to say, it is a matter of this type of allusive incitement.

4. Zhu Xi, *Sijizhuan*, commentary on the first poem. On this global change of perspective in the commentary of *Shijing*, see Steven Van Zoren, *Poetry and Personality: Reading, Exegesis, and Hermetics in Traditional China* (Stanford, CA: Stanford University Press, 1991).

5. *Zhuzi yulei*, ch. 80.

6. Two poems in *The Book of Songs* will allow us easily to understand the difference. The first (11) offers a reduced example of the incitatory mode (*xing*), since the natural image (or at least considered as such), the unicorn, opening each stanza is systematically followed by a development on the human plane (the family of the prince introduced according to the degrees of kinship), which makes up the subject of the poem:

The unicorn's hooves!

The duke's sons throng.

Alas for the unicorn!

In the other poem (5), the subject is never directly addressed, which brings us to a case of pure analogical functioning (*bi*):

The locusts' wings say "throng, throng."

Well may your sons and grandsons

Be a host innumerable

In each stanza, it is only a matter of locusts, with no mention of the human world (at least according to the interpretation of Zhu Xi); at the same time, this song honoring the locusts is seen as a praise sung to the queen, who, since she is not jealous, deserves a long posterity (the poem was allegedly composed by the palace women). The two figures can therefore be distinguished by their mode of functioning: the first uses indirect material, the second a transfer of meaning; in the first case, there is juxtaposition, in the second, substitution.

7. *Zhuzi yulei*, ch. 80.

8. Jean Cohen, *Structure du langage poétique* (Paris: Flammarion, 1966), p. 204; see also Michel Le Guern, *Sémantique de la métaphore et de la métonymie* (Paris: Larousse, 1973), p. 50.

9. This communal conception was particularly emphasized by Wang Fuzhi, *Jiangzhai shihua*, ed. Dai Hongsen, p. 33; on this subject, see my books *La valeur allusive* (Paris: Ecole Française d'Extrême-Orient, 1985), and *Procès ou création* (Paris: Seuil, 1989), ch. 16.

10. On this point, see Xu Fuguan, *Zhongguo wenxue lunji* (Taiwan: Xuesheng shuju), pp. 91ff.; in his analysis, however, the motivation and the semantic thrust are not clearly distinguished enough.

11. "Bi xing," in *Wenxin diaolong*.

12. "Quan fu," in *Wenxin diaolong*.

13. "Wu se," in *Wenxin diaolong*.

14. Liu Xie, *The Literary Mind and the Carving of Dragons*, trans. Vincent Yu-Chung Shih (Taipei: Chung Hwa, 1970), p. 353.

15. Aristotle's *Poetics* 17.1455A, in *Literary Criticism from Plato to Dryden*, ed. Allen H. Gilbert (Detroit, MI: Wayne State University Press, 1962), p. 94. All references to this work are from this edition and will be indicated by book in parentheses after each citation.

16. Longinus, "On Literary Excellence," in *Literary Criticism from Plato to Dryden*, p. 165.

17. *Ibid.*, p. 166.

18. Quintilian, *Institutio oratoria*, 6.2.

19. "Shense," in *Wenxin diaolong*.

20. Lu Ji, *Wenfu*.

21. Only the expression "He scrutinizes the mental representations (*yixiang*) and wields the ax [consequently]," from the chapter "Shense," goes in this direction, without our knowing, however, to what it corresponds (since it is due to the requirements of parallelism and is not taken up again later). In the beginning of the final *zan*, in any case, *xiang* takes on the meaning of phenomenon once more: "When the spirit is active, phenomena communicate" (*shen yong xiang tong*).

22. On this subject, see my study "Naissance de l'imagination: Essai de problématique au travers de la réflexion littéraire de la Chine et de l'Occident," *Extrême-orient, Extrême-occident* 7 (1985), pp. 24ff.

23. On the Homeric qualities emphasized by scholiasts, see Roos Meijering, *Literary and Rhetorical Theories in Greek Scholia* (Groningen: Egbert Forsten, 1987); on the notion of the imagination in Antiquity, see Gerard Watson, *Phantasia in Classical Thought* (Galway: Galway University Press, 1988).

24. "...I lose all control of my voice and my tongue has no power; my skin tingles as with fire; my eyes cannot see..." The author of *On the Sublime* has commented on these famous lines by Sappho: "Are you not amazed at the way she summons the spirit, the body, the ears, the tongue, the eyes, the color, as though all were apart from her..." (Longinus, "On Literary Excellence," ch. 10, in *Literary Criticism from Plato to Dryden*, pp. 159–60.

25. Aristotle, *Poetics*, in *Literary Criticism from Plato to Dryden*, p. 94.

26. It is true that among the Greek prose writers, like those in China, praise of the great men of the past served as a vehicle for projects of reform — and this out of a concern for reserve; see Jacqueline de Romilly, *Histoire et raison chez Thucydide* (Paris: Belles Lettres, 1956), p. 90.

27. See Aristotle, *Rhetoric* 1412A, trans. W. Rhys Roberts (New York: Modern Library, 1954), p. 191.

28. See Marsh H. McCall, *Ancient Rhetorical Theories of Simile and Comparison* (Cambridge, MA: Harvard University Press, 1969).

CHAPTER EIGHT: BEYOND THE LANDSCAPE

1. Arthur Waley is notable in this sense for his translation of *The Book of Songs*, or, more recently, C.H. Wang, *The Bell and the Drum* (Berkeley: University of California Press, 1974); similarly, Vincent Yu-chung Shih translates the title of the chapter "Bi xing" of *Wenxin diaolong* as "Metaphor and Allegory."

2. Only poem 5, which we have already read, uses the metaphor of locusts in this way (at least according to Zhu Xi's interpretation; the poem is considered, we remember, a eulogy of the queen and her many progenitors made by the palace women). The same goes for poem 155, which is entirely devoted to the description of a rapacious and destructive owl, although this was also interpreted historically (as the self-justification of the duke of Zhou for having led a punitive expedition against a group of rebels).

3. Or yet again, that the garden has hardwood trees but litter beneath them warns us of "the bad aspects of things we love" (or "the sage holds himself aloof, the good-for-nothing below"). Lastly, that the stones are good for grinding enjoins us to look for "the good aspects of things we detest" (or "to sharpen one's virtue" to gain wisdom).

4. Pauline Yu, *The Reading of Imagery in the Chinese Poetic Tradition* (Princeton, NJ: Princeton University Press, 1987), p. 76.

5. See Léonard Linsky commenting on Gottlob Frege: "The *reference* of an expression is the *object* named and denoted through it; and one must distinguish this object from the meaning of the expression," which "is grasped by anyone sufficiently familiar with the language."

6. See Zhu Ziqing, *Shi yan zhi bian*, ch. 2. It thus differs from the Greek tradition in that the poem is read not as the revelation of truth but as the indication of a value judgment, either positive or negative. (Pauline Yu, in my opinion, therefore has no grounds to state that the Chinese commentator seeks "not a metaphysical truth but the truth of his world" [*The Reading of Imagery*, p. 81]). Indeed, the Chinese commentator's concern is not truth at all (see the first poem in *The Book of Songs* read first as a poem of blame and then of praise): the important thing is that the poems become integrated, through a historical reference, into the moral and political order.

7. The commentary of Wang Yi of the Han; see You Guoen, *Li sao zuanyi* (Peking: Zhonghua, 1980), p. 31.

8. See You Guoen, *Li sao zuanyi*, p. 45 (ll. 21–22), p. 141 (ll. 89–90), p. 275 (ll. 205–206).

9. *Ibid.,* p. 160.

10. *Ibid.,* p. 289.

11. *Seventeen Old Poems,* in Arthur Waley, *Translations from the Chinese* (New York: Knopf, 1941), p. 37.

12. See Sui Shusen, *Gu shi shijiu shou ji shi* (Peking: Zhonghua shuju), p. 1; and Jean-Pierre Diény, *Les dix-neuf poèmes anciens* (Paris: Université de Paris VII, 1974), p. 49.

13. Yan Yanzhi, *Wenxuan*, ch. 23, commentary on the first poem.

14. Zhong Hong, part 1 of *Shipin*.

15. See Huang Jie, *Ruan Bubing yong huai shi zhu* (Peking: Renmin wenxue chubanshe, 1957).

16. Donald Holzman, *Poetry and Politics: The Life and Works of Juan Chi* (Oxford, UK: Cambridge University Press, 1976), pp. 229ff.

17. Fang Dongshu, *Zhaomei zhan yan*, ed. Wang Shaoying (Peking: Renmin wenxue chubanshe), p. 83.

18. Wang Fuzhi, *Gushi pingxuan*, ch. 4.

19. This implicit dimension, arising from the allusive value and constituting the perspective of Chinese poetry as a whole, was traditionally summarized by two lines of the Tang poet Sikong Tu:

Without directly writing a single word

Completely attaining "wind and waves" [poetic atmosphere]. ("Hanxu")

20. Holzman, *Poetry and Politics*, p. 232.

21. One is hardly surprised that in German romanticism the classical idea of representation gave way to that of infinity and that Europe began to discover a similar fecundity of allusion (*Anspielung*); see Friedrich Schlegel: "All work of art is an allusion to infinity"; and "The spark of the finite and the allusion to infinity flow into each other" ("Der Schein des Endlichen und die Anspielung aufs Unendliche fliessen ineinander"), *Kritische Ausgabe* 18, p. 416 [1140].

22. Those rare later poets, more or less openly breaking with the more common Chinese vision, sought to exploit the level of representation (see the discussion of Li He in ch. 3, above, and Li Shangyin's poem "Jinse"). We have seen, nonetheless, that traditional commentators would interpret their symbolism not as symbolism but as allusion.

In the beginning of the twentieth century, Chinese poets *discovered* symbolism (through contact with Western poetry); see the poems in modern Chinese by Lu Wun, such as "Him" (Ta), which are very different from his poems in classical Chinese.

23. As early as *The Book of Songs*, xing at times did not begin the poem; on this subject, see Zhu Ziqing, *Shi yan zhi bian*, p. 47; and Xu Fuguan, *Zhongguo wenxue lunju*, p. 113.

24. Words that are "simple," Mencius states, "while their meaning is far-reaching"[a] are "good words" (7.2.32). Instead of seeking to reveal mysteries or treat the most abstruse principles, the Chinese sage speaks only of the most ordinary things, those belonging to day-to-day experience; but these ordinary propositions give rise to an infinite depth. *The Book of Changes* is praised according to the same opposition: "Its terms are few but their analogic resonance vast;[b] its meaning is far-reaching, its expression harmonious."

25. *Shiji*, ch. 84, biography of Qu Yuan.

26. Liu Xie, "Bixing," in *Wenxin diaolong*.

27. In *Le Robert* dictionary, Buffon acknowledges this conventionality of the emblem as insufficiently justified in regard to the nature of the concrete: "The warbler was the emblem of inconstant love, just as the turtledove was of faithful love; however, the warbler, lively and gay, is neither less loving nor less faithful because of it, and the turtledove, sad and plaintive, is only all the more scandalously libertine."

28. Wang Bi, "Ming xiang," in *Zhouyi lüeli*.

29. Wang Fuzhi, *Jiangzhai shihua*, ed. Dai Hongsen, p. 8.

30. Sikong Tu, "Letter to Ji Pu."

31. Wu Qiao, *Weilu shihua*, ch. 1.

32. Chen Ting-zhuo, *Baiyuzhai cihua* (Peking: Renmin wenxue chubanshe, 1959), p. 158.

33. According to the philosopher Zhu Xi (twelfth century): "To be appreciated, poetry requires that one intone it so as to immerse oneself in it, to savor its meaning, to chew and masticate it to perceive its flavor." Also: "First one should intone the poem a great many times and only then read the notes; after having read the notes, one should intone the poem again a great many times so that the meaning may naturally dissolve and imbibe us — only then does one begin to understand the poem." On this subject, see my book *La valeur allusive* (Paris: Ecole Française d'Extrême-Orient, 1985), pp. 152ff.

34. We understand, finally, why China did not develop a theory of signs, *strictu sensu*, for, if there is no *mimesis*, can there be semiotics?

35. See Tzvetan Todorov, *Théories du symbole* (Paris: Seuil, 1977), p. 235.

36. Even if it signifies but indirectly, the symbol remains pointed toward generality. For example, Goethe states: "The objects represented in this way appear to be there only for themselves and are nonetheless significant in their deepest recesses, and this because of an ideal that always has a generality in its wake. If the symbolic indicates something else beyond representation, it is always indirectly" (*Oeuvres de Goethe*, Juhiläumansgaher, vol. 33, p. 94). With the symbol, the image presented is not transitive, "but he who senses this particular aspect keenly receives at the same time a general one, without being aware of it, or only later." In short, the symbol is inexhaustible: "The symbolic transforms the phenomenon into idea, the idea into image, and in such a way that the idea remains always infinitely active and inaccessible in the image that, though spoken in every language, remains unspeakable."

CHAPTER NINE: FROM THE MASTER TO THE DISCIPLE

1. Can one treat *Analects* as a single unity, without taking into account the different layers of tradition among the various sections of the collection, which philologists have taken great pains to bring to light (see Cui Shu at the end of the seventeenth century in his very interesting *Zhu Si kaoxin lu* and Kimura Eiichi, *Kōshi to Rongo* [Tokyo: Sōbunsha, 1971])? In Chinese thought, the various fragments have traditionally been credited to a single authority; nonetheless, we note the loss of meaning in the later sections of

the collection, which lack the subtle proposition attributed to Confucius.

The main commentary cited for this reading of *Analects* is Zhu Xi, *Sishu zhangju jizhu;* for the ancient period, He Yan and Huang Kan, *Lunyu jijie yishu,* was also used, as well as a few major neo-Confucian commentaries: Han Yu, *Lunyu bijie;* Zhang Shi, *Lunyu Zhang Xuan gong jie;* Chen Xiangdao, *Lunyu quan-jie;* and Hu Guang et al., *Lunyu jizhu daquan* (compiled in *Zhongguo zixue mingzhu jicheng*, vols. 3–5).

The paragraphs are cited according to their classic breaks: the translations to which I refer are those of James Legge, *Confucian Analects*, in *The Chinese Classics* (Taipei: SMC Publishing, 1994); Anne Cheng (Paris: Seuil, 1981); and Pierre Ryckmans (Paris: Gallimard, 1987).

2. From the gaze that the conscience turns inward on itself is born the Christian practice of confession, so different from the self-criticism once practiced in China: for the Chinese, it was a matter not of identifying an inner truth but of accommodating discourse to what one requires from others. Far from saying what one thinks to emerge from a crisis, one sacrifices to circumstance, which does not fool anyone. More generally, the Chinese tradition is not at all interested, given the absence of a theory of the self as subject, in *identifying* the phenomena of conscience through the power of speech. (Witness psychoanalysis, which, from a Chinese point of view, seems very dependent on a Western concept of speech, in which the object is to *make explicit*, whereas the value of speech in China is based on the implicit.)

3. Hegel, *Leçons sur l'histoire de la philosophie,* vol. 3, 5.1.

4. This indirect illumination based on the most minute aspect of conduct sometimes makes the proposition impossible to translate directly:

> The great officer, Hsien [Zhuan], who had been *family*-minister to Kung-shû Wan [Gong Shu], ascended to the Prince's *court* in company with Wan. The Master, having heard of it, said, "He deserved to be considered Wan (the accomplished)." (14.19)

To render the remark, the translator cannot stick to the indicative value of the scene and is forced to reintroduce a narrative element to serve as explanation. Therefore, he narrates more than he translates: "As soon as he was named by the duke of Wei, Kung-shû Wan [Gong Shu Wenzi] did not hesitate to present his own steward Hsien [Zhuan], who therefore was appointed the same rank at court" (A. Cheng, p. 114). The translator reconstructs the remark in this way not because he needs to say something contextual about the simple event indicated: one day, a great minister's steward appears at court with the same rank as he. A commentator has demonstrated well how such a detail of conduct suffices to reveal the moral exigency (justifying the praise pronounced by Confucius). That someone pleads the cause of his own steward so well to his prince that the officer is raised to the same rank as he "contains three essential qualities": knowing the other and appreciating his merits; forgetting oneself in the sacrifice of vanity; and best serving one's prince by helping him to surround himself with the most capable men.

5. The same is true for chapter 20 of *Analects*, in which the remarks concern the disciples of Confucius alone and are more normative, serving merely as illustration. In this short chapter, the second paragraph is but a catalog in the flat style of chapter 16 (the five excellent things and the four bad things; this method of conceptually closing off a series by a number still exists in China — for example, the four modernizations. As for the first paragraph, it repeats the solemn proclamations of the great founders of Chinese civilization: one commentator proposes reading it as a summary of the path of the Sage, which the "subtle remarks" gathered in the collection would endeavor to elucidate.

6. In a chapter such as "The Conduct of the Men of Letters" ("Ruxing," in *Liji*), the lesson attributed to Confucius takes the form of an oratorical development. (This chapter is even cited by Liu Xie as an example of the developed text; see "Zheng sheng," in *Wenxin diaolong*.) Confucius warns his listeners that it will be long and they should make themselves comfortable. While it is organized in series, the discourse leads to an absolute idealization of the Sage. This discourse is not allusive but does not demonstrate anything either and has no dialectical function, becoming a mere beatifying — and stupefying — inventory of moralism.

7. On *Kongzi jiayu*, refer to the classic study by R.P. Kramers, *K'ung Tzu Chia Yu: The School Sayings of Confucius* (Leiden: E.J. Brill, 1950).

8. For example, Confucius says:

The superior man has three preoccupations he can never forget: if, when young, he does not study, when he grows up, he will have no ability; if, when old, he does not teach, when he is dead, no one will think of him; if, when rich, he does not give to others, if he becomes poor, no one will come to his assistance. This is why the superior man, when he is young, thinks about when he will be grown up, and hence applies himself to his studies; when he is old, he thinks about his death and applies himself to teaching; and when he is rich, he thinks about when he will be poor and applies himself to giving ("The Three Reciprocities" [San shu], in Kongzi jiayu).

As one can see, the loss concerns both the saying and the said, expression and morality: the phrase has become alchemical (serial and repetitive), and the thought has lost its richness.

9. Ban Gu, *Hanshu* (Peking: Zhonghua shuju, 1962), ch. 30, p. 1701. Later, the expression *subtle proposition* (*wei yan*) becomes the classical formula for commenting on *Lunyu*; see Liu Xie, ch. 18.

10. Chen Kui, *Wenzi zhuyi* (Peking: Shumu wenxian chubanshe, 1987).

11. Brief forms have been the subject of many recent studies. See, in particular, *Formes brèves: De la gnōme à la pointe: Métamorphoses de la sententia* (La Licorne: Université de Poitiers, 1980); Jean Lafond, *Les formes brèves de la prose et le discours discontinu (XVI–XVII siècle)* (Paris: Vrin, 1984); and Philippe Lacoue-Labarthe and J.L. Nancy, *L'absolue littéraire: Théorie de la littérature du romantisme allemand* (Paris: Seuil, 1978).

12. Cicero, *Acad. Post* 1.4.15.

13. Vincent Y.C. Shih, "Lunyu de wenyi," *Zhongwai wenxue* (April 1975); Christoph Harbsmeier, "*Confucius Ridens*: Humor in the Analects," *Harvard Journal of Asiatic Studies* 50, no. 1 (1990).

14. The same is true for *Analects* 11.1: "The Master said, 'The men in former times, in the matters of ceremonies and music, were rustics, *it is said*, while the men of *these* later times, in ceremonies and music, are accomplished gentlemen. If I have occasion to use those things, I follow the men of former times.'" Instead of seeing the term *gentlemen* as ironic, as James Legge does, the Chinese com-

mentator thinks that here Confucius is citing a popular expression of his day; once again, the splitting used to interpret the literal contradiction is not seen as a feint opposing appearance and reality but rather as creating an opposition between the opinion of Confucius and that of others.

The remark would signify that in the past a perfect equilibrium was established between nature and culture but that with contemporary refinement this equilibrium appears too crude. Excess-flaw: the perspective is always that of regulation.

15. On the concept of regulation in China, see my book *Figures de l'immanence: Pour une lecture philosophique du* Yiking (Paris: Grasset, 1993), ch. 7, and my translation of *Zhong Yong* (Paris: Imprimerie nationale, 1993).

16. Pierre Ryckmans is wrong, in my opinion, to introduce the notion of *piège* (trap), as well as that of *but* (goal), into his translation of the remark (p. 50).

CHAPTER TEN: THERE IS NO PLANE OF ESSENCES

1. On the Socratic contribution, see, notably, Emile Boutroux, *Leçons sur Socrate* (Paris: Editions Universitaires, 1989); Emile Callot, *La doctrine de Socrate* (Paris: Marcel Rivière, 1970); V. De Magalhâes-Vilhena, *Le problème de Socrate: Le Socrate historique et le Socrate de Platon* (Paris: P.U.F., 1952); and W.K.C. Guthrie, *Socrates* (London: Cambridge University Press, 1971).

2. Plato, *Theaetetus*, trans. F.M. Cornford, in *The Collected Dialogues of Plato* (Princeton, NJ: Princeton University Press, 1961), p. 852.

3. This is my translation from *Analects* — TRANS.

4. In his note to *Analects* 6.23, James Legge explains that the term first designated a drinking vessel and later a wooden tablet. In Confucius's time, the form of the term was changed, while the name was kept — TRANS.

5. Since Legge translates *ren* as virtue, whereas Jullien gives it a broader definition, I have substituted "*ren*" or "humanness" in brackets in those places where Legge refers to virtue in his translation — TRANS.

6. See Pierre Ryckmans's explanatory note in his translation of *Entretiens (Analects)*, pp. 141–42. Derk Bodde, "A Perplexing Passage in *The Confucian Analects*," *Journal of the American Oriental Society* (1933), pp. 53–54; reprinted in

Essays on Chinese Civilization (Princeton, NJ: Princeton University Press, 1981), sums up the essential elements of the arguments in favor of an unorthodox reading of the passage. Contrary to Bodde's assertions, *yu* means "and also" in *Analects* (see 5.12 and 9.9); and the insistence in the coordination is justified all the more here since, from one term to the next, the reasons for which he "seldom spoke" are very different.

7. *The Book of Changes*, 2.6 — TRANS.

8. Two lines, one solid and the other broken (— and - -), can be used to express the polarity at work at the heart of the real. By following the play of their superpositions, we arrive at the following series of figures — either the fully developed form of sixty-four hexagrams or the condensed one of eight trigrams:

(yang waxing and yin waning)

(yin waxing and yang waning)

9. I wonder if the renowned Japanese poetic form, the haiku, does not embody an extreme example of this indicative capacity to realize globality from the outset.

10. To realize , as they say, is to realize — or not to realize — that someone is dead.

CHAPTER ELEVEN: ADVANCING TOWARD MATURATION

1. All references to Plato's *Letter 7* are taken from *The Collected Dialogues of Plato*, ed. Edith Hamilton and Huntington Cairns (Princeton, NJ: Princeton University Press, 1961), and are mentioned by line in parentheses after each citation.

2. Jacqueline de Romilly, *Histoire et raison chez Thucydide* (Paris: Belles Lettres, 1956), p. 101; cf. René Schaerer, *La question platonicienne* (Paris: Neuchâtel, 1938).

3. Chad Hansen, *A Daoist Theory of Chinese Thought: A Philosophical Interpretation* (New York: Oxford University Press, 1992), p. 157.

4. *Mencius*, trans. James Legge, in *The Chinese Classics* (Taipei: SMC Publishing, 1994), vol. 1. All references to this work are from this edition and will be

indicated by part and chapter in parentheses after each citation unless otherwise noted.

5. Mencius's double recommendation is too neglected by many modern commentators (who are only interested in the idea of *haoran zhi qi*). Tu Wei-Ming, for example, when he translates the passage, skips this expression; see *Confucian Thought: Selfhood as Creative Transformation* (Albany: State University of New York, 1985), p. 106.

6. *Mencius* ends with a final suspense that is along the same lines as *Annals*, emphasizing, by suggestion, the importance of the role undertaken by its author. We see the same periodic construction of historical events (Chinese history neither progresses nor repeats: it renews itself): here the rhythm is marked by the emergence of a sage every five hundred years; each time, the transmission of his wisdom is assured in such a way that another sage can later appear. Yet Mencius asks, "From Confucius downwards until now there are *only* 100 years and *somewhat* more. The distance in time from the sage is so far from being remote, and so very near at hand was the sage's residence. In these circumstances, is there no one *to transmit his doctrines*? Yea, is there no one *to do so?*" (7.2.38). These are the last words in the book. Mencius presents himself only through a detail that objective necessity makes impossible to overlook. But something that may appear a mark of modesty reinforces his position all the more. He attributes no merit to himself (that would distinguish his own personality), nor does he proclaim himself inspired (by invoking transcendence): only the immanent unfolding of events implies that he might fulfill the role that is his own.

7. Between the intransigence of one who wants to preserve his integrity at all costs (Yi Yin) and the other who is ready to serve the world at any cost (Hui of Liuxia), Confucius, according to Mencius, struck a balance by being able to act *according to the situation*: "When it was proper to go away quickly he did so; When it was proper to keep in retirement, he did so" (2.1.2 and 5.2.1). He is defined not by a (specific) quality but by the "moment" (that is, what was required of him in each situation during the course of things).

8. D.C. Lau, "On Mencius' Use of the Method of Analogy in Argument," *Asia Major*, n.s., 10 (1963); A.C. Graham, "The Background of the Mencian

Theory of Human Nature," *Tsing Hua Journal of Chinese Studies* 6, no. 1, 2 (1967).

9. Hansen, *Daoist Theory*, pp. 188ff.

10. I.A. Richards, *Mencius on the Mind* (London: Kegan Paul, 1932), pp. 43ff.

11. Wang Fuzhi, *Sishu xunyi: Chuan Shan quan shu* (Changsha: Yuelu shushe chuban, 1990), vol. 8, p. 676.

12. Mencius, who to us symbolizes the refusal of philosophical debate, and not in the name of wisdom (which is impossible to transmit directly), was judged negatively by the Japanese (neo-Confucian) thinkers as too confident of the value of explicit and argued discourse (this critical point of view becomes even more the case in their assessment of the Song commentators). For Sorai, the confidential relationship between the Master and his disciples is at the heart of teaching. He uses an argument from *Mencius* against Mencius himself: "holding" one point illuminates one aspect of things and "disregards a hundred others" (7.1.26). The argument is always biased and leads to illusion inasmuch as he who argues presupposes an opponent and tries to persuade him. Seen from Japan, the "Occident" (rhetoric) began in China. For the first elements, see Yoshikawa Kōjirō, *Jinsai, Sorai, Norinaga* (Tokyo: Tōhō gakkai, 1993).

13. Mencius excuses himself once for having spoken very directly to the prince, who consulted him about the role of the high ministers: if the prince commits grave faults, Mencius tells him, and the high ministers who are his relatives reproach him and he repeats his faults without listening to them, they can only dethrone him. The prince is disconcerted and changes color. "Let not your Majesty be offended," continues Mencius. "You asked me, and I dare not answer but according to truth" (5.2.9).

Mencius belonged to a time in which political speech in China was little censored; and let us not forget that, strategically, the *frontal* approach (when the other is expecting an oblique approach) can be a new way to be oblique with him.

14. On the relationships between Chan and language, see the rich study by Bernard Faure, *Chan Insights and Oversights* (Princeton, NJ: Princeton University Press, 1993): "An alternative solution was to use language in an essentially per-

formative and oblique way, thus acknowledging the failure of linear, sequential, discursive thinking. This may explain the breaking of syntax and logic in the koan" (p. 196). To my knowledge, the influence of the literary remark on the expression proper to Chan/Zen, although often mentioned, has not been sufficiently analyzed.

15. This is my translation of *Mencius* — TRANS.

16. Roland Barthes, *Empire of Signs*, trans. Richard Howard (New York: Hill and Wang, 1982), p. 74.

17. On the use of the expression "he bends without breaking," characterizing the teachings of the Master, see, for example, the commentary by Zhu Xi in the commentary by Cheng Yi on the passage in *Analects* 6.9.

18. See *Analects* 5.12 and 7.23.

19. *Heraclitus*, trans. Dennis Sweet (New York: University Press of America, 1995).

20. Jean Bollack and Heinz Wismann, *Héraclite ou la séparation* (Paris: Minuit, 1972), pp. 273ff.

21. Eric Weil, *Logique de la philosophie* (Paris: Vrin, 1950), p. 105.

CHAPTER TWELVE: THE GREAT IMAGE HAS NO SHAPE

1. Emile Bréhier, *La philosophic de Plotin* (Paris: Boivin, 1928).

2. Plotinus, *The Enneads*, trans. Stephen MacKenna (New York: Penguin, 1991), p. 380. All references to this work are cited from this translation.

3. Could this religious renewal be traced to the same source? According to Bréhier, in *La philosophie de Plotin,* ch. 7, the Orient that inspired Plotinus would have been the India of the Upanisads. In this case, the point of comparison emerges from the realm of fiction, and there would be a very indirect relationship — from Rome to China via India — between these thinkers.

4. The edition of Wang Bi's commentary used is Lou Yulie, *Wang Bi ji xiaoshi* (Peking: Zhonghua shuju, 1980). There is an English translation of his commentary by Ariane Rump in collaboration with Wing-tsit Chan (Honolulu: University Press of Hawaii, 1979), but it is very metaphysical.

5. All references to this text are taken from *Chinese Classics: Lao tzu*, trans.

D.C. Lau (Hong Kong: Chinese University Press, 1982), and will be referred to by number in parentheses.

6. Peter A. Boodberg, "Philological Notes on Chapter One of the *Lao tzu*," *Harvard Journal of Asiatic Studies* 20, no. 3–4 (1957), pp. 598–618; Chad Hansen, *A Daoist Theory of Chinese Thought: A Philosophical Interpretation* (New York: Oxford University Press, 1992), p. 215.

7. Mou Zongsan, *Caixing yu xuanli* (Taipei: Xuesheng shuju), p. 131; this chapter is the best philosophical study of Wang Bi's commentary I have read in Chinese.

8. Yulie, *Wang Bi ji xiaoshi*, p. 197; the text was translated and commented on by Rudolf G. Wagner, "Wang Bi: The Structure of the Laozi's Pointers (*Laozi weizhi lilüe*): A Philological Study and Translation," *T'oung Pao* 72, (1986), pp. 92ff.

9. *Zhilüe*, pp. 196 and 198.

10. Plato, *Parmenides*, trans. Mary Louise Gill and Paul Ryan (Indianapolis: Hackett, 1996); all references to this work are from this translation and will be noted in parentheses after each citation.

11. *Zhilüe*, p. 195.

12. This notion of sign (*zhao*[c]), which presages something to come, seems typical of ancient Chinese thought (which is that of a reality in process; see also, *The Book of Changes*). The sign is situated, in fact, in an intermediate, and precious, stage between reality not yet actualized and reality completely actualized and manifest; as such, it allows those who know how to detect it (sage or strategist) to intervene before the moment of actualization and thus in a more appropriate way (see chapter 2 and p. 301, above). The notion of sign, therefore, to some extent replaces the Western notion of symbol, which rests on a doubling of planes (sensible/intelligible) (see the originally *double* character of symbols already underscored by St. Augustine).

13. On *aporia* in the thought of Damascius, see the work of Joseph Combès, in particular, "La théologie aporétic de Damascius," *Néoplatonisme: Mélanges offerts à Jean Trouillard* (Fontenay aux Roses, France: E.N.S., 1981), pp. 125ff.

14. Although it is perfectly logical, this paradoxical expression has seemed suspicious on two fronts: that of Plotinus was corrected by Müller (but fortu-

nately defended by Emile Bréhier) and that of Wang Bi was judged "uncertain" (Wang Bi "hesitates"; see Isabelle Robinet, *Les commentaires du Tao To King jusqu'au VIIème siècle* [Paris: Mémoires de l'Institut des Hautes Etudes Chinoises, 1981], p. 72).

15. See Jean-Michel Charrue, *Plotin lecteur de Platon* (Paris: Belles Lettres, 1978), p. 62.

16. In a study on the idea of the void and the problem of radical origin in Greek Neoplatonism, *Etudes de philosophie antique* (Paris: P.U.F., 1955), Emile Bréhier has demonstrated the difficulty necessarily encountered in Neoplatonism, from Plotinus to Damascius, in separating the nonbeing conceived of as the origin and the source of being, and thus superior to being, and the nonbeing that is its antipode and the absolute negation of being. The failure of their conception, he concludes, comes from its attempting to unite the tradition of "Greek intellectualism," in which the intelligible is capable of expression, and the religious traditions of the East bringing the "notion of a supreme reality that cannot be the object of discourse" to the Greek world. In China, this difficulty is not an issue — it never comes up — for *wu* is not nonbeing, but it "does not have" the individuated character of *you* (it is not yet actualized or is returned to the undifferentiated). The void of the original undifferentiation from which reality proceeds is the same as the one I find in dissolving the concretization of things — which permits the vessel fashioned from earth to contain or the mark traced on white paper to become animated.

17. See Maurice de Gandillac, "Analogie et apophase," in *La sagesse de Plotin* (Paris: Hachette, 1952).

CHAPTER THIRTEEN: "NET" AND "FISH"

1. For Clement of Alexandria, the term is general, without his trying to distinguish between the figures: "Hence one could say that all peoples, Barbarians and Greeks, who treated divinity, hid the principles of things and transmitted truths through enigmas and symbols, using allegories and metaphors and other similar figures" (*Stromata* 5.21.4). At the beginning of *Stromata*, he makes this occultation the main principle of his work: "There are also things that my book

will mention only by allusion; it will stress some things, make mere mention of others, try to speak without appearing to do so, to look beneath the veil, and to make its point without saying a word" (1.15.1).

2. *Stromata* 5. On this subject, see Alain Le Boulluec, "Voile et ornement: Le texte et l'addition des sens selon Clément d'Alexandrie," in *Questions de sens* (Paris: Presses de l'Ecole Normale Supérieure, 1982), p. 52; see also Henri de Lubac, *Exégèse médiévale: Les quatre sens de l'Ecriture* (Paris: Aubier, 1964), vol. 4, especially p. 189.

3. For the sake of clarity, I have translated Jullien's French translations of this work — TRANS. "Waiwu," in *Zhuangzi*, ed. Guo Qingfan (Taipei: Shijie shuju), p. 944.

4. "Ming xiang," in *Zhouyi lüeli*, ed. Lou Yulie, *Wang Bi ji xiaoshi* (Peking: Zhonghua shuju, 1980), p. 609.

5. Wang Fuzhi, *Zhuangzi jie* (Hong Kong: Zhonghua shuju, 1976), p. 245.

6. "Tiandao," in *Zhuangzi*, p. 488.

7. "Qiushui," in *Zhuangzi*, p. 572.

8. "Zeyang," in *Zhuangzi*, p. 916.

9. In "Arrêt, vision et langage: Essai d'interprétation du *Ts'i Wou-louen* de Tchouang-Tseu." *Philosophie* 44, pp. 12–51, Jean-François Billeter has interpreted this phenomenon of vision as an *activity*, which corresponds to the anthropological model conceived of in China in which the dualism between mind and body dissolves. This is not the point of view I have chosen to follow, but it does not seem that one idea must preclude the other. Especially in regard to the Tao, one point of view does not preclude any other.

10. "Qiwulun," in *Zhuangzi*, p. 56.

11. *Ibid.*, p. 74.

12. "Xiaoyaoyou," in *Zhuangzi*, p. 2.

13. *Ibid.*, p. 26.

14. On Hui Shi, one might begin in French by reading Ignace Kou Pao-Koh, *Deux sophistes chinois: Houei Che et Kong-Souen Long* (Paris: Imprimerie nationale, 1953).

15. "Xiaoyaoyou," in *Zhuangzi*, p. 36.

16. *Ibid.*, p. 30.

17. For this, commentators cleverly set into play, from this opening chapter on, the argument of the "equalizing" of things and discourses that is developed in the second chapter of the work. But I believe this relativism is found only at the heart of ordinary language, not in these opening words of *Zhuangzi*.

18. Robert E. Allinson, *Chuang-Tzu for Spiritual Transformation* (Albany: State University of New York Press, 1989). However, I share neither the psychological orientation that Allinson leads up to (the myth brings us back to the "mind of the child") nor the analytic/aesthetics bipartition supposedly characterizing mental functioning.

19. "Tian xia," in *Zhuangzi*, p. 1098.

20. Clement of Alexandria, *Stromata* 1.21.1.

21. My translation of Proclus, *Commentaire sur la Republique*, 6th dissertation — TRANS.

22. "Yu yan," in *Zhuangzi*, p. 947.

23. "Xiaoyaoyou," in *Zhuangzi*, p. 28.

24. Allinson, "The Content of Myth," in *Chuang-Tzu*.

25. A.C. Graham gives only a brief mention of this; see *Chuang-tzu: The Seven Inner Chapters* (London: Allen and Unwin, 1981), p. 25. In his chapter on Zhuangzi, Chad Hansen, *A Daoist Theory of Chinese Thought: A Philosophical Interpretation* (New York: Oxford University Press, 1992), pp. 265–303, does not even mention it (although he treats the "flexibility" of his discourse).

26. On the image of the receptacle in ancient China, see the excellent study by D.C. Lau, "On the Term *ch'ih ying* and the Story Concerning the So-Called 'Tilting Vessel' (*ch'i ch'i*)," *Symposium on Chinese Studies* (Hong Kong: University of Hong Kong, 1968), p. 18; and the brief study by Kuang-Ming Wu, "Goblet Words, Dwelling Words, Opalescent Words — Philosophical Methodology of Chuang Tzu," *Journal of Chinese Philosophy* 15 (1988), pp. 1–7.

27. Wang Fuzhi, *Zhuangzi jie*, p. 246.

28. "Qiwulun," in *Zhuangzi*, p. 66.

CHAPTER FOURTEEN: THE CLOUDS AND THE MOON

1. Jin Shengtan, *Du di liu cai zi shu Xixiangji*, ed. Zhang Guoguang (Shang-hai: Shanghai guji chubanshe, 1986), no. 15, p. 13. Commentary on *Xixiangji*. Subsequent references will be referred to parenthetically in the text.

2. Jin Shengtan, "Qiao yi," in *Shishuo xinyu*, no. 4.

3. *The Western Room* 1.2.

4. Jin Shengtan, *Du shi jie* (Shanghai: Shanghai guji chubanshe, 1984), p. 46. Commentary on "Yu hua gong" by Du Fu.

5. "Wei qu," in *Vingt-quatre modes poétiques, Er shi si shi pin*. See also *Shi pin ji jie* and the 1983 edition of Qiao Li, *Er shi si shi pin tan wei* (Jinan: Qi lu shu she), p. 92.

6. Cited in *Jiangnan yuanlin zhi* (Peking: Zhongguo gongye chubanshe, 1963), p. 7.

7. On the art of the Chinese garden, see the basic text, *Yuanye* by Ji Cheng, edition with commentary: *Yuanye zhushi* (Peking: Jianzhu gongye chubanshe, 1988; English translation: A. Hardie, *The Craft of Gardens* [New Haven, CT: Yale University Press, 1988]); as well as the book by Chen Congzhou, *Shuo yuan* (Shanghai: Tongji daxue chubanshe, 1984). Among Western studies, see O. Siren, *Chinese Gardens* (New York: Ronald Press, 1948); and R. Stewart Johnston, *Scholar Gardens of China* (Cambridge, UK: Cambridge University Press, 1991).

8. "Consider the predilection for oil painting which, more than any other kind, allows the artist to attribute a distinct pictorial representation to each element of the object in the human face, or the search for signs which, when incorporated into the painting, would give the illusion of depth or volume through the play of light, foreshadowing, or chiaroscuro — the research into movement, forms, tactile values, and different sorts of material (think of the patient studies which brought to perfection the representation of velvet). These secrets, these processes discovered by a painter and augmented by each generation, are elements of a general technique of representation which at the limit would reach the thing itself, man himself, which cannot be imagined for a moment to contain any accident or vagueness....

"When the classical painter in front of his canvas looks for an expression of objects and beings that will preserve all their richness and lose none of their properties, it is because he wants to be as convincing as the things himself. It is because he can only reach us only the way they reach us, namely, by imposing upon *our senses* an unimpeachable spectacle" (Maurice Merleau-Ponty, *The Prose of the World*, trans. John O'Neil [Evanston, IL: Northeastern University Press, 1973], pp. 49–50).

CHAPTER FIFTEEN: THE ALLUSIVE DISTANCE

1. Du Yuankai, preface to *Zuozhuan*; cited in Liu Xizai, *Yigai*, ch. 1.

2. Lü Donglai, cited in Liu Xizai, *Yigai*.

3. Jin Shengtan, *Dushijie*, pp. 5–6.

4. On this subject, see my chapter "Lifelines Across a Landscape," in *The Propensity of Things*, trans. Janet Lloyd (New York: Zone Books, 1995), pp. 91–105.

5. Jin Shengtan, *Dushijie*, p. 18. Commentary on the poem "Deng Yanzhou chenglou."

6. *Ibid.*, p. 243. Commentary on the poem "Yu Wenchao shangshu zhi sheng Cui Yu siye zhi sun shangshu zhi zi chong fan Zheng jian qian hu."

7. *Ibid.*, p. 18. Commentary on the poem "Deng yanzhou chenglou."

8. *Ibid.*, p. 123. Commentary on the poem "Jiang shang zhi shui ru hai shi liao duan shu."

9. Shen Deqian, *Shuoshi zuiyu*, no. 22, p. 53.

10. Zhang Shi, pp. 53–54.

11. Liu Jin, p. 54.

12. The same technique is found, for example, in Wang Wei's quatrain "On the Ninth Day of the Ninth Month, in Remembering My Brothers in Shandong" ("Jiu yue jiu ri yi Shandong xiongyi").

13. Wang Fuzhi, *Jiangzhai shihua*, p. 94.

CONCLUSION: DETOUR OR SPLIT?

1. Pierre Fontanier, *Les figures du discours* (Paris: Flammarion, 1968), p. 125.

2. In the 1920s, psychoanalysis became a fashionable position and intrigued

certain minds. The great writer Lu Xun, who discovered it through the Japanese Kuriyagawa Hakusan, drew inspiration from Freud in writing his novella *Mending the Sky*. But one cannot help but notice that this interest never gained any substance, even before Communist censorship took hold (even Lu Xun did not keep to his original plan, since his novella progressively returns to the framework of traditional Chinese ideology). On this subject, see my book *Lu Xun: Ecriture et révolution* (Paris: Presses de l'Ecole Normale Supérieure, 1979), pp. 49ff.

Generally speaking, the writing of Lu Xun, who to my mind is the greatest Chinese writer of the twentieth century, offers a fascinating blend of two traditions: symbolism, which he borrowed from European literature, which he discovered during a stay in Japan, and allusive, indirect criticism, which he got from the indigenous literary tradition (as demonstrated particularly in his essays — *zawen* — which were collected in *Under the Flowered Canopy*; see *Ecriture et révolution*, pp. 91ff.).

Glossary of Chinese Expressions

Chapter Two: Frontal Versus Oblique Attack

a. Compare the expression *xin zhan* 心戰　with *bing zhan* 兵戰

b. *Zheng* and *qi* 正奇,　*zhi* and *yu* 直迂

c. *Xing yi ying xing, zheng ye* 刑（形）以應刑（形），正也
   Wu xing er zhi xing, qi ye 無刑（形）以裁（制）刑（形），奇也

d. *Yi yi wei qi* 以異爲奇

e. *Fa er wei zheng, qi wei fa zhe, qi ye* 發而爲正，其未發者，奇也

f. *Qi fa er bu bao, ze sheng yi* 奇發而不報，則勝矣

g. *You yu qi zhe* 有餘奇者

h. *Sheng dong ji xi* 聲東擊西

i. *Wenzhang congrong weiqu* 文章從容委曲

j. *Zhi ji ma gou;* 指雞罵狗；　*zhi sang ma huai* 指桑罵槐

k. *Pang qiao ce ji* 旁敲側擊

l. *Yi lan wu yi* 一覽無遺

m. *Quzhe hanxu* 曲折含蓄

Chapter Three: Under the Cover of the Image

a. *Wan dao wu qiong* 婉道無窮

b. *Chen gu er ci jin* 陳古而刺今

c. *Fu zhi yan pu* 賦之言鋪；
   zhi pu chen jin zhi zheng jiao shan wu 直鋪陳今之政敎善惡

d. *Bi, jian jin zhi shi, bu gan chi yan, qu bilei yi yan zhi* 比，見今之失，不敢斥言，取比類以言之

e. *Xing, jian jin zhi mei xian yu mei yu, qu shan shi yi yu quan zhi* 與，見今之美于媚諛，取善事以喻勸之

f. *Jiao* 敎

g. *Xian yiwei fengyu yi dong zhi, min jian kai wu, nai hou ming jiao* 先依違諷諭以動之，民漸開悟，乃後明敎

h. Compare the concept of *bian feng* 變風

i. *Zhu wen er jue jian* 主文而譎諫

j. *Feng-hua* 風化; *feng-ci* 風刺

k. *Bian jian yong bi hui bi you fa* 便見用筆迴避有法

Chapter Four: Quotations as Proxy

a. *Fu shi* 賦詩

b. *Ge ge bu yan er yu* 各各不言而喻

c. *Wan zhuan kai feng* 宛轉開諷

d. *Shi zhi shan yi ren qing* 詩之善移人情

e. *Yi wei yan xiang gan* 以微言相感

Chapter Five: Insinuating and Avoiding to Say

a. *Hui* 諱

b. *Yin* 隱

c. *Chunqiu bifa* 春秋筆法

d. *Wei er xian* 微而顯
   Zhi er hui 志而晦
   Wan er cheng zhang 婉而成章

e. *Chunqiu tui jian zhi yin* 春秋推見至隱

f. *Wei* 微

g. *Kong yan* 窆言; *kong wen* 空文

h. *Chunqiu yi zi yi bao bian* 春秋一字以褒貶

Chapter Six: The Impossibility of Dissidence

a. *Yin* 隱

b. *Youshi* 遊士

c. *Jian* 諫

d. *Guojia* 國家

e. *Ji jian* 幾諫 ; the concept of ji 幾

f. *Xun yan* 巽言

g. *Feng jian* 諷諫

h. *Jian er bu lu* 諫而不露

i. *Chen bu xian jian* 臣不顯諫

j. *Fang – shou* 放收

k. *Yi qi ci sui qing hui, yi gui yi zheng* 以其辭雖傾回，意歸義正，

l. *Mi ye zhe, hui hu qi ci, shi hun mi ye* 謎也者，回互其辭，使 昏迷也

m. *Wen – rou – dun – hou* 溫柔敦厚

n. *Wen – hou – he – ping* 溫厚和平

Chapter Seven: Between Emotion and Landscape

a. *Li* 理

b. *Fu, bi, xing* 賦，比，興

c. *Yu* 喻 , *you* 猶

d. *Xian yan ta wu yi yin qi suo yong zhi ci* 先言他物以引起所詠之詞

e. *Xing yi sui kuo er wei chang* 興意雖闊而味長

f. *Xing zhi bu jian bi* 興之不兼比

g. *Jing – qing* 景情

h. *Xing zai you yi wu yi zhi jian* 興在有意無意之間

i. *Chu wu yi qi qing, wei zhi xing, wu dong qing zhe ye* 觸物以起情，謂之興，物動情者也

j. *Qi qing zhe, yi wei yi ni yi* 起情者，依微以擬議

k. *Xing ze huan bi yi ji feng* 興則環譬以記諷

l. *Yan zai yu ci er yi ji yu bi* 言在于此而意寄于彼

m. *Ru xing* 入興

n. *Wu* 物   in relation to *xin* 心
o. *Shense* 神思
p. *Shen yu wu you* 神與物游
q. *Dong* 動

Chapter Eight: Beyond the Landscape

a. *Yu* 喻
b. *Xiang de* 象德
c. *Qing – jing* 情景
d. *Nei – wai* 內外 ; *xin – wu* 心物
e. *Shi jian zuo yong zhi gong* 始見作用之功
f. *Zheng yu jia xie* 正喻夾寫
g. *Wei er wan* 微而婉
h. *Bu po bu lu* 不迫不露
i. *Fan fu ling luan* 反覆零亂
j. *Xing ji wu duan* 興寄無端
k. *You zhi* 幽旨
l. *Chu ru zi de* 出入自得
m. In the sense of *han xu* 含畜
n. *Wen yi jin er yi you yu* 文己盡而意有餘
o. *Xiang* 象
p. *Xiang-zheng* 象征
q. *Xing-xiang* 興象
r. *Qi-xiang* 氣象
s. *Da xiang wu xing* 大象無形
t. *Jing sheng yu xiang wai* 境生于象外
u. *Shi zuo* 實作   悒   *xu zou* 虛作
v. *Wei* 味

Chapter Nine: From the Master to the Disciple

a. *Xing-yan* 行言
b. *Na* 訥 , *ren* 訒

c. *Ning* 佞

d. *Xin* 信

e. *Shi ren you suo wansuo er zi de zhi* 使人有所玩索而自得之

f. *Wei fa qi duan* 微發其端

g. *Sheng ren yan sui zhi jin, shang xia jie tong* 聖人言雖至近，上下皆通

h. *Yi shi zhi wei er zhong shan zhi ji* 一事之微而衆善之集

i. *Du zhe yi xiang wei zhi* 讀者宜詳味之

j. *Xu yao shi de sheng xian qi xiang* 須要識得聖賢氣象

k. *Ci zhang zhi yan, ming bai jian yue er qi zhi yi qu zhe fan fu* 此章之言，明白簡約而其意曲折反復

l. *Junzi – xiaoren* 君子，小人

m. *Shi – wei* 時位

n. *Zhong* 中 ; compare *Sheng ren zhi shi yi ge zhong de daoli* 聖人只是一個中的道理

o. *Wu fang ti* 無方體

p. *Xun xun ran* 循循然 ; compare *xia xue er shang da* 下學而上達

Chapter Ten: There Is No Plane of Essences

a. *Ci shengren kaishi zhi shen* 此聖人開示之深

b. *Shengren zhi yu, yin ren er bianhua* 聖人之語，因人而變化

c. *Jun jun, chen chen, fu fu, zi zi* 君君，臣臣，父父，子子

d. *Ren* 仁

e. *Ren yi li yan, tong hu shang xia* 仁以理言，通乎上下

f. *Ren zhi fang* 仁之方

g. *Han yan* 罕言 ; *han* in the sense of *shao* 少

h. *Fu zi wei chang zhi yan zhi* 夫子未嘗指言之

i. *Ya yan* 雅言 ; *ya* in the sense of *chang* 常

j. *Er* 而

k. *Wen-zhang* 文章

l. *Yi* 意

m. *Bi* 必

n. *Gu* 固

o. *Wu wo* 無我

p. *Wu ke wu bu ke* 無可無不可

q. *Quan* 權

r. *Da er hua zhi zhi wei sheng* 大而化之之謂聖

s. *Guan* 貫

t. *Sheng ren zhi xin, hunran yi li, er fan ying qu dang, yong ge bu tong,*
聖人之心，渾然一理，而泛應曲當，用各不同

u. *Qi yan qu er zhong* 其言曲而中　*Qi shi si er yin* 其事肆而隱

v. *Bu ke wei dian yao* 不可爲典要

w. *Shi xian er li wei* 事顯而理微

x. *Qu* 曲

y. *Qu er zhong* 曲而中

z. *Yu yi hunran, you ruo bu zhuan wei san jia fa zhe, suoyi wei shengren zhi yan,*
語意渾然，又若不專爲三家發者，所以爲聖人之言

aa. *Jie wei ru de zhi yao, ze you chu bu yi* 皆爲人德之要，則又初
不異

bb. *Ci shi che shang che xia yu* 此是徹上徹下語

cc. *Shengren chu wu er yu* 聖人初無二語

Chapter Eleven: Advancing Toward Maturation

a. *Fei yi xi er qu zhi* 非義襲而取之

b. *Ji yi suo sheng* 集義所生

c. In the sense of *zheng* 正；see *Zhu Xi: zheng zhi bu de* 正之不得

d. *Wu yu qi qi xiao* 勿預期其效

e. *Zheng zhu zhi bing* 正助之病

f. *Da zhe, zu yu ci er tong yu bi* 達者，足於此而通於彼

g. In the sense of *er* 而

h. *Bian* 辯

i. *Zhi* 執

j. *Zhi zhong wu quan* 執中無權

k. *Yue* 悅

420

l.   *Zhi* 直

m. *Zhi yan gong zhi* 直言攻之

n. *Zhi, jin yan yi xiang zheng ye* 直　盡言以相正也

o. *Yin er bu fa, yue ru ye* 引而不發　躍如也

p. *Yu bu neng xian, mo bu neng cang* 語不能顯　默不能藏

q. *Wen-zhang* 文章

Chapter Twelve: The Great Image Has No Shape

a. *Hun cheng* 混成

b. *Wu ming* 無名；*wu zhuang* 無狀；*wu wu* 無物
   Wan wu you zhi yi cheng 萬物由之以成

c. *Xu* 虛；*huang hu* 恍惚；*you ming* 幽冥

d. *Miao* 妙；for example, *zhong miao zhi men* 眾妙之門

e. *Gui wu* 貴無

f. *Xuan xue* 玄學

g. *Zhi shi zao xing* 指事造形

h. *Chang* 常

i. *You / wu* 有無

j. *Yong* 用

k. *Yong* 用 on the level of *wu* 無 becomes *li* 利 on the level of *you* 有

l. *Tong* 通

m. *You wei* 有爲；*you zhi* 有執

n. *Wu wei* 無爲

o. *Ming* 名；*wei* 謂

p. *Fen* 分

q. *Wu zhuang zhi zhuang, wu wu zhi xiang* 無狀之狀，無狀之象

r. *Da xiang wu xing* 大象無形

s. *Si bu xiao* 似不肖

t. *Qiang wei zhi rong* 強爲之容

u. *Pu* 樸；*su* 素

v. *Wu wei bu zu ting zhi yan, nai shi ziran zhi zhi yan* 無味不足聽之
   言，乃是自然之至言

Chapter Thirteen: "Net" and "Fish"

a. *Miao li* 妙理 ; *xuan li* 玄理

b. *Wu xing zhe* 無形者

c. *Yi qu* 一曲 ; *da fang* 大方

d. *Cheng xin* 成心

e. *Shi – fei* 是非

f. *Ming* 明

g. *Qi* 齊

h. *Bu yong er yu zhu yong* 不用而寓諸庸

i. *Xiu hu tian jun* 休乎天鈞

j. *Liang xing* 兩行

k. *Wei shi you feng* 未始有封

l. *Da er wu dang* 大而無當 ; *wang er bu fan* 往而不返 ; *wu ji* 無極

m. *Kuang* 狂

n. *Bu yi ji jian zhi* 不以觭見之

o. *Hu mo wu xing* 芴漠無形

p. *Yu yan* 寓言

q. *Ji yan* 寄言 ; *he yu* 合喻

r. *Zhong yan* 重言

s. *Zhi yan* 巵言

t. *Shi zizong* 時恣縱

u. *Yin shi yi* 因是以

v. *Bu yan ze qi* 不言則齊

w. *Wu wu bu ran, wu wu bu ke* 無物不然，無物不可

x. *Tian jun zhe tian ni ye* 天均者天倪也

y. *Wei yan jian chu, bian yan qu zhe, jie zhi yan ye* 微言間出，辯言曲折，皆巵言也

z. I am following the teaching: *yan wu yan, zhong shen yan, wei chang yan* 言無言，終身言，未嘗言

aa. *Shengren bu you er zhao zhi yu tian* 聖人不由而照之於天

Chapter Fourteen: The Clouds and the Moon

a. *Fa* 法

b. *Mu zhu bi chu, shou xie ci chu* 目注彼處，手寫此處

c. *Yili xie dao jiang zhi shi, bian qie zhu* 迤邐寫到將至時，便且住

d. *Zai bu fang tuo que bu qin zhu* 再不放脫卻不擒住

e. *Yu a du yi chu zhi si mian, jiang bi lai zuo pan you xuan* 於阿堵一處 之四面，將筆來左盤右旋

f. *Bian xu zi yi yao zhi ye zhi, bu de bian dao ti* 便須恣意搖之曳之， 不得便到題

g. *Yue du hui lang zhi fa* 月度回廊之法

h. *Wu xian ru yi ru li, ru yin ru yue bie yang miao jing* 無限如迤如邐， 如隱如躍別樣妙境

i. *Bi mo zui wei wei wan you hao zhi* 筆墨最為委婉有好致

j. *Yili fan xie qu qu si jing* 迤邐凡寫曲曲四境

k. *Jing* 壏； opposed to *jing* 景

l. *Wei qu* 委曲

m. *Zao yuan ru zuo shi wen, bi shi qu zhe you fa* 造園如作詩文，必 使曲折有法

n. *Ce bi* 側筆

o. *Hong yun tuo yue* 烘雲托月

Chapter Fifteen: The Allusive Distance

a. *Qi wen huan* 其文緩

b. *Wenzhang congrong weiqu er yi du zhi* 文章從容委曲而意獨至

c. *Wu wei* 無為

d. *Yu di* 餘地

e. *Hu yong* 互用

f. *Jing* 境 and *jing* 景

g. *Xie de yaoming danbo* 寫得杳冥澹泊

h. *Ling* 靈

i. *He bi ke yi shi pian* 何必刻意詩篇

j. *Duimian xiefa* 對面寫法

k. *Wu bi bu qu* 無筆不曲

l. *Miaoxie qingshi qu jin* 描寫情事曲盡

m. *Yu huan yu bei* 愈緩愈悲

n. *Qing yu neng yi zhuanzhe wei hanxu zhe, wei Du Ling ju sheng* 情語能以轉折爲含蓄者，唯杜陵居勝

Conclusion

a. *Hanxu* 含蓄

b. *Hu wen jian yi* 互文見義

c. *Yan sheng yu ci, yi sheng yu bi* 言生於此，意生於彼
wen jian yu ci, qi yi zai bi 文見於此，起義在彼

d. *Lixiang* 理想

Notes

a. *Yan jin er zhi yuan* 言近而指遠

b. *Qi cheng ming ye xiao, qi qu lei ye da* 其稱名也小，其取類也大

c. *Zhao* 兆

Designed by Bruce Mau with Barr Gilmore and Alan Belcher
Typeset by Archetype
Printed and bound by Maple-Vail on Sebago acid-free paper